*Sexuality
and
Feminism
in Shelley*

Sexuality and Feminism in Shelley

NATHANIEL BROWN

Harvard University Press
Cambridge, Massachusetts, and London, England
1979

Publication of this book has been aided by a grant from
the Andrew W. Mellon Foundation.

Library of Congress Cataloging in Publication Data

Brown, Nathaniel, 1929-
  Sexuality and Feminism in Shelley.

  Includes bibliographical references and index.
    1. Shelley, Percy Bysshe, 1792-1822—Criticism
and interpretation. 2. Sex in literature.
3. Women in literature. 4. Shelley, Percy Bysshe,
1792-1822. A discourse of the manners of the ancient
Greeks relative to the subject of love. I. Title.
PR5442.S47B76   821'.7   79-4634
ISBN 0-674-80285-3

Acknowledgments

I AM INDEBTED to the Pierpont Morgan Library, New York, for permission to quote from a previously unpublished Shelley fragment in his MS "On Life" (MA 408), and to the Bodleian Library, Oxford, for supplying a photocopy of the MS of Shelley's *A Discourse of the Manners of the Antient Greeks Relative to the Subject of Love* (MS Shelley adds. e. 6, pp. 4-59; e. 11, pp. 17-41). I also gratefully acknowledge permission from Alfred A. Knopf and Faber & Faber to quote from *The Esdaile Notebook: A Volume of Early Poems* by Percy Bysshe Shelley, ed. Kenneth Neill Cameron (1964); from the Clarendon Press of Oxford to quote from *The Letters of Percy Bysshe Shelley*, ed. Frederick L. Jones (1964); from Harvard University Press and John Murray, Publishers, to quote from *Byron's Letters and Journals*, ed. Leslie A. Marchand (1973-1978), vols. 1-8; and from The Carl and Lily Pforzheimer Foundation to quote from Shelley's MS letters and a section of Claire Clairmont's MS journals.

No formal acknowledgment can adequately express the extent of my gratitude to two leading Shelleyans, Carl Woodring and Donald Reiman. Without their assistance and encouragement these pages would most likely never have been written. Professor Woodring has been a source of guidance and inspiration ever since the days of my doctoral candidacy at Columbia University, and more recently Dr. Reiman has gone out of his way to offer me both personal and professional assistance in the face of heavy responsibilities of his own. Doucet Fischer, Dr. Reiman's associate at The Carl H. Pforzheimer Library, has also rendered valuable assistance. Another Shelleyan, Dr. Timothy Webb of the University of York, has been kind enough to answer questions concerning the texts of Shelley's translations; and Dr. William Kemp of Mary Washington College has been of great assistance in helping me decipher Shelley's sometimes illegible manuscripts. I am grateful to the administration of Mary Washington College for granting me a year's leave of absence in order to pursue work on this book. My thanks are also due to the staff of the Mary

Washington College Library, particularly to Mrs. Renna Cosner, for help in tracking down hard-to-locate books and articles that I despaired of finding myself. I especially wish to thank Dr. William H. Masters, Director of the Reproductive Biology Research Foundation, for answering questions about Shelley's sexual theories. Finally, I would like to acknowledge the patience and skill of my editor, Virginia LaPlante, in helping to turn my manuscript into a book.

Contents

Introduction 1

1. A Discourse on Love 5

2. Love's Typology 24

3. Love's Visible Link 45

4. Civilized Sex 75

5. Lawless Love 91

6. The Male Eros 117

7. Love's Dominion 150

8. In Defense of Women 164

9. The Eye of Sane Philosophy 197

10. The Detestable Distinctions of Sex 212

Abbreviations and Short Titles 231

Notes 235

Index 290

Sexuality
and
Feminism
in Shelley

Introduction

SYSTEMATIC EXAMINATION of human sexuality has been one of the major developments of the present century. The studies of Kinsey on the varieties and extent of contemporary sexual practice, the findings of Masters and Johnson on the physiology of sexual response, the investigations of John Money and his associates into the hormonal and psychogenetic aspects of sex, and those of Maccoby and Jacklin into the psychology of sex difference, mark some of the principal directions of modern sex research. The inquiries of sociologists and cultural historians into the roots and evolution of human sexuality have also greatly expanded present understanding. But the application of such investigation to the study of nineteenth-century literature is still relatively untrodden ground. While sexual love and sexual relationship are obviously important literary themes during the period, their expression has yet to receive intensive analytic treatment in light of the latest information. What exactly did sex mean for those writing in the early nineteenth century? Modern sex studies are beginning to supply the answers.

To choose Shelley as the focus of such an analysis, however, may appear something of a paradox. Of all the writers of the age he would seem least suited to such an approach. What is there to study? As everyone knows, two angels holding hands is the poet's notion of love. Physical passion is alien to his interests. Until quite recently, at least, this was the normal view. The discarnate Shelley is a truism experiencing substantial revision only in the last decade, and the angelic image of Victorian legacy still prevails with all but specialists. I well remember the shock that once greeted my suggestion that a famous passage in *Alastor* described a wet dream. Fortunately attitudes have changed significantly in the interim, and few academic Shelleyans would presently blanch at such an interpretation. The poet, far from ignoring the claims of the flesh, was actually a serious student of human psychosexuality, anticipating more than anyone else of his day the rise of twentieth-century sex research as an area of valid intellectual concern. Moreover, this theoretical bias was the immediate outgrowth of his own high valuation of sex. No bodiless angel, he joyously celebrated the pleasures of the senses. A knowledge of the sexual element in his work is thus indispensable to interpreting his significance. Furthermore, such a knowledge yields valuable insights into the sexual ethos of the era as a whole and still has meaning even for our own day.

Since the subject is relatively unexplored and Shelley's approach at times controversial, the treatment is necessarily detailed. Each point is demonstrated through the medium of the poet's own words and weighed against the evidence of his entire corpus. His judgments are placed within the framework of his total philosophy of sexual relationship. They are also studied against the backdrop of his presumed intellectual sources, both in the literature of the period and in the broader cultural milieu. Finally, his views are examined in the context of his personal experience and practice. Serving as counterpoint are the sexual attitudes and practice of his friend and fellow poet, Lord Byron. The two great poets emerge from a dissection of the sexual mores of the age as complementary extremes.

The study is developed primarily through the explication of a single text, Shelley's comparatively unknown essay on Greek love, *A Discourse of the Manners of the Antient Greeks.* Intended as an introduction to his translation of Plato's *Symposium,* the essay is a penetrating exploration of the differences between ancient and modern sexual attitudes and the evolution of those differences. But it is also a detailed and, for the period, surprisingly candid statement of the poet's own sexual attitudes—so candid that it was bowdlerized until well into our own century. This is a principal reason why the essay is still not widely known. Only in the last two decades has its utility as a guide to understanding Shelley become apparent, bringing it into the mainstream of his writings. Among the specific areas of Shelley's thought covered in the essay are his sexual psychology, antimatrimonialism, understanding of homosexuality, and attitude toward women. In particular the manuscript cancellations and false starts throw light on Shelley's intentions, often supplying information not available in the completed texts.

With the unexpurgated text of the essay as evidence, there can be little doubt that the poet possessed a coherent philosophy of sexual relationship. The key to this philosophy lies in his attitude toward women. With the emergence of the contemporary women's movement in the late 1960s and early 1970s it has been possible to see that Shelley's feminism supplies a framework for his philosophy, binding

Introduction

its various strands neatly into place. Shelley was the first major writer to experiment in literary consciousness-raising—a fact apparently little known to present-day feminists—and in his own sexual practice he incorporated a feminist ideal directly contradicting the period's sexist norms. But more important, his sexual philosophy presupposed an erotic psychology necessitating equality between the sexes, and this psychology was closely linked to the rise of feminist ideology during the succeeding years of the century.

Shelley the feminist is implicit in his attitude to woman's patriarchal subordination in ancient Athens and to its nineteenth-century counterpart in Catholic Italy, in his celebration of the courtly love of women during the Middle Ages as against the idealization of male love during antiquity, in his attack on the libertine sexual practice of his own day and his exposure of the period's sexual double standard, in his elevation of "sentimental" or romantic love over merely physical desire while nevertheless asserting women's right to complete erotic fulfillment, and in his indictment of patriarchal marriage as degrading to women and his preaching of "free love" as an alternative. All this prepared the way for the poet's deliberate championship of women against the sexist norms of his age.

Particularly vital for an understanding of Shelley's feminism is the recognition that it was rooted in the eighteenth-century doctrine of "sympathy," enunciated most prominently by David Hume and Adam Smith. This tradition stressed sympathetic correspondence or likeness as the epistemological basis of psychosocial cohesion. When the doctrine was applied to relations between the sexes—as it was by Shelley or by his mother-in-law, the pioneer feminist Mary Wollstonecraft—it played a crucial role in the emergence during the following century of a psychological alternative to the traditional polarization of the sexes into separate spheres and complementary identities. The doctrine of sympathy, which implied the dissolution of sex roles and gender stereotypes, was reflected, either consciously or unconsciously, in the preachments of feminists throughout the century, notably Fanny Wright, Margaret Fuller, and John Stuart Mill. The ramifications of this doctrine thus extend far beyond the understanding of Shelley, forecasting modern feminist ideals of unisexuality or androgyny and the creation of a society where gender has lost its significance. But Shelley remains seminal in the development of these ideals; and in both his person and practice he was their living embodiment to a degree unprecedented in his day, or perhaps since. The image of the "angelic" Shelley consequently takes on new meaning.

1

A Discourse on Love

SHELLEY'S *A Discourse of the Manners of the Antient Greeks Relative to the Subject of Love*, not published in its entirety until 1931 but set down over a century earlier, is a remarkable anticipation of modern psychological, sociological, and anthropological inquiry into the nature and history of sexual love. The characteristic zeitgeist of our own age has rendered us uniquely conscious of this love's multiform expressions, of how it penetrates even to the remotest corners of human concern. But Shelley was scarcely less sensitive to the multifarious operations of the winged god in all their morphological permutations. Behind man's smallest action he saw the guiding hand of Eros. Although admittedly an amateur, he was a surprisingly astute observer, able to ask himself the right questions. As a result, his investigation into the etiology and development of human sexuality is still very much alive today.

It is therefore unfortunate that the *Discourse* should have been known for so long only in its emasculated version, since the complete text would have done much to correct the incorporeal image of Shelley which until recently has obscured his thinking about sex. As it was, the version authorized by his wife in 1840 contained only the first and less interesting half under the title *Essay on the Literature, the Arts, and the Manners of the Athenians: A Fragment*, to which was subjoined a note explaining that the piece, though "intended to be a commentary on the *Symposium*, or *Banquet of Plato* . . . breaks off at the moment when the main subject is about to be discussed."[1] The core of the essay detailing Shelley's anatomization of the sex act and its role in the development of man's psychological and social history was omitted. Also omitted was a feminist passage containing the poet's most uncompromising and impassioned assertion of woman's intellectual and social parity with the male. Thus for nearly a century the *Discourse* appeared as little more than an intriguing fragment. But with the unabbreviated text at last available, the essay emerges as a self-contained whole.[2] The unmutilated version not only represents a striking forecast of modern findings about human psychosexuality but sheds important light on the author's own philosophy of sexual relations, with significance extending beyond the understanding of his work to the period that produced it, and even to certain aspects of life today.[3]

While visiting the Baths of Lucca in 1818 during his first summer in Italy, the self-exiled Shelley, temporarily adrift from his customary sources of poetic inspiration, took up the translation of Plato's *Symposium*. "I am employed just now having little better to do, in translating into my fainting & inefficient periods the divine eloquence of Plato's Symposium," he wrote to his new friends Maria and John Gisborne early in July: "only as an exercise," he explained, "or perhaps to give Mary [his wife] some idea of the manners & feelings of the Athenians—so different on many subjects from that of any other community that ever existed."[4] To the novelist Thomas Love Peacock in England he reported two weeks later: "I have lately found myself totally incapable of original composition. I employed my mornings, therefore, in translating the *Symposium*, which I accomplished in ten days. Mary is now transcribing it, and I am writing a prefatory essay."[5] In a letter on the same day to his father-in-law, William Godwin, he noted: "the Symposium of Plato, seems to me, one of the most valuable pieces of all antiquity whether we consider the intrinsic merit of the composition or the light which it throws on the inmost state of manners & opinions among the antient Greeks. I have occupied myself in translating this, & it has excited me to attempt an Essay upon the cause of some differences in sentiment between the antients & moderns with respect to the subject of the dialogue."[6] To Peacock he wrote again in the middle of August: "I am proceeding to employ myself on a discourse upon the subject of which the Symposium treats considering it with reference to the difference of sentiments respecting it existing between the Greeks and modern nations. A subject to be handled with that delicate caution which either I cannot or I will not practise in other matters, but which here I acknowledge to be necessary.—Not that I have any serious thought of publishing either this discourse or the Symposium—at least till I return to England when we may discuss the propriety of it."[7]

As Shelley's letters make plain, Plato's dialogue would require considerable elucidation and defense were he to offer a translation for the edification of a contemporary English audience. Plato was regarded at this date as morally suspect, and his work was little read even by the educated. "Plato, in his Symposium, discourseth very eloquently touching the Uranian and Pandemian Venus," observes the Rev. Dr.

Folliott in Peacock's *Crotchet Castle*, "but you must remember that, in our Universities, Plato is held to be little better than a misleader of youth; and they have shown their contempt for him, not only by never reading . . . but even by never printing a complete edition of him."[8] Although the eighteenth-century translations of André Dacier, Floyer Sydenham, and Thomas Taylor had made the dialogues more directly accessible than formerly, the popular effect was negligible. The reading public, if it concerned itself with Plato at all, preferred him in the safer guise of neo-Platonism than at firsthand. Prejudice against Plato's name continued into the Victorian period, contributing to the bowdlerization not only of Shelley's *Discourse* but of his translation of the *Symposium* as well.[9] The "propriety," therefore, of publishing a faithful Englishing of the dialogue was something for Shelley to weigh carefully. Only if the dialogue—"the most beautiful and perfect among all the works of Plato"—could be dissociated from vulgar notions of sexual obliquity would the project be feasible.[10] The execution of such a dissociation is clearly the intent of the *Discourse*. "Thus far," the essay concludes, "the translator has thought it his duty to overstep the jealous limits between what the learned and the unlearned know of the Greeks, and to indicate a system of reasoning which may enable the reader to form a liberal, consistent, and just judgment of the peculiarities of their domestic manners. This slight sketch was undertaken to induce the reader to cast off the cloak of his self-flattering prejudices and forbid the distinction of manners, which he has endeavored to preserve in the translation of the ensuing piece, interfere with his delights or his instruction."[11] If, in the process, the translator found it necessary to detail his own understanding of sexual manners or to speculate at length concerning the history of mankind's psychosexual evolution, so much the better for posterity.

Shelley opens the *Discourse* with his habitual apotheosis of classical Athens as at once the fountainhead and flower of Western civilization.[12] This elevation, while well-nigh obligatory whenever Shelley dwelt on the glories of Greek civilization, was here essential to his deeper purpose of uncovering the psychological roots of the Greek ethos. What were the buried human realities shaping the expression of Attic culture? Only by attempting to snatch a glimpse of the people themselves, "their daily actions, their familiar conversation . . . the tone of their society," could one discover the answer. For this reason, "whatever tends to afford a further illustration of the manners and opinions of those to whom we owe so much [is] infinitely valuable" (219). It is precisely here, as Shelley explained to Godwin, that the *Symposium* is such a significant document.

Sexuality and Feminism in Shelley

But it is not enough, holds the poet, to concentrate solely on the acknowledged strengths of the Greeks. Also necessary is an honest recognition of "their errors, their weaknesses." Only then can it be ascertained "how far the most admirable community ever formed was removed" from that "perfection" which the perfectibilitarian Shelley believes is the necessary goal of all human aspiration; only then can it be discovered "how great ought to be our hopes, how resolute our struggles" (219). Shelley himself is far from blind to the serious flaws in the Greek performance, aware that despite the magnitude of their achievements in government, philosophy, and the arts, the Greeks were far removed from perfection in the moral sphere. Yet this seemingly damaging knowledge is of value, since insight even into the low points of human behavior is a positive good: "There is no knowledge concerning what man has been and may be from partaking of which a person can depart without becoming in some degree more philosophical, tolerant, and just" (219). As the poet had written to his father in 1811 at the outset of his career, "*Truth* whatever it may be has never been known to be prejudicial to the best interests of mankind" (*L.I.51*). In the same months he announced the subversive *The Necessity of Atheism* with the characteristic declaration, "a love of truth is the only motive which actuates the Author of this little tract," since truth "has always been found to promote the best interests of mankind" (V.205). Only a few days before his death he was still confidently urging, "Let us see the truth whatever that may be" (*L.II.442*). Consequently it is hardly surprising in the *Discourse* to find him giving the unblinking pursuit of truth as justification for uncovering certain aspects of Greek social life not ordinarily discussed in modern letters. How else was he "to induce the reader to cast off the cloak of his self-flattering prejudices" and suggest "a system of reasoning" that might enable him "to form a liberal, consistent, and just judgment of the peculiarities" of Greek domestic manners. For the same reason Shelley condemns the pernicious "prudery" of his day, which rendered it virtually impossible to give an accurate picture of the ancient Greeks. No modern writer, he charges, has "dared to show" the Greeks "precisely as they were." Books professing to depict Greek social life are "all written for children, with the caution that no practice or sentiment highly inconsistent with our present manners should be mentioned, lest those manners should receive outrage and violence" (219). However, the fact that a "change . . . has been operated in certain conventional notions of morals" is no reason for allowing oneself to be scared off the liberalizing pursuit of truth.[13]

The *Discourse* singles out two writers in particular as bowing to the pressures of prudery—the Abbé Jean-Jacques Barthélemy, a French social historian and popularizer, and C. M. Wieland, the German novelist and poet—even though their writings in fact appear to have been principally behind the poet's own conspectus of Attic society and manners. Almost daily for a period of some two weeks in late June and early July 1818—only a month before he set to work on the *Discourse*—Shelley read conscientiously in Barthélemy's *Voyage du jeune Anacharsis en Grèce vers le milieu du quatrième siècle avant l'ère vulgaire*, a fictitious journal of life in fourth-century Greece by a namesake of the legendary Scythian Anacharsis.[14] But although the work is encyclopedic in scope and valuable as social history, the viewpoint is not authentically Greek. Barthélemy writes from the constricting viewpoint of a priggish eighteenth-century French cleric, never forgetting, in Shelley's words, "that he is a Christian and a Frenchman." Thus he anachronistically censures whatever clashes with his own values and shuts his eyes almost entirely to such a characteristically Greek institution as the love of boys. Barthélemy seeks to excuse his omissions, particularly with respect to "manners and customs," on the grounds that these "are often only indicated by ancient authors, and have given occasion to different opinions among modern critics. I have . . . suppressed a great part of them, and ought perhaps to have suppressed still more."[15] Inasmuch as Shelley was reading at the same time not only Plato but also Aristophanes—an almost invariable entry in his wife's *Journal* for this period being "Shelley reads Aristophanes and 'Anacharsis' "—he must have been disturbingly aware that what appeared to be the true Greek attitudes toward love, women, and sex were being slighted or distorted in the modern work.

This dissatisfaction was probably reinforced by another contemporary account of Greek social and cultural institutions, unmentioned in the *Discourse* but almost certainly present in its composition, August Wilhelm von Schlegel's *Über Dramatische Kunst und Literature* (1809-1811), translated into English by John Black in 1815 as *A Course of Lectures on Dramatic Art and Literature*. To allay the tedium while journeying through France on the way to Italy in the spring of 1818, Shelley on four separate occasions read "Schlegel aloud," in the words of Mary's *Journal*, to her and Claire Clairmont. The reference is undoubtedly to the *Lectures*, if for no other reason than that parallels between the *Discourse* and the German work are too extensive to be accidental.[16] For example, Schlegel writes, "We are yet in want of a work in which the entire poetic, artistic, scientific, and social culture of the Greeks should be painted as one grand harmonious whole . . . An attempt has indeed been made in a popular work . . . *Travels of the Younger Anacharsis* . . . but . . . it betrays more good-will to do justice to the Greeks, than ability to enter deeply into their spirit . . . and [is] disfigured by modern views. It is not the travels of a young Scythian, but of an old Parisian."[17] Here, almost certainly, is the origin of Shelley's interest in Barthélemy, for he took up the *Voyage* not long after. Schlegel also alerted him to the weaknesses in the account and hence to the need for a fuller, more objective rendering, one catching the authentic Greek spirit.[18]

As for Wieland, this author's "delightful novels," as they are termed in the *Discourse* (219), had long been favorites of Shelley's. Thomas Jefferson Hogg described his friend's enthusiasm at Bracknell in 1813 on being introduced by the Boinville circle to a French translation of Wieland's *History of Agathon,* which Shelley read again the following year with Mary, when the pair also read Wieland's *Peregrine Proteus.*[19] Both novels present a sympathetic if romanticized portrait of the ancient world. Another novel in the same vein, Wieland's *Aristippus,* which delineates life and thought in fifth-century Athens, Shelley had read in French translation only three months before the composition of the *Discourse.* "I am just reading a Novel of Wielands called Aristippus which I think you would like," he reports to Hogg on April 30, and Mary's *Journal* for May 2 notes, "Shelley finishes 'Aristippe.' " However, the poet was far from satisfied with the French version, because "the impudent translator has omitted much of the original, to accommodate it as he says to the 'fastidious taste & powerful understanding of his country men'!" (*S&C.*VI.584), which was precisely the sort of practice that Shelley would shortly by inveighing against in the *Discourse.* A particular problem in all of the novels is Wieland's handling of Greek sexual practice. Although he was no mean student of ancient eroticism, he deliberately suppressed one of its primary modes, refraining, in Shelley's words, from "diminishing the interest of his romances by painting sentiments in which no European of modern times can possibly sympathize" (219). Wieland was aware of the anachronism and, like Shelley, believed in the importance of accurately portraying the "manners" of cultures "beyond our little horizon" in order to "improve mankind," but he was not prepared to risk the taboo against homosexual portrayal.[20]

Not even the classical scholars of the day were prepared to confront head-on the challenge of the ancient attitude. In a review of Friedrich von Schlegel's *Lectures on the History of Literature, Ancient and Modern*—a review that Shelley no doubt read since the same journal contained John Taylor Coleridge's savaging of his own *The Revolt of*

Islam—the reviewer owns time and again that he is forced to circumlocution and suppression when speaking of "the difference of manners between the Greeks and ourselves," because "the decorousness of modern manners does not admit much allusion" to such things.[21] The reviewer's tone throughout is embarrassed and apologetic, where it is not indignant, and the same was true of classical scholarship generally, including Schlegel's *Lectures*.[22] Nowhere is there any suggestion that modern "decorousness" is mistaken, no protest against misguided prudery. Shelley's challenge of this prudery sets him significantly apart from his age.[23] Only in the present century have scholars begun to catch up with Shelley on this score.

Even Shelley, it must be admitted, is trapped into an uncharacteristic guardedness of language—that "delicate caution" which he acknowledged to Peacock as necessary—when he approaches the subject of Greek pederasty in the *Discourse*, and matters of the utmost importance for his argument go altogether unnamed. So carefully does he tread that close attention is demanded if the full import of his thought is not to be missed. Most of the time, however, his language is forthright and free of cant, leaving no doubt of his meaning. At no time, moreover, whether proceeding openly or by indirection, does he evade the manifest complexities of his subject or leave off pursuing their more baffling ramifications, regardless of the dark byways down which they lead him. In the process he succeeds in raising and, in some instances, partially answering a number of questions that are not wholly resolved even today. His analysis is frequently acute. Far from being merely an academic introduction to the *Symposium*, Shelley's essay is a genuine attempt at social history.[24]

"One of the chief distinctions between the manners of ancient Greece and modern Europe," holds Shelley in the *Discourse*, "consisted in the regulations and the sentiments respecting sexual intercourse" (219). Contributing foremost to this distinction was the Greek attitude toward women. Whereas "the male sex . . . received the highest cultivation and refinement . . . the other, so far as intellect is concerned, were educated as slaves and were raised but few degrees in all that related to moral or intellectual excellence above the condition of savages." Greek women, "thus degraded," acquired, "except with extraordinary exceptions, the habits and the qualities of slaves." This inferiority was institutionalized, built into the social system, "recognized by law and by opinion" (220-221).

In this view Shelley was at one with contemporary scholarly thinking, which held that the subordination of the upper-class matron in classical Athens was absolute, or "Oriental" in the stock phraseology of the day.[25] Shelley's sources here were not only Barthélemy and Schlegel but Madame de Staël's *De la littérature considérée dans ses rapports avec les institutions sociales* (1800), which he read in 1815 and which states that the Greeks "considered women in no other light than as slaves designed by nature for that unhappy state: and indeed the greater part of them were deserving of that appellation; their minds were not furnished with a single idea that could distinguish them from the brute creation."[26]

In such systematic moral and intellectual debasement Shelley discerned grave consequences for the Greek experience of love. What must have been the demoralizing effect upon the male psyche when the ordinarily "natural" object of its affection had to be judged fundamentally unworthy of it? What if a man's male companions were far more attractive, both in mind and body, than his wife or even his mistress? That this was the case Shelley had little doubt, especially in the Greece of the Periclean age.

In the first place, notes the poet, Greek women apparently suffered from a purely physical handicap. They "were probably not extremely beautiful," or "at least there was no such disproportion in the attraction of the external form between the female and male sex among the Greeks as exists among the modern Europeans." Even worse—and here woman's social subjection enters the equation—the Greek matron was "certainly devoid of that moral and intellectual loveliness with which the acquisition of knowledge and the cultivation of sentiment animates as with another life of overpowering grace the lineaments and the gestures of every form which it inhabits." The men of Greece, on the contrary, "corresponded in external form to the models which they have left as specimens of what they were. The firm yet flowing proportion of their forms; the winning unreserve and facility of their manners; the eloquence of their speech . . . their gestures animated at once with the delicacy and the boldness which the perpetual habit of persuading and governing themselves and others; and the poetry of their religious rites, inspired into their whole being—rendered the youth of Greece a race of beings something widely different from that of modern Europe." Not only were the men of classical Greece more attractive than their degenerate counterparts of a later age, but they even outshone the charms of their own women. "If my observation be correct," Shelley notes, "the word *kalos* (beautiful) is more frequently applied to the male sex, while *eueidēs* (handsome) denoted the attractiveness of a female."[27] Whether this difference was owing to "the climate," "the original constitution of the peculiar race of the Greeks," "the institutions and system of society," or "the mutual action of these several circumstances," Shelley is unclear (220-221). But of the fact he is virtually certain.

Modern research has shown that the poet's observations on the use of the word *kalos* were essentially correct. The so-called *kalos* inscriptions or "love-names" found in Attic literature and particularly on Attic vases contain numerous instances of the phrase *ho pais kalos* ("the boy is beautiful") but fewer of the feminine *ho pais kale*. As explained by David Robinson and Edward Fluck, the inscriptions "are formed by the addition of the adjective *kalos* to a proper-name." They refer "not only to attractive youths, but to worthy and popular men as well. Certainly throughout Greek literature it is not merely the ephebes who are called *kalos* . . . the adjective *kalos* could be and was used for males at almost any stage of their lives, if they deserved."[28] Significantly the term *kalos* denotes both beautiful and noble-minded. The Attic cultural ideal laid special stress on the development of the soul together with the body; this was the prized *kalokagathia*.[29] Bodily beauty was often conceived to be only the mirror of inner cultivation. It is to the incomparable power of Attic culture or *paideia* that Shelley alludes in the *Discourse* when proposing the institutions and structure of society as a possible source of male beauty. The difficulty, however, was that the benefits so lavishly bestowed on the male—the almost "*super*natural loveliness of his country's genius" (*L*.II.73)—were systematically denied the female, with a consequent diminution in her moral and intellectual loveliness and hence personal appeal. In sum, the very factors combining to enhance the romantic attractiveness of one sex were simultaneously operating to reduce that same quality in the other sex.

Like her Oriental subjection, the Athenian matron's allegedly inferior beauty was another commonplace when Shelley was writing, although the emphasis was more often on her physical than her spiritual defectiveness.[30] Shelley would have been familiar with this view from Wieland's *Agathon*, but his most likely source, whether direct or indirect, appears to have been the work of the French social historian Cornelius de Pauw, whose *Philosophical Dissertations on the Greeks* (1788) had long popularized the view. Although there is no record of Shelley's having read de Pauw, his speculation concerning the peculiar constitution of the Greeks echoes de Pauw's thesis that, "owing to some constitutional singularity," the youth of ancient Attica "were endowed with personal beauty more generally than women; and from this caprice of nature resulted a depravity in the common course of human passions."[31]

Shelley, while recognizing the possibility of such an explanation for Greek sexual tastes, plainly thought the problem was more complex. Whereas de Pauw attributed the peculiarities of Greek love to a physiological freak, Shelley saw them as embedded in the structure of the Greek ethos. The real difficulty was that Greek women were lacking in "intellectual" beauty and thus incapable of arousing the more elevated sentiments automatically elicited by the men. In this view Shelley had much to support him. Scholars have repeatedly insisted that owing to the intellectual inferiority of the women, there could have been little genuine affection between the sexes in ancient Athens.[32] A woman might serve as a convenient sexual outlet and she was certainly essential as a breeder for the state, but she could not expect to command the intellectual respect essential for the development of the higher emotions—hence the growth of pederasty.[33]

One element of Shelley's explanation for woman's inferior appeal is singularly his own and at the same time vital for an understanding of his sexual views. This is his indictment of the ocular deficiency of the Greek matron, whose "eyes could not have been deep and intricate from the workings of the mind and could have entangled no heart in soul-enwoven labyrinths" (220). To the uninitiate this charge might seem merely a rhetorical flourish, but Shelley's entire work discloses that he means precisely what he is saying, contrary to all contemporary scholarly opinion, which held that the Greeks were noted for the size and beauty of their eyes, no distinction being made in this instance between men and women.[34]

In Shelley's poetic universe, where all the heroines are intellectual beauties, it is their eyes which serve as a principal attraction for their lovers. They beam light from deep within: "dark, far, measureless,/ Orb within orb, and line through line inwoven"; whoso gazes" into them "faints, entangled in their mazes."[35] In Shelley's prose the story is the same. His heroines are remarkable for their radiant eyes, which serve as the magnetic focus of their spellbound lovers. Often his heroes similarly exhibit "eyes deep, like . . . wells of crystalline water" (*The Coliseum* [VI.300]). Shelley was himself notable for "brilliant" and prominent, even protuberant eyes, such as "are rarely beheld in the human or any other head."[36] And he was drawn to this feature in the women in his own life. Thus Harriet Westbrook's "radiant" eyes bind him to "worship the spirit within," of which they are the "sweet . . . index." It is the same with Mary Godwin, whose "bright" eyes "redeem" him. Within Claire Clairmont's eyes "a power like light doth lie." The "double Planet" of Sophia Stacey's deep eyes beguiles even "the wisest into madness" with its "soft clear fire." The "twin lights" of

A Discourse on Love

Emilia Viviani's eyes are the wells from which "the sunbeams . . . ever leap/Under the lightnings of the soul—too deep/For the brief fathom-line of thought or sense." The last words he ever wrote—to Jane Williams—were "only for the pleasure of tracing what will meet your eyes."[37]

What exactly was Shelley seeking when he gazed into the labyrinths of another's eyes? Some would say it was himself. Shelley's narcissism is overt in his sexual psychology, and in view of his own extraordinary ocular endowment, it is possible that he was looking for the counterpart of himself in another's eyes. But as with most of Shelley's "eccentricities," however open to psychological interpretation, he had in mind a perfectly logical rationale for his interest. The eyes spoke a language of their own, mutely conveying something of exceeding importance.[38] What Shelley thought he detected in the language of the eyes was the measure of a person's soul. The eyes marked both the portal to the inmost self and its egress.

The eye as the soul's window on the world is one of the hoariest of poetic conceits. But for Shelley it has special meaning. Principally what Shelley is looking for through the portal of the eyes is the quality of mind, the state of inward cultivation, lying behind them. The eyes are thus the gauge of whether a person possesses that "moral and intellectual loveliness" which the *Discourse* defines as quintessential for true beauty, and the infallible test for Shelley is their radiance, depth, and complexity. If the mind is deep, subtle, and full of light, so are the eyes. Ordinarily such beauty is the product of fortunate environment and right education, which in Shelleyan terms means an "enlightened" one, with the full etymological force of the word. It is no accident, for instance, that the intellectually beautiful Prince Athanase, described as possessing a pair of eyes "Through which his soul . . . shone, softly burning," had been an assiduous pupil of the old Socratic tutor Zonoras, whose outstanding feature was eyes "whose arrowy light/Shone like the reflex of a thousand minds./He was the last whom superstition's blight/Had spared in Greece."[39] But this potentiality can also be inherited if one is fortunate in one's parentage. A curious jotting in one of Shelley's notebooks shortly after the birth of Byron and Claire's Allegra on Jan. 12, 1817, begins: "To Alba [Allegra], eyes, depth, amicableness, like Albè [Byron]."[40] To Byron himself Shelley writes: "Her eyes are the most intelligent I ever saw in so young an infant."[41]

This potentiality has to be fostered and nourished if it is not to become blighted. Shelley stresses the fact that in infancy a child's eyes, hence its soul, are essentially passive, undeveloped, "the shrines of unawakened thought," and they must be deliberately brought to life by an enlightened upbringing.[42] At first the eyes are largely reflectors, mirroring back the light cast from without, or as expressed in *The Sensitive Plant*, they are like flowers opening up their petals in warm sunshine and "smiling" back to "Heaven" (I.59-65). If the nurture is right, through those smiling eyes one will have the pleasure of seeing "the growing soul beneath/Dawn in faint smiles" (*R&H*.382-383). Without the proper nurture, however, the inner light may never be kindled, and without continued nourishment, it may at any time find itself extinguished, either temporarily or permanently. When this happens, the eyes become glazed and cold, or glassy and glaring, or simply hollow.[43] When in *The Triumph of Life* Shelley encounters the mass of putrefaction that had once been Rousseau, he finds its eyes only burnt-out sockets, "the spark with which Heaven" had once lit its spirit now extinguished for lack of the "purer nutriment" which had fueled the fire of his youth (201-202).

In a series of revealing letters from Italy in 1818-1819 Shelley records his impressions of Italian women, which take on added fascination in the light of the *Discourse*, written during the same period. His remarks are nearly all unflattering: "The Italians . . . are a very different people from the French. They have less character; & the women especially seem a very inferior race of beings. Their manners so far as I can judge from their mien & physiognomy are at once prudish & coquettish, their features bony, their figures thin, & those who have any claims to beauty, have a beauty superficial, & of a cold & unfeeling character. Their voices have none of that winning persuasiveness of those of France, but are hard & without inflexion or variety of tone."[44] In both language and conception, Shelley's *Discourse* is here taking shape unconsciously. When the poet is actually writing the *Discourse*, he simultaneously writes to Godwin: "The modern Italians seem a miserable people—without sensibility or imagination or understanding. Their outside is polished & intercourse with them seems to proceed with much facility—though it ends in nothing & produces nothing. The women are particularly empty: and though possessed of the same kind of superficial grace, are devoid of any cultivation & refinement" (L.II.22). On the same day he writes to Peacock, "we have been over to the Casino [at Lucca], where I cannot say there is anything remarkable, the women being far removed from anything which the most liberal annotator could interpret' into beauty or grace, and apparently possessing no intellectual excellences to compensate the deficiency." But in an example of his low-keyed sexual humor he adds wryly: "I assure you it is well that it is so, for the dances, especially the waltz, are so exquisitely beautiful that it would be a little dangerous to the newly unfrozen senses and imagination of us migrators from the neighbourhood of the pole. As it is—except in the dark—there could be no peril" (*L*.II.25).

After a visit to Byron in Venice, Shelley's strictures take on real bite. "The fact is," he complains to Peacock, "the Italian women are perhaps the most contemptible of all who exist under the moon; the most ignorant the most disgusting, the most bigotted, the most filthy." His conclusion to Hogg is simply, "*I do not like the Italian women.*"[45] Although this aversion was undermined by Shelley's introduction to Roman society, its foundation remained intact, as shown by his observations to Peacock in which, whether consciously or not, he draws directly on the language and judgments of the *Discourse*: "the Romans please me much, especially the women: who though totally devoid of any kind of information or culture of the imagination or affections or understanding, & in this respect a kind of gentle savages yet contrive to be interesting. Their extreme innocence & naivete, the freedom & gentleness of their manners, the total absence of affectation makes an intercourse with them very like an intercourse with uncorrupted children . . . you must hear the common places which escape from them before they cease to be dangerous." Then follows the inevitable coda: "The only inferior part are the eyes, which though good & gentle, want the mazy depth of colour behind colour with which the intellectual females of England & Germany entangle the heart in soul-inwoven labyrinths."[46]

In Italy at this time, young girls were shut up in convents almost from infancy and kept there until they had reached a marriageable age. In Shelley's words, this kind of education produced a "sentimental, innocent, superficial Italian."[47] As early as 1810 in *St. Irvyne* the poet stigmatized a convent upbringing as "an erroneous system of education," stunting and narrowing to the intellect, rendering the mind *"comparatively imbecile"* (V.161-162). Visiting the convent where Byron had placed his daughter, Shelley reported that Allegra "yet retains the beauty of her deep blue eyes," but he had misgivings concerning the future. "Her intellect is not much cultivated here," he noted, and though the child "knows certain orazioni by heart & talks & *dreams* of Paradise & angels & all sorts of things—and has a prodigious list of saints—and is always talking of the Bambino . . . the idea of bringing up so sweet a creature in the midst of such trash till sixteen!—"[48]

It took a person with great natural force of character to surmount the evils implicit in such a system and to develop depth of mind. Such a person was Shelley's Beatrice Cenci, whose "deep," "life-darting eyes," her "awe-inspiring gaze," bespoke the "firm" and "subtle mind" within, producing that rare combination of "loveliness and wisdom" which magnetized to her will all those opposed to her in the climactic scenes of her life's sad drama.[49] Such a one too was Emilia Viviani who, though "imprisoned" in a convent, had "cultivated her mind," according tò Shelley, beyond anything he had ever encountered in Italian women.[50] Her intellectual, moral, and emotional development was exceptional. She was the only one who could vie in appeal with the intellectual women of England and Germany.[51] In the others, however, he could have no interest. Devoid of "moral and intellectual loveliness," eyes dull, shallow, and empty, like their ancient Greek counterparts, they stood hopelessly enslaved to the degrading manners and the patriarchal restraints of their religion and culture, and could not expect to win the love of a truly civilized man.

"I now understand why the Greeks were such great Poets," wrote Shelley after visiting Pompeii in 1819—"If such is Pompeii, what was Athens?"—and "above all I can account, it seems to me, for the harmony the unity the perfection the uniform excellence of all their works of art. They lived in a perpetual commerce with external nature and nourished themselves upon the spirit of its forms. Their theatres were all open to the mountains & the sky" (L.II.73-74). A favorable "climate" was, in Shelley's view, another distinguishing element of ancient Athens, which helped account not only for the unrivaled perfection of its artistic achievement but possibly even for the superior physical beauty of its male population.[52] Shelley himself was exceptionally sensitive to climatic variation, his health an unfailing barometer of meteorological change, and a temperate climate is one of the cardinal features of his poetic millennia, an indispensable prerequisite to physiological no less than sociological change. That Greece should be blessed in this respect was to be expected. Significantly the "halcyon" isle of his visionary flight in *Epipsychidion* is located in the "blue Aegean," cradled under "Ionian skies" and lapped in eternal springtime or summer; it is a solitary Eden but "for some pastoral people . . . /Who from the Elysian, clear, and golden air/Draw the last spirit of the age of gold" (410-430). Similarly in *Hellas* the "gold" in the "golden years" of the "world's great age" derives in no small measure from the light of Greece's "smiling" climate, spawning its lustrous youth (1060-1065).

A favorable climate should have worked to the benefit of both sexes equally, although there was the possible difference of the upper-class matron's indoor seclusion. However, while the element of climate did nothing to widen the gap between the sexes, neither did it reduce it.

When combined with the genetic and sociological factors determining the character of the sexes, the net effect was further to enhance the already overwhelming attractiveness of the male.

That Attica enjoyed an unusually favorable climate, leading to the mental and physical superiority of its inhabitants, was another commonplace of the period, maintained by both Schlegel and Wieland.[53] The most influential statement of this view was Johann Winckelmann's in *The History of Ancient Art*, where the perfection of the Greeks is ascribed to their climate.[54] Shelley is known to have read the *History* aloud to Mary in a French translation in the winter of 1818-1819, and its judgments colored his notes on Greek sculpture, written shortly afterward.[55] However, he may have read the *History* at an earlier date, specifically before composition of the *Discourse*. Since the *Lectures* of Schlegel, which were almost certainly behind Shelley's study of Barthélemy in the late spring of 1818, also made favorable mention of Winckelmann's *History*, there is the possibility of a companion study of Winckelmann which has gone unrecorded. If, as seems likely, Shelley first read the *Lectures* in England prior tc his departure for Italy, this would account for his having copies of ooth the *Voyage* and the *History* with him on the trip, at which time he no doubt anticipated ample leisure for reading.[56] During the following summer when he came to write his own disquisition on the ancient Greeks, he could thus have had the views of Winckelmann as well as of Barthélemy and Schlegel upon which to draw.

Internal evidence suggests that Winckelmann's *History* was indeed before Shelley as he set about composing the *Discourse*. In addition to reflecting its general tone of romantic enthusiasm for the Attic world, Shelley's essay bears the *History's* unmistakable impress in detailing the specific excellences of Greek culture. Like Winckelmann, the poet first admires the glories of Greek sculpture and then addresses himself to the subject of Greek pictorial art. Their paintings, he writes, were "full of delicacy and harmony," at least "according to Pliny and Pausanias" (217). The references are to Pliny's *Natural History*, Bk. 35, and Pausanias' *The Description of Greece*, two ancient compilations of classical culture. The former, according to Medwin, Shelley read and, on the testimony of Mary, translated during his Eton years. The latter, in a translation by Thomas Taylor, Shelley ordered from the Olliers in 1817. Whether the work was ever received does not appear, but there is no reason to suppose otherwise, especially as Peacock's *Rhododaphne*, written contemporaneously, evinces considerable knowledge of Pausanias, and Shelley and Peacock were then living in close proximity. Even though Shelley is not known to have read Pliny after Eton and his reading of Pausanias remains hypothetical, his appeal to the testimony of these authorities would appear to be in good faith except for one curious coincidence. In the *History*, Winckelmann, when tracing the growth of Greek painting, cites exactly the same two authorities (II.98). Such a yoking may reflect nothing more than a contemporary scholarly cliche', or it may be the sheerest chance.[57] Yet the striking similarity of context in which the two citations arise makes one suspicious that the words of the eminent German authority were not entirely unknown to Shelley. Since Winckelmann uses the evidence of "Pliny and Pausanias" to downgrade the importance attached by the Greeks to painting in comparison with their reverence of sculpture, Shelley may have thought of himself as redressing the imbalance, for he holds in the *Discourse* that Greek paintings "would probably bear the same relation as is confessedly borne by the sculptures to all succeeding ones" (217).

But most important for Shelley's understanding of Greek sexuality would have been precisely those pages in the *History* given over to praise of Greek sculpture, based on a study of the magnificent fragments of antique sculpture surviving in Italy. As Winckelmann argues, "Much that might seem ideal to us was natural" among the Greeks, and "it is reasonable to suppose" that in Greece nature "perfected man to the highest degree."[58] In the same way Shelley writes in the *Discourse* that Greek sculptures are "such as we in our presumption assume to be the models of ideal truth and beauty." Actually, he believes, the men of Greece "corresponded in external form to the models which they have left as specimens of what they were" (217, 221). This opinion persisted until the end of his career. The human form, he holds in the Preface to *Hellas*, reached a perfection in Greece "which has impressed its image on those faultess productions, whose very fragments are the despair of modern art, and has propagated impulses which cannot cease . . . to ennoble and delight mankind until the extinction of the race" (III.8).[59]

This opinion is confirmed again and again in the poet's statuary notes, also heavily indebted to Winckelmann, which he jotted down in Rome and Florence shortly after the composition of the *Discourse*.[60] The uncommon degree to which he found the classical formulation of male beauty genuinely moving and convincing is manifest. Significantly, the feature that elicits his warmest response and strikes him as characteristic of the people themselves is the epicene or androgynous element so prominent in the Greek aesthetic ideal, particularly in the Greco-Roman marbles of the decadent period that were his principal object of study, as they were Winckelmann's. He consistently praises the figures for their soft, flowing lines and their gestures "animated at once with delicacy and . . . boldness"—qualities of both masculine and feminine, though the latter predominate. It was in ancient Greece, he later writes in *Hellas*, that "fairest thoughts and limbs were built/To woman's growth" (996-998). Shelley's favorite sculptor was Praxiteles, whose work, of all the Greeks, is most noted for its androgynous qualities, and it was Praxiteles whom the Hellenistic sculptors took as their principal model. To this androgynous art Shelley in his statuary notes contrasts the more obviously masculine forms of later art, for which he felt much less enthusiasm. Shelley objects to the heavily muscled and proportioned figures of a more "scientific" anatomy, such as he found typified in what he considered the overrated paintings and sculptures of Michelangelo, which had "no temperance no modesty."[61] He prefers the "idealized" "beauty, virtue, and harmony" of Raphael, one of whose paintings he describes as "very sweet & lovely," or the delicate beauty of Titian, one of whose pictures had "the softest & most voluptuous form with languid & uplifted eyes & warm yet passive limbs."[62] These are the same qualities that riveted him to Hellenic sculpture.

He was responding, in other words, to the aesthetic ideal of Greek pederasty, as figured especially in the statues of Bacchus, Apollo, and Olinthus—"those sweet and gentle figures of adolescent youth in which the Greeks delighted" (VI.328). Boy-beauty was the principal object of attraction. Most striking in its revelation of this attraction is Shelley's impassioned description of a youthful Apollo that he examined in Rome, a figure whose androgynous grace particularly insinuated itself into his imagination. Recalling another statue he had seen earlier, he observes that it had been "difficult to conceive anything more delicately beautiful than the Ganymede"—another famous boy-beauty, who had inspired a violent pederastic passion in no less a luminary than the father of the gods.[63] But the Apollo surpassed it, possessing "a womanish vivacity of winning yet passive happiness and yet a boyish inexperience exceedingly delightful" (VI.327). This figure was the poet's "favourite," according to Mary, one that he admired far more than the "quantity of female figures in the attitude of the Venus di Medicis" abounding in Rome.[64] He describes the Apollo as "probably the most consummate personification of loveliness . . . with regard to its entire form that remains to us of Greek Antiquity" (VI.330).

Shelley would not have maintained that every antique sculpture should be regarded as a literal rendering from nature. His favorite, the Apollo, while embodying all that was finest in young Greek manhood, was nevertheless the representation of a god, not a human. This was beauty more than mortal, boy-beauty raised to its ideal perfection. As Winckelmann explains, for the Greeks the "highest conception of ideal male beauty is especially expressed in the Apollo, in whom the strength of adult years is found united with the soft forms of the most beautiful springtime of youth." Yet the Apollo was strictly "an ideality, adopted partly from the nature of eunuchs, and elevated by conformation surpassing that of humanity" (II.325,322). Another figure to which Shelley felt himself more than ordinarily attracted was the Bacchus. And Bacchus, as Winckelmann observes, was also a "kind of ideal youth," drawn, like the Apollo, "from the conformation of eunuchs," and "blended with masculine youth." Bacchus appeared under this form "always with delicate, round limbs, and the full, expanded hips of the female sex, for according to the fable, he was brought up a maiden" (II.329).

Winckelmann points out that the Greek worship of boy-beauty even molded its ideal of female beauty. Figures of women were relieved of most of their distinctively feminine characteristics, thereby converting them into further representations of boy-beauty. "The breast or bosom of female figures," he notes, "is never exuberant . . . The form of the breasts in the figures of divinities is virginal in the extreme . . . Virginal breasts are likened by the poets to a cluster of unripe grapes . . . On some figures of Venus . . . the breasts are compressed, and resemble hills whose summits run to a point; and this form of them appears to have been regarded as the most beautiful" (II.405).[65] Shelley's statuary note on the Venus Anadyomene reveals this equation plainly: it is a virtual duplication of his descriptions of the Apollo, to whom the figure is explicitly compared, the only difference being Venus' "pointed and pear-like bosom" (VI.321). This reduction of all sexual difference to one ideal form was also given expression in the openly bisexual figure of the hermaphrodite. "The great number" of these figures, explains Winckelmann, "shows that artists sought to express in the mixed nature of the two sexes an image of higher beauty; this image was ideal . . . All figures of this kind have maiden breasts, together with the male organs of generation; the form in other respects, as well as the features of the face, is feminine" (II.317-318).

Just how seriously the Greeks meant this ideal to be taken is open to question. The comic poets ridiculed it, and Plato derived considerable amusement from it through the mouth of Aristophanes in the *Symposium* (189D-192E). Once again, however, as with the Apollo and the Bacchus, Shelley appears to have been unusually drawn to this ideal.

A Discourse on Love

Familiar is the lovely fire-and-snow Hermaphroditus of *The Witch of Atlas*—a "sexless thing it was, and in its growth/It seemed to have developed no defect/Of either sex, yet all the grace of both" (xxxvi)—for which a variety of literary sources have been proposed. A passage from Shelley's "Lines Connected with *Epipsychidion*," however, suggests that at some point in his travels he had the chance to examine a hermaphroditic statue at firsthand: "that sweet marble monster of both sexes,/Which looks so sweet and gentle that it vexes/The very soul that the soul is gone/Which lifted from her limbs the veil of stone" (58-61).[66] Shelley's reaction reveals an unconscious assimilation of his attraction for the hermaphrodite to his worship of boy-beauty, in a manner not greatly different from the Greeks. Thus, in describing an Olinthus or seated youth that he viewed in Florence, he duplicates exactly the epithets of the *Epipsychidion* fragment, terming it "Another of those sweet and gentle figures of adolescent youth" (VI.328).[67] Just as his boyish Bacchae and Apollos are uniformly memorable for their "sweetness" and "gentleness," his unequivocally androgynous Hermaphroditus is no less lovely for its "gentle countenance" and limbs, the "youth" of its bosom, the "purity" of its expression, and its "sweet sighs" (*Witch*.xxvi, xl). The pervasiveness of this response is testimony to the intensity with which the poet was temperamentally attracted to the Greek pederastic ideal and explains why he was so ready to believe that the Greek male in fact surpassed the female in beauty. Antique sculpture proved it.

Small wonder that he should therefore conclude in the *Discourse* that in Greece of the classic period "beautiful persons of the male sex" became the "object of that sort of feelings, which are only cultivated at present as towards females" (221). Overwhelming personal beauty, when conjoined with the manifold intellectual graces of classical *paideia* and spotlighted against the backdrop of the mental and physical inferiority of women, could point to but one result—*paiderasteia*, or "the love of boys." To determine in more detail precisely what was meant by this curious passion becomes Shelley's primary concern in the remainder of his essay.

2

Love's Typology

"LET IT NOT BE IMAGINED," declares Shelley in the *Discourse*, "that because the Greeks were deprived of its legitimate object, they [were] incapable of sentimental love; and that this passion is the mere child of chivalry and the literature of modern times." On the contrary, this "object or its archetype forever exists in the mind" (220). Shelley's position is one of considerable theoretical consequence. Stated unequivocally, it makes for interesting comparison, not only with the thought of his own day, but with the findings of subsequent investigation. It also serves as a logical starting-point for the investigation of his own psychology of love, a subject crucial to understanding his philosophy of sexual relations.

In broadest terms, the question raised by the poet is whether the sort of emotional complex now labeled "romantic" is psychosexually innate, hence coexistent with human experience, or whether it is the product of cultural forces, hence unknown to many societies. More narrowly, the question is whether such passion was a common occurrence in the ancient world or whether it was a revolutionary development of medieval courtly society and thus an essentially alien strain in the sum total of man's psychosexual history. Of the two hypotheses, the second has found favor until recently—to the extent that feudal Europe was viewed as somehow the scene of an unprecedented upheaval in man's emotional evolution. In our own day the most influential exponent of this view has been C. S. Lewis, who maintained that French poets in the eleventh century "discovered or invented, or were the first to express, that romantic species of passion which English poets were still writing about in the nineteenth. They effected a change which has left no corner of our ethics, our imagination, or our daily life untouched, and they erected impassable barriers between us and the classical past." In ancient literature, "love seldom rises above the levels of merry sensuality or domestic comfort, except to be treated as a tragic madness . . . which plunges otherwise sane people (usually women) into crime and disgrace."[1]

This view has not gone unchallenged, however. Years ago John Addington Symonds noticed the similarity between the pederastic love celebrated in the Platonic dialogues and the love hymned by the troubadours in the medieval courts, a similarity resting on "something permanent in human nature."[2] William James questioned the validity of the traditional view, noting that there is a great difference between the way an emotion is experienced by a society and the way it is valued. He considered it unlikely that such a powerful emotion as romantic love could be of recent origin. Yet "our ideas *about* our emotions, and the esteem in which we hold them, differ very much from one generation to another."[3] Aldous Huxley considered it self-evident that "Love's psychological and physiological material remains the same." Every epoch simply treats the sentiment "in a different manner, just as every epoch cuts its unvarying cloth and silk and linen into garments of the most diverse fashion."[4] Maurice Valency observes that even were there no evidence of romantic love in antiquity, one would still "have to postulate its existence on the most fundamental psychological grounds," the psychic forces of this passion being such "that it is obviously impossible to assign any historical period to their resurgence . . . They must have existed everywhere and always, a basic attribute of human nature." Such a postulation is unnecessary, however, for it is "evident that the entire psychic and literary apparatus of romantic love was in existence among the ancients."[5]

Shelley's acuity in arriving at this conclusion one hundred and fifty years earlier is striking when one realizes that to hold such a view was in his day, even more than at present, to fly in the face of contemporary opinion, which was unanimous in regarding romantic passion as an evolutionary refinement, absent in the ancient world except as a comic weakness or psychological aberration. Especially was this the assumption of two of Shelley's major sources in the *Discourse*, Wieland and Schlegel, both of whom are at pains to uphold the orthodox interpretation of ancient sexuality. It has "long since [been] agreed," notes Wieland in *Agathon*, that the Greeks "had different ideas of love from the modern Europeans . . . They honoured conjugal attachment, but they had no idea of that romantic passion, we distinguish by the name of love, a passion, which numbers of romance writers among our neighbours on the other side of the Rhine, and in England, have endeavoured to elevate into an heroic virtue." The Greeks knew only the kind of love "which sports, kisses and is happy . . . that love which, with all the symptoms of a feverish delirium, overpowers the whole soul, was in their eyes one of the most odious vices" (III.101-104). In the *Lectures*, Schlegel argues that the Greeks "knew nothing of the gallantry of modern Europe, nor the union of love with enthusiastic veneration. All was sensual passion or marriage." However "highly the Greeks may have succeeded in the Beautiful, and even in the Moral, we cannot concede any higher character to their civilisation than that of a refined and ennobled sensuality" lacking all those spiritual graces that the advent of Christianity and chivalry introduced into human eroticism.[6]

To lay bare the insularity of such a view is Shelley's object in the *Discourse*. Sentimental love, far from being the creation of a certain period or culture, is a permanent impulse in the human psyche, though environmental factors influence the modes and frequency of its expression. It is this belief that elevates Shelley's picture of ancient Greece, so consonant in many ways with early nineteenth-century thinking, above the level of his age.[7]

From Shelley's viewpoint, what needed to be accounted for in the ancient world was not the absence of romantic passion but rather its peculiar bent. While he apparently agreed with Wieland and Schlegel that heterosexual love in the romantic sense was largely unknown in ancient times, he was distinguished from the others by his courage in pursuing the subject to its conclusion.[8] Only by challenging the traditional taboo was Shelley able to free himself from the parochial moral assumptions of an earlier period and arrive at the modern view that the potentiality for romantic passion does not represent the revolutionary advance of a more refined culture but is a psychological constant irrespective of object—an "archetype" in his expression, an inborn "psychic posture" in modern parlance. As Shelley recognized, an element of romantic longing has been present in all cultures, and Greece was no exception. In fact, owing to the unprecedented role attached to the life of the mind in Attic society, the Greeks were probably more susceptible to such feelings than any other people known to history (222-223). Because of the enforced inferiority of women, however, these feelings were generally barred from their natural outlet. This did not mean their cessation but simply their deflection toward "a compensation and substitute." As a result, "beautiful persons of the male sex" were "the object of that sort of feelings, which are only cultivated at present as towards females." Homosexual and heterosexual love, though outwardly polar opposites, were in reality one passion, opposite faces of a single impulse, which was itself unchanging.

Shelley's fascination with love is attested to by the number of times he sought to define it. It was not enough merely to know the passion from experience or even to portray it in operation; he had also to grasp it intellectually. "How you reason and philosophize about love," writes Mary Godwin to her lover in 1814 in the first months of their elopement; "do you know if I had been asked I could not have given one reason in its favour—yet I have as great an opinion as you concerning its exaltedness and love very tenderly to prove my theory."[9] Shelley's best-known definition appears in the essay *On Love*; the Preface to *Alastor* is also important. But most lucid and comprehensive is the definition set forth in the *Discourse*.[10] In addition to sketching the poet's characteristic schematization of love's psychology, the *Discourse* supplies a detailed commentary on the role of sex in love and on the place of love in humankind's social evolution.

First of all, love is a "profound and complicated sentiment." By "sentimental" Shelley means that love is a distinct emotion or "passion," not simply refined or ennobled sexual feeling, which was all the Greeks were supposedly capable of experiencing. Love is in fact a "universal thirst" for intercourse not just of the senses but of one's whole nature—"intellectual, imaginative, and sensitive" (220). This emotional complex would today be labeled "romantic" rather than "sentimental," which currently has an unfavorable connotation. Both terms were in use in the early nineteenth century, although *sentimental*, retaining its original sense of elevated or exalted, was probably the more common, and it was Shelley's exclusive choice.[11] The term was also applied in a more limited sense to literary compositions, especially to the medieval love-lyric and chivalric romance as well as the more recently developed "sentimental" novel and drama ("chivalry and the literature of modern times," in Shelley's phraseology), and it is because of this association that Shelley employs the term in the *Discourse*.[12] As he well knew, a whole literary tradition had flowered since the Middle Ages celebrating sentimental love. Its hierophants were among Shelley's favorite authors. Among eighteenth-century novelists, for example, he was particularly drawn to Jean Jacques Rousseau and Wieland. The love elevated in their work is quintessentially sentimental, stressing feeling, heart, sensibility, imagination, sympathy, and high moral aspiration, which is love as Shelley normally conceives it. His point, however, is that since the capacity for this emotion is universal, the moderns could hardly lay exclusive claim to it. It was no less common among the Greeks, albeit given a different sexual orientation.

Even in Shelley's day not everyone would have agreed that sentiment was a genuine emotion and not a mere sublimation of less ele-

vated desires. Byron has many cynical things to say about "sentiment." Reporting the Countess Guiccioli's demand that he discontinue
his mock-epic masterpiece *Don Juan*, he explains, "The reason . . .
arises from the wish of all women to exalt the *sentiment* of the passions—& keep up the illusion which is their empire." But *Don Juan*
laughs at sentiment and strips away the illusion. For Byron sentiment
is just a tinsel veil to cover "passions of grosser nature" and is "all
owing to Chivalry—& the Goths—the Greeks knew better."[13]

The historian Edward Gibbon, with whose work Shelley was familiar, also viewed sentiment as merely a sublimation of the physical
impulse. "Although the progress of civilization has undoubtedly contributed to assuage the fiercer passions of human nature," he writes,
"it seems to have been less favourable to the virtue of chastity . . .
The gross appetite of love becomes most dangerous when it is elevated,
or rather, indeed, disguised by sentimental passion. The elegance of
dress, of motion, and of manners, gives a lustre to beauty, and in-
flames the senses through the imagination."[14] Gibbon, who is here
referring to the differences separating the barbarian Germans from the
Romans under the Empire, puts his finger on a point that Shelley himself had to account for. If the archetype of love is universal, what
about its status in primitive societies? Gibbon clearly believed that the
passion was cultural in origin, dependent upon the development of
civilized institutions and manners.

Shelley too believed that the need for love "grows more powerful in
proportion to the development which our nature receives from civilization" and that the sexual impulse, though "only one and often a
small part" of the need, is still a "claim which even derives a strength
not its own from the accessory circumstances which surround it and
one which our nature thirsts to satisfy." As evidence, he cites "the
degree of intensity and durability of the love of the male towards the
female in animals and savages," which leads him to conclude that "all
the duration and intensity observable in the love of civilized beings
beyond that of savages" must be the result of other causes. As for "the
susceptibility of the external senses," the differences are probably
neglible (220-221). The incidence of sentimental love is therefore a
coefficient of a culture's social and intellectual advancement, even
though this love has an archetypal existence in the most primitive
societies.

In a state of total savagery, it is true, love must doubtless have been
a simple affair, the mere "gratification of the senses" (220). As Shelley
phrases it in his essay *On Marriage:* "Before the commencement of
human society, if such a state can be conceived to have existed, it is

probable that men like other animals used promiscuous concubinage . . . No moral affections arose from the indulgence of a physical
impulse" (VII.149). But this was before man was human, according to
the *Discourse*, for even in "his wildest state" man is "a social being."
Since "a certain degree of civilization and refinement ever produces
the want of sympathies still more intimate and complete," sensual
gratification can no longer be the sole object of sexual connection
(220). Because the poet links his archetype of love directly to man's
nature as a social animal, he places its origin at the dawn of human
society rather than farther up the evolutionary scale in some particular age or culture. Love exists from the moment people are aware
of others as persons like themselves with a whole spectrum of claims
or sympathies and with whom their entire being "thirsts" for communion. The sexual impulse soon becomes but a small part of this
amalgam, serving, from "its obvious and external nature," only as
"type or expression of the rest, as common basis, as acknowledged
and visible link," for the totality of "that profound and complicated
sentiment" which is love among social humankind (220).

The "social sympathies," observes Shelley in *A Defence of Poetry*—
those "laws" from which "as from its elements society results" and
which begin to develop "from the moment that two human beings
coexist"—serve as the foundation for all human motives, including
"love in the intercourse of kind" (VII.110). These laws, which underlie
the poet's reasoning in the *Discourse*, figured heavily in the thought of
the age.[15] The term *sympathy*, originally signifying compassion for
the suffering of others, during the eighteenth century came to denote
fellow feeling in general, an imaginative identification with the pleasures as well as the pains of others, and in this sense it became the
basis of much contemporary moral and social theory. Sympathy was
the impulse, whether considered innate or the product of association,
which enlarged the circle of the self, enabling the individual to interact
unselfishly or "disinterestedly," in the language of the day, with
others. It was thus the primary social impulse, the very "cement of
human society," in Lord Kames's much quoted phrase.[16]

In probably its most influential statement, this doctrine was given
extended treatment in Adam Smith's *The Theory of Moral Sentiments*
(1759), whose opening chapter, "Of Sympathy," explains: "How
selfish soever man may be supposed, there are evidently some principles in his nature, which interest him in the fortune of others, and
render their happiness necessary to him, though he derives nothing
from it, except the pleasure of seeing it. Of this kind is pity or compassion." The instrument of this emotion is the imagination. Since we can

never have any "immediate experience" of what another person feels, remaining forever locked within the boundaries of our own sensory perceptions, it is only through the imagination that we can surmount the limitations of the self. Through the imagination we place ourselves in the situation of another; "we enter as it were into his body, and become in some measure the same person with him, and thence form some idea of his sensations, and even feel something which, though weaker in degree, is not altogether unlike them," although it is "the impression of our own senses only, not those of his, which our imaginations copy." The effect of this imaginative identification is fellow feeling or the emotion called sympathy. Upon this psychology Smith rests his whole system of ethics: "We can never survey our sentiments and motives . . . unless we remove ourselves, as it were, from our own natural station, and endeavour to view them as at a certain distance from us." We become "the spectators of our behaviour, and endeavour to imagine what effect it would, in this light, produce on us. This is the only looking-glass by which we can, in some measure, with the eyes of other people, scrutinize the propriety of our own conduct." Smith's is clearly a social theory of ethics. "Were it possible that a human creature could grow up to manhood in some solitary place, without any communication with his own species, he could no more think of his own character, or the propriety or demerit of his own sentiments and conduct, than of the beauty or deformity of his own face." But society furnishes the necessary moral mirror, and sympathetic projection constitutes its psychological basis.[17]

David Hume, to whom Smith was greatly indebted, likewise placed social sympathy at the center of his ethics in *A Treatise of Human Nature* (1739).[18] Sympathy, he stresses, originates from the mental similarity of all humankind in "their feelings and operations; nor can any one be actuated by an affection of which all others are not in some degree susceptible." Yet because we know directly only our own sensations, "no passion of another discovers itself immediately to the mind. We are only sensible of its causes or effects." From these we can "infer" the passion, and this ability gives rise to sympathy. Men's minds, in short, are "mirrors to one another," and by the power of the imagination the individual enters into the interests of others and feels "the same satisfaction, that . . . objects naturally occasion" in them.[19]

Shelley claimed to have read Hume at Eton, though which work he does not specify; and it is possible that he became acquainted with Smith's theories at more or less the same time.[20] But these ideas need not be ascribed to a single source, since they were as much the common stock of educated people of the period as the theories of depth psychology are today, and they could have been encountered almost anywhere, including imaginative literature. Moreover, Shelley would have found them given sanction in Godwin's *Political Justice*, where they are clearly set forth, often directly echoing Adam Smith, and in the philosopher's later work, including the novels, where their importance is particularly stressed.

"Oh! lovely sympathy thou art indeed life's sweetest only solace" (*L.*I.191). From the outset sympathy played a central role for Shelley, whose own sympathetic sensibilities were pitched unusually high.[21] All his life he stressed the "sacred sympathies of soul and sense" (*QM.*IX.36) which draw man outside himself toward others, making him intensely social. These affections constitute for Shelley the "cement" of human nature (VI.222).

In the section entitled "Benevolence" of his fragmentary "Speculations on Morals" (VII.74-77), Shelley traces the psychological growth of the sympathetic impulse and its relation to the social organism. At birth, he holds, man is motivated solely by instinctual impulses, whose only object is self-preservation. As an infant and a young child, man thus directs all his energies to "extinction of the pains" with which he is "perpetually assailed." As these impulses are largely reflexive and unconscious, he has only "a very imperfect consciousness of the existence of other natures resembling" his own. If, for example, he feels no emotion while his nurse or his mother is "suffering acute pain, it is attributable rather to ignorance than insensibility."[22] In proportion, however, "as the mind acquires an active power," the scope of these original self-regarding impulses becomes limited. Eventually the child grows aware of being "surrounded by natures susceptible of sensations similar to its own." And when "the accents and gestures, significant of pain, are referred to the feelings which they express, they awaken in the mind of the beholder a desire that they should cease." In this way pain "is apprehended to be evil for its own sake." But until this time the infant, no less than the savage and the solitary beast, whose minds are incapable of receiving "an accurate intimation of the nature of pain" as existing in similar beings, is necessarily selfish. Conversely, the "inhabitant of a highly civilized community will more acutely sympathize with the sufferings of others" (VII.74-75), projecting beyond himself in an act of sympathetic reduplication. Hence the multiple benefits of civilized intercourse.

The faculty whereby the primal selfishness is eventually transcended is the "imagination," whose operations enable the individual mind to identify itself with the pains and pleasures of others, since the imagination is that faculty which "respects . . . the similitudes of things."[23] As man matures, collectively no less than individually, the imagination acquires through exercise the habit of "perceiving and abhorring evil" (VII.75), that is, pain. In this manner a moral sense is born, although as the poet notes in *On Marriage*, "the ideas of right and wrong must have subsisted from the moment that one human being could sympathize in the pains and pleasure of another" (VII.150). The sole distinction, therefore, "between the selfish man and the virtuous man is that the imagination of the former is confined within a narrow limit, while that of the latter embraces a comprehensive circumference" (VII.75). As explained in Shelley's fragmentary tale *The Coliseum*, "The internal nature of each being is surrounded by a circle, not to be surmounted by his fellows; and it is this repulsion which constitutes the misfortune of the condition of life. But there is a circle which comprehends, as well as one which mutually excludes, all things which feel. And, with respect to man, his public and his private happiness consists in diminishing the circumference which includes those resembling himself, until they become one with him and he with them" (VI.303-304). The selfish, however, never get beyond the inmost circle. Like the poet's Peter Bell the Third, who had a mind that was "At once circumference and centre/Of all he might or feel or know," and who had "as much imagination/As a pint-pot," so that he could never fancy any other situation "From which to dart his contemplation,/Than that wherein he stood," the selfish are bound "within the belt" of their own natures, cut off from sympathy with their fellows (273-302).

Paradoxically, then, it is from man's primary or "elementary" constitutional demands on others that he is led, by a mirroring or reduplicative act of the imagination, to altruistic sympathy for his fellows—and hence to love. For imaginative self-projection is clearly the basis of this impulse as Shelley understands it: "The great secret of morals is love, or a going out of our own nature and identification of ourselves with the beautiful which exists in thought, action, or person, not our own. A man, to be greatly good, must imagine intensely and comprehensively; he must put himself in the place of another and of many others; the pains and pleasures of his species must become his own. The great instrument of moral good is the imagination" (VII.118). As noted by Roy Male, Shelley in this passage from the *Defence* has merely substituted love for the sympathetic imagination.[24] Love is a psychological identification with the pleasures and pains of others beyond the circle of the self, or on the moral level, a benevolent sharing in mankind's common humanity.

Love's Typology

When we love, we place ourselves in the position of another, and through imaginative self-projection we actually become for the moment that other. But the important corollary is that our sympathy will be returned, that the other will also become us. Love results from tightening the imaginative circle around others who resemble the individual until they become identical (VI.303-304). This reciprocity is particularly vital at the emotional level. When sentimental love is not a sharing of sympathies, a mutual going out of the self, it is nothing, or "bitter ashes," as the poet writes in *On Beauty* of a sympathy that is not returned (VII.154). Indeed it is the sympathetic response, the seeking "to awaken in all things that are, a community with what we experience within ourselves," which receives principal stress in Shelley's verse, reflecting what he considers a primary human impulse. In the words of *On Love*, "We are born into the world, and there is something within us which, from the instant that we live, and move thirsts after its likeness" (VI.201).[25] But only through social intercourse, through the mirror of society, does man learn to reciprocate this drive, to give others that for which he himself thirsts.

Thirst is a key term for Shelley, present wherever he seeks to formulate his love psychology, just as it consistently characterizes the many lovers in his work, notorious for their all-consuming thirsts which, if not slaked, annihilate them. Shopworn though this usage is, Shelley manages to endue it with considerable resonance, as he so often does when using a stock expression, phrase, or metaphor. The motif of thirst reverberates through many contexts besides the erotic.[26] Essentially what the term means to Shelley is a fundamental impulse, drive, or desire, one that is intrinsic to the nature of a thing. Thirst is rich in possibilities for two reasons. First, of all the appetites it is the most imperative, the most immediate, and the most vital for sustaining life. Accordingly it is the perfect vehicle for representing a basic, primary, all-consuming want, which is the chief reason that Shelley generally chooses it to represent love over its principal alternative, love as hunger, "an insatiable famine" (VI.160). Thus in the spring, "All baser things pant with life's sacred thirst;/Diffuse themselves; and spend in love's delight,/The beauty and the joy of their renewèd might" (*Ado.*XIX). This is the instinctual, generative level of love, for Shelley employs "spend" in the popular sense of orgasmic overflow, a spilling of seed, and such love affects even the most refined natures, as he points out in the *Discourse* (220).[27]

But there is another "thirst" peculiar to man, one that in his developed state assimilates the purely instinctive or animal. This is the need for sentimental or sympathetic love, which is an "imperious want of the heart and of the mind" as well as of the body (221). As Shelley explains in *On Love*, if we reason, we desire to be understood. If we imagine, we desire that "the airy children of our brain [should be] born anew within another's." And if we feel, we desire that the other's nerves "vibrate to our own," that their glance "kindle at once and mix and melt into our own," that their lips "reply to lips quivering and burning with the heart's best blood" (VI.201).[28] This last powerful image of sensual feeling, as so often in Shelley, goes beyond the senses to what lies behind them. Just as the eyes are the locus of the intellect or spirit, so the lips are the dwelling place of the imagination: "Fine lips are never wholly bad and never belong to the expression of emotions completely selfish—lips being the seat of the imagination" (VI.326-327). Love is complicated precisely because the sexual affinities constantly suggest sympathies beyond themselves, standing as a "type and expression of the rest." Their total combination constitutes true love, the desire for which "grows more powerful in proportion to the development which our nature receives from civilization" (220), to such a degree that "in solitude, or in that deserted state when we are surrounded by human beings, and yet they sympathize not with us, we love the flowers, the grass, and the waters, and the sky" (VI.202). Nature too has its inner correspondences or "types" in man (*Alr*.508). Love is thus "the bond and the sanction which connects not only man with man but with everything which exists" (VI.201).

In summary, man is born thirsty: created with certain wants which demand immediate slaking if life is to be sustained. At first these are of the simplest instinctual or appetitive sort, and in his earliest years man is literally fulfilled if he is filled full. But as he matures, he grows aware of other elements of being which also demand fulfillment. He comes to learn that "the intellectual faculties, the imagination, the functions of sense" have each "their respective requisitions on the sympathy of corresponding powers in other human beings," and until these are satisfied, he experiences an emptiness, an inner "vacancy" (I.173-174), "the chasm of an insufficient void" (VI.201). Speaking from his own experience, Shelley recalls how in adolescence he grew conscious of a blighting "sense of loneliness," manifesting itself in a pining "thirst" for companionship, for a meeting with someone uniting "all sympathies in one" (*Rev.Is.*v-vii).

From a psychological point of view the most significant aspect of sentimental love is its premium on sympathetic affinity. The lover must find someone *like* himself if his love thirst or hunger is to be properly satisfied: "living beings who resemble your own nature and are bound to you by similarity of sensations are destined to be the instrument of your affections."[29] This requirement is built into the doctrine of sympathy by virtue of its foundation in eighteenth-century empirical philosophy and sensational psychology.[30] Because we are forever locked within the prison of our own sensory perceptions (VI.303), we can never truly sympathize with others except as they resemble us, except as their experience parallels or echoes our own. The nearer this correspondence, the easier is our imaginative projection and hence sympathetic identification. There is an *"immediate sympathy* which men have with characters similar to their own," asserts Hume. "They enter with more warmth into such sentiments, and feel more sensibly the pleasure, which arises from them." Hume explains that an "easy sympathy," which is common only to *"relation, acquaintance,* and *resemblance,"* leads directly to "love or affection." He illustrates this idea by reference to Plato's Aristophanic fable of the division of the sexes, according to which each is half of an original whole and forever searching for the other half or sympathetic double.[31] When Shelley defines the sentimental or sympathetic longing for likeness in his description of erotic attraction in *On Love,* he clearly has this fable in mind too, as his very personal rendering of the relevant passages in the *Symposium* (192C-193C) makes plain: "Whenever . . . any are impetuously struck, through the sentiment of their former union, with love and desire and the want of community, they are ever unwilling to be divided even for a moment . . . it is not merely the sensual delights of their intercourse for the sake of which they dedicate themselves to each other . . . but the soul of each manifestly thirsts for, from the other, something which there are no words to describe . . . [Each wants] intimately to mix and melt and to be melted together with his beloved, so that one should be made out of two . . . If this be the completion of felicity, that must necessarily approach nearest to it, in which we obtain the possession and society of those whose natures most intimately accord with our own."[32]

While the object of love, ethically speaking, is to enlarge the circle of the self to embrace the pains and pleasures of the whole species, only on the very broadest level is this possible and in the most general sort of way, as an identification with man's common humanity. Such an identification is only approximate at best. Our closest sympathies will always be for those most like ourselves. This is especially true of the sentiment of love, which demands a return of sympathy, a reciprocal identification, if it is to be complete. We experience certain things within ourselves and, as our social sympathies expand, become progressively more restless until that experience is shared, finding an "echo in another's mind." During childhood and early youth this desire is still largely unformed, but with the onset of puberty and the instinctive drive for sexual response, it becomes imperative: the mind, "suddenly awakened . . . thirsts for intercourse with an intelligence similar to itself."[33]

Ideally what the lover demands is a second or cognate self, an autotype, a twin soul or mirror image, but one purged so far as possible from his own faults and imperfections. The search for the approximation of this ideal shapes the psychodynamics of love as Shelley understands it. Love is one long quest to discover one's best self in another. In modern jargon, it is the attempt to externalize the individual's erotic ego ideal. "Thou wert my purer mind," writes Shelley in dedicating *Queen Mab* to Harriet Westbrook; and of Mary and himself after their elopement, he marvels: "so intimately are our natures now united, that I feel whilst I describe her excellencies as if I were an egoist expatiating upon his own perfections" (*L.*I.402).

As the poet elaborates the process in *On Love*, the sympathetic love affair with our environment, underway since birth, has by puberty produced within the self an indistinct mental image, a sort of hazy "miniature" or "portrait" of the entire self, free of all that we "condemn or despise, the ideal prototype of every thing excellent or lovely that we are capable of conceiving as belonging to the nature of man." This is the self raised to the highest pitch of perfection within our ability to "imagine" it in the light of our social and intellectual experience of the world. This miniature self is a mirror whose "surface reflects only the forms of purity and brightness"; it is a kind of "soul within our soul," encircling its own paradise "which pain, and sorrow, and evil dare not overleap." The notion applies not only to the physical self but to "the minutest particulars of which our nature is composed," to all its various elements or faculties (VI.201-202).[34] To this miniature we refer all our experience of the external world, "thirsting" for correspondences. The goal is to discover the miniature's replica or "antitype" (VI.202), a term employed in its root sense of a "corresponding form," responding "as an impression to the die," and thus "the person or thing represented or foreshadowed by an earlier type or symbol."[35] The psychodynamics of Shelleyan love are thus epitomized as the quest of the lover to match his ideal self-image or inner *type*, which is the *prototype* of all that the self can conceive as best in man, with its mirror image or *antitype*. This is love's typology, whose language and concepts are basic to the poet's work. Indeed, this system of types has the widest application in Shelley's thought, extending far beyond the confines of the strictly psychosexual.[36]

Love's Typology

Though reaching its fullest development in the years 1818-1819, Shelley's typology of love took shape as early as 1812, in some of his first letters to Godwin. Of his brief stay at Oxford, for instance, he reports: "I could not descend to common life. The sublime interest of poetry, lofty and exalted achievements, the proselytism of the world, the equalization of its inhabitants were to me the soul of my soul" (L.I.228). This is a description of his ideal prototype, the intellectual miniature reflecting "only the forms of purity and brightness," glimpsed in the process of formation. Three months later, reporting to Godwin his desire to purchase the property of Nantgwillt in Wales, he explains that he cannot view this "scenery, mountains & rocks seeming to form a barrier around this quiet valley which the tumult of the world may never overleap . . . without associating *your* presence with the idea, that of your wife, your children, & one other friend [Elizabether Hitchener] to complete the picture which mind has drawn to itself of felicity" (L.I.287). The soul within the soul, described in *On Love* as "a circle around its proper Paradise which pain, and sorrow, and evil dare not overleap," now freed from the common life of the university, has here found an Eden to realize its dreams. The miniature soul thus has a social analogue in the little world within the larger world, and the two often met in the poet's subsequent writings, as in the final section of *Epipsychidion*.

Several years passed before Shelley worked out this terminology to his satisfaction. In the Preface to *Alastor*, for example, he falls back on the inexact "prototype" where he plainly means "antitype" and is left with nothing to label the former conception as developed in subsequent definitions. Not until his Platonic studies in 1817-1818 does the useful *antitype* enter his vocabulary, borrowed from the philosopher's theory of Ideas, after which its appearance is frequent.[37] But by 1818 and *On Love* his analytic vocabulary is complete, with *type*, *prototype*, and *antitype* each having its assigned place in his typological scheme.

According to Shelley's erotic psychology, in sum, when the time finally dawns in adolescence that we are awakened sympathetically to the world about us and in consequence realize our personal insufficiency, we seek to elicit a community between our outer and inner experience, which applies to all levels of being—rational, imaginative, sensitive. The antitype promises such a community in proportion to the demands of the inner type or original ideal self-image: an understanding capable of "clearly estimating the deductions of our own," an imagination able to "enter into and seize upon the subtle and delicate peculiarities which we have delighted to cherish and unfold," and a body "whose nerves, like the chords of two exquisite lyres, strung to the accompaniment of one delightful voice, vibrate with the vibrations of our own" (VI.202).[38] What the lover wants is someone of his own type with whom to make sympathetic music. The quest for the embodiment of this ideal gives shape to some of Shelley's most characteristic work.[39]

But discovery of the perfect antitype, though love's goal, is "invisible and unattainable" (VI.202). It is an ideal only, whose realization has life solely in the imagination. The psychological impulse behind the creation of this ideal is described in the curious fragment "*Igniculus Desiderii*": "To thirst and find no fill—to wail and wander/With short unsteady steps—to pause and ponder—/Where busy thought and blind sensation mingle;/To nurse the image of unfelt caresses/Till dim imagination just possesses/The half created shadow, then all the night/Sick." In *Alastor* the formation of the antitype is "allegorized" (Pref.). With the coming of puberty, the protagonist, who is a young poet, imagines to himself the ideal lover, a veiled maid, who echoes in his erotic dreams, reduplicating and finally uniting with the ideal prototype he has formed of himself (154-161).[40] But when he seeks to find the ideal's human counterpart, "overleap[ing] the bounds" of the soul within the soul and "pursu[ing]/Beyond the realms of dream that fleeting shade," he is doomed to disappointment (205-207).

Yet while the incorporation of the dream is in the ideal sense impossible, this does not stop us from loving, from hoping against hope that our dream of love will somehow prove to be, in the arcane love rhetoric employed by Shelley's circle, the "pure anticipated cognition" of our antitype.[41] Indeed, once the antitypal ideal has been engendered, there is no escaping its demands, "no rest nor respite to the heart over which it rules," until we have succeeded in catching its reflection, however slight, in the external world, arresting its "faintest shadow" (VI.202). *Epipsychidion* describes the formation of the poet's own antitype and its consequences. In early youth he imagined a being, "a soul out of [his] soul," modeled sympathetically from all that was best in his own experience—love of nature, literature, philosophy —which became his "divinity." At first he thought, in the romantic naiveté of youth, to have found his antitype literally embodied: "from the caverns of my dreamy youth/I sprang . . . towards the lodestar of my desire." This was mere wish fulfillment, however, the desire of the moth for the star, and he soon realized that the ideal was purely a self-creation. The most he could hope to find was its pale approximation, its "shadow": "In many mortal forms I rashly sought/The shadow of that idol of my thought" (190-268).[42]

But how easy to forget, to imagine that in a Mary Godwin or an Emilia Viviani he had suddenly found, not a shadow or a simulacrum, but living substance, the "embodied vision of the brightest dream," "Youth's vision . . . made perfect"—only to experience inevitable disenchantment.[43] The foundation stone of love is precisely our ability to imagine, to identify our inner experience with what seems to be its counterpart in someone resembling us, and thus to sympathize with it. But imaginative projection is a tricky process at best, especially in an emotional transaction as complicated and subjective as love. All we ever truly know are our *own* sensations and their mental replicas, which we call ideas, and when we attempt to judge the experience of others, it can only be on the analogue of what we experience within ourselves. As Shelley explains in *On Life*, each individual "is at once the centre and the circumference, the point to which all things are referred, and the line in which all things are contained" (VI.194).[44] Forever locked within the prison of our own minds, we are easily seduced by superficial resemblances in others into sympathizing where there is little or no real basis for sympathy. "I know not the internal constitution of other men, nor even yours whom I now address," begins *On Love*: "I see that in some external attributes they resemble me, but when misled by that appearance I have thought to appeal to something in common and unburden my inmost soul to them, I have found my language misunderstood like one in a distant and savage land. The more opportunities they have afforded me for experience, the wider has appeared the interval between us, and to a greater distance have the points of sympathy been withdrawn" (VI.201).

The danger of going astray is particularly strong in love, owing to the idealizing nature of the experience. Beginning with the formulation of an imaginary ego ideal, love attempts to force all experience to fit its mold, even creating sympathies where they are nonexistent. Since the archetype of love is inborn, the mind inevitably proceeds to select "among those who resemble it that which most resembles it" and "instinctively fills up the interstices of the imperfect image in the same manner as the imagination moulds and completes the shapes in clouds, or in the fire, into the resemblances of whatever form, animal, building, &c., happens to be present to it" (220). What is at work here, as shown by a canceled section of *A Defence*, is the law of association, which governs the exercise of the imagination. Thus "when we look upon shapes in the fire or the clouds and imagine to ourselves the resemblance of familiar objects, we do no more than seize the relations of certain points of visible objects," filling in the outlines through association with our own experience (VII.107).[45] This tendency may be a good thing as regards poetry, which works to enlarge the circumference of the imagination "by replenishing it with thoughts of ever new delight" (VII.118); but when applied to love, it clearly has dangers. In associating to itself everything even remotely resembling it from the human world and then imaginatively, thus subjectively, filling in the imperfect outline, the sympathetic archetype often proves seriously delusive.

The danger is especially great in first love, where we have not yet learned to subdue our vision to the limitations or imperfections of reality, and hence our imagination often runs riot. As Shelley writes of the beauteous Henrietta in Godwin's novel *Mandeville*, no doubt thinking of his own Harriet Grove, she seems to be "all that a susceptible heart imagines in the object of its earliest passion. We scarcely can see her, she is so beautiful. There is a mist of dazzling loveliness which encircles her and shuts out from the sight all that is mortal in her transcendent charms" (VI.221-222).[46] The operative word is "imagines," which accounts for the misty, dreamlike quality of the experience, its atmosphere of light, duplicated in nearly all the poet's own renderings of love. In terms of Shelley's erotic typology, what the lover is seeing is in fact a dream, the diffused glow radiated by his own thirst of love, not the loved one. Rather than a real person, he is beholding a self-projection, the veiled maid, his imagined antitype, the replica of his miniature self reflecting only the forms of "purity and brightness." "You loved a being, an idea in your own mind which had no real existence," Shelley warns the adolescent Hogg of his blinding sentimental passion for Elizabeth Shelley. "You concreted this abstract of perfection, you annexed this fictitious quality to the idea presented by a *name*, the being whom that name signified was by no means worthy of this" (L.I.95). Shelley might well have profited from this advice himself, as has frequently been pointed out. Too often, like his Pan, he found himself pursuing a maiden and clasping a reed: "who is there that will not pursue phantoms, spend his choicest hours in hunting after dreams, and wake only to perceive his error and regret that death is so near?" But "Gods and men, we are all deluded thus!"[47]

Disenchantment was built into the very nature of sentimental love, as Shelley and every other Romantic recognized. The circumstance was symbolized by making the passion a form of nympholepsy, after the ancient malady supposed to have seized anyone beholding a nymph, a frenzied but unappeasable longing after the incarnation of the immortal ideal. "I think one is always in love with something or other," Shelley reflects shortly before his death, casting his gaze back over the history of his own love life: "the error, and I confess it is not easy for spirits cased in flesh and blood to avoid it, consists in seeking in a mortal image the likeness of what is perhaps eternal." The trouble is that "some of us have in a prior existence been in love with an Antigone, & that makes us find no full content in any mortal tie" (*L*.II.434,364). The nympholeptic theme is implicit throughout Shelley's poetry in the psychological symbolism of the unquenchable thirst for the nymphic veiled maid and her typological equivalents.[48]

The theme was a favorite of Shelley's friends. "Pray are you yet cured of your nympholepsy?" Shelley inquires of Peacock shortly after arriving in Italy in 1818; " 'Tis a sweet disease but one as obstinate & dangerous as any . . . Whether such be the case or not I hope your nympholeptic tale is not abandoned" (*S&C*.VI.657). The poet was most struck by the theme's treatment in Byron's *Childe Harold*—"those beautiful stanzas in the 4th Canto about the Nymph Egeria." The stanzas were in fact so Shelleyan that he felt obliged to disclaim a hand in their inspiration, though he was far from wishing to "suppress any thing nympholeptic" (*L*.II.44).[49] The difference between the two poets is that Byron, in his despair, reduced the thirst of love to its lowest common denominator, sex, cynically dismissing the rest as the "sentimental" self-deception of the ladies, while Shelley continued to the last to recognize the thirst's archetypal claims, even though acknowledging that they could never be entirely quenched. The realist, the antiromantic, might ridicule the self-deluding blindness of the sentimental lover, but for Shelley, to stifle the archetypal impulse was to deny what was best in human nature. It was to wither up or freeze man's full development as a civilized being, returning him to the level of the infant or savage, incapable of sympathy, whose claims are centered solely on the self. But man is ever a social being, and his sympathies continue to expand, unless blunted or deadened by selfish preoccupations, until he reaches that "epoch of refinement" where sentimental love becomes an imperative want of his whole multiplex nature. This want colors his entire view of human relations, implanting in his mind an ideal of perfection which impels him to seek out its faintest shadow in the external world and to create it where it is not. This ideal may often keep him from seeing the world as it actually is, and certainly it prevents him from accepting the world as it is. But as Shelley concludes in *On Love*, "So soon as this want or power is dead," the best part of man, his ideal prototype, dies too: "he becomes the living sepulchre of himself, and what yet survives is the mere husk of what once he was" (VI.202).

Shelley's typology of love, grounded in what he believes to be a universal psychological archetype, is a serious effort to formulate a sexual psychology, however rudimentary. Pieced out in the Preface to *Alastor, A. Treatise on Morals, The Discourse, The Coliseum*, and *On Love*, and dramatized in the poetry, it offers a coherent theory of the dynamics of psychosexual behavior. As such, it opens itself to comparison with modern theories on the subject, beneficiaries of over a century and a half of intensive investigation and speculation.

The claim has been made that in its scope and its emphasis on the complicated nature of love in civilized society, Shelley's psychology "anticipates in some respects such modern psychological theories as Freud's on the libido; for Shelley conceives of love as a unifying force with widely variant manifestations, biological, psychological, and social." Indeed the Freudian psychiatrist Karl Menninger argues that "One of the best definitions of love, and a very scientific one, was written by the poet Shelley."[50] Yet the affinity between Shelley and Freud is superficial at best. Freud was radically reductivist in his thinking, tracing amatory emotion back to the physical impulse and interpreting all higher manifestations of love, even where labeled "sentimental," as aim-inhibited sex.[51] For Freud, there is no escaping the primary motor power of the instinctual drives, however strenuously repressed or sublimated by the demands of society. Since these drives retain their original form in the unconscious life of the individual, their inhibition or deflection must be paid for at the often ruinous cost of psychological disorientation or neurosis. Civilization, built on just such inhibition, is therefore an infinitely fragile structure, held in precarious equipoise and forever on the verge of breakdown. A profound pessimism lies at the heart of Freud's thinking, thoroughly at odds with the perfectibilitarian outlook of a Shelley, whose thought is free of the bleak biological determinism circumscribing Freud's view of human behavior.

Much more congenial to Shelley's thinking are the omnibus theories of the Freudian revisionists, the so-called ego psychologists, such as Erich Fromm, Karen Horney, and Harry Stack Sullivan, who stress man's primary nature as a social animal with a whole range of personality claims to satisfy. These theories recognize love as not merely aim-inhibited sex but rather a distinct emotion, a discrete psychosexual state, incorporating the entire personality of the individual.

The truth of the matter, however, is that modern psychology has paid little attention to the emotional or psychic as opposed to the biological aspects of love. Freud himself, according to his pupil Theodor Reik, found the problem of love ultimately baffling, having to admit at the end of his life that we know "very little" about it, though it finally dawned on him that "love is a psychical power in its own right." Reik, who strongly believes that "sex and love are different in origin and nature," is one of the few to have made a systematic attempt to work out the psychodynamics of love as a discrete emotion, and his conceptual model, though far more elaborate than Shelley's, bears striking affinities with the poet's love typology. Like Shelley, Reik locates the basis of love, not in sex, but in ego fulfillment, the satisfaction of "ego-drives." Thus the first love-object is "a glorified ego, the phantom-self as we imagined it in our daydreams," a construct analogous to Shelley's prototype. The second love-object is "the embodiment of this desired image in a real person"—Shelley's antitype. Reciprocated love is therefore an interchange of ego ideals. Each person loves the ideal of himself in the other. Without this ego ideal there would be no love, according to Reik: "We fall in love because we cannot attain the image that is our better self and the best of our self." Not only is this unattainable ideal a phantom, but the love-object is also largely a phantom, "a peg on which we hang all the illusions of ourselves which we longed to fulfill," as Shelley too recognized. Because no one can remain forever concentrated on a phantom, to fall out of love means for Reik really to fall out of a dream, "the daydream of a better self."[52]

The most ambitious attempt to state the case for love as a separate emotion and to isolate its components has been made by the American psychologist Vernon Grant, much of whose argument is relevant to Shelley's love psychology.[53] Grant defines sexual love or "amorous emotion" as different, on the one hand, from sexual desire or sexual impulse, where the urge for genital satisfaction is largely indiscriminate in its choice of object. On the other hand, sexual love differs from benevolent love, concerned only with the well-being of the other person, where the factor of sexual desire does not enter. Amorous emotion is equivalent to what has traditionally been labeled romantic feeling. It is discriminating, concerned with the individuality of the object, and tends to include the entire personality of the object, while genital desire is focused narrowly on the body. Amorous emotion is longer in duration, persisting beyond sexual satisfaction; it is also generally slower in developing, since it depends on more than physical attraction and involves getting to know the loved one on more levels than the bodily.

Like Shelley, Grant rejects the view that amorous emotion is a "diluted or 'spiritualized' form of genital sex desire," making romantic behavior "a fairly recent event in human history" and reinforcing the presumed difference between civilized and primitive sexuality. Although anthropological evidence is scanty and ambiguous, Grant's position is that romantic emotion is dependent not on sublimation, but on individuation, the development of a sense of the personal uniqueness of others. This circumstance is not confined to any particular culture, though it is more common in advanced ones. Certainly the stress in modern Western society on the expression of individuality and on the cultivation of personality "may be related to the important role of amorous emotion in mating behavior." A perfect example, and one harking back to Shelley, lies in the emotional consequences seemingly attendant on the social status accorded woman in any given society. In cases where woman "is seen as mainly a breeder, a drudge, or a sexual toy, the incidence of the 'romantic emotion' is reportedly much lower than it is in cultures in which her status is relatively high. For an inferior one may feel affection, or sensual desire, but not the respect and adoration that is essential to amorous emotion as we know it in America, for example. Idealization requires a kind of minimum social valuation; woman as a sex must be acknowledged as *worthy* of strong feeling."[54]

Such theorizing is admittedly conjectural, and the scarcity of scientific data makes it as yet fundamentally *terra incognita*. According to Grant, "Despite the legitimacy of the problems of human amorous behavior, and the preoccupation of our culture with romantic themes, very few psychologists have been interested in it . . . The amorous emotion still awaits its Kinsey."[55] Shelley was no Kinsey. Yet it is clear he was listening to the same voice that summons us into the unknown a hundred and fifty years later.

3

Love's Visible Link

FOR SHELLEY the type or expression of love is the "sexual impulse." This is love's "common basis," in the language of the *Discourse*, its "acknowledged and visible link." And though it is only one, often small part of the total sentiment, it is nonetheless an impulse that demands satisfaction. While love in Shelley does not reduce to aim-inhibited sex, neither does it deny the impulse. The claims of the senses hold an honorable place in his anatomy of the total love experience. As he insists, the primordial archetype of love incorporates the intellectual, imaginative, and sensory elements of human nature, and each of these has its sympathies which must be fulfilled in order for the amatory experience to be complete. The senses have their legitimate claims, no less than the more elevated levels of the self.

Yet traditionally this level of Shelleyan love has been overlooked, the claims of the senses regularly ignored, their very existence often denied. The result has been to see his love poetry as disembodied, incorporeal, devoid of flesh-and-blood reality—which is very different from the way it was intended. Supposedly Shelley "hated the flesh like a puritan, but instead of mortifying it, he ignored its existence, and glorified love, not as a natural function, but as if it were an inspiration." He "rose but rarely into definite passion, nor [did] he often care to realize it." Though the words of late Victorian critics, these views have had a tendency to linger on.[1] Shelley "usually remains at a distance from the physical aspects of love," according to a recent writer, and often speaks in his love poems "like an exile from some other world."[2] This emasculate image has seriously damaged the poet's reputation during our own sexually obsessed century. He is accused of being a prude, a sexual hypocrite, "a poet of the averted gaze."[3] Sexual intercourse, "love's visible link," has thus for generations been the missing link in Shelleyan love.

Ironically, scarcely anyone in his own day would for a moment have thought of associating either Shelley or his poetry with discarnate love. On the contrary, it was the sensual element—"that abominable principle of *Shelley's*"—which was overstressed and condemned.[4] Typical of the reaction in his lifetime to the erotic in his work is a review of *Queen Mab* in *The Literary Gazette* for May 19, 1821: "A disciple following Shelley's tenets, would not hesitate to debauch, or, after debauching, to abandon any woman . . . Promiscuous intercourse of the sexes . . . to despise everything but the gratification of its own appetites: this is the millennium promised by the votaries of Shelley."

For the poet's work to survive into the Victorian period, a very different picture had to emerge. With the untiring efforts of his admirers, this is precisely what happened. Far from glorifying sensual indulgence, it was argued, Shelley scorned the fleshly. Soulmates, not bedmates, were love's goal. The poet himself had said that he did not deal in "real flesh & blood," that one "might as well go to a ginshop for a leg of mutton, as expect any thing human or earthly" from him (*L.*II.363). This view had the support of his wife, whose annotations to the verse did so much to shape the Victorian image of Shelley. Her husband "shrunk instinctively from portraying human passion," as she explained apropos of *The Witch of Atlas.* Variations on the theme appear whenever she refers to his attitudes toward love, and they fostered, and still foster, the view that the poetry as a whole is lacking in "human interest and passion."

The truth, however, is quite the reverse. Now that the distorting prism of Victorian sexual morality is a thing of the past, it is possible to look at the work without blinders. The result is to restore the claims of the flesh to their rightful place in the poet's overall anatomy of sexual relationship, and in the process to make the work more palatable to contemporary taste. Love's visible link is invisible only if one chooses not to see it.[5] Indeed a clear-eyed examination of the work discloses a rendering of human sexual response more psychogenically exact than that of almost any other poet. Shelley startlingly predicts the findings of twentieth-century sex research, especially those of Masters and Johnson. And in the personal attitudes which made possible such a rendering, he heralds the guilt-free attitudes toward the body defining modern sexual behavior. The celebration of liberated sexuality is a major theme of his life as well as his art.

Shelley's contempt for sexual prudery as expressed in the *Discourse* is enough to disprove the traditional view. But this attitude is not confined to the *Discourse:* it is reflected everywhere in his writing, and his personal life bore it constant witness. Anything smacking of bodily shame or the fear of natural impulse provoked his ire. "Curse these fig leaves"! he protested when examining the nude figure of a Greek athlete in Florence; "why is a round tin thing more decent than a cylindrical marble one?" (VI.315). At a time when the "horror of nakedness" was becoming "morbid," in the words of a modern historian, Shelley somehow managed to preserve an almost pagan delight in nudity.[6] Characteristic of his attitude is the episode reported by Claire Clairmont in the summer of 1814 during the poet's tour of the continent with Mary and herself: "On our way to Pontarlier, we came to a clear running shallow stream, and Shelley entreated the Driver to stop while he from under a bank could bathe himself—and he wanted Mary to do the same as the Bank sheltered one from every eye—but Mary would not . . . she said it would be indecent, and . . . how could he think of such a thing. The driver always looked at Shelley with a wondering stare as if he thought he was crazy . . . and refused to stop so Shelley could not bathe himself in the open air and in the middle of the day—just as if he were Adam in Paradise before his fall" (S&C.III.350). In 1818, while working on the *Discourse*, Shelley related to Peacock that it was his custom to undress and sit on the rocks of a pool, "reading Herodotus, until the perspiration . . . subsided, and then to leap from the edge of the rock into [the] fountain . . . I sometimes amuse myself by climbing when I bathe, and receiving the spray over all my body, whilst I clamber up the moist crags with difficulty" (L.II.26).[7]

In itself, perhaps, a sense of bodily modesty is hardly a cause for alarm. But to the degree that this kind of concealment reflects a deeper sense of sexual shame it was a serious evil to Shelley. By repudiating the innocent beauty of natural desires, prudery degrades the practitioner to "a kind of moral eunuch," as he declared of the self-righteous puritanism of the "unsexual" Wordsworth. The older poet "touched the hem of Nature's shift,/Felt faint—and never dared uplift/The closest, all concealing tunic." He knew not Nature's "deepest bliss," she favoring him only with "a sister's kiss" and admonishing him:

> " 'Tis you are cold—for I, not coy,
>   Yield love for love, frank, warm, and true;
> And Burns, a Scottish peasant boy—
> His errors prove it—knew my joy
>   More, learnèd friend, than you.
>
> "*Bocca bacciata non perde ventura,*
>   *Anzi rinnuova come fa la luna:—*

So thought Boccaccio, whose sweet words might cure a
Male prude, like you, from what you now endure, a
Low-tide in soul, like a stagnant laguna."[8]

The Italian, from the *Decameron* (ii.7), translates: "A mouth loses not
its freshness by kissing, but ever renews itself like the moon." Shelley
remarked to Leigh Hunt in 1819 that the application of this little
maxim "might do some good to the common narrow-minded conceptions of love." Boccaccio was "a moral casuist, the opposite of the
Christian, Stoical, ready made and worldly system of morals"
(L.II.122).

The fundamental gravity with which Shelley regarded the
consequences of sexual prudery is exhibited time and again in his
work. In *Prometheus Unbound* (1819), for example, when the Furies
flock together from the ends of the earth to torment the chained Titan,
they leave behind them "the self-contempt implanted/In young spirits,
sense-enchanted,/Misery's yet unkindled fuel" (I.510-512). In a world
still plunged in Christian darkness the awakening of adolescent sexual
desire is the certain prelude to shame and guilt. Impulses that in
themselves are wholly natural and good are poisoned and corrupted
by society's unnatural sexual taboos, until what should be the
harbinger of the greatest joy is the source only of bitterness and
distress.[9] Self-contempt is nearly always evil in Shelley, an "inward
stain," evidence of an unnatural sense of sin or worthlessness and a
loss of one's natural self-esteem. In the enlightened Promethean
world, all passion is "free from guilt or pain," and self-contempt is a
thing of the past. No longer is "ill shame" permitted to spoil the sweet
taste of the ecstasy of love.[10]

The theme is repeated more whimsically in *The Witch of Atlas*
(1820), which is an attack, in the name of a more natural morality, on
"the code of Custom's lawless law" inscribed, as in *Prometheus
Unbound,* upon "the brows of old and young" (541-542). The Witch is
the personification of natural as opposed to man-made law, and her
playful pranks are designed in part to break the bonds of sexual
custom. After a visit from the Witch, timid lovers who, like the poet's
Wordsworth, had been so "coy" that they "hardly knew whether they
loved or not" rise from their sleep and "take joy,/To the fulfillment of
their inmost thought" (649-656).

Shelley had little use for the sexual coyness demanded by
convention, which he mocks as "the loving game" in *Fiordispina.*[11] He
is severe on "the cold-hearted coquette, the lying and meretricious
prude."[12] His own lovers are frank and bold, the women no less than

the men. Once the thirst of love is kindled, nothing is allowed to stand in the way of its quenching. Shelley's women meet their lovers at least halfway. Often they are the sexual aggressors. Why, he demands in one of his earliest poems, cannot "impassioned tenderness . . . burst/ Cold prudery's bondage, owning all it [feels]"?[13] Fearless love is his ideal, and his writings are themselves meant to be sexually liberating: "marriageable maidens," formerly pining with love, will find in his work "a warmer zeal, a nobler hope." In his vision of the future, women, liberated from the taint of custom, freely express the passions they once dared not even feel.[14]

"There is nothing in itself vicious or wrong in sensual pleasure, or unworthy in passions," Shelley maintains.[15] So long as sex is not abused, it is a natural good, a pleasure to be enjoyed in its own right, and not an impulse to be feared or condemned.[16] The poet exhibited a lifelong abhorrence for the traditional asceticism of Christian teaching. He speaks of Christianity's "fanatical idea of mortifying the flesh for the love of God." The church makes nature and the flesh synonymous with "the Evil Spirit." Carnal indulgence condemns the sinner to hell-fire. Still worse is Christianity's "fanatical idea of chastity," which the poet dismisses as a "monkish and Evangelical superstition." Of the church's triumph in the ancient world he complains: "monstrous and detestable creeds poisoned and blighted the domestic charities. There was no appeal to natural love." He labels the "apathy to love and friendship" enjoined by Christian teaching "pernicious" and charges that, were it actually practiced, it "would speedily annihilate the human race."[17]

In Shelley's view ecclesiastical morality is at the deepest level inhuman, life-defeating. Nowhere is this more evident than in his running warfare with the population doctrines of the Reverend Thomas Malthus (originally advanced to rebut Godwinian schemes of social perfectibility) with their monkish appeal to sexual abstinence or "moral restraint" as a population check. Malthus holds that no one should marry "till he has a prospect of supporting his children" and that the interval before marriage should be passed in strict chastity.[18] Chastity not only eliminates serious social evils, such as promiscuity, prostitution, and children born out of wedlock, but is also enjoined by scripture. Transgressors are therefore offending against the will of God. The burden of these injunctions falls primarily on the poor, since they are the chief offenders. Moral restraint is for Malthus the only effective method of raising the condition of the poor, for whom he advocates a public campaign to educate them concerning their true interests. Meanwhile he urges the gradual abolition of the Poor Laws because these encourage the poor to marry and bring children into the world which they cannot support by their own efforts unaided.[19]

In his *Philosophical View of Reform*, Shelley exposes the essential inhumanity of such a solution, in some of the most savagely eloquent prose ever to issue from his pen. Malthus, he protests, has "the hardened insolence" to propose as a remedy for the population problem that the poor should be "compelled (for what except compulsion is a threat of the confiscation of those funds which by the institution of their country had been set apart for their sustenance in sickness or destitution?) to abstain from sexual intercourse, while the rich are to be permitted to add as many mouths to consume the products of the labor of the poor as they please." After the poor have been "stript naked by the tax-gatherer and reduced to bread and tea and fourteen hours of hard labor by their masters, and after the frost has bitten their defenceless limbs, and the cramp has wrung like a disease within their bones, and hunger . . . has stamped the ferocity of want like the mark of Cain upon their countenance," they are to be required to abstain from marrying "under penalty of starvation." This proposal would withhold from the mass of mankind its natural "birthright," would take away "the single alleviation of their sufferings and their scorns," and would obliterate "all the soothing, elevating, and harmonious gentleness of the sexual intercourse and the humanizing charities of domestic life which are its appendages," leaving them no compensation but the "insulting" advice to conquer "a propensity which persons of the most consummate wisdom have been unable to resist, and which it is difficult to admire a person for having resisted."[20] The proposal is in short a "cynical and unmanly contamination," an "anti-social cruelty," and the doctrine of a "eunuch" and a "tyrant," which is to say "a priest of course" (VII.32-33).[21] Strong language. But its very force should finally set to rest the slow-dying myth of Shelley's seraphic asceticism and asexuality. Sexual denial is in his eyes a first-class evil, and its elevation into the chief Christian virtue is cause only for lamentation.

Over against the Christian view Shelley sets the pagan, with its traditionally joyous celebration of nature and natural impulse. Shelley and his circle liked to think of themselves, only partly tongue-in-cheek, as a little band of pagan hierophants or Pan worshipers adrift in nineteenth-century England—"our contemporary Pagans," as Peacock labeled them.[22] In 1821 Hogg wrote to Shelley that on a hike through the countryside with Peacock, "we propitiated the far-darting King by a garland and an inscription, in Bisham Wood," to which the poet replied: "I am glad to hear that you do not neglect the rites of the true religion. Your letter awakened my sleeping devotion, & the same evening I ascended alone, the high mountain behind my house, & suspended a garland & raised a small turf altar to the mountain-walking Pan" (L.II.361). As Shelley explains in *On the Devil and Devils*, the sylvans and fauns, with their leader Pan, were "most poetical personages and were connected in the imaginations of the Pagans with all that could enliven and delight." Christianity, however, appropriated their horns, hoofs, tail, and ears to give to its "spirit of evil," thereby contriving to turn the Greek mythology to "purposes of deformity and falsehood" (VII.103).

Shelley was scarcely enthusiastic about some of the grosser elements accompanying pagan nature worship, especially the orgiastic revelry signifying possession by the godhead, which he termed "a monstrous superstition only capable of existing in Greece because there alone capable of combining ideal beauty and poetical and abstract enthusiasm with the wild errors from which it sprung" (VI.323). In general, the public madness and the ritual loss of control typified by the Bacchic or maenadic "orgasm" is an image of terror in Shelley.[23] Nevertheless, he much preferred the pagan deification of instinct and sensual release over their emasculating repression under the Christian dispensation.[24] The happy medium is presumably the world portrayed in *The Witch of Atlas* wherein the whole erotic pantheon of the ancients is shown subdued by love (viii-xii).[25]

Although the mature Shelley stressed the pagan innocence and tenderness of sexual connection as against the more Bacchic properties of the act, his career began with the Gothic, and the sexual element in his work never entirely lost the hectic, heavy-breathing cast of that once pervasive genre. His sexual imagination was permanently colored by the lurid lights of the cheap romances and "shilling shockers" or "blue books" of his day. Despite their often dissolving haze of perfervid emotionalism, the appeal of these works was in great part pornographic. There can be little doubt that in their pages Shelley released his earliest sexual emotions. As a schoolboy, he greatly admired Matthew Gregory Lewis, whose notorious *The Monk* was universally considered pornographic, drawing comparison with *Fanny Hill*. Though banned at Syon House, the novel became "an especial favorite with Shelley," according to his cousin Medwin. In the spring of 1811 Shelley seduced his cousin into reading the book himself. So shocked was the conventional Medwin that he "cut it up and tried to burn it."[26] Later, when Shelley eloped with the less straitlaced Mary Godwin, he made sure that she added the book to her reading list.

Shelley's own Gothic novels are scarcely pornographic, but neither are they virgin pure. Their author hardly appears as a prude. Although the novels purport to uphold an ideal of chaste love, so many pages are devoted to depicting the opposite that the author's motives are suspect.[27] Because Shelley is deliberately working within a genre and perhaps burlesquing it, it is hard to tell where his sympathies actually lie. But whatever the feigned attitude, the author in many of the steamier passages is clearly discharging his own adolescent sexual emotions: "Wild with passion, [Matilda] clasped Verezzi to her beating breast; and, overcome by an ecstasy of delirious passion, her senses were whirled round in confused and inexpressible delight. A new and fierce passion raged likewise in Verezzi's breast: he returned her embrace with ardour, and clasped her in fierce transports . . . An indefinable sensation, unfelt before, swelled through the passion-quivering frame of Megalena . . . Fiercer . . . flamed the passions of the devoted Olympia. Her brain was whirled round in the fiercest convulsions of expectant happiness; the anticipation of gratified voluptuousness swelled her bosom even to bursting" (V.75, 122, 144).

Zastrozzi (1809) and *St. Irvyne* (1810) were Shelley's juvenile attempts at literary eroticism, conveyed in the mode of the day and intended primarily for the amusement and titillation of himself and his friends, especially his sister and Harriet Grove. Their melodramatic posturing is absurd, though scarcely more so than in many comparable productions of the period. Yet the rhetorical conventions of the Gothic genre, however artificially expressed, once overlaid a genuine emotional experience. Shelley and his contemporaries often thought of sex in just these terms. Though the sex in *Zastrozzi* and *St. Irvyne* is patently spurious, literary rather than real, and the author's own sexual experience at the time was doubtless limited, the Gothic mode remained his vehicle of expression even after he had come to know the transports of sex at firsthand. And sex in the Gothic mode is a potent, all-consuming experience, a "frenzy" (L.I.191), a delirium, resulting in mental oblivion and emotional exhaustion. This is how it almost invariably appears in Shelley: "Soft, my dearest angel, stay,/Oh! you suck my soul away;/And streams of rapture drown my soul." This rhapsody from "Epithalamium" (82-86), purportedly by "a friend's *mistress*," was avowedly designed to make the volume *Posthumous Fragments of Margaret Nicholson* (1810) "sell like wildfire."[28] Shelley, and Hogg, the volume's coauthor, hoped to outrage with their "indelicacy" the bluenoses among their acquaintance, although the scandalous verses were carefully omitted from the copy sent Mrs. Shelley. Yet despite the deliberate sensation-mongering, the rhetoric and the sentiment are authentically Shelleyan, as are the less fevered, "I will kiss thine eyes so fair,/And I will clasp they form . . . And I will recline on thy marble neck/Till I mingle into thee" (91-96), which also describe the lovemaking. The lines are not to be dismissed as pure burlesque, as Hogg hoped they would be when he described their composition years later in the mid-Victorian period.[29] This same vein plainly persists into Shelley's mature verse, though less frantically and crudely expressed.

Even in this earliest period, Shelley professed to repudiate the strictly orgasmic in literature, the "hot sickly love" and "commonplace infatuation of novels and gay life" (*L.I.*192). Indeed his scorn of sex divorced from sentiment, whether in literature or life, was lifelong. But this did not mean that his amatory ideal precluded the sensual. The claims of the physical self were irresistible, "life's sacred thirst" in the vocabulary of *Adonais* (169), and must be quenched if one were not to experience psychological death. Thus the epithets "hot" and "sickly" precisely describe the sexual passion as it appears in his work. An overmastering flame, a conflagration of the senses and Gothic holocaust, the sexual urge was the primordial melodrama underlying all life.

In the real-life melodrama of Hogg's attempted seduction of Harriet Westbrook, Shelley had occasion to anatomize the power of the sexual drive in sober earnest. Deeply shocked by Hogg's making love behind his back to his bride of only two months, Shelley expelled him from their company. Although his friend pleaded to be allowed to return, claiming he would keep his feelings strictly under control, Shelley would not listen. "Sensation," he writes, is "something terribly strong." "If you have *loved*," he adds, "I can believe you have not felt it lightly." He himself knows well how "resistless" is this feeling, "how sophistical its inductions." What guarantee can Hogg give that if he is allowed to return he will not soon be passionately in love with Harriet again, yearning for love's "extremest consummation"? Indeed he would be driven to this "last consummation" by "exposure to Harriet's attractions"; her "*presence* without fullest satisfaction" would "terribly augment" his passion, kindling it to an "inextinguishable flame."[30] His imagination would dwell upon her charms, exciting "the wildest reveries of ungratified desire," until he would again be tempted to what he now regards with loathing. No one can be confident of virtuous intentions, Shelley concludes, after having once been exposed to the "tyranny" of sensation, the irresistible demands of the sexual impulse. Throughout the episode Shelley shows himself keenly aware of the immense force of the sexual drive and the serious psychological consequences attendant upon its repression. Hogg's "fall" obviously had a profound effect upon his thinking. Much as he wished to believe in the possibility of a love entirely free from the claims of the body, he was forced to concede that on the evidence of Hogg's behavior, love and sensuality were perhaps "inseparable" (*L.I.*181).

Whereas Shelley continued to envisage a love transcending sex, their union rather than their division receives chief emphasis in his work in the years to follow. The body's claims to fulfillment are as legitimate as are the soul's. When "every bond of sense" is "enamoured," when "Sensation all its wondrous rapture brings," man is vouchsafed a "foretaste of Heaven," and of nothing is this so true as of sexual love, "sensation's softest tie."[31] Thus it is not "blasphemy," he explains to Harriet not long after their elopement in 1811, to hope that heaven will provide more perfectly "those nameless joys/Which throb within the pulses of the blood." One "soul-reviving kiss" is "assurance that this Earth is Heaven/And Heaven the flower of that untainted seed/Which springeth here beneath such love as ours."[32]

Despite the self-styled "wild extacies" of Shelley's poems to Harriet, there remains a substantial doubt about the strength of his passion for her and a suspicion that much of the ecstasy is a mixture of romantic posturing and self-deception. The evidence is strong that the marriage was a relative failure sexually on both sides, though for some time unrecognized as such. In the beginning Shelley equated affection and compassion with love; if a genuinely passionate element was lacking, that was unimportant. He had married on the rebound from a truly passionate attachment to another Harriet, his cousin Harriet Grove. With her, according to "Melody to a Scene of Former Times," he had known two years of "speechless bliss" and one "blest day" of joys more fervid even than "passion's wildest ecstasy"—"Oh! I had never lived before" (18-23). Affecting now to scorn his former love as "the sottish idiotism of frenzy-nourished fools" (*L.I.*191), he set against it the "holy" and "ardent friendship" of his relationship with the "pure-minded" Harriet his bride, wherein a passionate love of the body apparently played only a minor role.[33] A letter to Hogg in late 1811 implies that Shelley would in fact have had no objection to relinquishing the marital prerogative altogether (*L.I.*175-176).

Harriet, for her part, probably did little to encourage any growth of sexual passion. Her upbringing was conventionally middle class and straitlaced. Her father was a "man of strict morals," who warned his daughter against "the vices of high society." From an early age she had learned all the rigid proprieties and "laws of feminine purity" typical of her class.[34] This training was reinforced by the narrow piety and sexual puritanism of the Methodist school where she spent most of her youth. Her girlish dream having been that if she married at all, it should be to a clergyman, she was profoundly shocked on first learning of Shelley's atheism. Although she subsequently abandoned Methodism and claimed to be "no longer shackled with idle fears" (*L.*I.273-274), the effects of such an education are not so easily eradicated, particularly in the sexual sphere.

Shelley demanded that a woman be aggressive and unashamed. But as noted by Clellan Ford and Frank Beach in their study of sexual behavior, "societies that severely restrict adolescent and preadolescent sex play, those that enjoin girls to be modest, retiring, and submissive appear to produce adult women that are incapable or at least unwilling to be sexually aggressive. The feminine products of such cultural training are likely to remain relatively inactive even during marital intercourse."[35] What Harriet's behavior was like on this intimate level can only be guessed. But her public behavior was exceptionally modest, even prudish. Hogg reports that whenever she went abroad, she was invariably the focus of attention, but instead of being flattered, she would "bashfully draw down her veil," and she was "always most unwilling to show her ankles." His picture suggests a rigid and repressed personality, the reverse of passionate.[36] Barely sixteen when she eloped, Harriet came to Shelley more child than bride, and it is unlikely the marriage ever generated much sexual heat. The couple were always more friends than lovers. With the birth of their daughter Ianthe in the summer of 1813, the sexual element may have withered away almost entirely.

In the ensuing spring, accordingly, when Shelley rediscovered the ecstasy of sexual passion, this time with the liberated Mary Godwin, the experience burst upon him with the force of a revelation, sweeping all before it. "Nothing that I have ever read in tale or history," remembered Peacock, "could present a more striking image of a sudden, violent, irresistible, uncontrollable passion."[37] Mary had come to meet the poet more than halfway. Because her affections had been preserved from "the corrupting contamination of vulgar superstitions," according to Shelley, in one "sublime & rapturous moment" in June she gave herself to him completely, overcoming his own half-hearted appeals to duty. The two "met with passion." From this moment Shelley dated his birth.[38]

In the preceding months Shelley had come to recognize the tragic error of a marriage devoid of passion—"my rash & heartless union," as he now acknowledged it. With the approach of spring and "the subduing voluptuousness" of its impulses which he had never before experienced so intensely and which produced in their train a host of erotic visions and phantasies almost palpable in their sensuousness, he realized that it was "no longer possible to practise self deception." He felt as if "a dead & living body had been linked together in loathsome & horrible communion."[39] He was left with the "revolting duty" of continuing to deceive Harriet about the true state of his affections (*L.*I.401-402), although managing to overcome his repugnance to the extent of fathering another child upon her.

In his torment and frustration he had earlier turned desperately to Cornelia Turner, whose "dewy looks" and "gentle words" had stirred the "poison" of pent-up desire in his breast, but had been able to suppress his feelings by "Duty's hard control."[40] With Mary Godwin, however, Shelley was soon lost beyond recall, and following the passionate avowal of her own feelings, he saw no further reason for preserving his hypocritical union with Harriet, which he now regarded as hopeless. He could no longer pretend what he did not feel and apparently had never felt. "It is no reproach to me," he explains to Harriet, "that you have never filled my heart with an all-sufficing passion." Perhaps "you are even yourself a stranger to these impulses," he conjectures, "which one day may be awakened by some nobler & worthier than me, and may you find a lover as passionate and faithful, as I shall ever be a friend affectionate & sincere!" Can it be, he inquires, that "your feelings for me differ, in their nature from those which I cherish towards you? Are you my lover whilst I am only your friend?" He thinks not, and concludes that "the purest & most perfect happiness is ours" if she will consent to live with him and Mary as a friend (*L.*I.389-390,402). Harriet indignantly refused, and when Shelley continued to reiterate the passionate nature of his attachment to Mary—"our spirits & [blank] are united" (*L.*I.395)—Harriet concluded that he had given himself up to the selfishness of animal lust and was no longer that "pure and good being he once was" but "profligate and sensual," a "vampire" (*L.*I.421-422).[41]

Confronted with a Shelley she had never known before, Harriet was baffled and dismayed. Shelley himself was at first dumbfounded by what had happened, hardly able to grasp the extent of his transformation. But what for Harriet was a bestial metamorphosis was for Shelley a heavenly transfiguration, the incorporation of a passion heretofore confined only to his dreams. Explaining his good fortune to Hogg, whom he had not seen since his elopement with Mary, Shelley marvels: "How wonderfully I am changed! Not a disembodied spirit can have undergone a stranger revolution! I never knew until now that contentment was any thing but a word denoting an unmeaning abstraction. I never before felt the integrity of my nature, its various dependencies, & learned to consider myself as an whole accurately united rather than an assemblage of inconsistent & discordant portions." After his former unhappiness, which had almost withered him to "idiotism"—"I have sunk into a premature old age of exhaustion, which renders me dead to everything," had been Shelley's despairing words back in March (*L.*I.383)—he now enjoys a happiness "the most perfect & exalted" in which it is possible for his "nature to participate," a "pure & celestial felicity." He is "restored to energy and enterprise" and has become again what he "once promised to become" (*L.*I.401-403). Born anew, Shelley luxuriates in his novel sense of power and well-being. His gratitude to her who made it possible repeatedly overflows in his letters, which are a record of a fully realized sexual passion.

The intensity of Shelley's passion revealed itself most nakedly in the moving letters exchanged by the couple in the fall of 1814, when the poet was forced into hiding to escape arrest for debt (*L.*I.407-418). "This separation is a calamity not to be endured patiently," he protests to Mary. "I cannot support your absence." "I so passionately love my own Mary that we must not be absent long." Yet the "*moments* bliss" of snatched meetings and the "divine rapture of the few & fleeting kisses" were the most that they could usually manage. "Oh my dearest love," he remonstrates, "why are our pleasures so short?" If only "I might hold you in my arms, & gaze on your dear eyes at will, & snatch momentary kisses in the midst of our happy hours, & sport in security with my entire & unbroken bliss." "How lonely & desolate are these solitary nights!" He can scarcely wait to "repossess to entirely engross my own treasured love." Mary is similarly impassioned and distressed: "Is this the way my beloved that we are to live till the sixth in the morning I look for you and when I awake I turn to look on you—dearest Shelley you are solitary and uncomfortable why cannot I be with you to cheer you and to press you to my heart." "May you sleep as well as though it were in my arms—but I know you wont." "Goodnight my love—tomorrow I will seal this blessing on your lips dear good creature press me to you and hug your own Mary to your heart . . . Take me—one kiss—well that is enough—tomorrow." Only on Sundays, when Shelley was immune from arrest, were the couple able to embrace in perfect security: "this is a day devoted to Love in idleness," Mary records in the *Journal* of one such occasion; "Go to sleep early in the evening." And of another she writes: "In the evening Shelley and I go to an inn in St. John's Street to sleep. Those that love cannot separate; Shelley could not have gone away without me again." Once they chanced an extra night together in another inn, the afterglow of which caused Shelley to exult: "the remembrance & expectation of such sweet moments as we experienced last night consoles strengthens & redeems me from despondency. There is *eternity in these moments*—they contain the true elixir of immortal life." This was "the antient language that love can alone translate."

In the months and years that followed Shelley was to translate his happiness with Mary into just such language in some of the most memorable scenes of his poetry. His verse is almost unsurpassed for its passionate evocation of the ecstasy of sexual communion. This happiness is first projected retrospectively in the dream of joy that is the high point of *Alastor* (1815), a poem in which Shelley portrays the psychological death-in-life of those unfortunate enough to be denied an "all-sufficing passion," as had been his own case until recently. The protagonist of the poem, a young poet, dreams of such happiness but, like Shelley, is withered to idiotism, sunk into a premature old age of exhaustion, when he cannot embody it. What he dreams, however, is what Shelley was at last experiencing with Mary—passionate union with a woman at once beautiful, intelligent, literary, politically liberated, socially enlightened, and sexually emancipated.

The dream begins with intellectual communion but soon turns sexual. The woman, a "veiled maid," fired by the sublimity of her own conversation, breaks into impassioned song, and then suddenly arises, her breath coming in tumultuous starts. The poet turns and sees "by the warm light of their own life" her limbs glowing through the filmy veil that encloses them. The maid reaches out to embrace him, her arms now bare, her lips open and "quivering eagerly," her eyes beamy. In delirious response the poet lifts his "shuddering limbs" and quells his "gasping breath," spreading his arms to meet her "panting bosom." The maid, momentarily drawing back, soon succumbs to "the irresistible joy" and with "frantic gesture" and "short breathless cry" at length folds him in her dissolving arms (151-187). The dream fades, and the poet awakens to the cold light of dawn. But he has been accorded a vision of bliss never to be forgotten, one which Shelley himself repeatedly portrayed after discovering it to be a waking possibility, not merely a wish-fulfilling fantasy. And the vision's language, which in his Gothic romances is simply the inflated rhetoric of a preposterous literary convention, now successfully evokes a genuine flesh-and-blood experience: "if we feel, we would that another's nerves should vibrate to our own, that the beams of their eyes should kindle at once and mix and melt into our own, that lips of motionless

Love's Visible Link

ice should not reply to lips quivering and burning with the heart's best blood. This is Love" (VI.201).

The Revolt of Islam, Shelley's next major poem, again epitomizes this love in the passionate dream sequence opening the poem, which introduces the poet's paradigmatic Woman to her archetypal lover, Lucifer. The dream is a model for the ensuing passion of the human lovers, Laon and Cythna—a passion whose consummation is the poem's centerpiece. Of Shelley's many evocations of sexual intercourse, this is his most extended and memorable one.[42] As nearly always in his work, the act takes place out of doors, far from society in the bosom of nature, which underscores the act's naturalness and innocence, the supreme physical expression of the rhythms binding the cosmos. "To the pure all things are pure!" is the episode's keynote (VI.xxx). The two lovers, reclining silently on a natural couch of leaves in a ruined, ivy-covered hall partially open to the sky, are seized by the thirst of love and, though it is autumn, long to make it spring, overcome by nature's animating principle which undergirds all thoughts, "like light beyond the atmosphere/Clothing its clouds with grace."[43] Spellbound by "wildering passion," the lovers are oblivious to all but the magic of each other's physical presence, now revealed by the flickering light of a wandering meteor or will-o'-the-wisp. Cythna's arms are "glowing" and "the thick ties/Of her soft hair" bend with their gathered weight Laon's neck near to hers, her dark and soul-enwoven eyes swimming in silent and "liquid ecstasies," her "eager lips" pale with their own fragrance, "like roses . . . which Spring but half uncloses." The meteor disappears, and the couple is plunged into darkness. The "beating of our veins" momentarily became still, recalls Laon,

> and then I felt the blood that burned
> Within her frame, mingle with mine, and fall
> Around my heart like fire; and over all
> A mist was spread, the sickness of a deep
> And speechless swoon of joy, as might befall
> Two disunited spirits when they leap
> In union from this earth's obscure and fading sleep. (VI.xxx-xxxiv)

"There is *eternity in these moments*," Shelley had written to Mary, "they contain the true elixir of immortal life." And in identical terms Laon recollects his rapture with Cythna. The two had been lost in "a wide and wild oblivion/Of tumult and tenderness" wherein the sense of time had been obliterated. They felt as if released from temporal process, floating high above the world, "two restless frames" blended in "one reposing soul." Upon regaining consciousness, they had no idea of the lapse of time. "Was it one moment," or rather ages, "such as make the moon and sun,/The seasons, and mankind their changes know," that had left "fear and time unfelt by us alone below?" At the same time the two had had no trouble recalling the fiery kisses or the "limb/Twined within limb" or "the quick dying gasps/Of the life meeting" in passionate caresses which had put a stop to time. When restored to consciousness, the lovers relaxed contentedly in one another's arms, basking in "the sweet peace of joy" that comes only to those who have fully quenched the burning thirst of the sexual impulse (VI.xxxv-xxxviii).

The couple felt wedded to one another, their ecstatic communion alone in nature the only rite necessary to sanctify their union. In the language of the *Discourse*, the satisfying of the sexual impulse had been the final pledge of their love, the external expression or type of a sentiment incorporating their entire natures—intellectual, imaginative, and sensitive. They needed no other more formal linking. So long as the complete range of their sympathies was mutually fulfilled, they were naturally pledged to each other for life.

In *Rosalind and Helen*, the poet's next extended treatment of the theme of sexual communion, the lovers are similarly pledged after consummating their love in the sanctity of nature. "We will have rites our faith to bind," explains Lionel to Helen, "But our church shall be the starry night,/Our altar the grassy earth outspread,/And our priest the muttering wind" (851-854). Imprisonment for blasphemy is Lionel's payment for this heretical nature worship. Upon his release, he leaves behind once and for all the "desert" of the city, where natural law goes unheeded (945-946), and accompanied by the faithful Helen, he escapes into the vernal June countryside, where, in the haven of evening,

> Like flowers, which on each other close
> Their languid leaves when daylight's gone,
> We lay, till new emotions came,
> Which seemed to make each mortal frame
> One soul of interwoven flame,
> A life in life, a second birth
> In worlds diviner far than earth,
> Which, like two strains of harmony
> That mingle in the silent sky
> Then slowly disunite, passed by
> And left the tenderness of tears,
> A soft oblivion of all fears,
> A sweet sleep. (968-987)

Love's Visible Link

The joys of sexual intercourse are raised to a cosmic level in *Prometheus Unbound*, which in its conclusion is a paean of universal eroticism. Earth's volcanic rebirth of love is repeatedly figured in terms of orgasmic release, with nature, at last resuscitated from its winter of sensual death in Christian repression, asceticism, and self-contempt, spending itself in love's delight. The release is both heralded and set in motion by the Titan's reawakened desire for Asia, his Aphrodisiac bride and nature's life principle, who, when first his "being overflowed," had been "like a golden chalice to bright wine" (I.809-810). The awakening is ingeniously symbolized by the Titan's erotic dream possession of Panthea, Asia's "shadow," who functions as the sympathetic intermediary between the couple. The episode draws heavily on the poet's standard coital imagery, translated into a dazzling similitude of natural process. Panthea, magnetized by the Titan's impassioned gaze and dizzied by the music of his intoxicating voice, is enveloped in an atmosphere of fire which wraps her in its "all-dissolving power,/As the warm aether of the morning sun/Wraps ere it drinks some cloud of wandering dew." She neither sees, nor hears, nor moves, only feels the Titan's presence "flow and mingle" through her blood until her being is absorbed into his (II.i.65-89). So completely are their persons intermingled that when Panthea later kisses her younger sister Ione, the Titan's presence is transferred along with the kiss, awakening Ione's hitherto dormant sexuality (II.i.95-106). Without realizing it, the adolescent Ione is awakened to the youthful "enchantment" of sense which, under the Christian dispensation, is a portent of misery. But now that Prometheus has thrown off this freezing morality and rediscovered a natural, enlightened attitude toward sex, Ione has nothing to fear. Panthea is already on her way to Asia, bearing the gift of the Titan's passionate dream, of which she is herself the enchanting and enchanted embodiment. When she arrives, Asia glimpses deep within her eyes the radiant presence of the Titan himself, whose smiles forecast their literal reunion in the regenerate world to come (II.i.120-126).

Ironically counterpointing the sympathetic intercourse of Prometheus and Asia is the loveless rape of Thetis by Jupiter, cold-bloodedly perpetrated in order to bring to life the "fatal child" who, according to the Aeschylean prophecy, will trample out the Titan's last spark of resistance. "Insufferable might!" Thetis had exclaimed: "God! Spare me! I sustain not the quick flames,/The penetrating presence; all my being/Like him whom the Numidian seps did thaw/Into a dew with poison, is dissolved,/Sinking through its foundations" (III.i.37-42). Thus it was, announces the tyrant, that "Two mighty spirits, mingling, made a third/Mightier than either," whose incarnation would seal the tyrant's victory (III.i.18-49). Jupiter is wrong, however, for the only birth actually in the offing is Prometheus', whose rebirth in love is necessarily fatal to self-willed and self-enslaving tyranny. With the jealous divinity's downfall and his relegation to the "darkness" that is his natural sphere (III.i.56), the sting or poison goes out of sex, no more to spoil the sweet taste of love.[44] No longer is humankind bound by the "dark and miserable," the unenlightened, code of Christian sexual morality (VI.214).

In the regenerate world, with Prometheus and Asia safely back together in one another's arms, the human mind ecstatically celebrates its sexual liberation.[45] Formerly "dusk, and obscene, and blind," it is now "an ocean/Of clear emotion,/A heaven of serene and mighty motion," whose depths are chambers of "wonder and bliss" formed of "woven caresses/Where lovers catch ye by your loose tresses" (IV.94-107). The last figure, suggesting maenadic abandon, is often the prelude to sexual intercourse in Shelley.

As the drama moves to its joyful conclusion, the very cosmos is depicted in orgasmic terms, Shelley playing on the idea of physical or gravitational attraction between the heavenly "bodies."[46] The earth and its satellite sister the moon join in a frenzied fertility dance that crowns the fructifying of their mutual attraction and prefigures mankind's reincorporation into the harmony of nature. "The joy, the triumph . . . the madness!" sings the rejuvenated earth. His "granite mass" is now "interpenetrate[d]" by love, an "animation of delight" that wraps him "like an atmosphere of light."[47] His enchanted bride responds:

> Some Spirit is darted like a beam from thee,
>   Which penetrates my frozen frame,
>   And passes with the warmth of flame,
> With love, and odour, and deep melody
>   Through me, through me!
> A spirit from my heart bursts forth,
> It clothes with unexpected birth
> My cold bare bosom! Oh! it must be thine
>   On mine, on mine!
>
>   Gazing on thee I feel, I know
>   Green stalks burst forth, and bright flowers grow,
> And living shapes upon my bosom move. (IV.319-370)

And just as on earth, "happy paramours" on the moon also wander through "newly-woven bowers" of bliss. The moon is herself the earth's "crystal paramour," a "most enamoured maiden," her mind faint and overladen with "the pleasure of her love." An "insatiate bride," she moves "Maniac-like" around her brother, gazing on his form from every side as if she were a maenad. But when the doting spheres meet in the intimacy of eclipse, then the female moon is "mute and still," "covered" by the shadow of her brother's powerful embrace, of his love "full, oh, too full!" (IV.427-475).

Prometheus Unbound represents the high watermark in Shelley's celebration of sex. Never again would he reach such a pitch of ecstatic and uninhibited sensuality. As the passion began to ebb from his own life and the original intensity of his relationship with Mary began to cool, speeded by a withdrawal of sympathy on her part, he came increasingly to view the claims of the body as a distracting nuisance, even a pernicious obstacle in the way of the higher claims of the spirit. He liked to maintain that he was himself no longer capable of giving "what men call love" but only a *l'amour de lointain*. His amatory rose, he insisted, was free of its wounding thorn.[48] By 1822 and the final, unfinished *Triumph of Life* physical love appears in a profoundly pessimistic light as one of the primary ways in which the world stains or conquers even its leading spirits, a Plato or a Rousseau. The maenadic dance of sex is now portrayed as "fierce and obscene"; the dancers mix wildly with each other in "tempestuous measure/To savage music," throwing back their heads in abandon and freeing their untamed locks, "tortured" and "convulsed" by the "agonizing pleasure." Intercourse itself is seemingly a species of spiritual death or "bright destruction" (137-160).

Shelley's retreat from the body was gradual, however, and despite himself, he often found his senses rekindled in the presence of female beauty. The charming Sophia Stacey, the ward of his uncle, Mr. Robert Parker, and more like his lost Harriet Grove than anyone he had known since, was the recipient of an outburst of playful but undisguised poetic eroticism in late 1819:

I

Good-night? no, love! the night is ill
   Which severs those it should unite;
Let us remain together still,
   Then it will be *good* night.

II

How were the night without thee good
   Though thy sweet wishes wing its flight?

> Be it not said, thought, understood—
> Then it will be—*good* night.

III

> The hearts that on each other beat
>   From evening close to morning light,
> Have nights as good as they are sweet,
>   But never *say* good night.[49]

"Good-Night" was transcribed into a copy of Leigh Hunt's *Literary Pocketbook* for 1819 and presented to Sophia the day before she left Florence. It was accompanied by another lyric, "Love's Philosophy" or "An Anacreontic," which had also been sent to Hunt for publication and which was in the same sportive vein, though less explicit:[50]

I

> The fountains mingle with the river
>   And the rivers with the Ocean,
> The winds of Heaven mix for ever
>   With a sweet emotion;
> Nothing in the world is single;
>   All things by a law divine
> In one spirit meet and mingle.
> [variant reading: In one another's being mingle]
>   Why not I with thine?—

II

> See the mountains kiss high Heaven
>   And the waves clasp one another;
> No sister flower would be forgiven
>   If it disdained to kiss its brother;

> And the sunlight clasps the earth
>   And the moonbeams kiss the sea;
> What is all this sweet work worth
>   If thou kiss not me?

The piece concludes at this point in the versions tendered to both Sophia and Hunt, but in a manuscript continuation the speaker's object is less innocent, if no less lightsomely expressed:

> Follow to the deep wood, sweetest,
> Follow to the wild-briar dingle,
>   . . . no eye thou there meetest
> When we sink to intermingle,
> And the violet tells no tale
> To the odour-scented gale,

> For they two have enough to do
> Of such work as I and you.[51]

Sophia was also the recipient of the impassioned "I arise from dreams of thee" and "To Sophia." Both lyrics repeat the fevered rhetoric of Shelley's erotic poetry, the speaker swooning from the intensity of feeling as if in the delirium of orgasm.

It has almost never been seriously argued that there was anything guilty in Shelley's relationship with Sophia. The two were simply "very close friends," in Sophia's words: the poet poured out to her his observations on religion and radicalism, love and death, as well as memories of his sisters and his youthful adventures, while she responded with her enchanting singing.[52] Yet the true nature of Shelley's impulses emerges plainly from the record of his poetry, however strenuously disguised, suppressed, or sublimated.

The same is true to an even greater degree of his infatuation with Emilia Viviani, the lovely Italian woman "imprisoned" in a convent in Pisa, whom the poet wished to save from the bleak fate of an arranged marriage. However he might represent his feelings, they were manifestly sexual. *Epipsychidion* (1821), the poetic record of this passion, is a highly erotic production, which moves at its close to a coital climax as powerful and explicit as anything that had yet issued from his pen. It is convincing confirmation of the truth of his youthful words of wisdom to Hogg that exposure to a beautiful woman's attractions without complete physical satisfaction triggers heated sexual reveries. What the poet really desired of Emilia appears with pathetic clarity in the long-suppressed "To Emilia Viviani" (1821):

> Thy gentle voice, Emilia dear,
>   At night seems hovering o'er mine.
> I feel thy trembling lips—I hear
>   The murmurs of thy voice divine.
> O God, why comes the morning blank
>   To quench in day this dream of peace
> From which the joys my being drank
>   Yet quiver thro' my burning face?[53]

This is the situation of *Alastor* all over again. But to abandon Mary, as he had Harriet, would be out of the question, as would the possibility of Mary and Emilia agreeing to another *ménage à trois*, although he clearly imagined it in the draft prefaces to *Epipsychidion*. In the poem itself he might rail against the deadening narrowness of marriage and bemoan the mischance that had kept him from meeting Emilia while he was still single, but he and Mary had yielded all to love. Whereas the passing years and the inevitable growth of domestic friction had damped their original ardor to the degree that Shelley could even disown the passion of their early relationship and charge Mary with an emotional frigidity and lack of sympathy from the start, they were morally obligated to each other for life.[54] The most, consequently, that he could permit himself with Emilia was a strictly Platonic relationship, which no doubt was all she sought in any case, and he struggled heroically, if not always successfully, to preserve the relationship on this level in his own mind. Thus, while reporting to Claire Clairmont that Emilia continues to enchant him, he is careful to explain that this is not an enchantment of the senses, though doubtless the world will interpret his feelings differently, "turn[ing] sweet food into poison; transforming all they touch into the corruption of their natures."[55]

Still, Emilia was a very beautiful woman, and when in *Epipsychidion* Shelley comes to hailing her charms through the vehicle of his customary high-powered erotic rhetoric, the world may be pardoned its suspicions, notwithstanding the pointed references to Dante's *Vita Nuova* and *Convito* in the poem's Advertisement.[56] Thus one reads of Emilia's trembling and burning limbs, her passion-breathing lips, her kindling eyes. True, her charms are treated as having no interest in themselves, as being merely the veil through which her interior beauty shines. If Emilia happens to resemble the poet's Asia or Cythna or the Veiled Maid, or if the language of his passion echoes that of *On Love*, this is deceptive. No longer is the reader to take sexual connection in the old way, as love's visible link, a type or expression of the rest. Now it is only a way of speaking, a convenient metaphor, much in the manner of the medieval mystic, for conveying something altogether beyond the senses. This is undoubtedly how Shelley means the reader to view the scene of passionate intercourse between himself and Emilia that concludes the poem—a scene, paradoxically, that has been the most visible of all the erotic passages in the poet's work, receiving more critical attention than the others combined. The trouble is that because Shelley really did want Emilia sexually, the scene takes on a reality, a literalness, impossible to ignore. Shelley clearly intends to portray the wedding of antitypes, making plain throughout that Emilia is the embodiment of his ideal prototype, his best self. The poet knows that he can never possess Emilia totally, but he can imagine it, as he does in one of "the wildest reveries of ungratified desire" on record. The conclusion is an impassioned vision of what might have been.

Love's Visible Link

Earthbound within the confines of marriage and family, Shelley nevertheless asks that Emilia fly with him in imaginary elopement, a union of ideal selves, which, since it transpires at the level of fantasy, no one can prevent. At this level, as he had written in *On Love*, the "soul within our soul . . . describes a circle around its proper Paradise which pain, and sorrow, and evil dare not overleap." Within this inner Eden of the imagination—a Grecian isle, appropriately, "Beautiful as a wreck of Paradise" (423)—Shelley and his bride consummate their love.[57] Since their mating is avowedly ideal, simply "the invisible and unattainable point to which Love tends" in the words of *On Love*, there is no harm in portraying the nuptials in his customary antitypal fashion. And so, by sleight of hand, the sexual connection is at once visible and invisible, in a masterstroke of poetic legerdemain.

For Shelley, the linking up of type with antitype at every level of intercourse represents the attempt to overcome, if only momentarily, the frustrating duality of human relationship, the separation of self from self that is the curse of mortality. Through a landscape, therefore, now alive with the divine law that "Nothing in the world is single;/All things . . . In one another's being mingle," the poet imagines leading his enravished mate, gradually merging the circle of his best self with hers. The charms of the landscape are first revealed in a sensational nuptial trope which in its ecdysiastical intensity rivals Keats's *Eve of St. Agnes*:

> And from the sea there rise, and from the sky
> There fall, clear exhalations, soft and bright,
> Veil after veil, each hiding some delight,
> Which Sun or Moon or zephyr draw aside,
> Till the isle's beauty, like a naked bride
> Glowing at once with love and loveliness,
> Blushes and trembles at its own excess. (470-476)

Wandering through this paradise, the pair will linger by the shore, which under "the quick, faint kisses of the sea/Trembles and sparkles as with ecstasy" (541-552). But eventually, like Laon and Cythna in the privacy of their ruin, or Prometheus and Asia in the security of their cave, they will in "some old cavern hoar" complete the merging of their antitypes:

> Our breath shall intermix, our bosoms bound,
> And our veins beat together; and our lips
> With other eloquence than words, eclipse
> The soul that burns between them, and the wells
> Which boil under our being's inmost cells,

> The fountains of our deepest life, shall be
> Confused in Passion's golden purity,
> As mountain-springs under the morning sun. (565-572)

Like Laon and Cythna at the height of their coital trance, the pair will lose all sense of division, the only thing preventing their total fusion being the brute fact of their biological discreteness. But the vision is too much, and as in the erotic dreaming of *Alastor*, the reverie abruptly collapses into orgasmic oblivion, the poet panting, sinking, trembling, and expiring.

Shelley's absorption with Emilia Viviani was a last-ditch attempt at the complete incorporation of his ideal of sentimental passion, even if unacknowledged as such. Following an inevitable revulsion of feeling, he seemingly abandoned the attempt as hopelessly visionary and sought to reconcile himself to imperfect reality: "I think one is always in love with something or other," he writes to Mr. Gisborne in 1822; "the error, and I confess it is not easy for spirits cased in flesh and blood to avoid it, consists in seeking in a mortal image the likeness of what is perhaps eternal." Just how imperfect that reality had become is revealed in the same letter: "I only feel the want of those who can feel, and understand me. Whether from proximity and the continuity of domestic intercourse, Mary does not . . . It is the curse of Tantalus, that a person possessing such excellent powers and so pure a mind as hers, should not excite the sympathy indispensable to their application to domestic life" (*L.*II.434-435). So much for the inestimable treasure who had once burst on his dazzled eyes as his dream mate, his perfect sympathetic antitype, making him feel for the first time the integrity of his nature as a united whole rather than an assemblage of inconsistent and discordant parts. Now his mate was no more than a pale and icy shadow of that vision. So life triumphed once again, holding out the cup and then withdrawing it, turning the fondest hopes to sand. Better to center our hope on eternity, looking beyond the sensual veil, however enchanting. Yet the archetype of love is also eternal, woven into our very nature as human beings, and so long as we are in fact "cased in flesh and blood" and not dead to their impulses, we will go on seeking its mortal likeness.

Jane Williams, common law wife of Shelley's friend Edward Williams, could by no stretch of the imagination be thought of as the poet's antitype, and this he knew as well as anyone. But she was a very pretty woman—Shelley speaks of "an elegance of form and motions that compensate in some degree for the lack of literary refinement" (*L.*II.435)—and she supplied a soothing companionship and an emotional sympathy denied him at the end by Mary. Inevitably the poet found himself turning her into his dream mate, his perfected self, so "imperious," in the words of the *Discourse,* is the necessity of sympathetic communion, "only to be satisfied by the complete or partial, actual or supposed fulfilment of its claims" (220). Jane represented a very partial fulfillment indeed. Nevertheless Shelley describes his satisfaction with her in the usual terms in his poetry, albeit more tentatively and with restraint. Imprisoned in his "cold home," excluded from the "Paradise" of antitypal communion, he beholds Jane emerge in his imagination as a promise of the renewed and passionate life of nature in the springtime, thawing out his frozen senses. Wandering with her through the "halcyon" calm and the "Elysian glow" of the Cascine pine forest outside Pisa—which in Shelley's mind was clearly a counterpart of the paradisal isle in *Epipsychidion*—he feels as if a magic circle has been traced around them, giving momentary respite to "mortal nature's strife," and in the center of the circle is "one fair form" who fills the air with love.[58]

As he had done with Emilia, Shelley associates Jane with the antitypal dream of his youth, feeling as if temporarily rejuvenated. If only she could be his in actuality, but she was devoted to her Edward. All he could hope for was pity, not love.[59] As with Emilia, he was forced to place the visible third of his antitype out of mind, though he was at times painfully conscious of how his sensual self was being stirred. Indeed, while claiming himself no longer capable of giving what men call love and staking his hopes on a supersensory ideal, he was far from dead sensually. Even with Mary, numbing though their relationship no doubt was to the senses, he had managed to conceive new life, just as he had with Harriet in similar circumstances years before, Mary miscarrying in June 1822. Under the influence of the radiant Jane his whole being now came quiveringly alive, and despite himself, he yearned to quench the thirst of love. In Jane's presence, it is true, his passions slept, made "weak and tame" by her soothing voice and touch. But when she was gone, the memory of these very attributes aroused his senses to fever pitch, the lingering sensations of her "vibrating" touch now electrifying him: "And thus, although she absent were,/Memory gave me all of her/That even Fancy dares to claim."[60]

Weak and disturbed, the "daemon" of the senses re-enthroned in his "faint heart," Shelley dared not speak his thoughts (28-30). But once, unexpectedly, his desire was momentarily returned, when Jane's lips met his in a fleeting but passionate caress:

> Sweet lips, could my soul not have hidden
>   That its life was consumed by you,
> Ye would not have then forbidden

> The death which a heart so true
> Sought in your burning dew.
> That methinks were little cost
> For a moment so found, so lost![61]

Though lasting for only an instant, this was enough to bind him to her irrevocably, the tying of the last strand in love's communion, its acknowledged and visible link: "If we feel, we would that another's nerves should vibrate to our own . . . that lips of motionless ice should not reply to lips quivering and burning with the heart's best blood."

Sexual intercourse leading to orgasm is possibly the intensest physical experience a human being can know. Breathing becomes extremely rapid and deep, with respiratory rates sometimes reaching a peak of forty per minute. Blood courses powerfully throughout the body, surcharging vessels and tissue, an effect often experienced subjectively as a throbbing or pulsating. The skin grows flushed and warm, suffused with blood. Heart action becomes excessively rapid, with rates as high as 180 beats per minute. Blood pressure is greatly elevated. The body experiences a massive increase in muscular tension, both voluntary and involuntary, exhibited by grimacing, contortion, gasping, semispastic clenching and clutching, muscle contraction and spasms. A perspiratory reaction often affects the limbs and sometimes the whole body. When fully aroused, the sexual organs become lubricious. At the peak of tension a loss of overall sensory awareness or acuity may occur, resulting in a subjective loss of conscious focus, a vertigo or partial blacking out. These are some of the principal physiological responses to orgasmic stimuli as observed in the modern laboratory by William Masters and Virginia Johnson. In their somewhat hermetic language, the orgasmic experience is defined as "total-body involvement through the processes of vasocongestion and myotonia," involving hyperventilation, tachycardia, and venous engorgement. The response cycle is subdivided into four stages—excitement, plateau, orgasm, and resolution—and orgasm itself is a "brief episode of physical release from the vasocongestive and myotonic increment developed in response to sexual stimuli."[62] However arcane in expression, these findings constitute the first truly objective data to be recorded about an experience which has been described subjectively from time immemorial, most memorably by imaginative writers.

No imaginative writer, whether in poetry or prose, has captured more completely than Shelley the intensity of human sexual response as established by Masters and Johnson nor sought to render its physiological components more faithfully. This assertion does not refer merely to organ response, descriptions of which have been common, but to the involvement of the whole body. As a poet, Shelley conveys the experience from within, as it is apprehended by the individual psyche. Masters and Johnson, as laboratory technicians, observe it impersonally from without. But both describe very nearly the same thing. Moreover, as Masters and Johnson make clear, "sexual function is not just a physical expression." Like Shelley, they emphasize that it is a total psychosensory experience, in which touch, smell, sound, and sight reflect "how men or women as sexual beings show what they feel and think," and the sum total is what brings "responsive meaning to the sexual act."[63]

Like modern science, Shelley too has his jargon, drawn not from the frigid vocabulary of the laboratory but from the fevered rotundities of Gothic romance. Twentieth-century critics, preferring the urbane elegance of the Elizabethan love lyric or the erotic "realism" of classical verse, have frequently found Shelley's style a source of embarrassment. Donald Davie in particular condemns Shelley's erotic vocabulary as confusingly emotive, producing a "hectic and strident tone."[64] Certainly Shelley's language produces a very different effect from the sort of verse now in vogue, but critics are mistaken in charging that he uses it vaguely or imprecisely. The diction, allowing for the period, is a workmanlike vehicle for detailing a real experience.

A composite portrait of sexual intercourse in Shelley, based largely on a systematic digest of his erotic terminology as extrapolated from individual acts of intercourse, demonstrates just how precisely and, in the light of modern investigation, how accurately he portrayed the act. For every term employed there exist nonsexual as well as sexual meanings, and often what is being conveyed is simply the physiology of any strong response. But the terms also have a specifically sexual denotation, by means of which Shelley vividly renders the act of human coitus.[65]

Ideally the act takes place in a secluded spot out of doors. Sitting or reclining, the couple talk quietly at first, then gradually fall silent, lapsing into passionate looks. Their mutually "kindling" eyes suggest a directly sensual level of response. The couple are very much aware of each other's physical presence, being wrapped or interpenetrated by their mutual atmosphere. Typically, the woman is veiled in the gauzy, diaphanous garments or vests of the period, which reveal as much as they conceal.[66] As she becomes aroused, her desire is stimulated. Her face flushes or blushes, her veins beat, and her limbs glow or burn, enflaming her lover, whose eyes have been roving over her charms, to a similar response. Loosening her clothes, she bares her outspread arms, pressing, clasping, enfolding her lover in a joyous embrace, which he returns, pillowing himself on her swelling, panting, trembling, heaving, leaping, throbbing, bounding bosom, formerly soft, full, deep, alabaster, marmoreal, now blushing or glowing. The woman's hair loosens and floats or streams about her, covering her lover as well. Sometimes she winds her locks round his neck, or he in turn binds his neck with her tresses. The two touch, sparking a fiery sensation; they caress; and particularly they kiss—sweetly, tenderly, moistly, lingeringly, quickly, quiveringly, tremblingly, warmly, deeply, passionately, breathlessly, frenziedly, burningly, never-ceasingly, close-mouthed and open-mouthed, sucking on the lips, the cheeks, and the eyelids.

All the while the couple are building up, in modern terms, a vasocongestive and cardiorespiratory response which is electric in its intensity. Their tumultuous breathing becomes labored—intermitting or intermitted. They pant and gasp, pouring their sweet, warm breath into one another's mouths. Their pulse rate mounts as the kindling blood surges through their burning veins, where it is felt like fire. The heart beats faster and louder; it flutters, trembles, throbs, and seems about to burst. The whole body is now alive, prickling and tingling, thrilling voluptuously to every sensation, its nerves quivering or vibrating, its limbs shaking or shuddering. The couple are by now locked in total embrace, their frames linked, their limbs intertwined or interwoven. Their passion is experienced as a wild, frantic, tumultuous, tempestuous rapture, ecstasy, or delirium—maddening, intoxicating, or rocking.

As their intercourse, mingling, mixing, commingling, intermingling, intertwining, interweaving, or simply embracing moves toward its crisis, the onset of the coital trance is experienced as an increasing vertigo and loss of sensory acuity, expressed by Shelley in a cluster of widely employed terms.[67] Surfeited with delicious or voluptuous sensation, the lovers grow giddy or dizzy. They feel weak, sick, or faint and experience a sinking, failing, drooping, or ebbing sensation.[68] Everything grows dim or misty, their eyes sometimes fill with tears, and they are overwhelmed by a sense of dissolution, as if fading, wasting, or melting. Finally, at the moment of climax and release, their pulses leap, their veins beat together, and the burning blood mingles.[69] As the fountains of their deepest life overflow, the entire body is shaken by the orgasmic spasm, as if convulsed by an earthquake or volcanic eruption. The lovers faint away or black out altogether in the darkness of eclipse—thought, sense, and feeling no longer distinct but confounded. The passion is annihilating; it is the little death, "the death which lovers love," and they "perish," "expire," or "die."

Shelley has little specifically to say about the resolution or postorgasmic phase of intercourse, the period of tension dispersal following sexual release, except to emphasize the atmosphere of peace and quiet joy, of unutterable closeness and tenderness, which wraps the lovers.[70] In this peace there is possibly a hint of the physical withdrawal and recuperation necessary to the male after emission—the "refractory period" or "temporary state of psychophysiologic resistance to sexual stimulation immediately following an orgasmic experience" defined by Masters and Johnson—but virtually none of the psychological letdown or withdrawal traditionally characterizing the male response, the ubiquitous postcoital sadness.[71] The one exception in the mature poetry is the reference to "love's sad satiety" in "To a Skylark." Here Shelley's meaning seems to be sexual, since he also speaks of "languor" and "annoyance" in contrast to "joy" (76-80), though conceivably the lines refer to the disillusionment springing from unsuccessful attempts to allay the thirst of sentimental, not sexual, love.[72]

Ordinarily, however, orgasmic release in Shelley's poetry is experienced as intensely satisfying, because the love evoking it is nearly always sympathetic, the lovers united at all levels simultaneously, so that when for the moment they retreat physically, they are still intimately bound emotionally and psychologically. These bonds are in fact strengthened by the memory of the physical linking. The lovers are thus exempt, to use the early rhetoric of the Gothic novels, from the "involuntary disgust" that follows an attachment "founded on the visionary fabric of passion or interest," which "sinks in the merited abyss of ennui, or is followed by apathy and carelessness." If a couple have nothing to hold them together except sex, they inevitably overindulge it and ultimately become satiated and hence bored or disgusted with one another: "Tired, at last, even with delight, which had become monotonous from long continuance." If they are sympathetically united, however, they feel "that innocent and calm pleasure which soothes the soul, and, calming each violent emotion, fills it with a serene happiness."[73] This thought is finely restated much later in Shelley's career in a statuary note. Limning the proportions of his favorite Bacchus, he equates their effect to "some fine strain of harmony" that enfolds the soul, leaving it "in the astonishment of a satisfaction, like the pleasure of love with one whom we most love, which having taken away desire, leaves pleasure, sweet pleasure" (VI.319-320). Toward the end of his life Shelley came to value this state more than intercourse itself: "When passion's trance is overpast," if only "tenderness and truth could last,/Or live, whilst all wild feelings keep/Some mortal slumber, dark and deep" (1-4). But most of his life he regarded postcoital satisfaction merely as a welcome pause while one relaxed in the company of the beloved and recouped one's powers. Sometimes the episode ended simply by the lovers drifting off into slumber, "the fresh dew of languid love," but this was a dew "Whose drops quench kisses" only "till they burn again" (*Epi.* 558-559).

Shelley's attitude toward sexual intercourse was for the most part positive and healthy. Intercourse appears in his work as a normally joyous experience.[74] The term *joy* occasionally even serves as the verbal equivalent of intercourse. This is a joy at once ecstatic and peaceful, tumultuous and tender. The intensity of the physical response is recognized and stressed, but also the serenity of the aftermath. However, the harmony of these responses, both psychological and physiological, even at the peak of somatic tension, defines the sex act at its best, making it truly the final bond of sympathetic interconnection, the type or expression of the rest.

4

Civilized Sex

WHILE THE EROTIC in Shelley's work expresses itself primarily in terms of human sexual response, the human is not its only area of expression. Sexual response is shown to operate at every level of the animate creation and, metaphorically, at the inanimate as well. Indeed, owing to the science of the day, the distinction between living and dead matter was essentially illusory. All matter was alive.[1] For this reason the poet had no hesitation in evoking the workings of the entire cosmos in the language of sex. Not only do his doe and his mimosa tremble and pant with the bliss of "love's sweet want," but so do his waves and stars—in short, his entire physico-poetic universe, whose presiding deity is the universal Pan.[2] All are responding to the sexual impulse, nature resolving itself into one vast act of coitus, from the minutest atom to the giant planetary bodies in interstellar space.[3] Nothing in the world is single; everything is merged and interpenetrated in one pantheistic whole. This commingling is projected as a universal sex dance in which fountains mingle with rivers and rivers with oceans, winds forever mix, mountains kiss the sky, flowers kiss each other, moonbeams kiss the sea, waves clasp one another, and sunlight clasps the earth. This is love's philosophy, and it makes Shelley's poetry a dense web of imagistic eroticism whose skeins insinuate themselves into the remotest corners of his work.[4]

Although love's philosophy rendered it logical for the poet to view the cosmos in sexual terms, he was also led to this perspective by his imagination which, freed of the normal inhibitions of the period, operated spontaneously through the medium of sexual tropes. No theoretical prompting was necessary; analogies from the world of sex matter-of-factly leapt into his head when he needed to make a point. Writing to Medwin, for example, from Pisa in 1820, he ends a paragraph expressing envy of his friend's mountain-climbing expeditions in the Alps with the casual interjection, "I see the mountains, the sky, and the trees from my windows, and recollect, as an old man does the mistress of his youth, the raptures of a more familiar intercourse."[5]

This sort of offhand sexual comparison appears continually in his work.

Often the analogies are justified by the context and develop or support the thought. When, for example, in *Hellas* the poet describes Hesperus fleeing the approach of night as a nymph would a satyr, "loveliness panting with wild desire/While it trembles with fear and delight" (1029-1040), the comparison is apt for both its erotic and its Greek associations. Or when in *The Sensitive Plant* the rose opens her petals "like a nymph to the bath addressed," unveiling "the depth of her glowing breast,/Till, fold after fold, to the fainting air/The soul of her beauty and love lay bare" (I.29-32), the figure is appropriate to a poem in which the loves of the plants are finding expression in human terms.[6] When much the same figure reappears in *Epipsychidion*, however, its appropriateness in a self-styled "soul" poem is open to question, although the problem of appropriateness involves the imagery of the poem as a whole.

It is not possible in every instance to distinguish sharply between images demanded by the content of a work and thus organic to it and images that are essentially illustrative or decorative or used for symbolic purposes. A marked feature of Shelley's writing, however, is his use of sexual comparisons in the most unlikely contexts. The figure of undressing, for instance, reappears in several elevated and serious passages of *A Defence of Poetry*, although by varying his terms, the poet conveys directly opposite meanings. Whereas high poetry is defined as "infinite"—"Veil after veil may be undrawn and the inmost naked beauty of the meaning never exposed"—it simultaneously "strips the veil of familiarity from the world" and "lays bare the naked and sleeping beauty, which is the spirit of its forms."[7] Similarly in *Prometheus Unbound* regenerate man is described as unveiling the physical mysteries of the universe as if by stripping it and laying bare its depths (IV.422-423). The frequency with which this figure recurs suggests the attraction of the author to its underlying reality. These analogies, though for the most part inorganic, are effective. Sometimes, however, Shelley introduces erotic comparisons which seem almost wholly gratuitous, such as this startling picture in the apparently innocent little nature lyric "The Question": "a sound of waters murmuring/Along a shelving bank of turf, which lay/Under a copse, and hardly dared to fling/Its green arms round the bosom of the stream,/But kissed it and then fled, as thou mightest in dream."

The poet was also keenly alive to the residual sexual meanings and connotations of language, with the result that he frequently revivified dead metaphors. When he speaks of "the shadows of the bosoms of

Civilized Sex

the hills," he means it. Or when he uses the hackneyed metaphor, "The balmy breath of soul-reviving dawn . . . kissèd the bosom of the waveless lake," he understands the precise cardiorespiratory response latent in the image. When at sunset "pallid Evening twines its beaming hair/In duskier braids around the languid eyes of Day," or when in the deep woods "meeting branches lean/Even from the Earth, to mingle the delight/Which lives within the light," concretely pictured erotic experience emerges beneath the tired rhetoric.[8] A powerful sexual imagination is at work in all these examples characteristic of the verse as a whole.

Yet despite this seeming monomania, Shelley did not elevate sex disproportionately. In both thought and practice he was the exact opposite of the voluptuary or the libertine. In his view physical pleasure represented only a small part of the total amalgam of the amatory experience. A truly "enlightened philosophy," the *Discourse* repeatedly stresses, "regards the senses as but a minute and subordinate portion of our complicated nature" (221). As an example, Shelley cites "that fine observer of the human heart," Samuel Richardson, who makes even the arch-libertine Robert Lovelace "express his contempt for the pleasure of the mere act of sexual intercourse."[9]

For Shelley few characters are more "degraded" than a habitual libertine, one who is accustomed to seek relief from the sexual impulse "divested of those associated sentiments which in a civilized state, precede, accompany, or follow such an act" (221). The sensualism that seems to characterize such poems as Shelley's "Love's Philosophy," Leigh Hunt explains, "must be understood with reference to the delicacy as well as freedom of Mr. Shelley's opinions, and not as supplying any excuse to that heartless libertinism which no man disdained more." Shelley "had no idea of love unconnected with sentiment."[10] For Shelley, sex in advanced societies had to engage the entire personality, or else it represented a step backward in mankind's psychosexual evolution, a negation of the higher sentimental communion for which humans yearn more strongly as they grow more civilized. Even the brutal Lovelace is forced to concede something like this, according to Shelley, when he finds "more truly delightful . . . the seduction progress than the crowned act: for that's a vapour, a bubble!"[11]

Libertinism had been a serious problem of English social life during the preceding century, as Richardson's novel attests. The careers of the real-life Lovelaces were not an edifying spectacle in a theoretically enlightened nation. Notwithstanding the rise of Evangelical morality, the problem persisted well into the nineteenth century. The Regency rake, personified in the Regent himself, was a prominent feature of the period and one seemingly tolerated by its mores. Francis Place, writing as late as 1832, found that almost "every young man considers girls of any grade below his own fair game for the debaucher. Success in this kind of iniquity [is] something to brag of amongst his associates; and, if unaccompanied by heavy pecuniary charges, [is] seldom thought much of by men of mature age—so little, indeed, as seldom to produce reprobation."[12]

Shelley, however, was in rebellion against such practices from his youth. *St. Irvyne* is notable for its violent attack on libertinism (V.178). He had to contend with elements of this tradition even in his own upbringing. His father, according to Medwin, was "a disciple of Chesterfield & La Rochefoucauld, reducing all politeness to forms, and moral virtue to expedience; as an instance of which, he once told his son Percy Bysshe, in my presence, that he would provide for as many natural children as he chose to get, but that he would never forgive his making a *mésalliance*."[13] Shelley nevertheless speaks of the libertine with scorn in a letter to his father in the fall of 1811 shortly after his elopement with Harriet Westbrook, though ironically, because of his "friendship" with Elizabeth Hitchener, he was already beginning to meet with the charges of libertine behavior, "of resembling *Lovelace*," that dogged him in later years.[14] In a poem at this time to Harriet he explains that his love for her is not that of "the Libertine," whose "breast must feel bliss with alloy/That is scorched by so selfish a flame."[15] *Queen Mab*, written in the following year, contains in Canto V a savage indictment of his society's loveless sexual code. The theme of the Canto is selfishness, which in sexual relations expresses itself in "frozen, unimpassioned, spiritless" sensualism and libertinism (V.25). The principal metaphor for selfishness is poison, which destroys "even the pulse/That kindles in the beating heart/To mingle with sensation," leaving "nothing but the sordid lust of self."[16] In an ironic twist at the end of the canto prophesying the eventual death of selfishness, Shelley has the old era living on "but in the memory of Time,/Who, like a penitent libertine, shall start,/Look back, and shudder at his younger years" (V.249-259).

Regardless of where the poet encountered libertine behavior, it invariably called down his reproof. In his otherwise laudatory review of Hogg's *Memoirs of Prince Alexy Haimatoff* (1814), he reprimands his friend for what he takes to be the novel's approval of libertine practice, "the loveless intercourse of brutal appetite." The author asserts that "a transient connection with a cultivated female may contribute to form the heart without essentially vitiating the sensibilities. It is our duty to protest against so pernicious and disgusting an opinion." To recommend indulging in "promiscuous concubinage" cannot be regarded "without horror and detestation" (VI.177-178). As Shelley remarks in *On Marriage*, promiscuous concubinage is the sexual norm of animals and savages with whom "no moral affections" arise "from the indulgence of the physical impulse" (VII.149). The indictment continues in the *Essay on Christianity*, which describes modern society as diseased by the "vices of sensuality and selfishness" and the "contamination of luxury and license."[17]

The essential violation to human nature that is involved in loveless sex is horrifyingly illustrated in *The Revolt of Islam* by Cythna's forcible abduction to the harem of the libertine Tyrant Othman. Attracting the Tyrant's attention, Cythna is borne off "a loveless victim" to his "secret bower"—not of bliss but of "cruel lust." What happens next is such an outrage to Cythna's nature, such a "loathsome agony" and mockery of "love's delight," ordinarily "great Nature's sacred power," that she is deprived of her senses. When the day breaks on her "awful frenzy," the Tyrant flees the sight, "aghast and pale" (VII.v-vi). The whole scene is a tragic parody of Cythna's nuptials with Laon. The effect is much the same in *The Cenci*, after the Count's diabolic attack on Beatrice, when her "brain is hurt," her "eyes are full of blood," and she feels as if the air "Is changed to vapours such as the dead breathe/ In charnel pits." A contaminating mist eats into her sinews and dissolves her flesh "to a pollution, poisoning/The subtle, pure, and inmost spirit of life!" (III.i.12,14-23). Through a deliberate subversion of his standard coital imagery in these two scenes Shelley achieves some of his most powerful effects.

Shelley had before him a striking real-life exemplum of the evils of libertinism in the career of Lord Byron. The running commentary in Shelley's letters shows him to have been profoundly disturbed by his friend's philanderings after leaving England. He was particularly upset by what seemed to him the consciously degraded and brutal character of Byron's sexual practice in Venice, which was the antithesis of his own ideal. Byron "is familiar with the lowest sort" of women, he writes to Peacock, "the people his gondolieri pick up in the streets. He allows fathers & mothers to bargain with him for their daughters, & though this is common enough in Italy, yet for an Englishman to encourage such sickening vice is a melancholy thing."[18] His report to Hogg is lighter in tone, but the disapproval is evident: Byron "is practising aphrodisiacs at a great rate & I should think must be as tired as Candide was of the mountain where the Deity is worshipped; but he will not own it." Later he writes to Horace Smith: "I dare say you have heard of the life [Byron] led at Venice, rivalling the wise Solomon almost, in the number of his concubines."[19]

Byron eventually did tire, as Shelley knew he must. By September of 1818 his "libertinism" had reached Olympian proportions, amounting by his own count to relations with "at least two hundred [women] of one sort or another" in the two years he had been in Venice, and he was ready to call a halt. His reform was completed the following year in his liaison with the "sentimental" Countess Guiccioli.[20] When Shelley visited Byron at Ravenna in August 1821, he was able to report to Peacock that his friend was now "in excellent cue both of health and spirits. He has got rid of all those melancholy and degrading habits which he indulged at Venice. He lives with one woman, a lady of rank here, to whom he is attached, and who is attached to him, and is in every respect an altered man." Back in Pisa he assured John Gisborne that Byron was "quite cured of his gross habits," but added the ominous qualification, "the perverse ideas on which they were founded are not yet eradicated."[21] It was precisely these perverse ideas which, after the two poets settled next to each other in Pisa at the end of the year, finally alienated Shelley from his friend. Byron's constant scoffing at sentimental love became more than Shelley could stomach. He had no desire to be dragged down to the level of the libertine even in thought.[22]

The prominence accorded in the *Discourse* to the evils of libertinism is therefore to a large extent a reaction to the sexual life of the period. Anyone writing at the time on the problems of human psychosexuality could not avoid seeing the question at least partly in these terms. But the practice of libertinism also served as a bridge in Shelley's mind to link the ancient world with the modern. From his translation of the *Symposium*, to which the *Discourse* is an introduction, it is obvious that he considered Plato's Pandemian or popular Venus simply libertinism in modern dress. The love inspired by this Venus "presides over *transient* and fortuitous connexions." Her votaries are interested only in the body and the satisfaction of their *"sensual necessities."* The opposite of the Pandemian Venus is the Uranian, whose worship "exempts us from wantonness and *libertinism."* The phrases in italics, which are Shelley's interpolations, suggest that he is attempting to rethink Plato's distinction, which also involves a discrimination between pederastic and heterosexual love, in the light of modern practice. Since Plato defines Pandemian love as common to the "vulgar" and "ignorant" but scorned by the cultivated elite, the distinction takes on considerable force in the light of Shelley's contemplated audience which, like Plato's, should be superior to the primitivism of Pandemian or libertine desire.[23]

Founded solely on the lowest sort of physical gratification, libertinism stood condemned of itself, a perversion—or quite literally a turning in the wrong direction, back down the evolutionary scale—of the archetype of sentimental love, which Shelley believed to be natural to civilized connection, whether ancient or modern. In this archetype the senses represent only a relatively small portion of man's complicated nature, all of whose claims demand fulfillment. The more civilized people grow, the more they will feel the claims of those higher faculties, the intellect and imagination, which dignify their nature as social beings.

Not content with a generic indictment, however, Shelley exposes libertinism on its own grounds. Constant and indiscriminate indulgence deadens the senses, bringing on satiety and ennui, while sentimental connection actually stimulates the senses. The pleasures of the senses are "weakened, not enhanced by repetition," which is especially true if they are pursued "unassociated with some principle from which they may participate in permanency and excellence" (221).[24] From his earliest work Shelley stresses the fleeting and dissatisfying quality of libertine intercourse—"the roses of momentary voluptuousness," "a transitory delirium of pleasure"—inevitably terminating in "disgust and lassitude." This transcience is compared to the longer, more joyous duration of sentimental connection.[25] Joy is the keynote of Shelleyan intercourse, while lust gives only "joys forlorn" (*Rev.Is.*II. xxxv.8). King Solomon, as Shelley often observed, though possessing a thousand concubines, nonetheless despaired that "all was vanity."[26] The final temptation offered the poet's Prometheus—a heaven of "voluptuous joy"—thus turns out to be no temptation at all (I.425-427).

Physiologically speaking, notes Shelley in the *Discourse*, there is probably no significant difference in the "susceptibility of the external senses" to sexual stimuli as between animals and savages on the one hand and civilized beings on the other. Sexual response is a biological constant admitting of little variation in the total yield of sheer organic pleasure. Yet it is an observable fact that "the degree of intensity and durability of the love of the male towards the female in animals and savages"—to whom "promiscuous concubinage" is the norm—is demonstrably less than in love between civilized beings. The causes must therefore be sought in the "accessory circumstances" attending the indulgence of the sexual impulse, from which it derives "a strength not its own."[27] These are the psychological and emotional factors which "in a civilized state precede, accompany, or follow such an act" and which confer on it some "principle [of] permanency and excellence" (220-221).

As ethologists now recognize, sexual bonding, except among humans, is normally of short duration. "The human's capacity for individualized affection" thus distinguishes him from the "so-called lower animals as much as anything else."[28] Anthropologists have similarly shown that many "primitive" societies tolerate a situation like Shelley's promiscuous concubinage in which no moral sentiment attends the indulgence of physical impulse. In advanced societies, in contrast, the accent is on the sentiments associated with the sex act. Although modern sex research by no means rules out entirely the influence of physiological or hormonal factors in accounting for variations in individual sexual response, it increasingly stresses the importance of psychological determinants.[29] Their exact composition varies widely from individual to individual and culture to culture, and their interrelationship is only now under serious investigation. Shelley himself is aware of both the personal and cultural factors, understanding them to be functionally interdependent. The more highly organized and complex a society, the more complicated is the individual personality structure, to the degree that the indulgence of the "instinctive sense" eventually constitutes only a small part of the individual's desire for total interpersonal communion—intellectual and imaginative as well as sensual. It is the addition of the intellectual and imaginative components, in fact, which gives the physical component a "strength not its own" and which lends it a permanency and excellence that set it off from the transient, repetitive, and ultimately joyless couplings of the libertine.

These views have received striking confirmation from the modern psychosexual investigations of A. H. Maslow. In studying the sex lives of what he labels "self-actualizing" people—those who are unusually mature, self-developed, and psychologically healthy—Maslow found that the orgasm "is simultaneously more important and less important than in average people. It is often a profound and almost mystical experience, and yet the absence of sexuality is more easily tolerated by these people. This is not a paradox or a contradiction. It follows from dynamic motivation theory. Loving at a higher need level makes the lower needs and their frustrations and satisfactions less important, less central, more easily neglected. But it also makes them more wholeheartedly enjoyed when gratified." Self-actualizing people, observes Maslow, "tend on the whole not to seek sex for its own sake, or to be satisfied with it alone when it comes." Unless united with love or affection, sex is generally eschewed by these people. Yet when the conditions are right, the self-actualizer is capable of enjoying sex with far greater intensity than the ordinary person.[30]

These views closely parallel Shelley's ideal of civilized sex and help explain why, without exception, the major coital episodes of his poetry are set within the framework of the participants' entire personality. The "moments of abandonment," as he writes in the *Discourse*, should be "by the entire consent of all the conscious portions of our being," so that the act itself stands as "the link and type of the highest emotions of our nature." The necessary corollary is "temperance in pleasure." Otherwise sex becomes an end in itself, degenerating, as with the habitual libertine, into a "diseased habit, equally pernicious to body and mind" (222). The higher elements of the personality are then forgotten in futile repetition of an act whose pleasures paradoxically diminish in proportion as they are pursued for their own sake, resulting in love's sad satiety—the postcoitum triste of lovers who have nothing to share except their sexuality.[31]

This distinction, which is intrinsic to the poet's philosophy, has the further purpose of throwing light on ancient Greek practice. Sexual moderation or temperance is also one of the maxims laid down by Plato in the *Symposium*. According to the dialogue, we should subject ourselves to the influence of sensual love only so far as "to derive pleasure from it without indulging to excess," in the same way that we should not overindulge in "the pleasures of the table." The Pandemian or libertine lover, however, is intemperate sexually and his conduct therefore censurable.[32]

Not only the libertine is guilty in this respect, adds Shelley, but nearly everyone. As evidence, he cites the story of Mrs. Shandy's clock, observing that after feeling a momentary amusement, one cannot but be "shocked at the picture it affords of the brutal prostitution of the most sacred impulses of our being" (222). Sterne's celebrated account of the night when Tristram Shandy was conceived, with Mrs. Shandy's ridiculous interruption at the crucial moment, "Pray, my Dear . . . have you not forgot to wind up the clock?" is shocking exactly because it is true.[33] This is not libertine sensuality but normal married love, the routine release of the physical impulse the world over. It offers a profoundly disquieting commentary on civilized sexual relations. Has man really progressed beyond the level of the brute or not? Scarcely, thinks Shelley, when most intercourse is nothing more than habit, the crude relieving of an instinct, incorporating none of the higher elements of the personality.

Shelley's reference to Sterne illustrates the earnestness with which the poet regarded sex. To treat it lightly or humorously or for its own sake was in itself a kind of intemperance, a profanation, depriving the instinct of its deeper meaning. In general Shelley did not find sex a laughing matter, and its discussion or portrayal was redeemed only insofar as it served some loftier aim. Otherwise it was indecent or obscene.[34]

The poet's friends remarked on the almost womanish modesty and purity of his own conversation and behavior. Medwin, for example, remembered that Shelley "never could enjoy obscenity in any form" and that "His converse was as chaste as his morals—all grossness he abominated." Hogg recalled that in Dublin the poet had been repelled by the profanity and lewd jesting of John Philpott Curran. Shelley, Hogg noted, was "in behavior modest; in conversation chaste . . . the gross and revolting indecency of an immoral wit wounded his sensitive nature." Horace Smith recollected that the poet evinced a mental "fastidious[ness] and delicacy; an innate purity which not even the licence of college habits and society could corrupt." Mary Shelley recorded that in Pisa Francesco Pacchiani disgusted her husband "by telling a dirty story." Shelley was also disgusted by Byron's "gross and indelicate" raillery during their last days together at Pisa [35]

It may be difficult to recognize in this almost Evangelical Shelley the same person who expresses himself repeatedly in sexual tropes and condemns his age for its prudery. But the inconsistency disappears if it is kept in mind that for Shelley the decisive factor is the attitude toward sex. While sex has undeniable claims, the other elements of the personality also have claims, and to treat the former in isolation, as an end in themselves, without regard to the total personality, is a violation of civilized nature. The language of the time, rooted in the vocabulary of eighteenth-century libertinism, seemed often to express just such a violation. Ford Brown writes of the vulgarity and foulness of speech which at the beginning of the nineteenth century was so common that it was "hardly noticed until the Evangelicals pointed it out. It was not found in the lower classes only. The speech of some ladies and gentlemen of the upper ranks, and even of the High Church clergy, was likely to contain expressions the following generation was to consider extremely offensive. Only a few years later such language was barred in circles of any respectability."[36] Shelley participated in this reaction at the same time that, paradoxically, he was reacting against the morality underlying the change. For him it was a question not of harkening back to the past to revive a repressive, puritanical Christianity but of looking to the future to create a more civilized and humane sexual sensibility.

"Obscenity," therefore—to employ his favorite term of opprobrium—no less than prudery, is a threat to this future precisely insofar as it reflects and perpetuates regressive attitudes and modes of behavior or speech. For obscenity, in the words of the *Discourse*, consists "in a capability of associating disgusting images with the act of the sexual instinct" (223); and in the more impassioned language of *A Defence*, obscenity is "ever blasphemy against the divine beauty in life" (VII.122). Significantly, obscenity is one of the principal elements darkening the human mind during the reign of Jupiter in *Prometheus Unbound*—transformed in the regenerate world into "an ocean/Of clear emotion" (IV.94-97). The libertine dance that precedes the triumphal car in *The Triumph of Life* is similarly "fierce and obscene" (154-155). Frequently in Shelley's poetry obscenity is associated with "the world's slow stain" of *Adonais*, which darkens or obscures the pure light of heaven with its filth.

Shelley was constantly on the watch for obscenity in the writings of others. Both the *Discourse* and *A Defence* contain capsule literary histories from this point of view. In the *Discourse*, he declares the Romans to have been "brutally obscene," as contrasted with the Greeks, who "seemed hardly capable of obscenity in a strict sense." Even Aristophanes' notorious *Lysistrata* is "innocent," he claims, compared with "the infamous perversions of Catullus!" (223).[37] This did not mean, however, that he approved of Greek indecencies. Extant is a letter from Hogg to Peacock which reports that Shelley "thinks A [ristophanes] coarse" (*S&C*.VI.919). And although Shelley does his best in the *Discourse* to defend Aristophanes at the expense of the Romans, it is plain that he found certain elements in the comedies grossly offensive.[38] Turning to the literature of his own country, Shelley finds the earlier dramatic writers to be even more obscene than the Romans. The explanation is fundamentally the same in each instance, the literary obscenity being merely a reflection of a wider social decay. Thus "Luxury produced for the Romans what the venereal disease did for the writers of James, and after the redeeming interval over which Milton presided the effects of both were united under Charles II to infect literature" (223). In *A Defence* Shelley explains that the Restoration witnessed the "grossest degradation" of the drama, when obscenity was not only more prevalent but more dangerous because veiled by the polished wit (VII.122). Shelley applied these distinctions even to sacred literature. The Old Testament, he charges in *A Refutation of Deism*, was disfigured by the "loathsome and minute obscenities to which the inspired writers perpetually descend, the filthy observances which God is described as personally instituting, the . . . contempt of the first principles of morality, manifested on the most public occasions by the chosen favorites of Heaven, [which] might corrupt, were they not so flagitious as to disgust" (VI.34). He notes the obscenity of having God command Moses to invade the Midianite nation and massacre its inhabitants, retaining "the maidens alone for concubinage and violation" (VI.34). Even the New Testament was obscene, according to

Shelley, precisely in its crucial article: the process of the Incarnation.[39]

Obscenity posed a particular problem for Shelley in his translations. How faithfully should he render passages of dubious propriety?
Shelley held no brief for bowdlerization. Yet he slightly softened
several crudely sexual or scatological passages in his own translations
and in one or two instances omitted words or lines altogether.[40] How
much such changes were in deference to contemporary taste and how
much to his own wish is not possible to determine, but it would seem
to involve a combination of the two. Goethe's *Faust*, for instance,
which he greatly admired, nevertheless contained "some scenes—
which the fastidiousness of our taste would wish erased."[41] These
scenes would have to be—if not erased—cleaned up, were the drama
to be translated into English. Coleridge, whom Shelley thought best
qualified for this task, had been deterred precisely because there were
parts which "could not be endured in English and by the English," and
he did not like to make the attempt with "the necessity of the smallest
mutilation."[42] The parts in question are the Walpurgisnacht scenes,
and when Shelley, who did make the attempt, came to them, he
prudently refrained from attempting a wholly faithful rendition,
though the changes are slight and the language franker than in later
versions during the century. But there was no point in translating
literally such lines as, "So geht es über Stein und Stock,/Es f . . . t die
Hexe, es st . . . t der Bock," even had he wanted to.[43] His awkward
substitute—"Hey over stock! and hey over stone!/Twixt witches and
incubi, what shall be done?/Tell it who dare! Tell it who dare!"
—suggests embarrassment and unease beneath the bantering mock
modesty. The scenes, in fact, must have elicited genuine distaste, for
they are from beginning to end unrelieved libertine sex of the most
"degraded" sort: naked witches "Dancing and drinking, making love"
around a hundred bonfires; Mephistopheles asking Faust to accompany him from fire to fire, with the explanation, "I'll be the Pimp,
and you shall be the Lover."[44] The passages, which are by definition
obscene, are plainly the model for the obscene dance of life in his own
poem.

Goethe's drama, however, was at least redeemed by elements of
profound philosophy and by the sentimental love story of Margaret
which Shelley found so moving. But what led him to translate Euripides' satyr play *The Cyclops* is more difficult to say. The drama is
generally gross, vinous, bawdy, and in his terms disgusting. It is little
calculated to support his view of the "innocent" Greeks. His rendering
reveals his discomfort, for he elevates the language and omits one
section containing such blunt matter as, "Why, when you're drunk,

you stand up stiff down here (*Gestures.*)/and then get yourself a fistful of breast/and browse on the soft field ready to your hands."[45] Although these lines could not in any case have been rendered faithfully in Shelley's day, they represent the very view of sex that he was determined to oppose.

Shelley was not totally incapable, however, of appreciating sex on its own terms or even enjoying a smile at its expense. Anyone who could recommend a dose of Boccaccio's the *Decameron* as a wholesome purgative for the narrowness of Christian sexual morality, or who could respond enthusiastically to the undisguised bawdiness of a Burns, an Apuleius, or a Lucian, was no Puritan, even though it was not the bawdy in these writers that particularly appealed to him.[46] While Shelley is not renowned for a sense of humor, a vein of mild sexual punning and raillery nonetheless runs throughout his letters, especially those to Leigh Hunt. Medwin recalled that Shelley was "endowed with a raciness of wit and a keen perception of the ridiculous, that showed itself not in what we call *humour*, that produces a rude and boisterious mirth, but begat a smile of intellectual enjoyment, much more delightful and refined."[47] An example is Shelley's remark to Peacock in a letter from Italy in which he describes the planet Jupiter as being almost as fine as Venus, "but it wants a certain silver and aerial radiance, and soft yet piercing splendour, which belongs, I suppose to the latter planet by virtue of its at once divine and female nature. I have forgotten to ask the ladies if Jupiter produces on them the same effect" (L.II.25). Another example is from Shelley's letter to Medwin on learning of his cousin's new friends the Williamses: "I hope . . . I may see the lovely lady & your friend— Though I have never had the ague, I have found these sort of beings, especially the former, of infinite service in the maladies to which I am subject; and I have no doubt, if it could be supposed that anyone would neglect to employ such a medicine, that the best physicians would prescribe them, although they have been entered in no pharmacopoeia" (L.II.184-185). Yet even this gentle levity causes Shelley characteristic unease, for he hastens to add, "Forgive my joking on what all poets ought to consider a sacred subject.—"

The instances of sexual levity in Shelley's poetry are few and, unlike the letters, generally occur as a heavy-handed, vulgar jocosity obviously unnatural to him. They are found mainly in his rare satires, such as *Peter Bell the Third*, and in his political spoofs, such as *The Devil's Walk*, one of whose witticisms is at the expense of the Prince Regent's broad backside, or *Swellfoot the Tyrant*, whose humor consists chiefly in variations on the conceit of Queen Caroline imitating

Pasiphaë with her lovers, necessitating a bill in Parliament excluding "all Minotaurs from the succession."[48] Shelley himself thought this sort of writing unworthy of him. He appears at his worst in his poetry, however, when he adopts the more natural pose of a maidenly coyness and mock modesty about sex. Particularly embarrassing to the modern reader is the archness concerning the facts of life in *Prometheus Unbound* (III.iv.85-94), where the Spirit of the Earth thinks that reproduction occurs through gazing on the loved one's eyes, or the coy whimsy in *Swellfoot*: "I saw all that sin does,/Which lamps hardly see/That burn in the night by the curtained bed,—/The impudent lamps! for they blushed not red."[49] In general the candid ribaldry of Byron in *Don Juan* is more acceptable than the usual Shelleyan sexual banter.

For all its libertine perversities Shelley was himself not immune to the merits of his friend's masterpiece and actively encouraged him to proceed with it. He especially liked Canto V with its teasingly risqué narrative of the Don's escapades in a Turkish harem—so different from the harem scenes in his own work—which he claimed had "the stamp of immortality."[50] This sort of humor was infinitely preferable to the coarse indecencies of Cantos I and II, some of which he would have liked to see canceled. On the other hand he was particularly drawn to Donna Julia's farewell love letter, recognizing it as an acute expression of female erotic psychology. Where, he quizzes Byron, did "you learn all these secrets? I should like to go to school there." But he is deeply disturbed by the use to which the letter is put when the seasick Don pukes over the side of the ship while reading it, since the humor is at the expense of Shelley's own ideal of sentimental love, which ought to be "sacred" to poets: "I cannot say . . . that I altogether think the bitter mockery of our common nature, of which this is one of the expressions, quite worthy of your genius. The power and the beauty and the wit, indeed, redeem all this—chiefly because they belie and refute it. Perhaps it is foolish to wish that there had been nothing to redeem" (L.II.357,198). But he obviously believes that his reaction is not foolish; and he is very severe on the second-rate imitators of Byron who perpetuate his obscenity but not his wit. Of Barry Cornwall's *Dramatic Scenes* (1819) he complains: "Is not the vulgarity of these wretched imitations of Lord Byron carried to a pitch of the sublime?" Worse, it is all affectation: Cornwall's "indecencies . . . both against sexual nature & against human nature in general sit very awkwardly upon him. He only affects the libertine." In Byron, at least, "all this has an analogy with the general system of his character, & the wit & poetry which surround, hide with their light the dark-

ness of the thing itself." But for a writer to be "at once filthy & dull—
is a crime against gods men & columns."[51] Once again libertine ex-
cesses are conveyed as an obscene stain obscuring the pure light of
man's civilized being.

For Shelley not only was temperance a necessity in sex, but so was
chastity. "An enlightened philosophy," holds the *Discourse*, suggests
"the propriety of habits of chastity in like manner with those of temperance" (221). Chastity bears a variety of meanings, the most usual
being sexual continence or denial, but here, as generally in Shelley, the
word signifies sexual constancy or fidelity. It thus denotes behavior
that is the reverse of promiscuous libertinism, bringing the sex act
under the principle of "permanency and excellence" so necessary for
its full enjoyment. Because chastity carries no absolute sanction, however, being merely a good "habit," its violation cannot be accounted a
sin or crime, as demanded by traditional morality, but is simply an
error or imprudence (*L.*II.319).

In view of *Queen Mab's* diatribe against chastity as "dull and selfish," the "virtue of the cheaply virtuous" (IX.84-86), it may seem that
Shelley's attitude underwent substantial revision as he matured. However, the poet never advocated sexual promiscuity, even in the palmi-
est days of his youthful radicalism. Chastity is the target in *Queen
Mab* because it is there synonymous with the depotism of marriage,
whose absolute claims Shelley sees as a thin device for sanctifying the
patriarchal intent of Christian sexual morality. A "fictitious merit" is
ascribed to chastity by traditional morality, he complains to the antimatrimonialist James Lawrence, which would not be so in a "rational
society," such as the polyandrous system outlined in Lawrence's *Empire of the Nairs*, but which at present makes its violation the "forerunner of the most terrible ruins" (*L.*I.323). For Shelley chastity is
matter of individual choice, not open to social or religious dictation.
One is chaste because it satisfies the laws of one's own sexual nature,
not otherwise. Indeed the attempt to limit sexual freedom arbitrarily
creates abuses worse than the original ones. An unwilling chastity is
"a greater foe to natural temperance even than unintellectual sensuality" (I.142).

Spontaneous chastity, on the contrary, yields the "advantages of
simple and pure affection" which it is the object of civilized morality
to promote, according to the poet's review of Hogg's *Memoirs of
Prince Alexy Haimatoff* (VI.178). Precisely because of its spontaneity,
however, such chastity must exist independently of marriage; it can
only wither under constraint, as proved by the unworkableness of the
traditional ideal in actual practice, of which the equally traditional

double standard in sex is tacit admission. But the double standard is scarcely an answer either, Shelley points out, since the basis of real chastity is mutual trust and affection. Chastity is a two-way proposition, as binding on the man as on the woman, and therefore it cannot exist when one partner is unfaithful: "Whatever may be the claims of chastity . . . these ties, these benefits are of equal obligation to either sex. Domestic relations depend for their integrity upon a complete reciprocity of duties" (VI.178). But this is a utopian ideal, and the obligation to chastity remains pre-eminently a female virtue, Shelley realistically concedes, for unless a woman is prepared to embrace certain and irremediable ruin, she has no alternative but to observe the obligation. "I think a regard to chastity," he writes Byron some years later concerning his friend's reluctance to have Allegra return to the Shelley household lest she be brought up to believe in free love, "is quite necessary, as things are, to a young female—that is, to her happiness." This is the prudential reason. But the more fundamental one is still the fact that, regardless of its social expediency, chastity is "at any time a good habit" (*L.*II.199).

The best way to assure habits of chastity, according to the *Discourse*, is to make certain that the object of sexual gratification is "as perfect and beautiful as possible, both in body and in mind, so that all sympathies may be harmoniously blended" (222). Generally speaking, mankind has valued only physical beauty, at the expense of the other elements of being. Shelley too was not immune to physical beauty. "Leda with a very ugly face," is his caustic comment on a Greek statue observed at the Pitti Palace in Florence; "I should be a long time before I should make love with her" (VI.329). All the women to whom he was sexually attracted were conspicuous for their good looks. But the totality of the sympathetic response was what he valued in sexual connection—"All thought, all sense, all feeling" confounded in "one unutterable power"—because this was what gave physical attraction its lasting value. "Delightful converse" is always the prelude to Shelleyan intercourse, and unlike the "unintellectual" couplings of the faithless libertine, it is what cements the connection once the physical impulse has been satisfied, thus making possible the enduring relationships of civilized sex.[52]

5

Lawless Love

THE SEXUAL ACT as a thing in itself—if indeed such a thing can be imagined—is "nothing," explains Shelley in the *Discourse*; it is of no greater moral consequence than such similarly appetitive functions as eating or drinking. It becomes ethically significant solely through the "mode" in which it is indulged (221).[1] The poet's position is thoroughly naturalistic. The morality of sexual indulgence is governed by two things only: "the indestructible laws of human nature" and "the complicated and arbitrary distinctions of society" (221). The difficulty is that the two have rarely coincided. Historically the expression of the sexual impulse has been unnaturally restricted by mankind's sexual codes, with widespread unhappiness as the result, and it is this very unhappiness that condemns them in Shelley's view. His own sexual code was avowedly hedonistic, grounded on the same pleasure-pain principle which shaped all his moral judgments. In the words of the *Discourse*, as regards the sexual act, "the one general law applicable to all other actions is applicable also to this: that nothing is to be done which, including your own being in the estimate, will produce, on the whole, greater pain than pleasure—in this sense adultery, seductions, etc., until mankind shall have enough" (222).

Shelley was never at any time a doctrinaire utilitarian. The frigid intellectualism of this school was unnatural to him. But on one point he remained faithful to utilitarian teaching: its ethical formula of the greatest happiness of the greatest number. Like virtually all moral philosophers of the day, no matter of what school, he also defined happiness hedonistically. Hedonism was the nearly universal standard of value, Epicureanism in modern dress, and it marked a radical departure from the asceticism of traditional Christian ethics. It represented an attempt to create a "scientific" morality on the model of the other natural sciences. As Shelley explains in his notes to *Queen Mab*, "it is not . . . until lately that mankind have admitted that happiness is the sole end of the science of ethics, as of all other sciences; and that the fanatical idea of mortifying the flesh for the love of God has been discarded" (I.141).

Sexuality and Feminism in Shelley

However, there is pleasure and pleasure. To weigh the morality of an action, holds Shelley, one must take into account not only "the greatest quantity" but also the "purest quality of happiness [that] will ensue" (VI.233). Shelley, like Godwin, embraced the notion of a qualitative hedonism, which drastically altered the outlines of the original formula. The distinguishing between different sorts of pleasure, and between those who seek them, was a primary concern of all Shelley's work. As he explains in *A Defence of Poetry* and its drafts, pleasure or good in a general sense is "that which the consciousness of a sensitive and intelligent being seeks and in which, when found, it acquiesces." But there are actually two kinds of pleasure, "one durable, universal, and permanent," the other "transitory and particular." One is produced by whatever "strengthens and purifies the affections, enlarges the imagination, and adds spirit to sense," the other simply by the satisfaction of our "animal" wants and the need for security. One relates to our "actual being," the other to our selfish ego drives. "Utility" can be employed to denote "the production and assurance" of either kind of pleasure, but only the former, pleasure in its "highest sense," can be labeled "true" utility.[2] These distinctions entail what may be denominated the doctrine of the "higher hedonism," and their connection with the distinctions promulgated in the *Discourse* is not difficult to perceive. They are based on the desires of different parts of the personality and explain the superiority of sentimental over libertine sex.

Shelley admits that in practice difficulties arise in accurately defining the pleasures of the higher hedonism, since these do not always come unmixed. Owing to some "inexplicable defect of harmony in the constitution of human nature, the pain of the inferior is frequently connected with the pleasures of the superior portions of our being" (VII.132-133). The inextricable "intertexture of good and evil" (VI.187), pleasure and pain, is one of Shelley's commonest complaints: "And good and ill like vines entangled are,/So that their grapes may oft be plucked together" ("Marenghi," X, 49-50). Yet luckily this entanglement is not always the case. The "ecstasy of the admiration of nature," the "joy of the perception and still more of the creation of poetry," and the "delight of love and friendship," are all of them pleasures "often wholly unalloyed" (VII.133). How to ensure that the third of these pleasures is true for the majority of mankind is the concern of the *Discourse*. Until mankind makes the practice of "true utility" a universal reality, it is argued, it will continue to suffer. So long as it persists in taking a lower pleasure for a higher, a "transitory and particular" one for "one durable, universal, and permanent," so long will it continue to create an overbalance of pain, manifested in the evils of adultery, seduction, and similar libertine abuses. Pain is always an element in the evil contemporary world of the poet's utopian visions, and an important element of that pain is sexual. In the same way pleasure, "that divinest birth" which at "the creation of the Earth" arose from "the soil of Heaven," is the keynote of his regenerate world where love reigns unalloyed. Mankind can never be wholly exempt from pain since it is human. But love is one of the primary areas where, if it sets its will aright, it can most nearly approximate this "Paradise."[3]

In a canceled portion of the *Discourse,* broken off after only a few disjointed sentences, Shelley attempts a brief survey of the manner in which society historically has treated such problems as adultery and seduction. Since his point of view is strictly hedonistic, it is scarcely a happy one. He is all on the side of chastity, but only as the practice gives pleasure, as it constitutes a worthwhile habit, corresponding with the primary laws of human nature, ultimately reducible to pleasure-pain. Man-made law, on the contrary, has often paid no heed to these dictates but raised "arbitrary and complicated distinctions" in direct conflict with hedonistic principles, however elevated. "The degree of criminality attached to the mode" in which a person resorts to sexual gratification, he begins, "must vary according to [the established modes institutions] a multitude of circumstances extant." For example, in ancient Greece, which is his primary concern in the *Discourse,* "the highest degree of criminality was conceived to attach, & the wrong depending on opinion did consequently attach to adultery." This attitude arose from the erroneous sentiment of preferring "to educate those children of which a man is the exciting physical cause, united with . . . a reluctance that . . . his female companion should be the source of pleasure to another."[4] The gravity with which the Athenians regarded adultery is briefly touched on in the *Symposium* (182), and this mention was no doubt responsible for Shelley's notice of the subject. The dialogue urges the enactment of a law to prevent corruption of youths blamable by "vulgar" or Pandemian lovers, contemptible for their "wantonness," "libertinism," and "intemperance," just "as we deter them with all the power of the laws from the love of free matrons."[5]

Shelley was as sensitive to the evils of adultery as were the Greeks. Yet not even the authority of Plato could justify the Greek attitude; it was much too harsh and absolute, the penalties far too severe and undiscriminating. Moreover, it was based on false premises, a selfish and primitive patriarchalism interfering with the primary law of pleasure-pain and unworthy of a civilized people. A "narrow & envious motive," Shelley held, underlay the Greek male's legal monopoly that allowed him to prevent his wife from being "the source of pleasure to another," and the motive was still in operation. Such a motive, he believed, was dependent on "elementary feelings in animals as well as men & like revenge avarice perverseness & pride" was weak in proportion to the "extent in intellectual cultivation."[6] One reason, possibly, that Shelley canceled the whole passage was its very inconsistency with his general picture of Attic culture. Were the Greeks the patterns of culture he maintained, it would seem to follow that their attitude toward adultery should not have evinced the retrograde and unenlightened inflexibility which was in fact the case. Shelley himself had been an adulterer. As he knew from firsthand experience, violation of the marriage oath did not invariably spring from base or libertine motives, nor did it inevitably result in an overbalance of pain. Quite the contrary, it sometimes led to a higher and more lasting pleasure. Far from requiring the automatic imposition of cruel and unyielding judicial sanctions, therefore, adultery was a matter best solved ad hoc, like all other moral questions, by the operation of the pleasure-pain principle, the laws of the higher utility. Like his Boccaccio, Shelley too was "a moral casuist," challenging the "Christian, Stoical, ready made and worldly system of morals," with its "narrow-minded conceptions of love."[7]

Seduction, while also to be left to the operations of the pleasure-pain principle, was clearly a much graver matter in Shelley's view, especially as it affected the innocent or unprotected, and he could appreciate the severity with which society has traditionally punished it: "The seduction of young virgins, a crime, which the consequences attached to it express even a darker strain, has ever been regarded as a high offence."[8] The passage breaks off abruptly, and the historical survey, such as it is, comes to a halt. But from two lines of Greek copied into the MS notebook containing the *Discourse*, one can deduce that Shelley planned to discuss the Greek attitude toward seduction in the same way as he had adultery, for the lines, from Euripides' *Hippolytus* (1004-1005), allude to this evil.[9] Shelley's description of seduction as a "darker stain" even than adultery vividly expresses his abhorrence of the act, showing that he connects seduction, as well as the more objectionable varieties of adultery, with the obscene "stain" of libertinism. "If there is any enormous and desolating crime, of which I should shudder to be accused," he confesses to James Lawrence, "it is seduction" (*L.*I.323). And seduction is ever a subject for condemnation in his work.

But seduction, while undeniably a serious evil, no more warranted the ferocious and inflexible retribution of society than adultery. Its correction was much better left to the free operation of the pleasure-pain principle—"until mankind shall have enough"—than to the imposition of the traditional remedies which were often founded on arbitrary and unreasonable moral distinctions worse than the evil itself and exacerbating it. In Christian societies, seduction had for the woman always been the "forerunner of the most terrible of [social] ruins."[10] The object of the evil was arbitrarily punished for the very act of which she was the victim. Shelley could only look to the future and hope for a truly utilitarian society where sexual relations would be governed solely by pleasure-pain.

For an "enlightened philosophy," affirms the *Discourse*, while agreeing with conventional morals in reprobating libertinism, intemperance, and infidelity, must nevertheless "condemn the laws by which an indulgence in the sexual instinct is regulated" (221).[11] Shelley's social philosophy was grounded in the rationalism and skepticism of the eighteenth-century Enlightenment, at which time "a ray of science burst through the clouds of bigotry that obscured the moral day of Europe" (V.264). Thus an "enlightened" philosophy for Shelley, in whose work the term always bears its full etymological force, was inevitably at war with the blind tyranny of the past and the eyeless forces of convention: faith, custom, and law. Especially was this true in the sexual sphere where its enemy was the "narrow and unenlightened morality of the Christian religion," enshrined in society's crippling marriage code (I.141).

Nothing in Shelley's career stirred up more universal hatred than his attack on his country's sexual institutions, and when he had the temerity to defy them in practice, he suffered the ultimate consequence, the imposition of those "high penalties" still attached to their violation, in his case the loss of his children by his first marriage.[12] In the central irony of his life, he found himself assailed and vilified on all sides as the personification of the very thing he most detested, the habitual libertine and seducer, and he ultimately had to abandon the country for his own safety.

The savagery of the attack is hard to imagine today. It is thus well to be reminded of its severity since it gives point to views which, while still controversial, scarcely seem so diabolically subversive as when he was alive. Because of his public flouting of his country's marriage laws and the unhappy consequences, he probably came as close as anyone during his day to occupying the archetypal role of "villain" in the popular mind, the unanimously "infamous Mr. Shelley." This image was compounded by his association with the satanic Lord Byron, his only serious rival for the distinction. Of the scandal provoked by their unorthodox domestic arrangements at Lake Geneva in 1816—Byron was living with Claire Clairmont and Shelley with Mary Godwin—Shelley later wrote: "These calumnies were monstrous, and really too infamous to leave us, their victims, even the refuge of contempt. The natives of Geneva and the English people who were living there did not hesitate to affirm that we were leading a life of the most unbridled libertinism. They said that we had formed a pact to outrage all that is regarded as most sacred in human society . . . The English papers did not delay to spread the scandal, and the people believed it."[13] This reputation was to pursue Shelley for the remainder of his life. "I am regarded by all who know or hear of me as a rare prodigy of crime & pollution whose look even might infect," he admits to Peacock in 1819. "My name is execrated by all who understand its entire import." He is, in short, "a thing whom moralists call worm."[14]

The image seemed justified by his writings, at least as interpreted by contemporary reviewers. For example, of the "enlightened" future envisioned in *Queen Mab*, the London *Literary Gazette* warned its readers in 1821: "there are to be no restraints on the passions, no laws to curb vice, no customs to mark with reprobation the grossest indulgence in sensuality and crime: that in the renovated order, chastity in women, and honour in men, are to be unknown or despised." It is "a frightful supposition" that the author's own life may have been "a fearful commentary upon his principles—principles, which in the balance of law and justice, happily deprived him of the superintendance of his infants, while they plunged an unfortunate wife and mother into ruin, prostitution, guilt, and suicide."[15] This reaction was the rule: alarmed protests at the poet's principles mixed with abusive ad hominem allusions to the conduct that purportedly inspired or illustrated them.[16]

Shelley had a scattering of defenders among the reviewers, notably Leigh Hunt in *The Examiner*, who was also suspect since he, like Shelley, believed that "the sexual intercourse might be altered much for the better, so as to diminish the dreadful evils to which it is now subject."[17] But the prevailing view on the part of both reviewers and public was that expressed by *The Gentlemen's Magazine and Historical Chronicle* on the occasion of Shelley's death: the poet belonged to "a junta, whose writings tend to make our sons profligates, and our daughters strumpets," and we ought "as justly to regret the decease of the Devil . . . as one of his coadjutors." The poet was "a fitter subject for a penitentiary dying speech, than a lauding elegy; for the muse of the rope, rather than that of the cypress."[18]

Lawless Love

Though totally misconstruing his motives, Shelley's contemporaries were correct in recognizing his goals as radically subversive of the accepted social fabric, the basis of which was the monogamous and indissoluble patriarchal family unit, institutionalized under law and sanctified by established religion. The law and the church were in this instance one. Still in effect were the sixteenth-century canon law regulations which gave jurisdiction over marriage to the Anglican Church and were administered by its Ecclesiastical Courts. These regulations insisted on the absolute bindingness of a validly contracted marriage. In actual practice, a civil remedy had developed through time for hopelessly unworkable marriages, but it was so difficult, so time-consuming, and so expensive to achieve that it was open to very few. Since the end of the seventeenth century it had been possible to obtain a bill of divorcement by a Private Act of Parliament setting aside canon law, dissolving the marriage, and allowing the right to re-marry—a ceremony that the church disingenuously never refused to perform, though plainly inconsistent with its own laws. The sole ground for suing was adultery; and in the case of the woman, the husband's infidelity had to be proved incestuous for good measure. Obviously not many women obtained divorces. But for the male the situation was little better. Prior to 1857 and the Matrimonial Causes Act, the number of divorces granted by Parliament had reached a total of three hundred and seventeen. In a society where the majority of marriages were arranged, mercenary, or the result of the most superficial kind of courtship, such a system produced untold suffering and hardship. It also led to untold hypocrisy. The prevailing double standard, which allowed the husband to commit adultery with impunity while insisting on the wife's absolute chastity, made a mockery of the marriage sacrament.

But the problem went beyond the sacramental. Marriage was the cornerstone of the property system. Not only were husband and wife bound to each other before the eyes of the patriarchal deity, but the wife was the husband's personal property, having no separate existence before the law. Thus her infidelity was first of all an offense against property, and it was this offense, not the sin of adultery, which enabled the husband to petition Parliament for divorce. In fact his first recourse at law was to sue his wife's "seducer," as he was technically labeled, in the civil courts for property damages. From the sociological point of view the laws, much as in ancient Greece, were patriarchal in design, concerned to preserve the purity of the family, the sanctity of property rights, and the inviolability of inheritance. As noted by O. R. McGregor, the original argument for instituting divorce by act of Parliament had been the need to "safeguard the inheritance of property and family succession endangered by a wife's adultery."[19]

For Shelley and his enlightened philosophy these were so many "complicated and arbitrary distinctions" which lost their authority when producing more pain than pleasure. To an unbiased observer it was clear that marriage as presently institutionalized was indeed producing more pain than pleasure; and from this realization it was but a short step to challenging the necessity of marriage in the formal sense at all. This is precisely where Shelley's "enlightened philosophy" led: "The system of society as it exists at present must be overthrown from the foundations with all its superstructure of maxims & of forms before we shall find anything but disappointment in our intercourse with any but a few select spirits" (L.II.191).

Shelley's antimatrimonialism, his preaching of "lawless love," begins with his earliest work, the two Gothic novels, and is reiterated in the major poems from *Queen Mab* through *Epipsychidion*.[20] Much the fullest, most systematic, and lucid statement of his antimatrimonial belief is the very early essay appended as a note to *Queen Mab* elaborating the charge from Canto V that "Even love is sold" (1. 189). As an explanation of his understanding of the social aspects of sex, it stands as a necessary supplement to the *Discourse* in piecing together his philosophy of sexual relationship.[21] Set down in 1811-1812, it is highly derivative in many points, borrowing directly from Godwin's *Political Justice* (Bk. VII, Ch. vi, "Of Cooperation, Cohabitation and Marriage"), James Lawrence's *The Empire of the Nairs* and "Love: An Allegory," and Mary Wollstonecraft's *A Vindication of the Rights of Woman*.[22] Nevertheless its argument as a whole is very much Shelley's own and continued substantially unchanged through the remainder of his career, though subject to modification in individual details.

Shelley's position is uncompromisingly utilitarian: "if happiness be the object of morality, of all human unions and disunions; if the worthiness of every action is to be estimated by the quantity of pleasurable sensation it is calculated to produce, then the connection of the sexes is so long sacred as it contributes to the comfort of the parties." Conversely, whenever the evils of a union outweigh its benefits, the connection is "naturally dissolved." There can be nothing "immoral" about this, holds Shelley, since constancy or fidelity has nothing virtuous in itself, "independently of the pleasure it confers." Indeed it constitutes a vice "in proportion as it endures tamely moral defects of magnitude" in the object of its mistaken choice (I.141). For the poet the basis of sexual connection is sentimental love, potentially one of the highest and most enduring of all the pleasures. But this is only when it engrosses the total personality, when it strengthens and purifies the affections, enlarges the imagination, and adds spirit to sense. To bind two people together forever as if the sexual link alone is what counts is to usurp the individual's right to fulfill the fundamental laws of his being, thus nullifying the doctrine of the higher hedonism, true utility, and convicting the traditional concept of marriage as by definition evil.

The realities of marriage were indeed cruelly evil, as Shelley notes: "the present system of constraint does no more in the majority of instances than make hypocrites or open enemies. Persons of delicacy and virtue, unhappily united to one whom they find it impossible to love, spend the loveliest season of their life in unproductive efforts to appear otherwise than they are, for the sake of the feelings of their partner or the welfare of their mutual offspring; those of less generosity and refinement openly avow their disappointment, and linger out the remnant of that union, which only death can dissolve, in a state of incurable bickering and hostility . . . The conviction that wedlock is indissoluble holds out the strongest of all temptations to the perverse; they indulge without restraint in acrimony and all the little tyrannies of domestic life, when they know that their victim is without appeal" (I.141-142). The children also suffer; their "early education . . . takes its color from the squabbles of the parents; they are nursed in a systematic school of ill-humor, violence, and falsehood." The alternative, though condemned by conventional morals, is far preferable. Had the couple been allowed to part "at the moment when indifference rendered their union irksome, they would have been spared many years of misery; they would have connected themselves more suitably, and would have found that happiness in the society of more congenial partners which is for ever denied them by the despotism of marriage" (I.142).

Not only the indissolubility of marriage but its institutionalized inequities produce evil, notes Shelley. Both religion and law give all the power to the male, thereby undermining the heart of the relationship, which is love. Love, as he explains, "is there most pure, perfect, and unlimited, where its votaries live in confidence, equality, and unreserve"; it is "compatible neither with obedience, jealousy, nor fear" (I.141). By its very conditions marriage often degenerates into male tyranny. "For God's sake . . . read the marriage service," Shelley expostulates to Hogg the year previously, "before you *think* of allowing an amiable beloved female to submit to such degradation" (L.I.81).

Allied with the patriarchal tyranny of marriage is its patriarchal exclusiveness. Marriage is a legal monopoly, the woman the husband's personal property. As Shelley notes in *On Marriage*, this capitalistic expropriation of the woman's person probably explains the origin of marriage. Wives were valuable to their husbands "in the same manner as their flocks and herds were valuable"; that is, the "circumstance of the pleasure being attached to the fulfilment of the sexual functions rendered that which was the object of their exercise a possession analogous in value to those articles of luxury or necessity which maintain or delight the existence of a savage." Consequently it was as necessary to men's interests that they retain "undisturbed possession" over women as over their other personal goods (VII.149). The same "narrow & envious motive," one appropriate to animals and savages but not to civilized human beings, continues as the underlying cause of modern marriage, striking "at the root of all domestic happiness" and consigning, in Shelley's hyperbolic computation in the "Love is sold" Note, "more than half of the human race to misery that some few may monopolize according to law" (I.142). Furthermore this patriarchal exclusiveness, when combined with the "fanatical" Christian ideal of prenuptial chastity which excludes young men "from the society of modest and accomplished women," results in the horrors of prostitution, destructive to both body and mind. A system, in short, "could not well have been devised more studiously hostile to human happiness than marriage." Indeed "religion and morality, as they now stand, compose a practical code of misery and servitude; the genius of human happiness must tear every leaf from the accursed book of God ere man can read the inscription on his heart" (I.142). The year before, Shelley had written to Hogg that "marriage is hateful detestable,—a kind of ineffable sickening disgust seizes my mind when I think of this most despotic most unrequired fetter which prejudice has forged to confine its energies. Yet this is Xtianity—& Xt *must* perish before this can fall . . . for anti-matrimonialism is as necessarily connected with infidelity as if Religion & marriage began their course together" (*L.I.80*). The connection between the sexes must be put on a "rational basis," he urges in "Love is sold" (I.142), one more in accord with an enlightened view of human nature and its indestructible laws.

But while love is the only legitimate basis for cohabitation, its expression is by its very nature "free"—the declaration is still not without its impact. Love is a "passion," stemming from the "involuntary affections" of man's nature and "inevitably consequent upon the perception of loveliness." To legislate "the indisciplinable wanderings" of this passion, to put it in "fetters," or to "imprison" it in the poet's favorite metaphor of marriage, can therefore result only in pain and evil. Love "withers under constraint; its very essence is liberty." Because the passion is inherently "capricious" and subjective, it is also peculiarly prone to error and self-deception and hence disillusion and change (I.141). What "an unstable deceitfull thing Love" is, a "pleasing delusion" but blinding to the strong, clear light of reason, Shelley had already proven for himself through the sudden, wrenching collapse of his once "eternal" love for Harriet Grove—a point doubly reinforced by the bewildering rapidity of Hogg's successive passions for Elizabeth Shelley and Harriet Westbrook (*L.*I.104,177). But the inner erotic autotype can never be stilled, in the psychodynamics of his more mature psychology, inexorably impelling one to continue to seek its mirror image or antitype in the person of others and instinctively filling in the imperfect image through imaginative or sympathetic self-projection even when it does not discover its exact duplicate or replica. To have to swear eternal fidelity to one person, as demanded by the marriage oath, and to be held to this by the state, is therefore not only immoral, since in the great majority of instances it will inevitably lead to an overbalance of pain, but self-limiting and irrational, according to the "Love is sold" Note: "to promise for ever to love the same woman is not less absurd than to promise to believe the same creed; such a vow in both cases excludes us from all inquiry" and amounts to saying that "the woman I now love may be infinitely inferior to many others; the creed I now profess may be a mass of errors and absurdities; but I exclude myself from all future information as to the amiability of the one and the truth of the other, resolving blindly and in spite of conviction to adhere to them" (I.141).

Well-aware that "free-love" may be misinterpreted as a plea for sexual license, the poet is careful to add the caveat, "I by no means assert that the intercouse would be promiscuous." On the contrary, unions would generally be of "long duration and marked above all others" with the same "generosity and self-devotion" that one finds on the part of the parent toward the child. At this point the topic is abruptly dismissed with the hardly satisfactory explanation that "this is a subject which it is perhaps premature to discuss" (I.142). But implicit throughout the essay is the belief, fundamental to Shelley's thinking, that natural constancy or fidelity will continue between partners who are truly "congenial" (I.142), combining all sympathies in one, and whose love is consequently sentimental, not libertine. Unions based on this sort of relationship yield a high and lasting pleasure and will not readily dissolve.

A letter a year later to Godwin, posted just about the time Shelley must have been working on "Love is sold," has often been read as giving a different answer to the question of fidelity, implying that in the regenerate state of the future, sexual intercourse will indeed be "promiscuous," though "under the present system of thinking" this practice would "inevitably lead to consequences the most injurious to the happiness of mankind" (L.I.314). Such an interpretation, however, would clearly contradict "Love is sold," not to mention Shelley's other pronouncements on the subject, as well as clashing with Godwin's own pronouncement in *Political Justice:* "It is a question of some moment, whether the intercourse of the sexes, in a reasonable state of society, would be promiscuous, or whether each man would select for himself a partner, to whom he will adhere, as long as that adherence shall continue to be the choice of both parties. Probability seems to be greatly in favour of the latter."[23] What Shelley actually appears to be alluding to in the letter is somewhat less sensational, if still a problem in the "present state of society"—the offense to personal modesty or "delicacy" involved in the promiscuous mingling of the sexes when undressing or retiring to bed (L.I.313-315).

That sexual promiscuity is the reverse of Shelley's vision for the future, he makes plain not only in "Love is sold" but also in the 1814 review of *Prince Alexy Haimatoff,* where "promiscuous concubinage" is denounced as brutalizing (VI.177), and in the fragmentary *On Marriage* (1817-1818), where promiscuous connection, treated from the historical viewpoint, is shown to be the norm of savage beast-man before the dawn of civilization when "no moral affections arose from the indulgence of a physical impulse" (VII.149).[24] The evolution of society has moved consistently toward the establishment of binding sexual relations. Shelley's only quarrel is with the arbitrary and absolute character of the legal and sacramental forms guaranteeing such relations, not with their value if based on the immutable laws of civilized human nature, which are in themselves binding. In the perfectibilitarian society of the future where love would be free of all legal sanction, "no lover would then be false to this mistress, no mistress could desert her lover," for purely utilitarian reasons, growing out of the free play of the laws of the higher hedonism (V.234).

So far as concerns the absolute character of the marriage contract, the movement of contemporary society has been in a direction the poet would have wholeheartedly approved. The loosening of the sacramental concept of marriage, its increasing secularization, the eradication of legal inequities within marriage, the growing ease and availability of divorce on thoroughly utilitarian grounds including simple incompatibility, and the generally more egalitarian view of the proper relationship between the sexes are developments Shelley would have welcomed. His desire to bring the marriage laws of his day more in line with "enlightened" opinion thus elicits sympathy today. But improving marriage law is one thing; doing away with it altogether is quite another. Despite the extraordinary growth in sexual freedom which has come to typify modern practice, to abolish marriage would still strike at the very foundations of the social system. Shelley's attack on the possessive or monopolistic aspects of marriage, indeed of any sexual relationship, is still a feature of his thought that is considerably ahead of all but the most advanced modern thinking and practice.

For Shelleyan love is truly free in the sense that it is free for all; it sets no limit on its participants. According to the poet, the individual can love more than one person at a time, and the same holds true for the recipients of his love. To monopolize the love of one person or to allow oneself to become so monopolized is to limit the possibilities of this experience. Love, like the intellect and the imagination—of which faculties it is compounded—is expansive, growing "bright," that is enlightened, as it focuses on more than a single object. "Narrow" is "the heart that loves," in the words of *Epipsychidion*, "the brain that contemplates,/The life that wears, the spirit that creates/One object, and one form, and builds thereby/A sepulchre for its eternity" (169-173). Such limitation is a form of death.[25] Paradoxically, to divide love is not to diminish but to increase it. The reasoning is fundamentally hedonistic, the emphasis on pleasure-pain: "If you divide pleasure and love and thought,/Each part exceeds the whole; and we know not/How much, while any yet remains unshared,/Of pleasure may be gained, of sorrow spared" (180-183). This is scarcely a plea for libertinism or general promiscuity, as so widely interpreted by Shelley's contemporaries. As always, "free love" is "true love," that is, love stemming from the elevated pleasures of "true utility," which embrace the total personality and make it naturally constant.[26] At the same time this constancy does not restrict love's ambience or operations. The individual may share sympathies in common with more than one other person concurrently, and so may the objects of that attachment. To deny the satisfaction of these sympathies, as demanded by traditional definitions of sexual relationship, is necessarily to create an overbalance of pain and suffering, which renders the traditional definitions immoral and nugatory, while their opposite can lead to an increase in pleasure and thus represents a higher morality.

Free or unlimited love has in fact had some eminent authorities in its "commendation," Shelley ironically observes in the draft version of *Epipsychidion:*

Why there is first the God in heaven above,
Who wrote a book called Nature, 'tis to be

Reviewed, I hear, in the next Quarterly;
And Socrates, the Jesus Christ of Greece,
And Jesus Christ Himself, did never cease
To urge all living things to love each other.[27]

Western patriarchal society, however, has continually stained or clouded the pure light of these sources with its "narrow and unenlightened" concepts of love, preventing the "fit and natural arrangement of sexual connection." The "ready made and worldly system" of traditional sexual morality, "dressed up in stiff stays and finery," would start back in horror, the poet exclaims in the "Love is sold" Note, from its "own disgusting image" should it ever behold itself in "the mirror of nature" (I.142). Shelley was proclaiming the calamitous consequences of such an unnatural and self-limiting morality until the end of his life:

I never was attached to that great sect,
Whose doctrine is, that each one should select
Out of the crowd a mistress or a friend,
And all the rest, though fair and wise, commend
To cold oblivion, though it is the code
Of modern morals, and the beaten road
Which those poor slaves with weary footsteps tread,
Who travel to their home among the dead
By the broad highway of the world, and so
With one chained friend, perhaps a jealous foe,
The dreariest and the longest journey go. (Epi.149-159)

The draft version of these lines reads, "With one sad friend, and many a jealous foe." The subsequent change seems directly aimed at Mary Shelley and her intense jealousy of her husband's "true love" for Emilia Viviani.[28] In both versions jealousy is shown to be one of the inevitable evils attendant on marriage and, as Shelley had written in "Love is sold," is incompatible with the highest sort of connection.

No doubt one of the most controversial elements of Shelleyan love is its rejection of sexual jealousy—the "narrow & envious motive" that prevents a person from desiring his partner to be the source of "pleasure" to another and which will disappear in a regenerate world (Pr.Unb.III.iv.161-163). As the poet explains to Elizabeth Hitchener, jealousy is animal in origin, its "parent" the love whose source is "sensation." This love is "self-centered self devoted self-interested"; "it desires its *own* interest . . . its object is the plaything which it desires to monopolize—selfishness, monopoly is its very soul, & to communicate to others part of this love were to d[es]troy its essence, to annihilate this chain of straw."[29] Jealousy is thus a primitive emotion, weakening, he believes, with the development of man's intellectual powers.

Though hard data are lacking, authorities today would be more likely to attribute jealousy to social determinants since the phenomenon is not cross-culturally universal. Polygamous and polyandrous societies have existed, many of them "primitive," where sexual exclusiveness or possessiveness has been rare and jealousy no problem. The question is thus not one of "elementary animal feelings," as asserted by Shelley.[30] Indeed Shelley tacitly recognizes this in *On Marriage* where he postulates an original primitive state of "promiscuous concubinage" before the dawn of organized society. As he notes there, the development of personal property instincts is the true source of sexual jealousy. In strongly patriarchal societies, such as ancient Greece or western Christianity, habits of possessiveness are so ingrained as to seem elementary, and sexual jealousy consequently prevails among all except the most emancipated and enlightened— those marked by the extent of their "intellectual cultivation," according to the *Discourse*. For those cultivated enough to grasp the virtues of communal property sharing and the evils of the proprietary family unit, the sharing of sexual favors presents no difficulty, especially since in their pursuit of the higher hedonism, the true utility, sensual gratification plays a subordinate role in any event.[31]

Perhaps the best way to get a sense of how Shelley's free love was intended to operate in practice is to examine one or two examples from his own practice, as these events appeared to him. In the fall of 1811 Shelley was stunned to learn that his best friend Hogg had secretly been trying to make love to his bride of two months, Harriet Westbrook. Here was a situation putting Shelley's principles directly to the test. Though married, he had remained loud in the defense of the abstract justice of his antimatrimonial precepts, explaining that he, "an *Atheist*," had chosen to subject himself to "the ceremony of *marriage*" solely for the sake of the woman who, in challenging conventional morality, was forced to make a disproportionate sacrifice in comparison with the male, who in such cases was considered a man of "gallantry and spirit" whereas the woman lost her reputation forever. Moreover, placing herself beyond the law, the woman yielded up her "political rights"—that is, those legal safeguards which, however imperfect, would accrue to her and her children were she married. Expediency thus dictated that, until society was differently arranged, the "experimentalist" should bow to the traditional forms. But this did not negate the intrinsic "unholiness of matrimony," a "villainous" and unnatural incarceration of love that could have no place in a regenerate society.[32]

To find Hogg taking him *au pied de la lettre*, however, was something for which Shelley was unprepared. But his dismay, far from exposing his inconsistency or hypocrisy, rather reinforces the sensitivity of his practice. He was upset initially because he thought Hogg had betrayed his good faith, playing the part of the conventional libertine or "seducer," motivated by "the commonplace infatuation of novels and gay life." It was in this light that Shelley first attempted to explain his friend's otherwise inexplicable behavior. Scarcely two months previously Hogg had been protesting his undying love for Elizabeth Shelley and now he was lavishing the same apparently deceitful flattery on Harriet, all merely to satisfy his selfish physical lusts.[33]

Hogg sought to defend himself on two grounds. First, he sincerely loved Harriet and was not trying to take advantage of her innocence for his own selfish gratification; second, he had only been putting into practice Shelley's own often reiterated doctrine of free love, not attempting to play the libertine traitor to him. Before long Shelley absolved Hogg of deliberate criminality but dubbed his action a "mistake" and a "terrible" one. It was plain to Shelley that Hogg had no real conception of his own rarefied notions of sentimental connection, the only legitimate basis for a free love union, and was simply letting his sexual desires run away with his emotions. Conceding for the sake of argument, however, that Hogg genuinely loved Harriet, Shelley personally had no objection to his living with them and sharing Harriet's sexual favors. He was not backing down on his principles. "I attach little value to the monopoly of exclusive cohabitation. You know that I frequently have spoken slightly of it"—undoubtedly what had caused Hogg's "mistake" in the first place; "were this to have been yielded to you & the sentiments with which we regarded each other still to have remained unchanged suppose not that I would have envied you what I too might share, what I should not much care utterly to resign." Hogg was "welcome to even this, the dearest." Not for Shelley the narrow and envious motive that induces a man to want to prevent his female companion from being a source of pleasure to another: "Jealousy has no place in my bosom . . . would I be so sottish a slave to opinion as to endeavour to monopolize what if participated would give my friend pleasure without diminishing my own?" Shelley's love for Harriet far transcended the animal desire to monopolize in love. Could he have trusted Hogg, the sharing of Harriet's person, far from dividing them, would have cemented their friendship. Sadly, Shelley could not.[34]

But even if he could have, it was still out of the question, for there was another person's happiness to consider as well as their own. Utility, as always, was the ultimate moral criterion. As Shelley told Hogg time and again, and as Hogg so rudely discovered for himself, Harriet could not return his love and had no desire to yield up her person to him, nor even to live under the same roof with him. Shelley could not consent "to the destruction of Harriet's peace." This was basic. And if Hogg sincerely loved Harriet as a person, rather than selfishly as a sex object, he would recognize this too and abandon his suit.[35]

Hogg claimed that were he allowed to live with the couple again, he would keep his feelings strictly under control. But Hogg knew this to be untrue, retorted Shelley. The renewed presence of Harriet's charms would inevitably reillumine his passion, causing him to resume his gross designs on her person. Simply from the point of view of his "safety," his own "happiness," morality demanded that he not live with them any longer. In any case Shelley had no intention of trading Harriet's happiness for his "short-lived pleasure." He owed it to Harriet's happiness and Hogg's reformation that the relationship should be broken off entirely. While he personally favored "the Godwinian plan" of cohabitation, "particularly since the late events," the world did not. Shelley doubted that Hogg himself was wholly free of conventional "prejudice" and able to enter into such a relationship as the one proposed without experiencing a revulsion of shame and guilt. Shelley was not even sure that, emotionally speaking, he was entirely free of the old morality himself. But he did know—and this was "the last the greatest consideration"—that Harriet still cherished the traditional sanctions "as a prejudice interwoven with the fibres of her being," and they must not play with her feelings. Harriet was not a Rousseauistically liberated Heloisa, even were he a St. Preux. If she were convinced of the innocence of their proposal, it would be a different matter, and Shelley hoped that she would not always be so prejudiced, but until then, "on her opinions of right & wrong alone does the morality of the present case depend." Thus even were Harriet inclined to return Hogg's love, she "*ought* to stifle her desire to do so," as long as yielding to it would involve her in feelings of guilt and remorse.[36]

Finally there was the question of Shelley and Harriet's own love for each other. Hogg's devious and erratic behavior and Shelley's attempts to account for and extenuate it had made Harriet suspect Shelley's love. He could not risk destroying Harriet's faith in the sincerity of those feelings that constituted the foundation of their relationship. The decision was inescapable. The two must part. The happiness of the whole demanded it. If Shelley were free, it would be otherwise; but he was Harriet's and "devoted to her happiness."[37] Thus ended the poet's first encounter with the realities of communal loving.

In the months following, Shelley continued to be devoted to Harriet's happiness—Hogg was kept at a safe distance—but almost immediately Shelley put her "prejudices" to the test in another way. While the Godwinian plan of communal loving might be immoral under the present circumstances, entailing an overbalance of pain when the feelings of the group as a whole were weighed against each other, there was nothing to stop an experiment in the Godwinian plan of communal living. Obliged for the good of the whole to relinquish his male friend, Shelley at once set about introducing his female "friend," the emancipated schoolteacher Elizabeth Hitchener, into his domestic circle. Since he was married, there would be no risk of "worldly impropriety," he felt, in such a move. Elizabeth was not so sure, but Shelley belittled her fears. They should not care what the world said. They were not accountable for its "silly notions." Come, he urged her, "lose in our little circle the tenets of the unthinking . . . *I* ought to count myself a favored mortal with such a wife and friend (these human names and distinctions *perhaps are necessary* in the present state of society)." "Let us attempt to form this Paradise," he concluded, "and defy the destroyers." Even the "prejudiced" Harriet bravely did her best to go along with the plan, dutifully seconding Shelley's invitation and expounding the Shelleyan doctrine that jealousy was quite out of place in such an enlightened group as theirs. Though oversanguine as to the manner in which the world would view this arrangement—already gossip had it that he was unfaithful to Harriet, seduced by "a female Hogg" intent on becoming his "*Mistress*"—Shelley went ahead with his plans, and Elizabeth, steeling her "breast to the poison shafts of calumny," finally moved in.[38] The paradise was thus complete, the destroyers defied.

Unhappily, the sequel proved to be nearly as disappointing as the imbroglio with Hogg, the arrangement foundering on the imperfections of human nature not yet ready for such a visionary reordering of human relationship. "Bessy," as Hitchener was now known, turned out to be not at all the person she represented herself to be but rather the illiberal and designing woman rumored by the world. "She built all her hopes on being able to separate me from my dearly beloved Percy," wrote Harriet, "and had the artfulness to say that Percy was really in love with her, and [it] was only his being married that could keep her within bounds now." Elementary passions still ruled the day.

Neither woman had any intention of abolishing the distinction between wife and friend, so for the happiness of the whole Bessy had to leave. As was not the case with Hogg, the decision was an easy one for Shelley since he retained no feelings of friendship for the one expelled, though he acknowledged the obligation to reimburse her for the loss of her job and reputation, both sacrificed to his scheme.[39]

While continuing to place Harriet's happiness first during this period and moderating his practice to the demands of existing morals, the poet still remained vocal in the defense of his principles. Love was free, marriage a prison, and if love seemed "inclined to stay in the prison," it was, he often reminded Harriet, a voluntary commitment only, not otherwise binding.[40] Many years later Robert Southey, in condemning Shelley's matrimonial history, was forced to concede that Harriet had at least been given ample warning of what might come: "I will do you justice, sir. While you were at Keswick you told your bride that you regarded marriage as a mere ceremony, and would live with her no longer than you liked her. I dare say you told her this before the ceremony." Not that Southey believed that Shelley at this time anticipated ending their union, for he was not "wicked by disposition"; rather, "corrupted" by his speculations, he had reasoned himself into "a state of mind so pernicious" that he had deliberately "tampered [with his] own heart."[41]

Though wrong about the reasons for Shelley's subsequent behavior, Southey was doubtless correct that he had no idea of abandoning Harriet at the time of these pronouncements. He still "liked" her and was only trying to maintain his intellectual integrity. However, the time came when he no longer liked her, and when this occurred, as far as he was concerned the marriage was terminated. The reasons for this estrangement are complex, but the clinching determinant for Shelley was simply his increasing realization, disguise it as he might, that he had made a horrible mistake in the "object of [his] indiscreet choice," to use the language of "Love is sold." Harriet, he now knew, was far from fulfilling the range of his sympathies, intellectual, imaginative, and sensitive, however much he might try to convince himself of the opposite, and the imperious erotic autotype within was growing increasingly restive and discontent. Consequently what seemed depraved to Southey appeared to Shelley perfectly natural and inevitable: "if happiness be the object of morality, of all human unions and disunions, then the connection of the sexes is so long sacred as it contributes to the comfort of the parties, and is naturally dissolved when its evils are greater than its benefits" (I.141).

For a brief period longer, the poet remained bound to Harriet physically, even if he could not contain "the indisciplinable wanderings" of his emotions.[42] But he knew in his heart that this fidelity partook of "the temporizing spirit of vice"—the "hypocrisy" of "Love is sold"—and when another appeared on the scene more "suited to [his] taste," as Southey put it (*L*.II.232), Shelley was true to his principles, finding "that happiness in the society of a more congenial partner" which would forever have been denied him by the despotism of marriage. The unprejudiced Mary Wollstonecraft Godwin, both of whose parents had written against the evils of marriage and for a time defied the institution in practice, had not been afraid in her "young wisdom" to "burst and rend in twain" the "mortal chain/Of Custom" and walk "as free as light the clouds among,/Which many an envious slave then breathed in vain/From his dim dungeon" (*Rev.Is.*vii). This was because her understanding had been illuminated by "a spirit that sees into the truth of things," and her affections preserved "pure & sacred from the corrupting contaminations of vulgar superstitions" (*L*.I.403).

Shelley's elopement with Mary in the summer of 1814 was a blow struck in defense of the higher hedonism and, as such, was fully justified in the poet's own thinking. But it raised certain practical considerations, untouched in his theoretical pronouncements, which now pressed in from all sides. The chief problem was what to do about Harriet. Implicit in Shelley's thinking was that separation would be by mutual consent. But suppose one of the parties did not consent? Harriet still loved her husband, despite the coolness and friction that had entered their marriage, and had no intention of giving him up. For Shelley, the marriage was naturally dissolved since he loved someone else. Harriet ought therefore to be "virtuous" enough, "generous" enough, to place his happiness with Mary above her own, particularly since it was happiness of the highest sort, deriving from sentimental communion. Yet he also recognized an obligation to Harriet's happiness. This had been entrusted to him when they married, and even now he was constantly occupied in determining how he could be "permanently & truly useful" to her. "Remember Dear Harriet," he admonishes her, "that such attachment as I profess for you, is always to be counted upon" (*L*.I.394-406). It was this sort of enduring obligation even after the cessation of love that set his free love at the opposite pole from libertine connection.

His initial solution went well beyond this obligation, however, and although alternately shocking or amusing to posterity, was perfectly in tune with his own elevated view of civilized sexual relationship where wife and friend were "unmeaning distinctions." In short, following the elopement he proposed setting up a *ménage à trois* such as the one tried with Elizabeth Hitchener but with Harriet now in the role of "friend" or "sister," while Mary replaced her as "wife" (L.I.421). Shelley thought that on this basis their attachment would acquire "even a deeper & more lasting character"; it would, echoing "Love is sold," be "less exposed than ever to the fluctuations of phantasy or caprice." He recognized now that their connection was never "one of passion & impulse. Friendship was its basis, & on this basis it has enlarged & strengthened." If Harriet could accept this truth and live with him and Mary as a friend "the purest & most perfect happiness is ours." He urged her to join them in Switzerland, "where you will at least find one firm & constant friend, to whom your interests will be always dear, by whom your feelings will never wilfully be injured. From none can you expect this but me" (L.I.389-392).

Harriet indignantly rejected any such arrangement. Her view of the affair was understandably conventional. Mary was the female Hogg, "determined to seduce" her husband. According to Harriet, Shelley at first resisted Mary's protestations, but she "then told him she would die—he had rejected her, and what appeared to her as the sublimest virtue was to him a crime." It was at this point that the "monstrous" idea had occurred to Shelley of their all living together: "He had the folly to believe this possible." His excuse was Godwin's *Political Justice*. "The very great evil that book has done," Harriet lamented, "is not to be told. The false doctrines there contained have poisoned many a young and virtuous mind" (L.I.421). Although Harriet had been suspicious of this book from the beginning, having sent Shelley shortly before their marriage Amelia Opie's novelistic exposure of its antimatrimonial doctrines, *Adeline Mowbray*, she had been willing to tolerate its doctrines in theory; but reduced to practice, she saw them as the rationalization for libertinism and sexual license.[43] Shelley had become "profligate and sensual," and she had no intention of sanctioning his unlawful love. Far from recognizing the claims of lawless love, she planned to enforce her legal claims as a wife if he did not abandon his paramour and return to her side as a dutiful spouse (L.I.42).

Such attitudes, Shelley saw, ended all possibility of his remaining connected to her even by friendship—that is, the friendship based on mutual sympathies which cements any relationship in other than a worldly sense. As regards their worldly tie, Harriet could still rely on his concern. Shelley carefully explains to her the distinction, which went to the heart of his sexual philosophy: "To sympathise in our principles and views to have common pursuits & habits of feeling is the origin of friendship & the attendant of every species of affection. I shall never cease to interest myself in your welfare—you were my wife, you are the mother of my child: you will bear another to me. But these are ties which only bind to worldly matters where sympathy in the great questions of human happiness is wanting . . . There are probably many & very excellent persons in the world who are capable of being to you as the brother of your soul who can participate your feelings, your tastes & your opinions—you justly remark that I am not that person. I shall watch over your interests, mark the progress of your future life, be useful to you, be your protector . . . but as friends, as equals those who do not sympathise can never meet" (L.I.404).

If Harriet persisted in taking legal action against him, however, even worldly friendship would be at an end and he would have no other recourse but to consider her "as an enemy." He began to suspect that he had been mistaken about her even from the beginning. The Harriet whom he had once considered "the partner of my thoughts and feelings" had all along been merely wearing "the mask of friendship & affection." Now that the occasion had arisen to prove her emancipation, so far from demonstrating her contempt for the narrow and unenlightened code of modern morals, she insisted on its being obeyed to the letter. Unless she changed her views and the "narrow" conduct they produced, she was lost to him forever. But he foresaw no likelihood of change. In her heart she had apparently "always been enslaved to the vilest superstitions."[44]

Shelley and Mary, together with her stepsister Claire Clairmont who had accompanied the couple, suffered nearly complete social ostracism following their return to London in the fall of 1814. This was to be expected from the ignorant and slavish, according to Shelley, when regulating one's "domestic arrangements without deferring to the notions of the vulgar."[45] But it was a severe disappointment coming from the more enlightened among their acquaintance. That the author of *Political Justice* should himself turn upon them, however, was as unexpected as it was unjust. In the episode's crowning irony Godwin, who was rumored by the world to have sold Mary and Claire to Shelley, interpreted the elopement in the most worldly terms.[46] His version differed little from Harriet's, except for the reversal of the principal offenders. Thus according to Godwin, Shelley in pursuit of his "licentious love" had "seduced" Mary, "played the traitor" to him, and "deserted" his wife. Consequently, the philosopher had broken off, "with bitter invective & keen injustice" in Shelley's resentful words, all further communication with the delinquent couple.[47]

As Shelley was undoubtedly aware, Godwin had softened his opposition to marriage over the years, increasingly stressing that the abolition of this institution applied only to regenerate society. Under existing social conditions "an accurate morality will direct us to comply" with current matrimonial practice, even while recognizing its evils.[48] Shelley remonstrated that this qualification did not mean that "a young family, innocent and benevolent and united," should be confused with "prostitutes and seducers." The elopement might be ill-advised from a worldly point of view, but it was still the offspring of Godwinian principles, however prematurely applied, and if the philosopher who had once had the "daring to announce the true foundation of morals" (VI.220) retained any measure of self-respect, it was his particular duty to see that his disciples were treated fairly (L.I.459). But Godwin was now more concerned with his worldly reputation than with his intellectual, and he remained unrelenting in his condemnation.[49]

One of the very few not to desert Shelley was Hogg, restored to his friend's good graces two years previously but never entirely forgiven by Harriet. The persistence of his wife's "narrow and prejudiced" behavior toward Hogg had remained a continuing hurt to Shelley (L.I.370), and now that he had burned all his bridges to the conventional world, he decided to give Hogg his due.[50] The Godwinian plan might be premature for society at large but not within his own little circle of the enlightened, released from the bondage of custom. Here at one stroke was his chance to make amends to Hogg, free him of prejudice, demonstrate his own lack of prejudice, and prove that in his new love he did not possess another slavish Harriet. To the astonishment of posterity, Shelley now set about making a reality of what had hitherto been simply theory. While the knowledge of what happened next is sketchier than in the earlier affair, it is sufficient to leave beyond any doubt that Shelley was in fact above the "narrow & envious motive" of the uncultivated and not "so sottish a slave to opinion as to endeavour to monopolize what if participated would give my friend pleasure without diminishing my own."

Exactly who was the first to propose the idea is uncertain. What is certain, however, is that once Hogg fell in love with Mary, as was apparently inevitable, Shelley encouraged her to return his love—"If you divide pleasure and love and thought,/Each part exceeds the whole"—and himself gladly resigned his exclusive conjugal rights over her: Hogg was "welcome to even this, the dearest." The evidence consists chiefly of Mary's letters to Hogg, the texts of which only came to light within the present century, and Shelley and Mary's *Journal*.[51] These documents show that from the outset the extent of Hogg's "enlightenment" was to be put to the test by the renegade couple. Following Hogg's first call after their return to London, Shelley concluded in the *Journal*: "perhaps he still may be my friend, in spite of the radical differences of sympathy between us; he was pleased with Mary; this was the test by which I had previously determined to judge his character."

Apparently Hogg continued to be pleased with Mary, for he called several times a week in the months ensuing, often when Shelley was out. Mary for her part did her best to return this interest. Much of their time was spent in arguing, the "emancipated" Mary trying to talk the more "worldly" Hogg, now a respectable legal apprentice, out of his growing conservatism. Hope of his reclamation was originally tenuous. But as Hogg grew more at ease in this strange situation, he gradually relaxed the guard of his self-protective irony and lost his stuffiness. For the first time Mary began to discover a thread of sympathy drawing her toward him, and soon their talk embraced such interesting topics as "the different intercourse of sexes, &c," which no doubt included praise of those enlightened few who were courageous enough to break the chains of custom and rise above the narrow and envious motive enslaving the vast majority of humankind. Growing to "like" Hogg better each time he called, Mary was at the same time experiencing "odd dreams" about him. Eventually even Shelley was having "odd dreams" after his friend's visits. Evidently Hogg's attentions were becoming less disguised, for on December 29 Claire teased Mary about them: "Hear Jane talk nonsense about Hogg." Finally on New Year's Day, 1815, Hogg openly declared his love. Written in Shelley's hand, the first entry in the couple's *Journal* for the new year records, "A note and present from Hogg to the own Maie."

Mary's response was at first a trifle hesitant. Although she was flattered, the two had known each other such a short time, and she had not thought about "love." However, given time, "*that* also will come," she reassured him. Soon she would return his love with "the passion you deserve." There was a bright prospect before them if only he would be patient. He could count on both herself and Shelley absolutely. Meanwhile he must content himself with "the affection" which she felt from the bottom of her heart and with which he himself out of his very goodness and disinterestedness had already said he was "quite happy" (*S&C*.III.435). No deceiving libertine this time, bent on satisfying his selfish lusts, but holding Mary's happiness above his own, Hogg would receive the reward he justly deserved. That Hogg could count on Shelley was no illusion. Amply atoning for his past slavishness, the poet was diligent in promoting his friend's interest, even abetting the two lovers in their desire to be alone together.[52]

Despite these efforts, Mary's love obstinately persisted in remaining affection, the feelings of a friend, not a mistress, and Hogg's "happiness" was incomplete. As she explained, "My affection for you, although it is not now exactly as you would wish, will I think dayly become more so." She asked "but for time, time which for other causes beside this—physical causes that must be given—Shelley will be subject to these also & this, dear Hogg, will give time for that love to spring up which you deserve and will one day have" (*S&C*.III.339-340). Mary, who was several months pregnant, imagined the "exquisite pleasure" the approaching summer would hold when she was safely delivered of her baby and able to respond properly to the "tenderness" of Hogg's passion. But their "still greater happiness will be in Shelley—I who love him so tenderly & entirely, whose life hangs on the beam of his eye, and whose whole soul is entirely wrapped up in him—you who have so sincere a friendship for him to make him happy" (*S&C*.III.447-448). Clearly Mary's sexual feelings—*tender* was the code word in the Shelley circle for romantic sexual emotion—were still totally engrossed by Shelley. In promising to submit to Hogg physically, she was forcing her emotions, not for the sake of Hogg's happiness, but for Shelley's.

What actually happened is not known. Certainly there was no summer of happiness. Born prematurely on February 12, the baby lived only a short while. For weeks afterward Mary was morbidly depressed, and with the coming of summer the couple left London while Hogg remained at his law apprenticeship. Whether in the interim the affair was consummated remains conjectural. Several pages from the *Journal* are missing, including all those for May 14, 1815, through July 20, 1816, and the letters are few and inconclusive. The risqué note that sounds through the letters is open to more than one interpretation, but it is all so light and bantering as scarcely to suggest a serious liaison.[53] The letters do reveal that Hogg was by this time in possession of Shelley's own love-names for Mary, "the Maie" and "the Dormouse." The most compromising evidence from the period is a letter by Shelley himself to Hogg which seems to picture the Godwinian plan as at last materialized: "My dear Friend/I shall be very happy to see you again, & to give you your share of our common treasure of which you have been cheated for several days. The Maie knows how highly you prize this exquisite possession, & takes occasion to quiz you in saying that it is necessary for me to be absent from London, from your sensibility to its value. Do not fear. [*A few months canceled*] We will not again be deprived of this participated pleasure."[54] The reverberations are considerable, especially when this letter is compared with Shelley's earlier letters to Hogg on sexual possession and sexual jealousy or to lines 180-183 of *Epipsychidion*. Despite the sensational phrasing, however, Shelley is likely describing nothing more heterodox than sharing with Hogg the renewed pleasure of Mary's company.[55] But whether or not Mary literally yielded up her person is ultimately immaterial. The fact remains that she was ready to do so in principle and with the clear encouragement of her lover.

Such an arrangement was no doubt doomed to failure. Aside from the disapprobation of society, it is unrealistic to imagine the cautious Hogg overcoming his essential worldliness or Mary her natural monogamousness.[56] Even in this little oasis of enlightenment the shifting sands of imperfect human advancement could hardly be stilled. But within Shelley himself at least the last chain dividing him from the Promethean world of lawless love had been rent asunder. Beautiful idealisms of moral excellence are all very well. But it is out of such real-life redirections of the will that the future is born.

6

The Male Eros

WHILE REJECTING the laws of society, with their "complicated and arbitrary distinctions," Shelleyan love yields unconditionally to the laws of human nature. These, according to their definitive exposition in the *Discourse*, are "indestructible" (221) and in the sex act require both temperance and a harmony of sympathies if the pleasure derived from the act is to be lasting. But this is not the whole story. A third "proposition" falls under this category which, though inadequately and tautologously defined, is nonetheless of central importance in completing Shelley's objective, the comparison of ancient sexual practice with modern. "Thirdly," then, the sex act "ought to be indulged *according to nature.*" A "volume of definitions and limitations belong to this maxim," Shelley continues, but then breaks off abruptly with the lame qualification that these "may here be passed over" (222).

Though Shelley speaks sarcastically in the *Discourse* of the sexual prudery of the period that prevents writers from dealing openly with Greek love and elsewhere describes the difference between Greek sexual practice and modern as merely a change in "certain conventional notions of morals," he actually shared many of the prejudices of his contemporaries toward homosexuality. Notwithstanding the remarkable open-mindedness of his thinking in most respects, he was still child enough of his age and his cultural heritage that an "enlightened philosophy" did not extend to the toleration of practices deemed sexually unnatural, as nature had been defined by three thousand years of Judeo-Christian teaching. For Shelley, as for his contemporaries—with a handful of subversive exceptions such as Byron—sex was a pleasure to be enjoyed between men and women or not at all. While Shelley's allusions to homosexuality are few and comparatively veiled, there is no mistaking the intensity of his aversion. Best-known in this connection is the passage from a letter to Peacock in which he describes Byron's notorious Venetian debaucheries, including the association with male prostitutes—"wretches," he shudders, "who seem almost to have lost the gait & physiognomy of man, & who do not scruple to avow practices which are not only not named, but I believe seldom even conceived in England."[1] In the same letter he tells of a Greek statue he has just seen in the Studii Museum at Naples depicting a scene of pederastic lovemaking—a satyr embracing a youth—only the supreme artistry of which makes it possible to "overcome one's repugnance to the subject."[2] For the more grossly physical expression of male lovemaking Shelley's repugnance knew no bounds. In the Preface to *The Cenci* he notes that the Count, in addition to the abomination of incest, had been repeatedly guilty of "capital crimes of the most enormous and unspeakable kind."[3] This is the conventional formula for referring to sodomy, a crime "the very mention of which is a disgrace to human nature," according to the language of English jurisprudence, and "in its very indictments, [one] not to be named," but there is no reason to suppose that the poet did not himself subscribe to its terms.[4] The *Discourse* discloses exactly the same revulsion. Such an act is "ridiculous and disgusting," "operose and diabolical," fraught with "images of pain and horror," in short a monstrously "detestable violation" (222-223).

The force of this language leaves no doubt as to the depth of Shelley's feeling. Homosexual practice is a satanic travesty of natural desire, not to be endured under any circumstances. Accordingly, when he finally reaches the copestone of his argument in the *Discourse*, the application of his "propositions" to the practice of the ancient Greeks, he plays up its emotional and spiritual aspects while downplaying its physical. Were his favorites ever to be rescued from the depths of obloquy to which they had fallen in the eyes of the modern world, their sexual conduct had to be restated so as not to violate completely the norms of nineteenth-century practice. To perform this delicate operation was admittedly difficult, but not impossible. What was required was to rethink the Greek experience in the light of the higher hedonism, whose psychosexual implications he had carefully anatomized in advance.

First of all, Shelley makes no attempt to deny that by modern standards Greek love was far from normal. The "passion which their poets and philosophers described and felt seems inconsistent" with the laws of nature "in a degree inconceivable to the imagination of a modern European." At the same time, he insists, it will not do to "exaggerate the matter." Rarely was there anything criminal about the attachments in the modern sense. Greek pederasty was an affair primarily of the mind and the emotions, not the senses. Its dominating impulse was sentimental, a point underscored in the manuscript of the *Discourse* by the substitution of the key word "felt" for "practised" to describe

the Greek experience.[5] "We are not," he concedes, "exactly aware—
and the laws of modern composition scarcely permit a modest writer
to investigate the subject with philosophical accuracy—what that
action was by which the Greeks expressed this passion." Nevertheless
it was "totally different from the ridiculous and disgusting conceptions
which the vulgar have formed on the subject, at least except among
the more debased and abandoned of mankind" (222).

Shelley would have liked to exculpate Greek love entirely from the
vulgar imputation, as is clear from the original text, where "ever" first
appears in place of "usually."[6] However, a regard for historical
accuracy forces a reluctant tempering of this judgment. At the same
time, to suppose that its expression could ordinarily have
approximated "so operose and diabolical a machination as that
usually described" is inconceivable to his way of thinking. Apart from
the inherent perversion of such an act, it was scarcely calculated to
have a wide appeal, being too laborious and discomforting, in fact
downright painful. Shelley is apparently employing the word
"operose" in this root sense. No lover in his right mind would care to
be remembered in a context of "pain and horror." Purely for
utilitarian considerations, therefore—the reasoning is quintessentially
Shelleyan—the vulgar interpretation had to be rejected and a less
gross conception substituted in its stead.

The "laws of modern composition" hardly prevent even the most
modest of writers nowadays from investigating the problem of Greek
love with a maximum of philosophical accuracy. Investigation in the
long interval since Shelley wrote has been extensive, and knowledge
greatly enlarged. Nor do moralistic considerations any longer stand in
the way of an objective examination and weighing of the evidence. Yet
even today the problem remains elusive, and scholarly opinion is still
divided or uncertain. This is primarily because the evidence itself is
inconclusive. Laws against homosexual practice existed everywhere in
Greece, with the exception of Elis, and the very language associated
the act of sodomy with defilement and dishonor, scorn being
particularly reserved for the passive partner or catamite. On the other
hand, male brothels were part of the scene in Athens and homosexual
street solicitation was not uncommon. Obviously some kind of erotic
relationship between males was widespread throughout Greece,
especially among the upper-classes, which under the name of
paiderasteia was extensively celebrated in its legends and history and
had the sanction of a number of its philosophers. Institutionalized,
this relationship was the basis of upper-class education in many of the
city-states. In the loves of the Gods the relationship had been

apotheosized, virtually the entire Olympian pantheon being, in classical idiom, ambidextrous. And pederasty was a principal subject of Greek literature and art.

The difficulty in interpreting the literary and artistic evidence is that so little of it is explicitly sexual, although the Greek vases can occasionally be startlingly frank in their depiction of clinical details. But for the most part a veil descends whenever the direct expression of Greek love is in question, so that little is known as to the incidence of an undisguisedly physical element. Nevertheless, modern scholars, no longer blinded by the parochial assumptions which hindered earlier generations from admitting the existence of such an element lest they besmirch the reputation of the Greeks, can now view without alarm the likelihood of full sexual connection in Greek love.[7]

Shelley based his views entirely on his reading of ancient literature, where the evidence is admittedly ambiguous. Even here, however, he was forced to acknowledge certain difficulties. For one thing he had to dissociate Greek homosexual practice from that current elsewhere in the ancient world. He also had to dissociate it from postclassical practice, when the pederastic ideal had sunk into the most sordid "vice."[8] But primarily he had to dissociate it from the practice of the "licentious Romans." Here it was useless to deny the presence of inferior feelings. Roman literature was too explicit, "brutally obscene," time and again "associating disgusting images with the act of the sexual instinct." Especially offensive in this regard were the works of Catullus, Martial, Juvenal, and Suetonius which, according to Shelley, were full of "infamous perversions" (222-223). Certainly it is true that these writers do not hesitate to supply or suggest the most candid details, not excluding buggery, which is often described as pleasurable even for the passive partner. "A crowd of disgraceful passages will force themselves on the memory of the classic reader," observes the incomparable Gibbon.[9] Exactly what these are may be gleaned from Friedrich Karl Forberg's nineteenth-century compilation, *De Figuris Veneris: The Manual of Classical Erotology*, the nature of whose contents is indicated by the chapter headings: "Of Copulation," "Of Pedication," "Of Irrumation," "Of Masturbation," "Of Cunnilingus," "Of Tribads," "Of Intercourse with Animals," "Of Spintrian Postures."[10] Authorities from Shelley's time to our own have been unanimous in condemning Roman sexual practice, including pederastic, as of the lowest kind imaginable compared with Greek, unredeemed by the least element of higher feeling or sentimental refinement.

Despite the overwhelming mass of evidence, flagrant examples of which he himself cites, Shelley nonetheless insists that even in the revolting travesty of Greek love that was Roman eroticism—"the horrible commentary which the imitation" of Greek manners "produced upon the text"—pederastic practice could rarely have approximated the brutal violation of the modern conception. To support this assertion, he adduces the further example of Petronius' the *Satyricon*, maintaining that the notorious homosexuality which is the binding thread of the romance's action stops short of anal intercourse. In his words, that pederastic connection "could seldom have approached to a resemblance the vulgar imputation with even among the more gross and unrefined Romans, I appeal to a passage of Petronius, well known to every scholar, in which Giton, the pathic, is represented to talk the language of a woman receiving pleasure from the embraces of Encolpius. This, even as a piece of meretricious flattery, is wholly inconsistent with the vulgar notion" (222).[11]

The reference is apparently to the dramatic shipwreck scene off Croton, in which the panic-stricken lovers, seeing themselves in imminent danger of drowning, clutch each other in a last desperate embrace. As narrated by Encolpius: "I embraced Giton, and wept and cried aloud . . . As I spoke Giton took off his clothes, and I covered him with my shirt as he put up his head to be kissed. And that no envious wave should pull us apart as we clung to each other, he put his belt round us both and tied it tight, saying, 'Whatever happens to us, at least we shall be locked together a long while as the sea carries us, and if the sea has pity [it] will cast us up on the same shore.'"[12] Exactly what is going on here is perhaps open to question, the more intimate details being left discreetly to the imagination. An earlier scene is equally inconclusive (1-3).[13] But whatever is happening, Shelley will not let it be buggery. Not even the habitually deceitful Giton, he thinks, would be capable of the guile necessary to counterfeit the rapturous ardor of the shipwreck rhapsody were he undergoing the painful violation of the vulgar imputation, the operose and diabolical machination. Petronius must therefore have in mind some less violent, though unspecified, operation.

Although the example of Petronius is equivocal and hardly a convincing counterweight to the poet's other literary examples, his real point is that the Romans must not be taken as an accurate measure of Greek practice: "The ideas suggested by Catullus, Martial, Juvenal, and Suetonius never occur among the Greeks; or even among those Romans who, like Lucretius, Virgil, Horace, imitated them."[14] Consequently there were doubtless "innumerable instances among that exalted and refined people in which never any circumstance happened to the lover and his beloved by which natural modesty was wronged" (222-223).

Even here honesty compels Shelley to some qualification; he acknowledges that the evidence is not entirely on one side. Although during revision this admission was suppressed, it appears plainly in the MS text. Thus immediately preceding the assertion beginning, "We are not exactly aware" in what manner pederastic connection actually expressed itself, is found the canceled phrase, "That some acts of . . ." Again, after the declaration that pederasty could seldom have approached the vulgar notion, comes the concession in another canceled passage: "it is known[?] that Theocritus & Aristophanes contain refine some gross allusions to the vulgar idea."[15] Of these allusions, the poet would have been uncomfortably aware, having a month prior to starting work on the *Discourse* read through a major portion of the comedies; and the *Idylls* formed part of his daily study for the week of August 7-13, 1818, during the actual writing of the essay. But when set against the undoubted elevation of Greek behavior in most other respects, this evidence was apparently not enough to undermine his faith in the fundamental purity of their sexual practice when taken as a whole, especially when the great majority of ancient literary sources remain silent concerning any physical violation.[16]

Encouraging Shelley in this interpretation was his understanding of Plato, whose Eros he saw not only as a metaphysical ideal but as a working model of Greek love. In one of the dialogues he even thought he detected metaphorically unveiled the baffling enigma of its precise physical expression—the answer to the seemingly insoluble paradox of a violently homosexual passion at once openly indulged and yet inoffensive to sexual modesty. How accurately Shelley's explanation translates the philosopher's intent is open to question. But that it could have been arrived at only by someone thoroughly familiar with the dialogues is self-evident.

First falling under Plato's spell in 1817 at Marlow when he embarked upon a serious study of the dialogues in the original, Shelley was particularly attracted to his love doctrines as expressed in the *Symposium* and the *Phaedrus*. Upon leaving for Italy the following spring, he took with him the first and tenth volumes of his Bipont Plato, in the second of which were both the dialogues on love (*S&C*.VI.549). It was to these that he first turned when finding leisure to take up once more the study of the philosopher's work. Although he was eventually to become steeped in the metaphysics of Platonic love, what chiefly drew him to the dialogues at this period was not their philosophical content but rather, as his letters indicate, the unparalleled insight they seemed to offer into the actual expression of the Greek Eros. What was the human reality underlying the strange passion celebrated again and again in Attic literature? Plato's twin love colloquies seemed to supply the clue.

Accordingly, when in the summer of 1818 Shelley came to piece out his own exposition of Athenian manners and mores, it was principally to the *Symposium* and the *Phaedrus* that he looked for guidance. The former he knew practically by heart from his recent translation. Significantly, in his Preface to the translation, composed shortly afterward at the same time that he was working on the *Discourse* and integrally bound to it, he breaks off with the remark that the dialogue's introductory scenes describing the occasion of the banquet afford "the most lively conception of refined Athenian manners" (VII.162). Associating the Preface verbally with the title of the *Discourse*, this observation once again suggests that Shelley's primary interest in Plato's dialogue, at least at this juncture in his career, was as a social document, not a philosophic treatise—he also refers to it as a "drama," for "so the lively distinction of character and the various well-wrought circumstances of the story entitle it to be called" (VII.162).[17] The *Phaedrus* Shelley read for two days on August 4 and 5, not long after beginning work on the *Discourse*, and he refers to the dialogue enthusiastically to Peacock a fortnight later while well along on his essay's composition (*L.II.29*). Presumably his object in re-reading the *Phaedrus* was the desire to refresh his memory concerning the degree to which the picture of love presented in the two dialogues is mutually consistent. That the argument of the *Phaedrus* as well as the *Symposium* was indeed in his mind's eye as he developed his own picture of Greek sexuality is clear from the evidence of the *Discourse*.

If Greek love were too refined to include the "operose and diabolical machination," then precisely what *did* take place when two lovers found themselves alone together, the tides of passion mounting? Shelley's ingenious answer throws fresh light on his own work. If, he argues, "we consider the facility with which certain phenomena connected with sleep, at the age of puberty, associate themselves with those images which are the object of our waking desires; and even that in some persons of an exalted state of sensibility that a similar process may take place in reverie, it will not be difficult to conceive the almost involuntary consequences of a state of abandonment in the society of a person of surpassing attractions, when the sexual connection cannot exist . . . This is the result apparently alluded to by Plato" (222). Exactly how all this relates to Plato is revealed in certain passages from the *Phaedrus.*

Midway through the dialogue is a section relating the soul-shaking effect on the Uranian pederast of the sight of his *erômenos* or "loved one." So ardent is his response that magically his soul begins sprouting feathers as if it were the winged Eros himself. In its frenzy, continues Plato, the soul of the lover "cannot sleep at night or stay in any one place by day, but it is filled with longing and hastens wherever it hopes to see the beautiful one. And when it sees him and is bathed with the waters of yearning, the passages that were sealed are opened, the soul has respite from the stings and is eased of its pain."[18]

The perfervid tumult of the lover's emotions is further conveyed through the metaphor of two hostile steeds, one squat, dark, and ugly, figuring unruly pride and desire, the other upright, light, and clean-limbed, figuring honorable "temperance and modesty," the two contending with each other under the watchful eyes of the charioteer, reason. When the lover comes into the presence of the loved one "and his whole soul is warmed by the sight, and is full of the ticklings and prickings of yearning, the horse that is obedient to the charioteer, constrained then as always by modesty, controls himself and does not leap on the beloved." The other horse, ignoring the charioteer, springs wildly toward the beloved, proposing "the joys of love." "Terrible and unlawful deeds" are on the verge of being committed; but in the nick of time the charioteer, remembering the true nature of beauty, seeing it standing "with modesty upon a pedestal of chastity," pulls the reins so violently backward "as to bring both horses upon their haunches, the one quite willing . . . but the unruly beast very unwilling. And as they go away, [the modest] horse in his shame and wonder wets all the soul with sweat" (254-254C). Through repeated checks, the unruly horse is gradually tamed and humbled, eventually becoming obedient to the charioteer (254E). But what the unruly horse desires of the beloved is left in no doubt. Standing for unbridled lust, the joys he proposes are bluntly carnal. Not satisfied with merely touching, kissing, lying down with, and caressing the beloved, as is the modest horse, "he would not refuse his lover any favour, if he asked it." Plato notes that it is only the very few, governed by nobility and philosophy, who can keep the unruly horse completely in check. Even those governed by honor, when drinking or otherwise off their guard, may be surprised by the unruly horse "and accomplish that which is by the many accounted blissful; and when this has once been done, they continue the practice, but infrequently, since what they are doing is not approved by the whole mind" (255E-256). None of this is greatly comforting to the Shelleyan view.

Nevertheless, in the original draft of the *Discourse* Shelley twice interpolates "Phaedrus" into his discussion of the physical aspects of Greek love, over the words, "But let us not exaggerate the matter," and after, "This is the result apparently alluded to by Plato."[19] What Shelley appears to have in mind is the possible sexual symbolism in the behavior of Plato's second or "modest" horse. Far-fetched though such a reading may be, coupled with his references to erotic dreaming and erotic reverie, Shelley is almost certainly inferring from these passages the experience of spontaneous or involuntary orgasm, in which rather singular fashion the Uranian pederast transcended the necessity for full sexual connection, thereby making possible Shelley's confident assertion that there were probably "innumerable instances" among the refined Greeks in which pederastic love expressed itself without the violation of natural "modesty." This is Shelley's answer to the riddle of what "action" the Greeks employed to express the mysterious passion of pederastic desire. While disclaiming the possibility of accurately investigating such a subject under the laws of modern composition, he nonetheless proceeds, in characteristically headlong fashion, to do just that.

Shelley assumes that a refined and "exalted" people such as the Greeks of the classic period would naturally exhibit "an exalted state of sensibility" which, when expressed psychosexually, would obviate the necessity of gross physical contact for complete erotic gratification. The mechanism of release is no different from that triggering the adolescent nocturnal emission. The operative stimulus is similarly inward, emotional and psychological, rather than physical—what Masters and Johnson term a "psychogenic" response.[20] Leaving behind him the intractable external world, the fantasist retreats to the more malleable world of the imagination where all things are possible, no joys forbidden. In such a state of intense psychogenic abandon, direct physical stimulus is supererogatory. The nerve ends respond automatically, and orgasm is at last the involuntary result. Of their own accord, the passages which were formerly "sealed," in Plato's words, are now "opened." "Bathed with the waters of yearning," the entire being at last experiences "respite from the stings" of desire and is "eased of its pain."

The immense appeal of such an explanation to Shelley may be guessed from the evidence of his own abnormally exalted sensibility which, as recalled by Mary Shelley, "rendered his mind keenly alive to every perception of outward object, as well as to his internal sensations."[21] This sensibility, coupled with a pathologically high-strung nervous system, made for a life of almost unendurable intensity, rendered yet more intense by a hyperactive fantasy life in which dreams and reverie played an important part. Sometimes these served as autistic release from the pressures of his conscious life, but more often they were probably a continuation of the pressures. Medwin noted that from childhood the poet had been given to overpowering "waking dreams."[22] Occasionally the barrier between dream and reality gave way altogether, and Shelley's hallucinations were the result. Testimony of the thin line dividing the two is the exclamation, "Here I was obliged to leave off, overcome by thrilling horrors," which interrupts his prose fragment "On Dreams" and apparently signified its abandonment (VII.67).

As the fragment itself indicates, the poet was imbued with a modern desire to decipher the exact nature of the dream state and interpret its implications for the waking. Medwin recalled that in his Poland Street days his cousin was even then "in the habit of noting down" and "systematising" his dreams.[23] By tracing and analyzing his own experience, he hoped to illuminate for others some of the mysterious interconnections between dream states and waking—how, for example, in dreams "images acquire associations" to the waking life. He exhibited a similar interest in unlocking the significance of the waking dream, attaching exceptional importance to this state. "Those who are subject to the state called reverie," he explains in his essay *On Life*, "feel as if their nature were dissolved into the surrounding universe, or as if the surrounding universe were absorbed into their being. They are conscious of no distinction. And these are states which precede or accompany or follow an unusually intense and vivid apprehension of life." The psychology of this state is natural to childhood, when "we less habitually distinguished all that we saw and felt from ourselves. They seemed as it were to constitute one mass." However, as people grow up, this power, with rare exceptions, "commonly decays, and they become mechanical and habitual agents" (VI.195-196). The exceptions, as appears from the MS text of the essay, are "Poets & Persons of a peculiar enthusiasm"—persons, that is, like himself subject to visionary illuminations of the nature described in his *Hymn to Intellectual Beauty*, to which the essay stands as a gloss.[24]

The parallel with Wordsworth's "Ode: Intimations of Immortality" and "Lines: Composed a Few Miles Above Tintern Abbey" is striking. Wordsworth's moments of sublimity wherein the body is laid asleep and one becomes "a living soul" seem a close counterpart of Shelley's visionary reveries and apparently grow out of much the same understanding of childhood vision and its relation to adult perception. As recalled by Wordsworth in the Fenwick notes to the "Intimations Ode," when he was a child, he was "often unable to think of external things as having external existence," and he communed with all that he saw as something "not apart from, but inherent in," his own "immaterial nature." This sensation lent to all objects of sight a mysterious "dream-like vividness and splendor," which haloed them in a light not their own but rather emanated from within himself. The experience, which he labeled an "abyss of idealism," so frightened him at the time that he was compelled to grasp at a wall or tree in order to reassure himself of the material reality of the external world. In later life, however, when only too conscious of this reality, of its "heavy and weary weight" in the dolorous words of "Tintern Abbey," he welcomed recollections or momentary revivals of the earlier state and took them as comforting evidence of a spiritual reality transcending the physical.

Shelley interpreted the experience in similar terms, finding in it confirmation of the essential immateriality of things (*On Life* [VI.196]). His interest, like Wordsworth's, went beyond the psychological to the metaphysical. Wordsworth's "abyss of idealism" effectively suggests Shelley's mature metaphysics, which was a sort of skeptical version of philosophic idealism, a dream philosophy in which mind or thought—that is, mental impressions or images—existed as the only knowable reality, thus making life and thought synonymous. Derived from Hume and Berkeley by way of Godwin and Sir William Drummond, this "intellectual philosophy" or "system," as Shelley refers to it, did away with the "vulgar" distinction between mind and matter, objects internal and external: "Nothing exists but as it is perceived."[25] The notion of a world of "things" different from the perceiver was therefore illusory: "By the word *things* is to be understood any object of thought—that is, any thought upon which any other thought is employed with an apprehension of distinction." It follows that hallucinations and dreams are quite as "real" as so-called *"real, or external objects."*[26]

All metaphysics is thus ultimately reducible to "the great study of ourselves," to an "inquiry concerning those things belonging to, or concerned with, the internal nature of man." Metaphysics is the "science of mind," and we are ourselves the "depositories of the evidence" we would consider. Consequently, writes Shelley, "If it were possible that a person should give a faithful history of his being from the earliest epochs of his recollections, a picture would be presented such as the world has never contemplated before. A mirror would be held up to all men in which they might behold their own recollections and, in dim perspective, their shadowy hopes and fears—all that they dare not, or that daring and desiring, they could not expose to the open eyes of day." But for mind to operate on itself in this fashion, to pass from "sensation to reflection—from a state of passive perception to voluntary contemplation" without vital loss, is doomed by the nature of things to ineluctable frustration. Thought is "like a river whose rapid and perpetual stream flows outwards," and so it "can with difficulty visit the intricate and winding chambers which it inhabits." Yet it is precisely to the "rigid examination of itself" that we must compel the mind if we are ever to advance the boundaries of existential knowledge.[27]

Holding such a metaphysics and endowed—or cursed—with such a psychological sensibility, Shelley was naturally led to devote a large proportion of his own poetry to the portrayal of mental phenomena and to take as its base a faithful history of his own mind. As he insisted throughout his career, his poems were first of all accurate pictures of their author's inner life, and whatever their defects, this was their ultimate justification, making them as mirrors in which the reader might see reflected the mysterious recesses of the interior world. In view of this orientation, it was natural that the dreams and reveries which constituted such an active part of his life should find their way into his poetry, and that the greater portion should to some degree be erotic in character. For the powerful claims of the sexual self to a place in human consciousness was a fundamental Shelleyan premise, and the prevalence of erotic fantasy in his poetry is tacit admission of the power of these claims to a place in his own consciousness.

Again and again Shelley exposes the dark places of his mental life for the reader's illumination. That deeply felt experience and not simply fanciful embellishment is going into these pictures is continually revealed by the personal lyrics. In giving so prominent a place to the erotic dream and fantasy, Shelley is simply mirroring the truth as everyone knows it: for better or worse these longings make up a great part of a person's inner life from puberty onward and reveal the deepest self. Not to portray this dream world would be to falsify the picture of the mind he was intent on building up through the vehicle of his poetry—one mind, the type of all, with its recollections, its shadowy hopes and fears, all that the individual dare not or cannot expose to the eyes of day. "Nature is her own pornographer," explains the modern sex researcher John Money. "Particularly in the case of the male, at the time of puberty, she institutes her own movie shows," images over which he has little or no conscious control, and these persist, though less urgently, throughout his adult life.[28] It is self-evident, Money notes further, that "the only erotic imagery to which an observer has direct access is his own. The solipsism of imagery keeps it forever private and unknown to others except through verbal report."[29]

As Shelley observes in the *Discourse*, one of the phenomena characteristically heralding the birth of adult sexuality is the noctural emission or wet dream.[30] Given the poet's desire to trace faithfully the history of his own psychoerotic growth, it would be unusual were he to omit instances of the experience from his work. And given his own peculiarly sensitive and high-strung psychological organization, it would be equally unusual were these not vivid and intense. As modern sex research has shown, "the frequencies of nocturnal dreams of any sort, sexual or otherwise, appear to have some correlation with the imaginative capacities of an individual."[31]

The adolescent erotic dream plays a prominent role in Shelley's work, from the Gothic novels and the earliest poetry onward, frequently evoked with great intensity and often manifestly implying orgasmic release.[32] For Shelley such release must have figured importantly in his own adolescent sexuality and perhaps continued well into his adult life.[33] At the time of his death he was still only in his twenties, and all his work, even the most mature, reflects the psychosexuality of a still young man. To take the most obvious example, the dream vision of the veiled maid in *Alastor*, whose nature has caused so much debate through the years, is literally defined by the "certain phenomena connected with sleep, at the age of puberty" of the *Discourse*, even to the "shock" of emission which ends the dream and jolts the young poet awake from his "trance," and would long ago have been accepted as such were the physical element not regularly denied his work.[34] As Shelley states unambiguously in his Preface, the poem, though developed symbolically, is psychological in intent—"allegorical of one of the most interesting situations of the human mind"—and concerns itself with the adolescent sexual awakening, and its consequences, of a youth much like himself.

The awakening, besides having psychological validity in terms of sympathetic love, has psychosexual validity by virtue of its occurring in a wet dream. Time and again Shelley realistically depicts the "thirst" for sympathetic response as originating at puberty. His psychology is rooted in the observed realities of human experience. Before we start combing the physical world for possession of our sympathetic antitypes, we have already been granted a foretaste of this possession through intercourse with their shadows or "images" and are therefore under no illusions as to what we are looking for.[35] As explained by modern sex research, since people cannot consciously will changes in the imagery of dreams and fantasies, they have no alternative but to live with this imagery "and, probably, one day, put it into action in real-life experience."[36] Shelley's recognition of this truth makes nonsense of the many attempts to present his love psychology as essentially transsensual or avoiding the senses. As he knows, the thirst for sympathetic communion is grounded in the senses and only becomes imperative with their hormonal activation at puberty. It is the very physicality of the ideal which makes these "dreams of joy" at once so exhilarating and so frustrating, shadowing forth what the external world could be but so often is not. Except for the infrequent periods in our lives when shadow and substance are one, the sexual dream, though giving a kind of satisfaction, is ultimately a wasting experience, as Shelley must have felt. Certainly this is the message of *Alastor*, where the young poet, unable to find in the real world the erotic "image" he had formed in his mind, experiences psychological death, and it is true of a number of the other poems as well: "lovely dreams" are always fading, "ere morning's chilling light," into "sad realities."[37]

More difficult to assess are the ramifications of the erotic daydream or reverie in Shelley. In view of the uncommon frequency of such states in his verse and his own "exalted sensibility," they could conceivably betoken a psychosexuality like that described in the *Discourse*, capable of spontaneous sexual release even when awake. For example, his remarks on "the state called reverie" in *On Life*, which clearly apply to himself, could be extended to account for the psychological process triggering this release. The dreamer, experiencing "an unusually intense and vivid apprehension of life," feels himself "dissolved into the surrounding universe" or feels it "absorbed" into him so that the two merge, leaving him "conscious of no distinction" (VI.195). Having momentarily achieved fusion with the images of his desire, he suddenly finds that psychological reality has become surprisingly physical. Such an interpretation would go a long way to making human and concrete all those "I die! I faint! I fail!" effusions which have been the bane of Shelley readers for generations because of their seemingly pointless vehemence. Connecting the frenzied rant of such passages with the psychological state described in *On Life*, one could view the language as Shelley's deliberate attempt not only to convey the psychogenic intensity of the visionary reverie but even to evoke it, when appropriate, in sexual terms. Such rhetoric, with its associative word clusters—"sinking," "perishing," "expiring," "dying"—is often consciously employed by Shelley in a sexual sense as the verbal equivalent of orgasmic annihilation.

The interpretation could also work backward, suggesting that in orgasm Shelley felt a breaking down of barriers and an intensity of vision akin to the moments of sublimity connected with the reverie state when the distinction between the individual self and the external universe is annihilated and one can see into the life of things. This reading would give sexual response its final and most magnificent level of meaning, and it is exactly what seems to be implied in the nuptial stanzas of *Laon and Cythna*. The same implication marks the psychoerotic finale of *Epipsychidion* in which Shelley imagines the results of being alone with Emilia Viviani on the paradisal isle of his daydreams. What is even more intriguing are the psychoerotic effects of Shelley's efforts to convey such fantasy: "Woe is me!/The wingèd words on which my soul would pierce/Into the height of Love's rare Universe,/Are chains of lead around its flight of fire—/I pant, I sink, I tremble, I expire!" (587-591).[38] The poet's life is ebbing, swooning, collapsing, dying because in the intensity of his effort to surmount the boundaries of the self he is experiencing sensations equivalent on the one hand to the visionary reverie and on the other to orgasm. Whether he has also literally experienced orgasm can only be guessed.

Encouraging speculation even further is the astonishing last stanza of "The Boat on the Serchio":

> The Serchio, twisting
> Between the marble barriers which it clove
> At Ripafratta, leads through the dread chasm
> The wave that died the death which lovers love,
> Living in what it sought; as if this spasm
> Had not yet passed, the toppling mountains cling,
> But the clear stream in full enthusiasm
> Pours itself on the plain. (105-112)[39]

It is tempting to find in these lines a sort of Rosetta stone to the interpretation of Shelley's verse. No longer does the reader have to wonder what on earth can account for so many swooning, dissolving lovers. The reality is clear. Passages formerly blurred by a gushy sentimentality or a mawkish vapidity snap into focus. When, for example, the impatient Cosimo of the fragment "Fiordispina" faints on the morning of his wedding day, "dissolved into a sea of love" because overcome by the "ardours of a vision which obscures/The very idol of its portraiture" (21-25), the problem is obvious. And when Shelley adverts to his own experience, the story is the same. Lines previously insubstantial or inflated take on concrete substance. No longer does the vehement language of "To Constantia [Singing]," for example, seem out of proportion to the experience evoked, ludicrously overheated—

"As morning dew, that in the sunbeam dies,/I am dissolved in these consuming extacies./I have no life, Constantia, but in thee." On the contrary, the language stands as a psychogenically faithful record of the experience. "I faint, I perish with my love!" Shelley protests elsewhere: "I grow/Frail as a cloud whose [splendours] pale/Under the evening's ever-changing glow:/I die like mist upon the gale,/And like a wave under the calm I fail."[40] This is either elaborate nonsense or the evocaton of something very real, namely "the almost involuntary consequences of a state of abandonment in the society of a person of surpassing attractions, where the sexual connection cannot exist."

Though the notorious "Indian Serenade" is not a personal lyric, as readers have often assumed to Shelley's detriment, but an imitation of an Oriental love song with the speaker an "Indian girl," it exactly parallels the experience elicited in the personal lyrics, thus suggesting the virtually interchangeable orgasmic effects in either sex under intense psychogenic stress.[41] Opening with the speaker rising "wild & joyous" from erotic dreams of her lover—with whom she had been making love earlier, as a MS variant shows—the poem follows her to a station on the lawn outside his bedroom window where, wrapped in profound reverie, she feels herself begin to dissolve into the night scene or to find it absorbed into her.[42] Falling back on the grass, she discovers all nature joining her in a sympathetic swoon: the wandering airs "faint," the champak odours "fail," the nightingale's complaint "dies" upon her heart, as she feels she must soon die if she is unable to wrench herself back to reality. Powerless to lift herself, however, she is left to moan in helpless ecstacy: "I die! I faint! I fail!" The situation is psychosexually equivalent to the contemporaneously written "Ode to the West Wind." And if, like Shelley with his wind, the girl's lover does not respond immediately to her prayer, lifting her to his breast, she will no doubt "die away" altogether, as she does in the MS draft, dissolving like mist or failing like a wave, her substance spent—not in love's delight, but in its agonizing counterfeit.[43] Modern sex research shows that spontaneous sexual release in the woman most often follows direct physiological arousal, such as the girl would have just experienced with her lover.[44] On this reading, the poem, far from being squishily sentimental, is almost painfully clinical, an authentic and powerful psychosexual minidrama.

While the hypothesis is appealing, it is admittedly tenuous and impossible of verification. Moreover, were it to be substantiated, most people's enjoyment of the poetry would not necessarily be greatly enhanced, spontaneous sexual release being in any period out of the mainstream of human experience and scarcely of wide appeal. And despite its value in explaining Shelley's personal psychosexuality, it was likely outside the flow of his immediate experience as well. At least this is the necessary inference from the text of the *Discourse* itself, which is the only documentary evidence. Here, as initially drafted, the question of involuntary orgasm is clearly speculative, Shelley writing that "perhaps" this release may occur in some persons of exalted sensibility. Yet even if such release is beyond the bounds of his own experience, he leaves no doubt that it is fully within the realm of human possibility, given the proper circumstances: "how easy in an exalted state of the external senses," begins the canceled opening of the discussion, to trigger spontaneous sexual release without the super-addition of external stimulus.[45] With the exalted Greeks, such stimulus would have been unnecessary, so that even in the farthest reaches of passion their pederastic practice as described by Plato would have preserved its essential purity.

Despite the ingenuity of this explanation, it was clearly not a subject on which Shelley relished expressing himself. In the same notebook containing this section of the *Discourse* appears a detached passage, perhaps intended as a footnote, which suggests that he felt more than a little disquieted about the extent of sexual detail to which the discussion had led him: "in the human world one of the commonest expressions of love is sexual intercourse, and in describing the deepest effects of abstract love the author could not avoid the danger of exciting some ideas connected with this mode of expression. In this he has exposed himself to the danger of awakening ludicrous or unauthorized images; but in obedience to an impulse."[46] With considerable relief, therefore, he finally disposes of the physical side of Greek love and turns to its more elevated manifestations, which he again saw exemplified in the pages of Plato.

In his view Plato's love was primarily social, a view widely shared by modern scholarship. The "educational Eros" is "glorified in the *Symposium*," stresses the classicist Werner Jaeger. *Paideia*, "true culture," was its goal.[47] As argued by Pausanias in the dialogue, the paideutic element justified the Athenians and Spartans in elevating pederastic attachment above the grosser varieties of male love that were supposedly the norm elsewhere in ancient Greece (*Symp.* 181C-185C). The theme is raised to a higher plane in Socrates' concluding speech where, through the inspired lips of the prophetess Diotima, it is explained that they who would beget immortal progeny, namely sobriety and justice, those virtues most important "to the regulation of cities and habitations," must learn to submit themselves to the paideutic Eros and take in hand the education of beautiful boys (*Symp.* 209B-D).

Such a view of Eros must have appealed enormously to Shelley, explaining why he so much desired to free it from the taint of the sexually perverse.[48] A similar pedagogic or tutorial Eros occupied an equally prominent place in his own erotic psychology, though directed toward young women not youths.[49] To render the Greek version of this Eros more palatable, however, he was forced to elevate its practice to the highest plane imaginable, one probably not envisioned even by Plato as more than a utopian possibility. But then for Shelley the Greeks were not like other peoples, and one could not hope to measure their behavior by what he labelled "our own feeble conceptions of the intensity of disinterested love" (222). In the presence of his loved one the Athenian pederast was ordinarily immune to those baser passions governing the remainder of mankind, which he satisfied with his "wife or his slave"; rather he was "engrossed in such lofty thoughts and feelings as admitted of no compromise between them and less intense emotions" (223).

Shelley warns against applying the psychological yardstick of feeble modern conceptions of the intensity of disinterested love to the understanding of Greek pederasty. In essence, however, precisely this transvaluation is going on in the *Discourse*. The poet's interpretation of Greek love is a thorough reworking of the ancient experience in terms of contemporary doctrines of disinterested love and friendship. His rendering of the older male Eros has a most English coloring.

As Notopoulos has noted, the "concept of disinterested love is so pervasive in Shelley's thinking that we can truly call it an *idée fixe.*"[50] The concept derived from the ethical benevolism of the preceding century elaborated by Shaftesbury, Bishop Butler, Hutcheson, and Hume, in which the virtues of "disinterestedness" played a key role.[51] This so-called "moral sense school" postulated that mankind, far from being motivated exclusively by self-regarding impulses as maintained by Hobbes and later by the more rigid Utilitarians, is in reality endowed with a variety of affections, including sympathy, compassion, and benevolence, which make possible spontaneously disinterested actions. The "selfish school" denied this postulate, arguing, in the words of Hume, that "whatever one may feel or imagine he feels for others, no passion is or can be disinterested; that the most generous friendship, however sincere, is a modification of self-love." But this view goes against common experience which testifies to the reality of such affections as "love, friendship, compassion, gratitude." There are countless instances of "a general benevolence in human nature, where no *real* interest binds us to the object." Such propensities as those for "benevolence and friendship" must consequently be built into "the original frame of our temper."[52]

The Male Eros

This view coincided closely with Shelley's. The poet found the view reinforced by the imaginative literature of the day, which was soaked in the vocabulary of benevolism and its stress on the virtues of disinterested love and friendship, as in *Tom Jones*, whose phraseology Shelley echoes in his own work, or in *Clarissa*, or *Julie*, or Wieland's romances. Shelley's friend Hogg, who was an exponent of the selfish school, pressed Shelley on this subject in their early letters, and in defending himself, Shelley revealed the benevolist foundations of his position. "You have very well drawn your line of distinction between instinctive & rational motives of action," runs one letter: "the *former* are not in our own power, yet we may doubt if even those are *purely* selfish, as congeniality sympathy unaccountable attractions of intellect wc arise independent frequently of any considerations of yr own interest, operating violently in contradiction to it, & bringing on wretchedness which your reason plainly foresees, which yet although yr judgement disapproves of you take no pains to obviate.—all this is not selfish" (*S&C*.II.715). Shelley is echoing Hume, though no doubt his position is also the consequence of personal observation as well as self-examination. The association of disinterestedness with congeniality, sympathy, and intellectual attraction unmistakably heralds his mature archetype of sentimental love. Disinterested love and friendship are already seen to be taking shape as basic constituents of an all-embracing sexual psychology.

From the beginning Shelley was clear that most so-called love is merely another name for selfish desire. "Ah! poor deluded Eloise," he exclaims of the cold-hearted seduction of the heroine in his second novel *St. Irvyne*, "didst thou think a *man* would merit thy love through disinterestedness." Yet not all men are ipso facto seducers, as shown later in the novel: in the Chevalier Mountfort, Eloise has "a most warm, disinterested friend."[53] Since the Chevalier is a professed "libertine" and Eloise is a beautiful woman completely in his power, this disinterestedness presumably takes some doing. Shelley's point is that innate "compassion," or sympathy, can sometimes prove stronger than the selfishness of lust (V.188).

Just how great a strain intense sexual passion puts on disinterestedness the poet was soon to discover personally in the collapse of his engagement to Harriet Grove. No matter how hard he tried to place Harriet's happiness before his own, he could not help returning to his own loss, his own sorrow. Again and again he lamented his selfishness, but it could not be helped: "I am afraid there is selfishness in the passion of Love for I cannot avoid feeling every instant as if my soul was bursting, but I *will* feel no more! it is selfish." He trusts that his love for Harriet is not based merely on her "person, the embodied identity," and that his despair is not the result of "the hot sickly love which enflames the admirers of Sterne or Moore," but that he loves "what is superior what is excellent," her spirit, and for the happiness of which he would defy the torments of hell. Yet he cannot be certain. So he remains a "sceptic" about love, wishing he could either believe in it as traditionally represented or disbelieve in it totally, but unable to do either (*L.*I. 36, 44).

Shelley's hurt made him shy away from passionate love for some time. Love, he claimed, could be trusted only if dissociated from passion—a point he reiterated when trying to discourage Hogg's growing passion for Elizabeth Shelley. Why, he asks, "should you love her? A disinterested appreciation of what is in itself excellent. this is good if it is so . . . but what you feel is a *passion* it is I *suppose* involuntary . . . passion can evidently be neither interested or its opposite" (*S&C*.II.847). Disinterestedness is coming to be identified in Shelley's thinking with dispassionate intellectual communion to which the physical self is a threat. Friendship now tends to substitute for love, which, he grudgingly admits, may in fact be "inseparable" from "sensation" (*L.*I.181).[54]

What happened to his thinking in this respect as he matured is difficult to know with certainty, possibly owing to the poet's own uncertainty. At times he allowed the claims of the body honorable restoration through the medium of his archetype of sentimental love; at others he seems to have despaired. There is the further question of whether or not he modified the strictly benevolist base of his position, owing to his increasing contact with Godwin. While a universal reign of disinterested benevolence was the goal of Godwin's philosophical system, he appears to have believed that the qualities producing this are learned, not innate; human beings are originally self-regarding. The key to their improvement lies in the expansion of the sympathetic imagination. The growth of society necessitates this expansion. People learn to overcome their native selfishness through imaginative self-projection, sympathetically identifying with the pleasures and pains of others, thereby overleaping the boundaries of the self and forming genuinely other-regarding habits. Insofar as these habits, once learned, are seen as reflexive or involuntary in their operations, Godwin is ranging himself against the selfish school—the "advocates of the system of self-love"—and on the side of the benevolists.[55] In practice there is little real difference between Godwin's position and Hume's.

Since Shelley's mature views, as expressed in his "Speculations on Morals," parallel Godwin's, the difference between his early letter to

Hogg, in which he links instinctive motives of "congeniality sympathy unaccountable attractions of intellect" with disinterestedness, and his later position is more apparent than real.[56] The elementary emotions of "disinterestedness" are still those "we feel to constitute the majesty of our nature," and their development is guaranteed by our life as a social creature which necessitates the growth of the sympathetic imagination, the foundation of disinterested emotion. Thus "disinterested benevolence" is the product of a "cultivated imagination," and love "possesses so extraordinary a power over the human heart, only because disinterestedness is united with the natural propensities. These propensities themselves are comparatively impotent in cases where the imagination of pleasure to be given, as well as to be received, does not enter into the account."[57] We must give in order to get, as Masters and Johnson maintain in the more prosaic language of modern sex research. Experiencing another's pleasure is the passport to our own and holds out the panacea for humanity's sexual ills.

Yet there remains an irreducible core of self buried in all sexual relationships which prevents them from ever approaching perfect disinterestedness. To this extent passionate physical love can never be wholly free of the pain inherent in clashing human desire. As Shelley came ever more pessimistically to recognize, love based on sense is one of the ways in which the world keeps mankind chained to her wheels. Perhaps a dissociation of the two is after all the only solution.

Disinterested love need not be confined exclusively to relations *between* the sexes, however. Shelley's early letters to Hogg reveal feelings at least as intense as anything he was expressing for women. This was the "noble," the "disinterested" Hogg of his student days, before the "fall" of Hogg's attempted seduction of Harriet (*L.*I.186), and Shelley's relationship with him has considerable bearing on his attitude to the boy-love of the Greeks. That Shelley felt love and not just friendship, as this term is commonly understood, is indisputable from the letters, which have proved an embarrassment to later generations, less inclined to believe in the disinterestedness of such attachments. Shelley himself was not a little uneasy at the intensity of his emotions.

Idealizing Hogg, the poet saw in his friend both "the brother of his soul" and a "superior being." At the university he increasingly yielded to Hogg's intellectual tutelage, isolating himself from the vulgar herd of his fellow undergraduates. After his expulsion, Shelley adamantly refused to break off the friendship, though this was one of the principal conditions laid down by his father for reconciliation with the family. Shelley hoped to bind Hogg even closer by encouraging his union with his beloved sister Elizabeth Shelley. When eloping with Harriet Westbrook, Shelley continued to place his friendship with Hogg first, including him in the bridal tour of Scotland. According to Hogg, when he arrived in Edinburgh, the poet exclaimed: "We have met at last once more! and we will never part again! You must have a bed in the house!"[58]

So tied up was Shelley with his friend emotionally that when the idyll was shattered by Hogg's attempted seduction of Harriet, the resulting turmoil had all the force of a lovers' quarrel, and Shelley was able to declare just how much his friend had come to mean to him, both friends speaking in passionate terms. "Oh! how I have loved you," Shelley wails. "I was even ashamed to tell you how!" Now to have to break off *"forever*—no, not forever," is too much to bear. Hogg must rejoin them: "Will you come—dearest, best beloved of friends, will *you* come. Will you share my fortunes, enter into my schemes—love me as I love you; be inseparable as once I fondly hoped you were." But grim reality reasserts itself: " 'Tis past all past, like a dream of the sick man which leaves but bitterness 'tis a fleeting vision." And so Shelley debates with himself, struggling to resist Hogg's frantic appeals while seeking to regain control over his own emotions. He dare not see Hogg again, "lest I convert disinterestedness into selfishness" (*S&C*.III.41). Eventually he cools off enough to view the situation in a more dispassionate light, explaining to his new friend Elizabeth Hitchener: "How I have loved him *you* can *feel*—but he is no longer the being whom perhaps twas the [warmth?] of my imagination that pictured. I love no longer what is not that which I loved" (*L*.I.213). But while the relationship simmered down to the proportions of a more conventional friendship, subject at times to considerable strain, Shelley continued to find Hogg necessary for his happiness, and Hogg was only too ready to be needed. Until the end, Hogg remained first among the poet's friends, and in *The Revolt of Islam* Shelley sought to make amends for the rupture by commemorating their early attachment in the most glowing terms.[59] He "always loved you the best," wrote the grieving Mary to Hogg after Shelley's death, just as Hogg she knew, had ever been "most singularly attached" in return.[60]

It may be imagined what modern commentators have made of such a "friendship." Hardly any argue for an overtly homosexual attachment, the mere thought of which would have revolted Shelley, but most recognize some sort of latent homosexual feeling, underscored by Shelley's seeming compulsion to share his women with Hogg and Hogg's ready acquiescence. In the light of twentieth-century psychoanalytic theory this conclusion has some plausibility.[61] Placing the relationship within the context of nineteenth-century psychosocial patterns, however, yields a different explanation, one filling in an important area of the poet's love psychology.

Shelley's friendship with Hogg was not the first of such attachments. At the age of eleven or twelve he had formed a similar attachment to a schoolmate at Syon House or Eton, which bore all the earmarks of romantic passion except the "sensual" element.[62] So intense were the emotions aroused that they still haunted him fifteen years later. In such attachments he detects an important key to the interpretation of human psychosexuality. "The object of these sentiments," he explains in "On Friendship," "was a boy about my own age, of a character eminently generous, brave, and gentle . . . There was a delicacy and a simplicity in his manner inexpressibly attractive." Particularly memorable were the tones of his voice, which were "so soft and winning that every word pierced into my heart, and their pathos was so deep that in listening to him the tears often have involuntarily gushed from my eyes." The "involuntary" orgasm of Greek pederasty would seem to be part of the same basic psychosexual response as Shelley imagines it. This boy was the first person for whom he experienced the "sacred sentiments of friendship." Like two lovers, they used "to walk the whole play-hours up and down by some moss-covered palings, pouring out our hearts in youthful talk" and confirming each other in "everlasting fidelity." Their friendship seemed "exquisitely beautiful." Every night when they parted for bed, they "kissed each other."[63] In his naiveté, he recalls, he wrote his mother about the attachment, but "I suppose she thought me out of my wits, for she returned no answer to my letter" (VII.143-144).[64]

From beautiful friendships to beautiful pederasty is but a short step, and it must have been one that Shelley in effect took in his imagination when seeking to interpret the Greek Eros. The association, for instance, is plainly disclosed in one of his 1819 statuary notes. "Less beautiful than that in the royal collection of Naples," he writes of a Bacchus and Ampelus, "and yet infinitely lovely." In epithets directly recalling "On Friendship" and subsuming both accounts under his paradigm of boy-beauty, the figures are depicted as strolling with "a sauntering and idle pace and talking to each other . . . One arm of Bacchus rests on the shoulder of Ampelus . . . [who] half embraces the waist of Bacchus"—just "as you may have seen (yet how seldom from their dissevering and tyrannical institutions do you see) a younger and older boy at school walking in some remote grassy spot of their playground with that tender friendship towards each other which has so much of love." The description then becomes an open parody of heterosexual love, Ampelus, the coquette and flirt, deliberately provoking the masculine protectiveness of Bacchus (VI.319). The entire note gives a version of Greek pederasty consciously refashioned in the image of the playing fields of Eton and Harrow.[65]

For Shelley, as perhaps for the age, the archetype of that disinterested love which he claimed for the Greeks approximates most nearly the sort of delicate, romantic fervor engendered in the traditional adolescent attachments at the English public schools. In such attachments, the poet believed, it was possible to recognize a bond of affection so strong that it could legitimately bear the name of love yet still remain sexually innocent, "pure," and consequently free of the claims of the physical self. While such sentimental liaisons in Shelley's day were not precisely encouraged, as witness his caustic interjection about dissevering and tyrannical institutions, they were nonetheless implicitly condoned and played, as they have continued to play, an important, sometimes decisive role in the emotional life of the English upper classes. What makes Shelley exceptional is that he was the first to explore the psychological foundations of this passion and set it in the perspective of mankind's developing psychosexual history.

Many of his contemporaries would have been in sympathy with his conclusions on the basis of their own experience. Wordsworth, for example, recalling the happiness of his Hawkshead schooldays in *The Prelude*, confesses that this period was made especially dear because he had at his side "a Friend,/Then passionately loved," the thought of whom even in later years still warms his heart (Bk.II.333-334). Apparently he saw nothing guilty in such sentiments, any more than did Leigh Hunt in those experienced for several of his schoolmates at Christ's Hospital: "if ever I tasted disembodied transport on earth, it was those friendships which I entertained at school. I shall never forget the impression it first made on me. I loved my friend for his gentleness, his candour, his truth . . . I thought him a kind of angel."[66] The sentiments tying Byron to several school and college friends in what he calls "*sentimental* friendships" were remembered in similar terms.[67] For John Edleston, for instance, a Cambridge chorister, Byron experienced a "violent, though *pure*, love and passion," and these feelings, combined with his friendship for his Harrow schoolmate Edward Noel Long, made the "then romance of the most romantic period of my life."[68] "School friendships were with me *passions*," as the impassioned "Childish Recollections," a sort of poetic "On Friendship," bears striking witness. A roll call of his Harrow crushes, the verses memorialize those happy

Hours of my youth! when, nurtured in my breast,
To love a stranger, friendship made me blest, —
Friendship, the dear peculiar bond of youth,
When every artless bosom throbs with truth;
Untaught by worldly wisdom how to feign,
And check each impulse with prudential rein;
When all we feel, our honest souls disclose—
In love to friends. (55-62)

Nor did these crushes entirely lose their force in later years. The "sentimental" intensity of his feelings toward at least one of his Harrow friends, Lord Clare, persisted unabated until his death.[69]

The evidence of Byron is admittedly weakened by a possibly real homosexual bias. His attachments apparently did not always stop at the level of the emotions.[70] Yet if he is the exception, tainted by practice condemned as criminal by his age, the innocent picture of schoolboy romance encouraged by Shelley still does not altogether fit the facts. What went on behind the scenes at such institutions as Harrow and Eton when the boys were out of sight of their masters was not always just harmless kissing: "as many kisses as would have sufficed for a boarding school," Byron writes of his parting with the Greek youth Eustathius.[71] It was not, in short, entirely the harmless relationship postulated of the ancient Greeks.

Homosexual practice of one sort or another was in fact rampant in the nineteenth-century public school, with little attempt to control it. Only when, as with Byron, such behavior carried over into the adult world was it severely penalized. There was a double standard at work, which was exposed at the end of the century with the conviction of Oscar Wilde. Observers pointed out the contrast between "the universal execration heaped upon" the writer and "the universal acquiescence of the very same public in the same kind of vice in our public schools." In the sardonic words of W. T. Stead: "If all the persons guilty of Oscar Wilde's offences were to be clapped into gaol, there would be a very surprising exodus from Eton and Harrow, Rugby and Winchester, to Pentonville and Holloway . . . public schoolboys are allowed to indulge with impunity in practices which, when they leave school, would consign them to hard labour."[72]

At Eton boys traditionally slept three to a bed, and "Filth, tortures, sin, etc., were all rampant," admit school chroniclers Anthony Cheetham and Derek Parfit. They quote from a letter in 1850 from the Provost of King's College, Cambridge, to the Provost of Eton, bewailing the horrendous prevalence of "vice" at Eton during the first half of the century: "I shall be borne out by the consciences of my contemporaries when I say, that a few years ago it was almost impossible for a boy to pass through College without acquiring an acquaintance with Evil that is perfectly fearful to contemplate in boys of such tender age. It required little short of miraculous intervention to prevent them from becoming thoroughly contaminated . . . The depth of the pollution they had contracted . . . he only can know who has struggled patiently for years to unlearn the evil lessons of his schoolboy days."[73] The situation was apparently no different at Harrow, as revealed in Phyllis Grosskurth's life of John Addington Symonds, drawing on his still unpublished memoirs. When Symonds arrived at the school, he was "stunned by its sexual immorality . . . It was the common practice for every good-looking boy to be addressed by a female name; he was regarded either as public property or as the 'bitch' of an older boy." Growing up, like Shelley, in a predominantly feminine household, Symonds found the talk among the boys "incredibly obscene, and he could not help seeing innumerable scenes of crude carnality."[74] Montgomery Hyde, also drawing on the memoirs, confirms that the "talk in the dormitories and studies was of the grossest character, with repulsive scenes of onanism, mutual masturbation and obscene orgies of naked boys in bed together. There was no refinement, just animal lust."[75]

All this, though a half-century after the Harrow of Byron's experience, gives the impression of a continuing tradition.[76] It was still the same school that had been the "grave" of his "moral being," as Byron confessed to his wife Annabella.[77] Even in the twentieth century the host of memoirs, confessions, and novels dealing with the subject shows that things have not greatly changed at the public schools.[78] Their walls conceal a thriving homosexuality which remains a shaping influence on English emotional life.

There is no way of knowing just what Shelley's experience was at Eton. But it cannot have been wholly innocent. With his girlish good looks he could hardly have escaped attracting homosexual overtures. Perhaps his later abhorrence of such behavior reflects such an advance. At the very least he must have been aware of homosexual activity among his schoolmates.[79] His knowledge of sodomy, as reflected in the *Discourse*, seems authentic, though such practice was no doubt rare at the secondary school level.[80]

Yet while Shelley's picture of schoolboy friendship is deliberately one-sided, overlooking a number of the seamier realities with which he must have been acquainted, it still contains a measure of truth. There undoubtedly existed numerous instances of friendship where the relationship was in fact pure, or "exempt," in the poet's characteristic phraseology, "from the smallest alloy of sensuality," yet love in every other sense of the word. Michael Campbell, dealing fictionally with schoolboy friendships in the modern public school, describes many such attachments as "romantic," intensely emotional, and in no way different from heterosexual love. The couples hold hands, embrace, kiss, write passionate love notes and letters to each other, and think of their love as eternal. There may be sex play, but by no means always. Many relationships are entirely free of sexual feeling, the emphasis exclusively on sentiment.[81] It was this variant that Shelley took as characteristic and in turn sought to apply to the ancient Greeks.

It seems likely that "On Friendship" did grow out of Shelley's interest in the Greek Eros, possibly as an attempt to generalize some of the arguments initiated in the *Discourse*.[82] Both essays seek to demonstrate the possibility of ardent sentimental attachments between members of the same sex which, though bearing all the earmarks of heterosexual passion, give no hint of sexual violation. In the *Discourse* Shelley postulates the archetypal nature of sentimental love. Inasmuch as its psychological model is inborn, we are all constitutionally predisposed to desire sentimental gratification. Consequently everyone we meet is potentially the embodiment of our psychosexual needs: the question of gender does not at first figure significantly. This is particularly the case in advanced societies where intellectual and imaginative claims automatically assume pre-eminence over physical. In civilized love the desire for sexual gratification, even on the heterosexual level, is simply the ultimate step in a long emotional and spiritual interchange, a mere type or expression of the more elevated levels of attraction. Much the same thing is postulated in "On Friendship," which states that generically little if any difference exists between sentimental friendship and sentimental love, for the simple reason that both participate in the same psychological archetype.

"The nature of Love and Friendship is very little understood," the essay begins, and the distinctions between the two "ill established." The latter "feeling"—"at least, a profound and sentimental attachment to one of the same sex, wholly divested of the smallest alloy of sensual intermixture—often precedes the former. It is not right to say, merely, that it is exempt from the smallest alloy of sensuality. It rejects with disdain all thoughts but those of an elevated and imaginative character and the process by which the attachment between two persons of different sexes terminates in a sensual union has not yet begun" (VII.143).[83] This assertion could serve as a gloss on the *Discourse*—the Greek pederast "engrossed in such lofty thoughts and feelings as ad-

mitted of no compromise between them and less intense emotions."
Furthermore, as Shelley points out in the *Discourse*, the cultivation of
such attachments was not confined exclusively to ancient Athens.
Attachments of a similar sort were apparently widespread during the
English Renaissance: "in the golden age of our own literature a certain
sentimental attachment towards persons of the same sex was not uncommon."[84] A signal example is Shakespeare, who "devoted the impassioned and profound poetry of his sonnets to commemorate an
attachment of this kind, which we cannot question was wholly divested of any unworthy alloy" (223).[85] Pederastic and Renaissance
attachment are also associated in one of the "Fragments Connected
with *Epipsychidion*":

> If any should be curious to discover
> Whether to you I am a friend or lover,
> Let them read Shakespeare's sonnets, taking thence
> A whetstone for their dull intelligence
> . . . or let them guess
> How Diotima, the wise prophetess,
> Instructed the instructor, and why he
> Rebuked the infant spirit of melody
> On Agathon's sweet lips. (97-105)

Shelley concedes that where the form of such attachments is grasped
but not their substance, they may quickly degenerate into something
less innocent, into "licentiousness" and gross perversion, as happened
with the ancient Romans in the last years of the Republic, or with the
English during the reign of Charles II (222-223). He will not allow,
however, that in the two golden ages of man's history sentimental
attachment could have been anything other than disinterested.

The *Discourse* and "On Friendship" are linked not only thematical-
ly, but also verbally. Phraseological echoes rebound between the two
essays, most strikingly in the passages describing male love or friendship. The sentimental attachments of male love—"wholly divested of
any unworthy alloy"—become in male friendship, "wholly divested of
the smallest alloy of sensual intermixture," "exempt from the smallest
alloy of sensuality." Both essays are thus describing the same experience. But the echoes reverberate even further, reaching out to embrace *A Defence of Poetry* in such a way as to bring all three essays
directly into line with a governing principle of Shelley's thought, the
universal omnipotence of pleasure-pain. He distinguishes in the *Defence* between two sorts of pleasure, one "durable, universal, and
permanent," the other "transitory and particular." The former arises

from whatever "strengthens and purifies the affections, enlarges the imagination, and adds spirit to sense," and only the production and assurance of this pleasure deserves the name of "true utility." Unfortunately, because of some "inexplicable defect of harmony in the constitution of human nature," this pleasure generally does not come unmixed; "the pain of the inferior is frequently connected with the pleasure of the superior portions of our being." But some experiences are exempt from this limitation, and among these is "the delight of love and friendship," a pleasure "often wholly unalloyed" (VII.133).

Love and friendship become synonymous precisely at the level of the higher hedonism. So long as love retains an "alloy of sensual intermixture," so long does it retain an element of the "inferior" portion of the being and thus risks the almost inevitable intrusion of pain. This is because the demands of sense introduce an ineluctable particle of self. Love on this level cannot be wholly disinterested. Yet disinterestedness is the highest of all pleasures, as Shelley had learned from Godwin, because it contains no admixture of pain, and disinterestedness is the essence of friendship.[86] Therefore, only as love leaves behind the burr of self and merges its identity with friendship does it raise itself to the plane of pleasure unalloyed and become lasting. It is precisely because of their essential identity at this level that Shelley can describe love and friendship as a single pleasure, "*the* delight of love and friendship," and find no difficulty in translating Greek love into romantic friendship. A people accustomed to seeking only the highest species of pleasure in every other domain of experience would scarcely content itself with an inferior pleasure, involving "images of pain and horror," in the crowning experience of all.[87]

Shelley's exact meaning can be detected in the startling simile with which he concludes the statuary note on the Bacchus and Ampelus. The flowing proportions of the Bacchus seem a sort of voluptuous music which enfolds the soul and leaves it in "soft astonishment of a satisfaction; like the pleasure of love with one whom we most love, which having taken away desire, leaves pleasure, sweet pleasure" (VI.319-320). This is that unalloyed pleasure which comes from a love whose self-interested physical demands have for the moment been allayed and the lovers can relax in each other's presence as if they were simply affectionate friends. Shelley viewed modern schoolboy attachment in the same light. The difference between the Greek relationship and the modern is that in the modern the archetypal attraction, though still intense, has never consciously reached the physical level except in the harmless guise of an aesthetic appreciation of the loved one's beauty, cemented by an innocent kiss or two, and thus is by its nature disinterested, free from the claims of self. The Greek relationship, while not so innocent, preserved its essential purity by restricting the claims of the self to spontaneous sexual release, freeing the loved one from having to submit to onerous physical demands.

Strengthening Shelley's equation between Greek love and the doctrine of the higher hedonism was the *Symposium*. The verbal affinities between the Shelleyan Eros and the Platonic indicate that the poet had the dialogue in mind when working out his own distinctions, though he begins well up the scale of the philosopher's erotic calculus rather than at the bottom. According to the dialogue's prophetess, when a man "by the right method of boy-loving" ascends step by step from particular beauties to general until he descries at last the wondrous vision of essential beauty itself timeless and unchanging, then will he find it "truly worthwhile to live." This beauty, once glimpsed, "will outshine your gold and your vesture, your beautiful boys and striplings, whose aspect now so astounds you and makes you and many another, at the sight and constant society of your darlings, ready to do without either food or drink if that were any way possible, and only gaze upon and have their company."[88] Revealing the exact point where the Platonic Eros and the Shelleyan connect, she concludes that a man who has "the fortune to look upon essential beauty entire, pure and unalloyed; not infected with the flesh and colour of humanity, and ever so much more of mortal trash . . . is destined to win the friendship of Heaven; he, above all men, is immortal."[89] In these words the doctrine of the higher hedonism, the pursuit of pleasure unalloyed, and the doctrine of eternal Forms, the ascent to that "beauty absolute" which is at once the ultimate resting place in the Platonic quest for reality and the culmination of the Greek experience of love, momentarily coincide.

Because of the archetypal identity of love and friendship at the highest level, Shelley uses the terms interchangeably in his last work. In *Epipsychidion*, love and friendship are one and the same, which explains why there is no incongruity in both Socrates and Christ defending free love, as they do in the poem's drafts. What they are defending is *philia*, friendship, fraternity.[90] Thus in the poem proper "free love" becomes "True Love"—that is, love founded on the pleasures of "true utility," which are unalloyed, universal, and permanent. The Platonic as well as the utilitarian sources of the language are evident: this love involves a separation of the "baser from the nobler; the impure/And frail, from what is clear and must endure."[91] Only when one divides up or shares this sort of "pleasure and love and thought" does one end up with more than one started with and have something that endures. But the other love, based on the senses with their "suffering and dross," is easily diminished when divided, until it is "consumed away" altogether.[92] It is the lower pleasure of the *Defence*, "transitory and particular." In sum, Shelley's free love doctrine has evolved into a defense of disinterested love or romantic friendship. Thus what he felt for Emilia Viviani is what he had felt for his friend at school or Hogg at college or what the Greek pederasts felt for each other in the gymnasium, "a profound and sentimental attachment," free from the least taint of sensuality, "disdain[ing] all thoughts but those of an elevated and imaginative character," because an expression of the higher hedonism.

The difficulty was that while love and friendship both participated in the same psychological archetype and, on the level of both the higher hedonism and the upper reaches of the Platonic Eros, were identical, this archetype did not exclude the senses. One might disdain all thoughts but those of an elevated and imaginative character. Yet like it or not, everyone inherits at birth a bodily "disguise," as Shelley's Rousseau dolefully explains in *The Triumph of Life*, which is subject to the world's "corruption," too often staining with its sensual alloy the pure light of the spirit (201–205). However much Shelley might resist it, there was a flesh-and-blood poet who yearned for more than romantic friendship in the society of an Emilia Viviani or a Jane Williams, just as there was a real-life Plato not content solely with the disembodied pleasures of Platonic love. While the object of both men was to leave the lowest level of the archetype behind, the level of "dull mortality" in the words of *Epipsychidion* (389), and achieve the plane of abiding value, this was perhaps not possible for "spirits cased in flesh and blood," and both men were condemned to atone for the joys of the lower self, "all that was mortal" in the explanation of *The Triumph of Life* (254), through pain and sorrow.

That Shelley believed Plato's practice fell short of the Platonic ideal is evident from *The Triumph of Life* where the philosopher is depicted as one of those chained to the Car of Life, expiating "the joy and woe his master knew not" because the "star [Aster] that ruled his doom was far too fair—/And Life. . ./Conquered that heart by love which gold or pain/Or age or sloth or slavery could subdue not" (254–259). In 1814 Shelley had read and annotated Diogenes Laertius' *Lives of Eminent Philosophers*, which reports Plato's love—and not just Platonic—for a number of handsome youths, among whom are Dion, Phaedrus, Agathon, and Aster (III.29). The poet was doubly familiar with this account because the same "Life of Plato" was appended to his

Bipont edition of the philosopher's *Works*. From this account he translated two Platonic epigrams, addressed to Aster and Agathon, the second of which describes kissing which is no mere schoolboys'. The philosopher's relations with his pupils thus could not have been wholly disinterested.[93] This did not mean that the lofty ideals of the dialogues were counterfeit, however, or impossible of attainment. There was still the example of Socrates, the spectacle of whose supremely disinterested love for the seductive Alcibiades, even under the most extreme provocation, shone forth from the *Symposium* (217-220). It was doubtless on the basis of the dialogue that Socrates was granted the instant glorification denied to the pupil in *The Triumph of Life* (128-135,255), Shelley's last will and testament on love. Free from the "pollutions of mortality and all the colours and vanities of human life," the master was one with the "true beauty simple and divine" and unalloyed.

This view took some defending, as Shelley was well aware. Only three years earlier it had been severely challenged in two of his country's leading journals. "In a late number of the Quarterly Review," Shelley had written at the time to Leigh Hunt, "I observe an attack on the character of Socrates, which appearing to proceed from the pen of an accomplished scholar gave me the severer pain. A portion of Cumberland's Observer is dedicated to the same purpose of defaming that illustrious person by taking advantage against him of a change which has been operated in certain conventional notions of morals, which he is accused, but as I feel myself prepared to prove, falsely accused, of having violated" (L.II.145). The *Quarterly Review* article, by Thomas Mitchell, was occasioned by a translation of Friedrich von Schlegel's *Lectures* (1818). Mitchell paints a portrait of Socrates drawn from a detailed knowledge of Plato's dialogues as well as a number of other ancient sources. Since his object is to account for Aristophanes' satiric portrait in *The Clouds*, he attempts to show the philosopher as he must have appeared to his contemporaries, warts and all. "On the side of manners and morals," Mitchell concludes, as opposed to "intellect," the Socrates who comes down to us in history leaves something to be desired "both in purity and dignity."[94]

A far more damning indictment was Richard Cumberland's account in the *Observer*, originally published in 1807-1808 but reprinted in *The British Essayists* for 1819. Cumberland notes that the philosopher's character was not so "sacred" in his own day as it has since become, it now being considered sacrilege to impugn the "unspotted purity" of Socrates. But the truth is that the school of Socrates grew in such disrepute because of "the infamous characters of many of his disciples, and of the disgraceful attachments he was known to have," and it was at one time virtually deserted. Of Alcibiades, Cumberland comments, "the stories of Socrates' attachment to him are such as need not be enlarged upon; they obtain so generally, that he was vulgarly called Alcibiades' Silenus." Popular opinion viewed the relationship as being of "the impurest nature."[95]

For Shelley this charge was the grossest slander, a defamation of one whom he firmly believed "to have been the author of some of the most elevated truths of ethical philosophy" and to have personally presented "a grand & simple model of much of what we can conceive, & more than in any other instance we have seen realized, of all that is eminent & excellent in man" (L.II.145-146). Shelley took his stand with the Socrates of the *Symposium* and the *Phaedrus* rather than the Socrates of "coarse" Aristophanes, though the only defense he ever got round to writing was *The Triumph of Life*.[96] What had happened meanwhile to his earlier confident assumption of the "innumerable" instances of disinterested pederastic practice "among that exalted and refined people" can only be guessed.

7

Love's Dominion

EVEN THE EXAMPLE of Socrates, insofar as it hypostatized the highest ideals of the Greek Eros, was still a far cry from incorporating the standard of amatory behavior betokening the Shelleyan ideal. And though the sage's great disciple could be considered one of mankind's mightiest exponents of Eros, whatever his practice—"Love . . . found a worthy poet in Plato alone of all the ancients" (VII.128)—his testimony could not stand as the subject's last word. For idealize it as one might, this love had its origin in the lust for boys. Intercourse *between* the sexes was banished to the service of the common or popular Aphrodite, a goddess inspiring a love with no discrimination, such as is seen in "the meaner sort of men" who "love women as well as boys" and prize "the body more than the soul." An erotic ideal which, however refined, left no room for the sentimental love of women was hardly one to appeal to the poet's imagination under the best of circumstances. But when rooted in the systematic depreciation of womankind, it was bound to be judged not merely imperfect, but positively mistaken. Accordingly, in his disquisition on Greek love, Shelley follows up the eulogy of the exemplary disinterestedness and self-control allegedly exercized by the Greek male in his practice of boy-love with a scathing assault on the Greek Eros as a principle. "Represent this passion as you will," he insists, "there is something totally irreconcilable in its cultivation to the beautiful order of social life, to an equal participation in which all human beings have an indefeasible claim and from which half of the human race by the Greek arrangement were excluded" (223).

This is the familiar argument from utility. A pleasure not geared to producing the greatest happiness of the greatest number is a priori evil. Even if Greek pederastic practice were predominantly disinterested, as he believed, it was still far too limited and discriminatory in its expression to warrant social encouragement, denying to one half of humanity the joys of sentimental gratification that were its birthright. But the basic problem was that Greek love, even if disinterested, still repressed a physical component, and to this degree it was a sexual perversion. In modern Europe, on the contrary, "the sexual and intellectual claims, by the more equal cultivation of the two sexes, so far converge towards one point as to produce, in the attempt to unite them, no gross violation in the established nature of man" (221), and thus the sentimental archetype can fulfill itself without going astray, especially where the "intellectual females of England & Germany" are its object.[1]

It was to this rerouting of sentiment and the conditions responsible for it—together with the abolition of personal slavery—that Shelley looked for the only real evidence of moral progress since the age of Pericles (220). The sexual "practices and customs of modern Europe" are "essentially different from and incomparably less pernicious" than those of either ancient Greece or Rome—"however remote," the visionary in him adds, "from what an enlightened mind cannot fail to desire as the future destiny of human beings" (221). Shelley's efforts to account for this startling metamorphosis, one that has drawn the interest of modern social and literary historians likewise, tie together many of the major themes of his philosophy of sexual relationship.

At its most rudimentary, Shelley's answer lay in the comparative liberation of the female intellect and personality which may be assumed to have taken place since classical times. This liberation was far from complete, as he was unhappily aware. Still, there was no longer the immense gap that had separated the sexes in ancient Athens. This gap had been narrowed to the point where, apparently for the first time in history, women were capable of eliciting respect as individuals, not simply as breeders or domestics. Coupled with the normal biological instinct, this change rendered them the focus of sentimental or romantic feelings, connate in the human psyche, which were formerly reserved for men. No longer must such feelings seek "a compensation and a substitute." Women were able to provide a measure of amatory gratification at the imaginative and intellectual levels as well as the sensual.

But if this was the simplest explanation for the rechanneling of the sentimental impulse, the problem went deeper, as Shelley recognized. Conceding woman's increasing intellectual and social emancipation, the more difficult question of accounting for the complex course this development had taken remained unexplored. The historical forces behind woman's growing freedom were not easy to pinpoint, nor were the psychological and sociological roots implicit in her increased erotic elevation. Shelley admitted he had no satisfactory answers to these questions. Nevertheless, during the course of a brief survey in the

Discourse of developing sexual attitudes between ancient and modern times, he hazards a few possibilities.

His investigation takes as its starting point the same sharply drawn picture of sexual inequality in ancient Athens outlined earlier in the *Discourse*, the men receiving all the mainfold benefits that a highly refined classical *paideia* could bestow, while the women, "so far as intellect is concerned," were "educated as slaves" and hence "raised but a few degrees in all that related to moral or intellectual excellence above the condition of savages" (221). Yet if classical Greece marked the absolute nadir of woman's position in Western society, the subsequent "gradations" in her history "present us with slow improvement." For example, Roman women seemingly held a "higher consideration in society and were esteemed almost as the equal partners with their husbands in the regulation of domestic economy and the education of their children" (221).

Such faith was doubtless over-sanguine, for woman's progress has not been uniformly upward. Nevertheless Shelley's estimation of her relative eminence in the Roman world, at least in the late Republic and early Empire, is not exaggerated. Authorities are nearly all agreed that her status was certainly far superior to that in ancient Greece. There is in fact reason to believe that woman's condition attained to a height in Rome which it was not to reach again in the Western world until modern times. Only in our own era has woman's position caught up with and surpassed the ancient Roman's.[2]

In view of this freedom, it might be supposed that the Roman matron occupied a lofty erotic status, that she was the frequent object of idealized passion or romantic sentiment. But this was not the case. Despite woman's growing equality, neither of the sexes appears to have been in the least moved to refine or spiritualize its physical relations. Authorities are virtually unanimous in agreeing that Roman eroticism gives little evidence of ever having risen above a rather low level of sensuality.[3]

Traditionally this curious absence of higher feeling has been blamed on the Roman character. The Roman is "by nature a coarse sensualist," explains Otto Kiefer; "in a sense he is brutish and savage." The Romans "lack the spiritual equipment for the finer types of love." W. E. H. Lecky speaks of the "extreme coarseness of the Roman disposition [which] prevented sensuality from assuming that aesthetic character which had made it in Greece the parent of art and had very profoundly modified its influence."[4] Shelley too recognized this coarseness and found it repellent. The Romans were "licentious" and, in a way the Greeks could never be, "brutally obscene" (222-223).

Love's Dominion

Under the Empire, "Refinement in arts and letters, became subservient to lust . . . sensual pleasures occupied the interest of mankind," and the socially elite became habituated "to the most monstrous and complicated perversities of appetite and sentiment . . . man lived like a beast of prey among his fellowmen." The Roman bedchamber was a "chasm for devils," where people kept "darkest revels."[5]

Yet paradoxically, despite this unrelieved sexual barbarism, Roman women were much further along the road to full intellectual and social emancipation than their Athenian counterparts. Shelley's problem was how to account for the low level of Roman sexual relationship, because his argument seemed to demand just the opposite, the appearance of a more refined, more sentimental species of eroticism. The answer resides in what he considered the rooted inferiority of Roman culture and intellectual life generally. Granted that under the Empire the sexes were tolerably equal, but this equality actually amounted to little. Nothing in the character of either of the sexes was likely to awaken the intellectual admiration or love of the other. The two were united on a dead level of intellectual mediocrity. It is true that Shelley believed the archetype of romantic or sentimental eroticism constituted a permanent fixture in the human psyche, rather than being a creation of environment. But the influence of environment was nonetheless of first importance. Were the archetype to receive other than incidental expression, the prerequisite was a society incorporating relatively refined cultural ideals, and one to which the cultivation of the higher elements of personality was therefore not peripheral but central. Roman civilization was plainly not of this high caliber. In the ancient world such a distinction was reserved solely for classical Greece, to which Rome stood as the pale "shadow," in the words of *A Defence of Poetry* (VII.125). And when the Romans sought to imitate or "mirror" the Greeks directly, the inevitable result was coarse travesty, for with rare exceptions the inner spirit of Greek *paideia* escaped the Roman mind.[6] Consequently the Romans got the sort of love they deserved.

The question for Shelley was what therefore took place in the ensuing epoch to make possible the sentimentalization of erotic relations between the sexes characteristic of modern times. He was familiar with the tradition, widespread in his day, that the refining of heterosexual passion occurred in the heart of the Middle Ages, in eleventh- and twelfth-century France, a period when neither the general level of culture nor the position of all but a few women could by any stretch of the imagination be pictured as fundamentally elevated. Yet it was precisely at this juncture that the worship of woman seemingly found encouragement as a social ideal and the sentimental love of her was celebrated in story and song. A whole literature of heterosexual passion, known today as "courtly love," magnificently flowered in this apparently arid soil.

Shelley was himself perplexed at the development. While noticing a variety of possible explanations, drawn from contemporary scholarly theory, he conceded in the end that there was much to learn before a satisfying answer could be given. But that the attainment of such an answer is of real psychological and sociological importance, he had no doubt. Thus regardless of whether "the difference . . . in the regulations and the sentiments respecting sexual intercourse" between the ancient world and the modern originates from "some imperfect influence of the doctrines of Jesus Christ, who alleges the absolute and unconditional equality of all human beings, or from the institutions of chivalry, or from a certain fundamental difference of physical nature existing in the Celts, or from a combination of all or any of these causes acting on each other," there is no denying that this question is "worthy of voluminous investigation" (219-220).

That the question continued to intrigue his imagination is evident from *A Defence* where he returns to it *in extenso*, having in the meantime discovered the apparently central importance of the troubadour love lyric. He finds that the subjugation of women in ancient Greece, one of the "many imperfections" that "deformed" the society, was subsequently eradicated from the customs and institutions of modern society by the "poetry" or moral imagination inhering in chivalry and Christianity. The "true relation to each other by the sexes into which humankind is distributed" has now become "less misunderstood; and if the error which confounded diversity with inequality of the powers of the two sexes has been partially recognized in the opinions and institutions of modern Europe, we owe the great benefit to the worship of which Chivalry was the law, and the poets the prophets." Chivalric poets created "forms of opinion and action never before conceived, which copied into the imagination of men became as generals to the bewildered armies of their thoughts."[7] Chivalry in its turn was apparently owing to the survival of "the poetry in the doctrines of Jesus Christ and the mythology and institutions of the Celtic conquerors of the Roman empire," following the collapse of the "exhausted" Greco-Roman world. The result was the abolition of "personal and domestic slavery and the emancipation of women from a great part of the degrading restraints of antiquity." It was not, however, until the eleventh century that the effects of these changes began to make themselves felt, at which time the "freedom of women produced the poetry of sexual love." Then it was that love became "a religion the idols of whose worship were ever present" (VII.118-129).

These reflections ignite one of those spectacular bursts of impassioned and figurative rhetoric encountered whenever Shelley's imagination dwells on the unsurpassable delights of heterosexual communion. Thus, he marvels, it was as if "the statues of Apollo," his aesthetic ideal, and "the Muses had been endowed with life and motion and had walked forth among their worshippers; so that earth became peopled by the inhabitants of a diviner world. The familiar appearance and proceedings of life became wonderful and heavenly, and a paradise was created as out of the wrecks of Eden" (VII.128). Shelley sketches the astonishing growth of this new kind of religion, how it took root and flourished in the pages of medieval literature and was carried throughout Europe in the magnificent love poetry of the Renaissance, ultimately creating those romantic attitudes woven into the very fabric of Western emotional patterns. First there were the delicate love lyrics of the French troubadours, the "Provençal Trouveurs, or inventors," as Shelley calls them, mixing up the troubadours with their northern France imitators, the *trouvères*, or *trouveurs*, as they were sometimes termed.[8] Then there were the rapturous *canzone* of Petrarch, verses which are "as spells which unseal the inmost enchanted fountains of the delight which is in the grief of love," and which make it "superfluous to explain how the gentleness and the elevation of mind connected with those sacred emotions can render men more amiable, and generous, and wise, and lift them out of the dull vapors of the little world of self."[9] Above all, there was Dante, "who understood the secret things of love even more than Petrarch," whose *Paradiso* is "a perpetual hymn of everlasting love" and whose "apotheosis of Beatrice in Paradise, and the gradations of his own love and loveliness, by which as by steps he feigns himself to have ascended to the throne of the Supreme Cause, is the most glorious imagination of modern poetry."[10] Shelley calls the roll of that great company—Ariosto, Tasso, Spenser, Shakespeare, Calderón, Rousseau—who straight up through modern times have "celebrated the dominion of love, planting as it were trophies in the human mind of that sublimest victory over sensuality and force."

Scarcely anyone has written more beautifully or excitingly of these matters than Shelley. Yet once the witchery of his language has released its spell, his argument loses force when set against the results of modern scholarship. As Shelley hoped, investigation has been "voluminous." And while the underlying problem has yet to yield up a fully convincing solution—indeed "there are almost as many theories about 'the origins of courtly love' as there are scholars who have studied it"—enough has been learned to render doubtful the hypotheses proposed by Shelley.[11] These can now persuade only on the basis of largely untenable assumptions.

The view, for instance, that there was something inherent in the "mythology and institutions of the Celtic conquerors of the Roman empire," or even in their physiological makeup, which predisposed them to a more elevated concept of women than existed elsewhere in antiquity, though once popular, is no longer generally accepted. It rested on nothing more solid than certain passages of dubious reliability in Tacitus' *Germania* praising the sexual morality of the Teutonic barbarians, such as that the women "are the witnesses that a man reverences most, to them he looks for his highest praise [in battle]."[12] From these attitudes were supposed to have arisen the sentiments later enshrined in chivalry and courtly love. Shelley read *Germania* in 1816, having earlier found Tacitus' account summarized in Gibbon, and it is conceivable that this summary caused him to turn to the original.[13]

But for the direct linking of the Teutonic attitude toward women with the development of chivalry and the doctrines of medieval love Shelley would have had to go beyond either Gibbon or of course Tacitus. The idea was much in the air by the end of the eighteenth century, and he could have encountered it, usually subsumed under the name of Germanic "gallantry" to women, in any number of places. The English medievalists Thomas Percy, Richard Hurd, and Thomas Warton, for example, subscribed to it.[14] While there is no record of Shelley's having read any of their work, their contemporary eminence makes it probable that he was familiar with the writings of at least one of them. His most likely source was Continental, however, not English. Paul-Henri Mallet's *Northern Antiquities* was the most influential contemporary statement of the "northern" thesis, and it is Mallet's version that Shelley seems to have followed specifically, though whether at firsthand or indirectly remains uncertain. Mallet argues that the northern "Celts," as opposed to the southern nations (Greeks, Romans, Egyptians), "did not so much consider the other sex as made for their pleasure, as to be their equals and companions." The chivalric or knightly service of women originated with these tribes, he believes, and this same spirit produced "that polite gallantry so peculiarly observable in our manners" which—in language almost forecasting Shelley's—"unites the lasting charms of sentiment, regard and friendship with the fleeting fire of love, which tempers and animates one by the other, adds to their number, power and duration, and which cherishes and unfolds sensibility, that most choice gift of nature, without which neither decorum, propriety, chaste friendship nor true generosity can exist among men." It would be unnecessary to prove, he concludes, "that we are not indebted for this manner of thinking to the ancient Romans. We may appeal for this to all who known any thing of their character."[15]

As Bishop Percy points out in the English edition of the *Antiquities*, Mallet's otherwise valuable account is marred by the repeated confusion of the Celtic with the Gothic or Germanic tribes: this "opinion . . . has been a great source of mistake . . . to many learned writers of the ancient history of Europe; viz that of supposing the ancient Gauls and Germans, the Britons and Saxons, to have been all originally one and the same people; thus confounding the antiquities of the Gothic and Celtic nations," when in fact these were "two distinct people, very unlike in their manners, customs, religion and laws."[16] Shelley ordered the English version, but if he read it, he ignored Percy, who makes the correction of this error his especial object in the Preface and notes, and in the text he substitutes Gothic or Germanic wherever Mallet uses Celtic.[17]

Whatever Shelley's source, the fact remains that whether the tribes are called Celtic, Germanic, Teutonic, or Gothic, this northern theory of origins, once so widespread, has largely disappeared from view. As pointed out by the modern medievalist Sidney Painter, Tacitus' picture "is in accord neither with what one would expect from a people in the state of civilization which had been reached by the Germans nor with what we know of the Germans themselves four centuries later." The latter were a "brutal, lustful people who objected to adultery with their wives or violence to their daughters as serious infringements on their property rights."[18] C. S. Lewis explains that "what Tacitus describes is a primitive awe of women as uncanny and probably prophetic beings, which is as remote from our comprehension as the primitive reverence for lunacy or the primitive horror of twins." Consequently there is no real reason to connect it with the medieval service of women.[19]

Neither does Shelley's guess as to the influence of the "doctrines of Jesus Christ" fare much better in the light of the latest opinion. It was customary during Shelley's day to derive the medieval elevation of women not only from the peculiar temperament of the Germans but from the spread of Christianity, the combination of the two producing chivalry and a new concept of love. Typical of this thinking is Schlegel's *Lectures*, which is probably the immediate origin of Shelley's speculations, especially since he was reading it not long before sitting down to write the *Discourse*. With the triumph of Christianity, Schlegel explains, the ancient world was regenerated from "its state of exhaustion and debasement." This development, when added to the "rough, but honest heroism of the northern conquerors . . . gave rise to chivalry," which was associated with "a new and purer spirit of love, an inspired homage for genuine female worth . . . now revered as the acme of human excellence, and maintained by religion itself under the image of a virgin mother, infus[ing] into all hearts a mysterious sense of the purity of love." Out of these conditions arose a poetry "founded on adoration of women and a very great freedom in their social lives."[20] Most of Shelley's hypotheses are here: the injection of a fresh vitality and a new spirit into the exhausted Latin peoples by the conquering northern tribes, the diffusion of a more humane and equitable notion of the worth of the individual through the triumph of Christianity, the formulation of a chivalric code of courtly virtues arising from the combination of these two developments, and the emergence of a poetry of sexual love founded on the consequent freedom of women, all uniting to produce a purer concept of love, with woman as its object. The only point lacking in Schlegel is Shelley's insistence, following the French school, on "Celtic" rather than "Germanic" as the proper label for the conquering barbarians. Conversely, there in nothing in Shelley's account about the cult of the Virgin. Otherwise the two explanatons are substantially the same.

No longer, however, is it possible to view the victory of Christianity as a victory for feminism. Authorities are for the most part agreed that the teachings of the early church intensified rather than softened the endemic misogyny of the ancient world. Certainly patristic literature does little to encourage an idealistic concept of woman.[21] Nor was this misogynistic bias lessened to any significant degree by the ideology or practice of the medieval church.[22] Scholastic philosophy underscored woman's biological inferiority, and the Pauline doctrine of male headship governed man's domestic relations with woman. The wife's obedience to her husband was absolute.[23] In one respect Christian sexual practice represented a change from antiquity. Pederastic relationships were effectively outlawed. The opposite sex became the sole legitimate outlet for the sexual impulse.[24] But this did not mean that the church encouraged love between the sexes. The object of marriage was procreation. Romantic passion was an idolatrous misdirection of energies which ought to be absorbed exclusively in love of the divine.[25] Moreover the notion, once common, that Mariolatry had something to do with the changed attitude toward woman, thus marking a feminist plus for Christianity, is now viewed dubiously by most authorities. If anything, the worship of the Virgin was colored by medieval love poetry and not the other way around.[26]

Even though Shelley was familiar with the depreciation of women by the early church, as outlined in Gibbon, and with their Pauline subjection, as established in the New Testament, he nonetheless embraced the possibility that the spread of Christian belief had an ameliorating effect on woman's condition. In his view the growth of institutionalized Christianity simply obscured the fundamental Christian teaching of the "absolute and unconditional equality of all human beings" (220).[27] This "imperfect influence," he assumes, was at work beneath the murky surface of early medieval life helping to raise the position of women. The addition of the mythology and institutions of the Celtic conquerors of the Roman Empire led to the development of medieval chivalry and the freedom of women, events mirrored in the sudden efflorescence of the poetry of "sexual," or "courtly," love.

A fundamental objection to this theory, based on modern investigation, is the lack of evidence that courtly poetry, or for that matter the chivalric service of woman, represents an accurate reflection of woman's status in the Middle Ages. "My knowledge of the chivalric age is small," admitted Shelley to Godwin in 1812, adding confidently, "Do not conceive that I intend it to remain so" (*L*.I.303). In the following years, Shelley did expand his knowledge of the age considerably. About the institution of chivalry itself he probably relied primarily on Gibbon and on Hume's *History of England*. Gibbon typically traces the institution back to "Tacitus and the woods of Germany" and explains that, according to the laws of chivalry, the knight as "champion of God and the ladies . . . devoted himself to speak the truth; to maintain the right; to protect the distressed; to practice *courtesy*, a virtue less familiar to the ancients."[28] Hume notes merely that in the Middle Ages "ideas of chivalry infected the writings, conversation, and behaviour of men . . . and even after they were, in a great measure, banished by the revival of learning, they left modern gallantry and the point of honour, which still maintain their influence, and are the genuine offspring of those ancient affectations."[29]

Both accounts derive from the French antiquarian La Curne de Sainte-Palaye, whose *Mémoires sur l'ancienne chevalerie* (1751) and *Histoire littéraire des troubadours* (1774) were the definitive treatments of chivalry and the troubadour love lyric during the eighteenth century. It is thus of first importance that Saint-Palaye interpreted chivalry in the light of an authentic institution. "The trouble with Sainte-Palaye's view of chivalry," notes his biographer Lionel Gossman, "was not simply that he took the romances and the theoretical manuals" that made up his sources literally, but also that "he took the code as it was elaborated in late manuals and apologies to be the original *goal* of chivalry, and he therefore assumed that the 'laws' described in them were intended to govern a real *institution,*" instead of being "devised . . . by later generations to provide a rationale for the social form or title which chivalry had become."[30] Sainte-Palaye assumes that chivalry was responsible for the poetic attitudes which followed—that the literature of the medieval love lyric and romance constituted a direct reflection of once living social ideals: "From the precepts included in the oath of Chivalry, branch forth all those morals spread throughout the works of the ancient French poets and romance writers"; "the poets and romance writers . . . *were the echos of the historians.*" Life and literature merge as one.[31]

This view dominated the literary scene by the end of the century, and Shelley was clearly one of its adherents. At the same time his direct knowledge of the medieval "poetry of sexual love" was sketchy. Besides confusing the *troubadours* with their northern imitators the *trouvères,* so far as is known he never read the writings of either. In fact he appears to have been unacquainted with any medieval French love poetry at firsthand.[32] His only direct contact with the "system of courtly love," as it was later styled, was through Chaucer's *Troilus and Criseyde,* and this contact came late.[33] His reading in courtly literature was apparently confined almost entirely to the Italian *stil nuovists.*

Precisely how Shelley came to know of the troubadours and their contribution thus remains obscure. There is no evidence that he read Sainte-Palaye, either his account of chivalry or his history of the troubadours. The principal repository of knowledge in England about the troubadours prior to Sainte-Palaye was Warton's *History of English Poetry* (1774), which Shelley could have read at some point in his career. However, Warton takes a dim view of the troubadours—"an idle and unsettled race," "the fables of the Provençal poets"—little consonant with Shelley's picture of them.[34] Shelley could also have read Hazlitt's review of Simonde de Sismondi's *De la littérature du Midi de l'Europe* (1813), from which Hazlitt quoted liberally. Sismondi gives a full account of troubadour poetry and the ideals of chivalry, but unlike Shelley, he sees no relationship between them and feudal reality.[35]

It is probable, therefore, that Shelley's knowledge of the subject, such as it was, proceeded from sources less scholarly—from Hunt, or Hogg, or Peacock, or even Southey, all of whom knew something, however inaccurate, about the "chivalric age," which they idealized, and the troubadours.[36] Shelley's *A Defence*, where he first mentions the Provençal love lyric, is written in response to Peacock's *The Four Ages of Poetry*, which glancingly refers to "the songs of the troubadours."[37] But unlike Shelley, Peacock does not confuse *troubadour* with *trouvère*.

Shelley's knowledge of terminology is indeed hazy enough to suggest conversation as a source, rather than printed authority. Conceivably Coleridge's 1818 lectures on literature were an influence. Shelley could have attended these or at least heard them reported.[38] The third lecture would have struck him as especially interesting, since it traces in broad terms the development of medieval and Renaissance love literature from its birthplace in the feudal courts of twelfth-century Provence. Coleridge notes the "love of the marvellous, the deeper sensibility, the characteristic spirit of sentiment and courtesy," which distinguished the "Gothic conquerors" of the Roman Empire and set them off from the Latin peoples whose culture they had supplanted, making possible a chivalric sensibility new to Western history. Coleridge also distinguishes between "the Troubadours or Love-singers of Provence" and "the Trouveurs, Trouveres, or Norman-French poets," who "merited their name of . . . inventors," and traces the development of a chivalric sensibility through Dante, Petrarch, Ariosto, Tasso, Chaucer, and Spenser.[39] It may be that when Shelley came to write of these matters himself, the remarks of his esteemed fellow poet served as his model, albeit the lecturer's exact terminology had become a trifle garbled in his memory.

It is also conceivable that Shelley debated these matters with Byron, who was fairly learned in the subject, more so than Shelley, though he took a quite different view. So different was Byron's view that it might even have generated some heat between the two poets. Characteristically Byron, in an Addition to the Preface of *Childe Harold's Pilgrimage*, attacks chivalric or courtly sentiment for women as a myth, claiming that the reality was far different. The Addition was prompted by a review of the poem in the *Quarterly Review* criticizing its author for making the Childe's attitude toward women ungallant—"a scoffer at the fair sex"—and thus unknightly and anachronistic.[40] In reply, Byron charges that the "vows of chivalry were no better kept than any other vows whatsoever; and the songs of the Troubadours were not more decent, and certainly were much less refined, than those of Ovid." The supposedly "good old times" were "the most profligate of all centuries . . . So much for chivalry."[41] Obviously Shelley was on the side of the *Quarterly Review* for once, not of Byron. And in this he would have had the support of his age.

History has been on the side of Byron, however. For whatever Shelley's sources, the confident assumption of his day that an emerging "freedom of women" caused "the poetry of sexual love" cannot be sustained in the light of subsequent knowledge. "With regard to the social background," observes Maurice Valency, "all that can be stated with confidence is that we know of nothing in the objective relationships of men and women in the Middle Ages which might conceivably motivate the strain of love-poetry which the troubadours developed in the Midi of France."[42] "Spiritual and canonistic writing, medical treatises, penitentials, letters, chronicles, law codes, court cases, all paint a quite different picture from the poetry," points out John Benton.[43] The courtly code was thus little more than "a veneer," and the romantic passion celebrated in the poetry of courtly love was not a passion at all but merely the rhetoric of a novel literary fashion, having little to do with the love of any real person.[44] In short, the older interpretation probably reversed the true sequence of events. Several centuries would have to pass before the revolutionary attitudes embodied in medieval love poetry could take hold as normal sexual practice.

Yet even if Shelley's efforts to explain exactly what went on at the bottom of the dark gulf separating the ancient and modern worlds must in the end be largely rejected in the light of subsequent knowledge, the attempt itself was laudable. A genuine reorganization in the structure of erotic attitudes, making love as it is experienced today a widely different thing from what it was in antiquity, unquestionably began to disclose itself in the Middle Ages, even though not in just the way or for just the reasons he supposed. Moreover, if Shelley was unable to piece together a fully satisfactory explanation, neither has posterity. The problem still baffles solution.[45]

In any case, he advanced his hypotheses only tentatively, submitting them as the jumping-off point for further scholarly inquiry. In the considerations adduced he was naturally influenced by prevailing scholarly theory, which sought at all costs to preserve the apparent sincerity of emotion expressed in courtly literature. With such an aim, Shelley would have been in entire sympathy. He could have small use for mere poeticizing, for poetry that was not a cry from the heart. His own romantic sensibility would in all likelihood have found the conventions of medieval love poetry singularly convincing. He always personally yielded "chivalric submission" to "the great general laws of antique courtesy," an obedience that was in fact his "religion" (L.II.335). Both to raise up and to humble himself before the women in his life was in his case second nature. As he once explained to Hogg of his feelings for Mary: "most sensibly do I perceive the truth of my entire

worthlessness but as depending on another. And I am deeply per-
suaded that thus ennobled, [I shall] become a more true & constant
friend, a more useful lover of mankind, a more ardent asserter of truth
& virtue—above all more consistent, more intelligible more true"
(*L.*I.403). A knight to his lady could have little to add.

Thus predisposed, the poet must have experienced scant difficulty
in embracing the authenticity of the sentiments so enchantingly set
forth in the medieval love poem. Nor is it surprising that he should
have taken these to reflect the authentic facts of feudal experience. A
society capable of producing the splendid love goddesses hymned in
its romances and songs could only have been a society in which the
women were truly free. To suppose anything otherwise was patently
absurd.

Beyond Shelley's strictly temperamental considerations for assuming courtly literature to give an accurate picture of medieval life
were his deeper ideological grounds for making the assumption. The
upholding of an organic relationship between the poetry of a society
and its manners was indispensable to the preservation of his faith in
the underlying perfectibility of humankind. Were the magnificent love
songs of the Middle Ages a sham, nothing but the false flowers of an
artificial literary convention, there could be no necessary correlation
between the cultural attainments of a society and its inner moral perfection. Shelley's carefully constructed scheme of the increasing refinement of man's erotic instincts would thus collapse, Socrates becoming just another dreary pederast and Dante a common adulterer.
Shelley could not have rested even remotely content with such a
cheerless conclusion.

8

In Defense of Women

DESPITE SHELLEY's confidence in woman's improving erotic status since its degrading nadir in antiquity—"an improvement the most decisive in the regulation of human society"—he recognized that her status in most other respects still left much to be desired (220). While now the object of idealized male desire, she nevertheless remained the auxiliary sex. Thus, in the *Discourse* Shelley broadens his charge against the inequalities of Greek sexual practice to include the very principle of sexual inequality itself, branding it as one unworthy of civilized manners. In this respect not only do the ancient Greeks stand convicted, but so too the moderns, and with much less justification: "This invidious distinction of humankind as a class of beings [of] intellectual nature into two sexes is a remnant of savage barbarism which we have less excuse than they for not having totally abolished." Because of this distinction, half the human race had been excluded from Greek social life. But equal participation in the social life of a community is an "indefeasible claim" of all human beings, protests Shelley, irrespective of sex (223). And modern women were still subject to gross sexual discrimination. The existential realities of their position in fact differed little from those of the ancient Greeks, however greater their freedom of social movement. It would have been nearly as accurate to write of Shelley's own age that inferiority of women was "recognized by law and by opinion" or that women were "educated as slaves," as it was to charge this of the ancient Athenians. Notwithstanding woman's superior erotic status, the system remained broadly patriarchal, woman being confined almost exclusively to the domestic and maternal roles. Crippled by legal disabilities, denied political rights, severely restricted in both economic and educational opportunities, she could no more claim true independence than could her "degraded" sister in ancient Athens. The injustice of such a lot provided the poet with the impetus for his lifelong campaign to elevate woman's social and intellectual status.

Shelley's defense of women is an integral feature of his work, once recognized as such, but generally lost sight of with the apparent winning of women's freedom in the opening decades of the twentieth century.[1] Until a few years ago the feminist element in his work was dismissed as of merely academic interest or overlooked entirely. But with the modern resurgence of feminism, Shelley's championship of women has taken on renewed vitality. His philosophy of sexual relationship anticipates much that is valuable in the latest feminist teaching. Not that all his thinking would pass inspection by the standards of the current woman's movement. He was no more prepared than were Mary Wollstonecraft or William Godwin, his fellow proponents of women, to envisage contraception or abortion as fundamental planks in the feminist platform. In a number of other ways his thinking was limited by the prejudices of his period. Yet of all the major imaginative writers in the language, male or female, he remains to this day the most eloquent advocate of woman's overriding human right, the opportunity to develop her personality with the same freedom as the male. He also holds the distinction of being its first major advocate in literature. His work can be viewed as the earliest deliberate attempt by a writer of the first rank at literary consciousness-raising, with effects extending throughout the nineteenth century.[2] Not only did his work help create a climate of opinion favorable to feminism among the general reading public, but it influenced the history of the movement proper: both the feminist Owenites and John Stuart Mill acknowledged their indebtedness to Shelley's championship of women.[3] Bertrand Russell ranked Shelley with Wollstonecraft and Mill, both of whose contributions are universally acknowledged, as one of the movements founders.[4] The significance of his contribution thus warrants renewed affirmation.

Shelley's earliest experience was largely of women. His father, already middle-aged, remained patriarchally aloof, seldom seeking a more intimate relationship with his son.[5] Throughout childhood Shelley was far closer to his considerably younger and more affectionate mother. A striking beauty, Mrs. Shelley was considered clever with a masculine understanding, although no intellectual, and Shelley not only loved but genuinely admired and respected her.[6] Her example doubtless did much to mold his sympathetic view of women.[7] He was also surrounded by four younger sisters; a brother did not appear on the scene until Shelley was well into adolescence. Until the time he left home for school women were virtually his sole companions and playmates. It was thus an essentially women-centered world that the poet knew for the first ten years of his existence, one lacking, as Kenneth Neill Cameron phrases it, a strong "male ideal" or model.[8]

As a consequence, Shelley developed pronounced feminine interests and personality traits, which were reinforced by a strikingly effeminate morphological structure. Meek-looking, delicate, narrow-chested, beardless, small-featured, long-haired, shrill-voiced, and expressive-eyed, the youthful Shelley could almost be mistaken for a girl. All his life he retained a feminine gentleness and softness which, with the etherealizing of his reputation during the Victorian period, made it possible for subsequent generations to relieve him of his manhood altogether.[9] Yet there was a masculine side to Shelley too, as these qualities have traditionally been defined. He displayed considerable physical and moral courage, intellectual nonconformity, social independence, and a love of learning and the rigors of intellectual debate for their own sake. All his friends emphasized his essential manliness, despite the deceptively girlish appearance and mannerisms. Quite possibly, however, he never completely developed a sense of fixed or exclusive gender identity such as is characteristic of normal sexual development, according to modern research, but retained the dualistic potential of the sexes at birth.[10] This resulted in a lifelong androgynous merging of the traditionally masculine with the traditionally feminine. Lacking a firm sense of gender constancy, he was thus much freer than most people of ordinary sex-typing characteristics and behavior.

It must in any case have been a savage shock when the poet was introduced to the all-male world of the English public school, with its coarseness, insensitivity, sanctioned aggression, and disregard for the rights of others. Medwin remembered that his cousin was made game of for his "girlishness" at Syon House. Provoked or cornered, he would shriek hysterically and fight open-handed, "like a girl in boy's clothes." When flogged, recalls another classmate, he would roll on the floor, "not from pain, but from a sense of the indignity."[11] All his life he could easily identify, or "sympathize" in his terminology, with the indignities heaped upon women by male sexism and brutality. In his own heart he knew what it was to be a woman.

During this time his chief associate and intellectual companion was not one of his schoolmates but his sister Elizabeth, with whom he collaborated on his first literary publication, *Original Poetry* by "Victor and Cazire," and upon whose assistance he relied for his tentative first efforts at combatting religious and social tyranny. Accounting her one of the enlightened, Shelley subsequently destined her for a free love union with his exalted Oxford friend Hogg—testimony to both his high evaluation of her intellectual powers and his belief in her sexual emancipation. Following his expulsion from the university, he was bitterly disappointed to find Elizabeth renege on her liberated views, spurning both Hogg's attentions and his own free-thinking principles. "I will not deceive you," he writes to Hogg in the spring of 1811: "she is lost, lost to every thing, Xtianity has tainted her, she talks of God & Xt . . . A young female, who only once, only for a short space asserted her claim to an unfettered use of reason."[12] Particularly frustrating was that Elizabeth's change of view was dictated solely by prudential concerns: she is "no more a Xtian than I am, but . . . regards as a sacred criterion the opinion of the world" (*L*.I.90). Losing her nerve, Elizabeth retreated back into the bigoted, worldly, narrowly pietistic domain which was the destiny of most women of her class.

Even though Elizabeth was lost, Shelley persisted for several years in nourishing hopes of rescuing his younger sisters from a similar fate. At the same time he maintained a continuing scheme of adopting and educating a girl of his own. These plans came to nothing; but he did succeed in liberating Harriet Westbrook, Mary Godwin, and her stepsister Claire Clairmont. There can be little doubt that in eloping with Harriet, and later Mary, accompainied by Claire, Shelley in part thought of himself as emancipating them from their traditional fate as women.

The experiment with Harriet was ultimately a tragic failure. No more than Elizabeth was she prepared either by birth or upbringing to lead the emancipated existence anticipated by Shelley. But with Mary the experiment was brilliantly successful, primarily owing to her extraordinary heritage. Daughter of the leading radical philosopher of the day and the foremost feminist, she had been educated from birth to meet someone like Shelley on his own terms, and the poet had no intention of letting the opportunity go to waste. In a day when women's education was domestic, ornamental, and heavily larded with religion, Mary and Claire had been nourished on radical social philosophy and drilled in Roman, Greek, and English history. They had been expected to vie with men as their intellectual equals. As remembered by Claire, simple goodness of character and industriousness were not enough to satisfy the standards of the Godwin household; "in our family, if you cannot write an epic poem or novel that by its originality knocks all other novels on the head, you are a despicable creature, not worth acknowledging."[13]

Describing Mary to Hogg shortly after his elopement in 1814, Shelley emphasized the "originality and loveliness" of her character and genius. She was all that his fondest dreams had pictured of womanhood (*L*.I.402). By this he did not mean what was usually understood by womanhood, the conventional ideal of softness, weakness, delicacy, modesty, docility, and ignorance of all but domestic accomplishments. As noted by Janet Dunbar, "Husbands did not as a rule require brains in their wives, they demanded charm, a high sense of domestic duty, admiration for and submission to themselves."[14] Shelley's stress is precisely on Mary's mental strength. It is her intellectual beauty that constitutes the principal source of his satisfaction and solidifies their union. He draws no distinction between her capabilities and his own. At first indeed he feels inferior in this respect, confessing himself "far surpassed in originality, in genuine elevation & magnificence of the intellectual nature." Mary is possessed of the "subtlest & most exquisitely fashioned intelligence"; "among women there is no equal mind" to hers.[15] Moreover, Mary was far from retiring and modest in their courtship; she was the aggressor, going out to meet him more than halfway and taking the lead in declaring her love. In both appearance and actions Mary was at this time the very antithesis of the common womanly ideal; she was mannish in aspect, bold in behavior, unkempt in dress. Nor did she have either domestic accomplishments or any interest in acquiring them. She was "never, like most of her female contemporaries, taught the arts of womanliness," explains her biographer Muriel Spark.[16] But it was exactly this "womanliness" from which Shelley wanted to rescue women. In Mary he thought he saw the promise of what it was possible for woman to become.

From the beginning the couple shared a journal in which they recorded their intellectual pursuits. Mary was expected to be just as intellectually active as her lover, keeping pace with his reading and studies, learning new languages, translating, transcribing, even trying her hand at imaginative writing.[17] Whatever Shelley could do, so could Mary. In his own life the poet drew no "invidious distinction of humankind as a class of beings [of] intellectual nature into two sexes." The difference between Mary and most women is shown some years after their marriage when Shelley compares her with his new acquaintance Mrs. Hoppner, who is "so good so beautiful so angelically mild that were she wise too, she would be quite a Mary. But she is not very accomplis[hed]" (*L.*II.38). Shelley is not using "accomplished" in the conventional sense, for Mary's accomplishments were not ornamental but solidly grounded on genuine intellectual achievement. Until the last, Shelley constantly urged her on, encouraging her to live up to her best self, helping her realize her talents to the fullest. Of her novel in progress, *Valperga*, he writes glowingly, "I flatter myself you have composed something unequalled in its kind, & that not content with the honours of your birth & your hereditary aristocracy, you will add still higher renown to your name." "Be severe in your corrections," he adds, "& expect severity from me, your sincere admirer."[18]

Shelley's treatment of Claire Clairmont was little different. Though lacking in Mary's intellectual endowments, erratic, and at the mercy of her emotions, she was nevertheless clever, witty, good at languages, and intellectually aggressive.[19] Shelley valued her as a companion, encouraging her mental development just as he did Mary's. In fact, in her masculine courage, her tough-minded independence, her fiery scorn of worldly opinion, and her indomitable spirit, Claire was more nearly the reverse of the womanly ideal than Mary, more the prototype of the future feminist.[20] Always on the lookout for evidence of woman's intellectual equality with man, Claire waxed ecstatic at the apprearance in 1818 of her stepsister's *Frankenstein*, regarding it as a triumph for the cause of women: "I cannot bear that women should be outdone in virtue and knowledge by men." Whatever her personal feelings "at not being able to do so well" herself, all envy yielded when she considered that Mary "is a woman & will prove in time an ornament & an argument in our favour. How I delight in a lovely woman of strong and cultivated intellect. How I delight to hear all the intracacies of mind & argument hanging on her lips!"[21] Claire was indignant at the sexist tutelage given Sophie in *Emile*, Rousseau's influential treatise on the proper education of the sexes, and in words that echo Wollstonecraft protests: "Sophie is the most finished of Coquettes—Emile is astonished at her infidelity—'he is sure that as Sophie has proved weak there can be no truth in Woman.' It is indeed partial to judge the whole sex by the conduct of one whose very education tended to fit her more for a Seraglio than the friend & equal of Man." Claire was for complete sexual equality—"Sex ought to be abolished"—believing, with Wollstonecraft, in "the necessity of Woman's being free that Man may walk, unencumbered by his fair clog, more freely towards a noble destiny."[22]

With the encouragement of Shelley, Claire too kept a journal, recording her reading, which was considerable and serious, her thoughts, which though not profound were often perceptive and spiky, and her creative attempts, which showed undeveloped natural talent. She was particularly sensitive to the battle of the sexes, resisting all views of women, however superficially flattering, that reduced them to the level of mere sex objects. Some of her character sketches of Byron are especially devastating. For a good part of her life she flatly refused to play the role of the dependent female. Her especial hatred was marriage, which she viewed as the ultimate step in female bondage and degradation.[23] Courageous enough to bear a child out of wedlock, she refused to barter her independence for the security of marriage. But she was forced to pay the consequences—twenty-five years of loneliness and drudgery superintending the education of other people's children. Claire preserved her integrity at the expense of a life largely wasted, owing to the narrow, male-centered views of her society.

Not all the women in Shelley's life were conscious intellectuals or feminists. Sophia Stacey and Jane Williams, for example, were no more than conventionally accomplished and were content to play the domestic role assigned them by society.[24] Shelley could enjoy their company and even be stirred by them emotionally but on the deepest level he could not find them wholly satisfying. He was fortunate, however, in discovering several women in his acquaintance who had surmounted the intellectual limitations usual in the female education of the period and developed their minds along the lines of the male. The tradition of the eighteenth-century bluestocking, though on the wane, survived in muted form among certain of his older married acquaintance. These women were of necessity largely self-educated, yet their learning was substantial. It was not always Shelley's lot to come to a woman as her tutor; sometimes he was the pupil. The genuinely cultivated Maria Gisborne, who had been the friend of both Wollstonecraft and Godwin and the object at one point of the philosopher's marital intentions, served as Shelley's mentor, with whom he studied Calderón in the original. His letters and verses to Maria show that he considered her his intellectual equal, often treating her to discussions of his literary projects. Another woman of this sort was Mrs. Mason, the former Lady Mountcashell and once the pupil of Wollstonecraft, whom Shelley describes to Leigh Hunt as "everything that is amiable and wise."[25] Supposedly the model for the Lady in *The Sensitive Plant*, she soon had him reading Aeschylus' *Agamemnon* under her guidance. The prototype of these women was Mrs. Boinville, to whose circle Shelley had been admitted in 1813 and whose effect he never forgot. He writes to Hogg in 1819 that Maria Gisborne "resembles Mrs. Boinville in her acquirements, her freedom from certain prejudices and the gentleness of her manners," but "she does not approach our lost friend in the elegance and delicate sensibility of her mind." Her daughter Cornelia Turner, with whom he fell briefly in love in 1814, he remembered as giving indications at age eighteen of "her mother's excellencies," though "less fascinating."[26]

Mother and daughter had in fact burst upon Shelley's consciousness as a revelation. Hitherto he had never known women who combined enlightened political and social beliefs with literary and artistic interests, without sacrificing feminine elegance of appearance and manner. As he explained to Hogg at the time, "The contemplation of female excellence is the favorite food of my imagination." Previously he had been "unaccustomed to the mildness the intelligence the delicacy of a cultivated female," but at Bracknell there was "ample scope for admiration." The effect was irresistible, and the contrast with the unteachable schoolgirl who was his wife was almost more than he could bear (*L.*I.401).

Before his introduction to the circle at Bracknell, the only remotely educated woman he had known was the ill-fated Elizabeth Hitchener, who in 1811 at the age of twenty-nine was seemingly doomed to the lot of a spinster schoolmistress. Though their relationship would ultimately strike the poet as a disaster, for a crucial year in his life, 1811-1812, she was the closest thing he possessed to an intellectual companion, helpmate, and confidante. For a time he poured forth his deepest self to her, as if she were indeed the "partner of his thoughts," the "sister of his soul," his "second self," his intellectual double.[27] Though she insisted on holding herself in a position of discipleship, Shelley would not hear of it. They were equals. Possessed of a "tongue of energy" and an "eye of fire," she evinced "the embryon of a mighty intellect which may one day enlighten thousands." With a "pen so overflowing so demonstrative, so impassioned," she ought "to trace characters for a nations perusal," not merely "mark grammar books for children." "Have confidence in yourself" was his adjuration, "dare to believe 'I am great' "—words which might stand as his lifelong injunction to all women.[28]

Of the many women with whom Shelley associated himself, Elizabeth Hitchener was most professedly the feminist, or in Medwin's words "an *esprit fort, cerulean blue*" and "great stickler for the rights of her sex." In both appearance and manner she was the personification of the feminist stereotype as this image would take shape in the public consciousness during the closing years of the nineteenth century. In Hogg's malicious but presumably accurate description, she was "tall and thin, bony and masculine, of a dark complexion; and the symbol of male wisdom, a beard, was not entirely wanting. She was neither young nor old; not handsome—not absolutely ill-looking." Her manner and speech were "prim, formal, didactic."[29] Elizabeth herself admitted her deficiency in traditional feminine beauty. Shelley initially dismissed this lack as of scant importance: "tho' the sleekness of your skin, the symmetry of your form might not attract the courtiers of Dublin castle," yet her mental energies were more than adequate to prosecuting the cause of justice and benevolence. He had no intention of yielding to patriarchal notions of sexual distinction. A woman's mental beauty, not her physical, was what counted. As for all arbitrary sexual differentiation, in "a future state of being" "these detestable distinctions will surely be abolished" (*L*.240,195).

The development of Shelley's relationship with Elizabeth put this ideal severely to the test. Whatever the case in a future existence, in the present life mental beauty was not enough. To be alive at all was to be a prisoner of sex. A woman's physical self was an inextricable part of her total makeup, to which Shelley could not remain wholly indifferent. Faced with the daily presence of Elizabeth in the flesh, Shelley was repelled. His reaction is instructive. His ideal might be asexual, but in actual practice a woman must be a woman. It was all very well to assert woman's parity with the male, but for a woman to *be* a male—this "ugly, hermaphroditical beast of a woman"—was carrying feminism too far, and Shelley retreated in revulsion: "What would Hell be, were such a woman in Heaven?" (*S&C*.III.110). With the distancing of time he saw the episode as absurd, sometimes quoting, while laughing so hard "the tears ran down his cheek," the first line of a poem in which his one-time soulmate defended women's rights: "All, all are men—*women* and all."[30]

Whereas Shelley desired women to preserve intact some semblance of their traditional femininity, he found himself from the first in active conflict with the prevailing sexual norm of the age which elevated women as physical objects but otherwise belittled or denied their powers. While the triumph of the chivalric conception of woman, of which the contemporary sexual code was heir, might have been crucial in rechanneling erotic sentiment from its unnatural course in antiquity, it had not fundamentally altered the underlying reality of woman's patriarchal subordination. The ritualization of the courtly attitude to women in the practice of "gallantry," as this homage was termed in the cant of the period, was thus inherently false, resulting either in outright male hypocrisy or, more often, in confused or ambivalent attitudes. Either way the consequence was an inaccurate, unrealistic, and distorted image of women, who were the chief sufferers.

In *A Vindication of the Rights of Woman*, a work that was to function as a handbook for Shelley on the proper relations between the sexes, Wollstonecraft drives directly to the heart of the dilemma: "If love have made some women wretched—how many more has the cold unmeaning intercourse of gallantry rendered vain and useless! yet this heartless attention to the sex is reckoned so manly, so polite that, till society is very differently organized, I fear this vestige of gothic manners will not be done away by a more reasonable and affectionate mode of conduct." The "homage of gallantry," with its rigamarole of respectful sighs, is too often only a mask for male appetite on the one hand and an excuse for female vanity on the other: "When a man squeezes the hand of a pretty woman, handing her to a carriage, whom he has never seen before, she will consider such an impertinent freedom in the light of an insult, if she have any true delicacy, instead of being flattered by this unmeaning homage to beauty."[31] In the same way Shelley complains in *Peter Bell the Third* of gallants, whom he calls "Things," "whose trade is, over ladies/To lean, and flirt, and stare, and simper,/Till all that is divine in woman/Grows cruel, courteous, smooth, inhuman,/Crucified 'twixt a smile and whimper" (III.x).

So debased had the chivalric tradition become by the end of the eighteenth century that the term *gallantry* had for many users degenerated into a synonym for *libertinism* or *adultery*, the terms often being employed interchangeably. "What men call gallantry, and gods adultery," writes Byron bluntly in *Don Juan*, stripping the code of its cant (I.xliii.7). Shelley applies the term in the blunt sense of libertinism to Byron himself when reporting his friend's temporary reformation at the hands of Teresa Guiccioli: "Lord Byron is reformed, as far as gallantry goes, and lives with a beautiful and sentimental lady, who is as much attached to him as may be" (*L*.II.345). Byron's amatory career epitomized the corrupting sexist attitudes Shelley was determined to expose and overturn.

Because of the complexity of his personality, Byron is possibly a dangerous example. The paradoxes in his behavior are real, and the tortured relationship with his mother, added to his consciously acknowledged attraction to members of his own sex, make him hardly typical. Yet a number of the seeming contradictions in his attitudes are resolved when seen in the light of the prevailing sexual code. Byron the romantic idealizer of women and Byron their cynical denigrator are equally consistent with the period's sexual values. The Regency rake, while encouraged by tradition to profess romantic feelings for women, was nevertheless worldly enough and practiced enough to see them as they really were, second-class citizens in a system designed exclusively for the comfort of men. He might pay lip service to the courtly code of manners in his role of the gallant, but it was all surface politesse with no real meaning. Beneath the service of gallantry lay an ill-concealed contempt for woman as not worth man's serious attention and good only for sexual and domestic service.[32] Unlike Shelley, he had no desire to change this system, not only finding it to his advantage but also considering it fixed in the nature of things.

Byron the romantic is enshrined in the love lyrics and Eastern tales, but Byron the realist is revealed in the later work, such as *Don Juan*, and in the letters. This is the Byron who prides himself on his low or skeptical view of women, scorning their feminine weakness, mocking their womanly emotions, and ridiculing their intellectual pretensions. To this Byron, women are so much "cunt," and all he wants from them is their bodies.[33] This Byron boasts of intercourse in Venice with over two hundred women in eighteen months, at which point he stops counting—a course record in "gallantry" that horrified Shelley. This Byron considers love "utter nonsense, a mere jargon of compliments, romance, and deceit."[34] This Byron is contemptuous of the whole courtly tradition and its modern ritualization in gallantry, despite the lip service he pays it in his popular poetry.[35]

Romantic realism or skepticism was in fact built into the period's attitudes precisely because of the absurd overestimation of women demanded by the gallant code. A little contact with worldly reality bred an emotional cynicism that undermined the possibility of meaningful homage to women. A misogynistic skepticism regarding women's worth was thus endemic in the period's sexual attitudes.

But neither would the male want a female who seriously lived up to the letter of the ideal. This was the deeper reality. The genuine elevation of women would have constituted a direct threat to patriarchal ascendancy. Typically, Byron is suspicious of any woman who shows signs of rising above her sphere intellectually. For a woman to be "clever" is a great defect. Bluestockings especially are anathema.[36] "Thank God you are not a blue-stocking," he writes his sister Augusta. "I only want a woman to laugh," he tells his "blue" wife Annabella, "and don't care what she is besides." Of his teenage mistress Caroline he complains that she has "only two faults, unpardonable in a woman,—she can read and write."[37] A woman who publishes is even worse: "Of all Bitches dead or alive a scribbling woman is the most canine."[38] If a woman is to be cultivated at all, her talents should be "general," that is, ornamental. Much better, however, is the Turkish arrangement: "in the East women are in their proper sphere, & one has—no conversation at all."[39] In European society, as he explains to Medwin, women "are in an unnatural state . . . The Turks and Eastern people manage these matters better than we do. They lock them up, and they are much happier. Give a woman a looking-glass and a few sugar-plums, and she will be satisfied."[40]

At heart Byron, like most men, viewed any assertion of female will with alarm: "Oh! ye lords of ladies intellectual,/Inform us truly, have they not henpeck'd you all?"[41] A woman's duty was to know her place and not impinge on man's consciousness except when bidden. Like most of his contemporaries, despite the facade of courtliness, Byron saw women as inferior in kind—the "absurd womankind" was one of his favorite phrases—and any attempt to bridge sexual difference threatened a weakening of masculine self-esteem. Given the sum of these attitudes, Byron, in absolute contradistinction to Shelley, was particularly drawn to the ancient Greek settlement of the woman question. While both poets placed their cultural ideal in fifth-century Athens, Byron found most attractive what Shelley found most abhorrent. His view of women was quintessentially classical. As he jotted down in his journal toward the end of his life, the state of women under the ancient Greeks was "convenient enough," whereas the present state was "a remnant of the barbarism of the chivalric and feudal ages—artificial and unnatural. They ought to mind home—and be well fed and clothed—but not mixed in society. Well educated, too, in religion—but to read neither poetry nor politics—nothing but books of piety and cookery. Music—drawing—also a little gardening and ploughing now and then."[42]

Yet if a society educates women as inferiors or "slaves," in Shelleyan terminology, and has use for them only in a sexual and domestic capacity, they will indeed be "silly," "absurd," and "bores in their disposition," as Byron said of them, and men will be forced to look elsewhere for true companionship, sentiment, and love.[43] Byron did not hesitate to express the logic of this belief in action. But a sublimated homosexuality was in fact endemic in English social life throughout the century. As in ancient Greece, the position of women necessitated it. The difference was that the Greeks allowed male love out into the open and institutionalized it, whereas in modern times it was rigidly suppressed and so could express itself only in guilty, tortured, or self-deceptive forms. Women were still the principal sufferers, victims of the emasculated or openly misogynous emotional life of their "lovers."

Even though Byron, unlike most of his contemporaries, gave uninhibited expression to the left-handed or homoerotic side of his nature released by the underlying conditions of his society and freely acknowledged his basic contempt for women, whatever he might pretend in his popular poetry, he was by no means uniformly woman's enemy or wholly insensitive to her lot.[44] One of the best-known passages in all his verse poignantly adumbrates the limitations of the life to which woman is ordinarily confined by patriarchal custom—the speaker is Don Juan's mistress Donna Julia:

> "Man's love is of man's life a thing apart,
> 'Tis woman's whole existence; man may range
> The court, camp, church, the vessel, and the mart;
> Sword, gown, gain, glory, offer in exchange
> Pride, fame, ambition, to fill up his heart,
> And few there are whom these cannot estrange;
> Men have all these resources, we but one,
> To love again, and be again undone." (I.cxciv)

The lines are immediately undercut, much to Shelley's disgust, by Byron's hint at the conscious attitudinizing that may underlie a heartrending display of female sentiment. But there must have been a part of Byron, for all his love of exposing romantic posturing, that was genuinely moved, for he returns to the question twice more, admitting that no man can project himself fully into woman's situation: "Poor thing of usages! coerced, compell'd,/Victim when wrong, and martyr oft when right,/Condemn'd to child-bed . . . who can penetrate/The real sufferings of their she condition?" So woeful is their lot that any woman of mature experience would willingly exchange it for the lowliest man's.[45]

Nowhere, however, does Byron really challenge patriarchal definitions of woman and assert her right to lead an independent existence on equal terms with man. When he sympathizes with her lot, he does not envisage changing it. And when he exalts womankind, the elevation is founded on courtly conceptions, not egalitarian. Woman is morally superior, purer and more spiritual, an angel redeeming man from his animal grossness and vice. This is a literal rendering of the code of gallantry which, supported by Evangelical antisexual attitudes, would later come to typify Victorian definitions of woman, making her an "angel in the house." Byron is clearly subscribing to this view when he writes to Annabella, "What can you *know* (or what can a *good woman* know) of strong passions &c."[46]

The fundamental inhumanity and self-deception of such an ideal is laid bare by John Stuart Mill in *The Subjection of Women*. Women are declared to be "better than men," he maintains, but this amounts to "an empty compliment, which must provoke a bitter smile from every woman of spirit, since there is no situation in life in which it is the established order, and considered quite natural and suitable, that the better should obey the worse." Indeed "we are perpetually told that women are better than men, by those who are totally opposed to treating them as if they were as good, so that the saying has passed into a piece of tiresome cant, intended to put a complimentary face upon an injury." Women are taught from infancy that they are created for self-sacrifice. But what is needed is for woman to develop herself, not sacrifice it, and to this end she must be granted full equality of rights. "We have had the morality of submission," concludes Mill, "and that of chivalry . . . but the time is now come for the morality of justice."[47]

This was Shelley's plea also, and it meant setting himself against the combined weight of ubiquitous patriarchal custom and the hypocritical conventions of male gallantry. Steering clear of the twin fallacies of sexist depreciation and courtly flattery, Shelley committed himself from the outset to the goal of full sexual equality. Hogg recalls a dinner party attended by the two friends during the Oxford period at which Shelley spoke "with great animation" in defense of women's character and abilities in spite of the gentlemanly condescension and sneers of his dinner companions.[48] All his life Shelley was on the watch for objective testimony to validate his high opinion of woman's potentiality. "Gibbon VIII.284 on the eminence of women" reads a characteristic memo in one of his notebooks from the Italian period, marking the historian's description of the enhanced status achieved by women in the early empire, when "the Roman matrons became the equal and voluntary companions of their lords," an opinion subsequently finding its way into his brief history of sexual attitudes in the *Discourse*.[49]

It was easy enough to expose the injustice of the traditional depreciation of womankind, but more difficult to cope with woman's recent artificial elevation by man. Required was the stripping away of widespread dishonesty and self-deception on the part of both sexes and the demonstration that what purported to be homage to women was in reality another way of keeping them in fetters. This was a major point in the feminism of both Wollstonecraft and Mill and is re-emphasized by modern feminists. "To succeed, the Woman's Movement . . . would have to unmask chivalry and expose its courtesies as subtle manipulation," stresses Kate Millett.[50] Shulamith Firestone notes that while "gallantry has been commonly defined as 'excessive attention to women without serious purpose,' " its purpose is very serious: "through a false flattery, to keep women from awareness of their lower-class condition." Because "the distinguishing characteristic of woman's exploitation as a class is sexual, a special means must be found to make them unaware that they are considered all alike sexually ('cunts')." This is the function of romanticism.[51] Ironically, the very tradition which had seemingly liberated women from their degrading status in antiquity was now pivotal in their continuing subjection, preventing them from perceiving their exploitation as a class and hence from uniting to act as a class.

This important insight of modern feminism was shared by Shelley a century and a half earlier, though he could not place it so firmly in the ideological framework of sexual politics. That he understood the hypocritical foundations of the contemporary homage to women, how it disguised the realities of their sexist depreciation and exploitation by men, is apparent from his running battle with Hogg over the question in his early letters and in his 1814 review of his friend's *Memoirs of Prince Alexy Haimatoff*. In the review, while praising Hogg for the "delicacy and truth" with which he has noticed some "peculiarities of female character," Shelley nonetheless recognizes certain fatal "deficiencies." Hogg is not free from "the fashionable superstitions of gallantry," not "exempt from the sordid feelings which with blind idolatry worship the image and blaspheme the deity, reverence the type, and degrade the reality of which it is an emblem." This is the same Hogg who can give his sanction to "promiscuous concubinage," that is, to libertinism (VI.177,181–182).

From the outset Shelley perceived in his friend's mind a confusion of sexual motives with courtly idolatry. "I confess," he remarks ironically, "that I cannot mark female excellence, or its degrees, by a print of the foot, a waving of vesture, etc., as you can." Something more than physical testimony is required.[52] Hogg's infatuated pursuit of Elizabeth Shelley long after she had given proof that she was no longer worth pursuit made plain his true feelings. Originally, Hogg's attachment had been justified, based solely on respect for her intellectual powers ("coincidence of intellect") as evidenced in her letters, poetry, and Shelley's reports of her advanced opinions.[53] But when these powers yielded to female weakness, Hogg's continued worship was exposed as merely a rationalization of sexual desire. Shelley makes the contradictions in Hogg's position syllogistically plain: "You loved a being. The being whom you loved is not what she was, consequently as love appertains to mind & not body she exists no longer" (L.I.195). When Hogg persists in his passion, reinforced by one enflaming glimpse of Elizabeth through the Warnham Church windows, Shelley reiterates his argument: "I am truly surprised! The peep at Warnham Church cannot have influenced you one way or the other but it *may*; for it is the only sensual intelligence that you have received of this fair one. I cannot call it intellectual, as even in the short view of her face which you had, you cannot pretend to guess her moral qualities" (*L.I.*124). The emphasis is on Elizabeth's intellectual and moral rather than personal beauty, as it should be if the homage of gallantry is to have any real meaning. But as Hogg's behavior reveals, this exaltation of women more often than not is merely a cloak or disguise for less noble feelings, reducing the elevated compliments of gallantry to self-seeking, hypocritical flattery.

No sooner had Shelley weaned Hogg of his attachment to Elizabeth than he was forced to agonize through the whole sophistic performance again with respect to Hogg's feelings for Harriet. This time, however, beneath all Hogg's gallant gush, the true nature of his feelings was exposed at last. It was absurd from the beginning, Shelley points out, to lavish on Harriet, whatever might have been the case with Elizabeth, the inflated encomiums of courtly rhetoric, which Hogg knows to be sheer hogwash, empty "compliment (I will not say a piece of flattery)," dictated by the force of his passion. Harriet knows it too and recognizes its source. Shelley asks that his friend examine the source of his own feelings, his "*adoration,*" which he will find derives principally from "sensation." Hogg's sophistical abasement before Harriet, Shelley adds, is not only insulting to her but demeaning to himself.[54] As Shelley perceives, the gallant mentality was dishonest at the core, falsifying the intercourse of the sexes, which should rest on a foundation of genuine equality, not self-deluding or hypocritical conventions of sexual exaltation and abasement.

It could be argued that Shelley himself was not exempt from the "fashionable superstitions of gallantry." As Hogg enviously notes, his manner toward women was that of the gallant.[55] Shelley himself states that the laws of chivalric courtesy to women are his "religion." The great difference with Shelley's practice of gallantry was that he rendered an honest deference to women as human beings, not simply the sexual homage exacted by the brief period of courtship. Hogg, despite the inflated rhetoric, was basically conservative in his attitude toward women. He had no desire to disturb the fundamental relationship of the sexes. He might pay lip service to women as superior beings and even put them on a moral pedestal as ministering angels of hearth and home, but he was not ready to elevate them outside this sphere. He knew perfectly well the way of the world and was content to let it stay that way. Shelley, on the contrary, believed in women as equals, or as potential equals. He always dealt with both men and women in terms of their best selves, encouraging them to live up to the implied compliment.[56] Believing that women were worthy of real respect, not just sexual homage, he treated them with real respect. Hogg observes that it was Shelley the conversationalist who "was found to be especially attractive and enchanting by all females, particularly by the young and intellectual."[57] The poet often sat up half the night keeping a circle of female admirers spellbound with talk. What appealed most to Shelley in the relations of the sexes was plainly the possibility of full intellectual companionship. Enough therefore of Hogg's "divinities," he cries; it is foolish to talk in terms of sexual superiority. Both sexes should work toward the ideal of human perfectibility, with men assisting women, even if the goal itself can never be fully attained.[58]

In attempting to imagine a program for the future of the women's liberation movement, Firestone points to the extreme difficulty of the task, lamenting not only the lack of "precedents in history for feminist revolution" in the root sense, but the lack even of "a literary image of this future society; there is not even a *utopian* feminist literature in existence."[59] Utopian feminism, however, is precisely what Shelley offers in his literary prophecies of the future. Were his feminism better known to the modern women's movement, his poetry could stand as a welcome inspiration, as it once did to nineteenth-century feminists. The liberation of women occupies a central position in all three of his major verse forecasts of futurity.

The apocalyptic *Queen Mab* discloses the revolutionary spectacle of "Woman and man, in confidence and love,/Equal and free and pure," treading together the "mountain-paths of virtue," both sexes now rid of the patriarchal shackles of law and custom which have hitherto hobbled their intercourse (IX.89-92). The vision fades, but the poem's heroine is expected to keep its promise alive in her breast and work for its future actualization in the real world. As always in Shelley's utopian forecasts, the vision is reinforced in practical terms by demonstrating the ecstatic effects of emancipation upon the erotic relations of the poem's hero and heroine (IX.190-208).

This vision is triumphantly repeated in the millennial restructuring of the social order following upon release of the chained titan in Shelley's Aeschylean prophecy, *Prometheus Unbound*:

> And women, too, frank, beautiful, and kind
> As the free heaven which rains fresh light and dew
> On the wide earth; gentle radiant forms,
> From custom's evil taint exempt and pure;
> Speaking the wisdom once they could not think,
> Looking emotions once they feared to feel,
> And changed to all which once they dared not be,
> Yet being now, made earth like heaven. (III.iv.153-159)

Shelley prophesies nothing less than woman's total emancipation—sexual, social, intellectual, moral, and spiritual—from centuries of male tyranny. What the female was up against is graphically mirrored in the contemporary journalistic reaction to just such a forecast: "the very decencies of our nature are to vanish beneath the magic wand of the licentious REFORMER. Every modest feeling, which now constitutes the sweetest charm of society is to be annihilated—and *women are to be—what God and nature never designed them to.*"[60]

The poisonous effect on female nature of such an ideology is illustrated in the poem when, under the patriarchal rule of Jupiter, women are seen to be the "ugliest of all things evil," disfigured behind their "foul masks" of falsity and frowning—though even here they possess the potentiality of being "fair," like the exiled Asia, when "good and kind, free and sincere" (III.iv.44-49). With the downfall of Jupiter, the deification of the male principle ends. Once Asia returns to Prometheus' side, the natural order is restored, and women resume their "radiant forms," free from the corrupting taint of custom.

Precisely how this result is to be achieved receives its fullest statement in *The Revolt of Islam*, the most powerful feminist poem in the language and, except for Tennyson's *The Princess*, the most thoroughly grounded in the realities of the woman question. Whereas Tennyson opts for the Victorian solution of sexual complementarity, equal but separate spheres of operation, Shelley comes down on the side of full sexual integration, men and women sharing all opportunities equally. In Tennyson the woman returns to the home, glad to be relieved of the burdens of her feminist consciousness; in Shelley the woman's home is the world, and she gladly sacrifices her life in defending her claim to it. Shelley's feminism is militant, his program radical, his battle cry sexual revolution.

In this "Epic of Woman," as Shelley's poem has been called, the symbolism of social regeneration is focused, as it is not in Shelley's other millennial prophecies, squarely on the efforts of the subject sex to cast off the chains of male supremacy.[61] Appropriately, the palm of victory is awarded, not to the poem's hero, but to its heroine Cythna. In Cythna is realized "a new female type," according to the Victorian feminist Mathilde Blind, hitherto absent from literature, one who considers it at once "her right and her duty to take an active share in the general concerns of humanity, and to influence them, not only indirectly through others, but directly by her own thoughts and actions . . . Cythna, prophet, reformer, and martyr . . . is a creation unique in the whole range" of literature. Previously, Blind observes, "all poets creating ideals of woman, however pure or lofty these might be, had depicted her invariably in her relation as either wife or mistress, mother or daughter—that is, as a supplement to man's nature."[62] But Cythna is fully the equal of the male.

That the "revolt" of the poem is in no small measure the revolt of women against male oppression is signaled many times in the text and is underscored by the title, the world of Islam figuring as the type of man's brutal subjugation of woman to patriarchal values.[63] The Moslem seraglio embodies the institutionalization of woman's sexual, social, and religious subjection at its most extreme, and by extension it stands for her still universal thralldom to sexist values. The scene, for example, in which Cythna is seized by the Tyrant's minions and forcibly borne off to languish for years in his sordid harem is much more than just a melodramatic plot device: it functions as a vivid metaphor of woman's condition everywhere, victim to male tyranny and lust. Unlike most men, however, who in their hearts still favor the "Eastern solution," as Byron was frank enough to admit, Shelley favors throwing wide the doors of the harem and setting the inmates free.

Cythna's progress through the narrative represents Shelley's deliberate allegory of the awakening of the female intellect and will to their real powers and capabilities: Cythna, within whose "fairest form, the female mind/Untainted by the poison-clouds which rest/On the dark world, a sacred home did find" (II.xxxv). Even as a child, Cythna participates equally in the intellectual pursuits of her brother Laon, keeping him to his task when his own energies flag. After death, the pair are still conversing of "wisdom" as well as "love," reunited in their eternal abode of the human spirit. Underlining the fact that woman herself must take the lead in bringing about her emancipation, Cythna is the first to raise her brother's consciousness to full-fledged abhorrence of sexual as well as political and religious tyranny, so that he experiences "a wider sympathy"— formerly Laon had felt woman's misery "but coldly"—and mourns with her "the servitude/In which the half of humankind were mewed/Victims of lust and hate, the slaves of slaves" (II.xxxvi). Can man himself "be free," Cythna protests, "if woman be a slave?" (II.xliii). Knowing full well the answer, she vows to dedicate her life to the cause of women, releasing "degraded woman's greatness" (VII. xxxvi). Her brother himself has much to gain, she points out: "Nor wilt thou at poor Cythna's pride repine,/If she should lead a happy female train/To meet thee over the rejoicing plain." With his help she can dare anything, even mortal combat (II.xxxviii-xxxix).

The reason Cythna is so "undaunted," so free of the submissive psychology stamped on women in a patriarchal society, is that from earliest childhood her brother has allowed her to develop her full powers of mind, instead of keeping them shackled to traditionally female pursuits. Thus she has evolved an intelligence and will similar to his own. Throughout the land, thinks Cythna, there must be many like herself who, could they have such an education, "would fear no more" (II.xl). Accordingly, Cythna's plan is to descend "where'er in abjectness/Woman with some vile slave her tyrant dwells" and "disenchant the captives," for woman has become "the child of scorn,/The outcast of a desolated home;/Falsehood, and fear, and toil, like waves have worn/Channels upon her cheek, which smiles adorn,/As calm decks the false Ocean" (VIII.xv).[64]

Cythna's plan is realized when, metamorphosed into the militant Laone, she arrives at the Golden City (London) to unseat the patriarchal Tyrant, having in the meantime grown "Wise in all human wisdom" through years of study (VII.xxxi). At first she is hailed as a female Redeemer, "the child of God, sent down to save/Women from bonds and death." But soon her "human" words elicit "sympathy/In human hearts" (IX.viii-x). In proclaiming "the law of truth and freedom," she finds that it is "chiefly women" who respond to the message:

> The wild-eyed women throng around her path
>   From their luxurious dungeons, from the dust
> Of meaner thralls, from the oppressor's wrath,
>   Or the caresses of his sated lust
>   They congregate:—in her they put their trust;
> . . . .
> Thus she doth equal laws and justice teach
>   To woman, outraged and polluted long;
> Gathering the sweetest fruit in human reach
>   For those fair hands now free, while armèd wrong
> Trembles before her look, though it be strong;
> Thousands thus dwell beside her, virgins bright,
>   And matrons with their babes, a stately throng! (IV.xx-xxii)

Cythna's preachments awaken women from "their cold, careless, willing slavery" to men, releasing them, in the language of modern feminism, from the privatism that has traditionally kept them isolated and powerless and binding them in a sense of pride and sisterhood. From the moment that the import of her words sinks in, the women's shackles magically drop away and they find themselves "free!": "Their many tyrants sitting desolately/In slave-deserted halls, could none restrain;/For wrath's red fire had withered in the eye,/Whose lightning once was death,—nor fear, nor gain/Could tempt one captive now to lock another's chain" (IX.x).

Ray Strachey, writing of the climate of opinion faced by the pioneering feminists of the early nineteenth century, observes that women were conditioned to believe that "ambition, achievement, and independence were unfeminine attributes, and that obedience, humility, and unselfishness were what was really required." Women "brought up on this convention grew accustomed to it, and loved it. They sheltered under the irresponsibility it gave them and they hugged the 'chains' which seemed so protective."[65] The women's liberationist Florynce Kennedy advances the principle of the "circularity of oppression" to explain the "brainwashed consensual condition" of women: "no really pervasive system of oppression" can exist "without the consent of the oppressed. People who have not withdrawn consent usually deny that they are oppressed." Women thus act out their submissive role "without any noticeable pressure from anyone."[66]

This consensual submission is precisely Shelley's target in *The Revolt of Islam*. As always in his work, the level of the struggle is psychological, the drama inward: before an evil can be uprooted, it must be experienced as evil; before corrupting institutions can undergo radical change, the necessity of such change must be internalized. But once this has taken place, change will inevitably follow, according to Shelley's necessitarian social philosophy. In the case of women, they must truly want their condition changed; few men will desire it. All meaningful reform begins at the level of the individual self, in a primary redirection of the will. Shelley understood this truth; it was recognized by the first feminists; and it is central to the feminist movement today with its program of consciousness-raising. The "arena of sexual revolution is within human consciousness even more pre-eminently than it is within human institutions," insists Kate Millett. "So deeply imbedded is patriarchy that the character structure it creates . . . is perhaps even more a habit of mind and a way of life than a political system."[67] *The Revolt of Islam* is a pioneering attempt at just such consciousness-changing, with its primary object the revolutionizing of the female will.

What such a revolution might mean is envisaged in the poem when the women celebrate their freedom. The inauguration of the new order is solemnized in rites about a marble pyramid, atop which is enthroned the dazzling Cythna, high priestess of the occasion. The steps leading upward are thronged with "female choirs . . . the loveliest/Among the free" (V.xl-xliv). At the apex, encircling the throne, appear the carven images of three allegorical figures, emblematic of Wisdom, Love, and Equality. The place of honor is assigned to "divine Equality!/Wisdom and Love are but the slaves of thee" (V.xli.3). This ordering indicates the supreme importance attached to female liberation. As an ideal, equality, particularly sexual equality, is placed at the very center of the poem.[68] Wherever true equality is absent, wherever one half of humankind is crucified as a subordinate class of being by "Faith" or institutionalized religion, there can be no true wisdom or love (V.xlix-l). Viewed in this light, the profoundly personal experience celebrated a short while later in the mountain-top nuptials of the poem's hero and heroine, who are both lovers and brother and sister, assumes a wider, universal meaning. Shadowed forth is the perfect mating of man and womankind, wholly equal, wholly loving, and wholly deserving of one another's love. The epitome of Shelleyan intercourse, all sympathies harmoniously blended, their love stands as the perfected type of all sexual relationship.

Yet Shelley does not end with this picture, for he knows that the barriers standing in the way of its realization outside the world of poetry are formidable. Not until it becomes a reality in the minds and hearts of the vast majority of humankind can it be anything but a tantalizing dream, one of those "beautiful idealisms of moral excellence" to the propagation of which his poetry is dedicated. There is a Jupiter, a Tyrant, a patriarch, enthroned in the heart of each of us who has to be unseated before the victory can be secure, the new order made lasting. Even in the exultant conclusion of *Prometheus Unbound*, a discordant warning is sounded: the victory may be reversed, humankind lose its nerve, the old order be restored. Humankind can change for ill as well as good. Mutability is one of the givens of existence, however much Shelley would like to arrest the will permanently when once set in the right direction. Thus the action of the poet's feminist epic takes a sharply pessimistic turn, just when hope is running highest. The forces of tradition are far too powerfully entrenched at this stage in history to make the feminist dream a reality in the minds of more than a handful of scattered and unorganized visionaries. Lacking leaders, a program, or even a general consciousness of grievance, feminism as a social movement can as yet represent only a dream of the future. Shelley has no recourse but to show the new order overthrown in its turn, the Tyrant restored, Laon and Cythna captured and martyred.

Even in the hour of triumph there are ominous portents of patriarchal reaction. Though temporarily bereft of power, the Tyrant has not yielded inwardly. Thus "priests [are sent] throughout the streets" to "curse the rebels," and "grave and hoary men" are bribed to spread poisonous, sophistical lies about the dangers of freedom and the necessity of returning to the traditional "peace of slavery." There are "yet obscener slaves with smoother brow,/And sneers on their strait lips, thin, blue and wide," who insinuate that "the rule of men" is "over now,/And hence, the subject world to woman's will must bow" (IX.xiii-xvi). Yet for the moment this sort of reasoning has lost its force, the patriarchal mentality is on the decline, so the Tyrant goes unheeded and the churches grow emptier, "till the priests stood alone within the fane" (IX.xviii).

The victory is short-lived because the forces of reaction are too strong, tradition too ingrained. Regrouping his scattered legions, "willing slaves to Custom old," the Tyrant returns to the city, spreading panic and destruction (XI.xvii). The defenders of freedom, outnumbered, are overwhelmed and annihilated, their leaders burned to death, though significantly for the future they do not go unmourned: "one by one, that night, young maidens came,/Beauteous and calm," and "by the flame/Which shrank as overgorged, they laid them down,/And sung a low sweet song, of which alone/One word was heard, and that was Liberty" (X.xlviii). Laon and Cythna, escaping temporarily, are at last apprehended and in a public execution burnt at the stake as atheists, sacrificed to appease "the withering ire/Of God," even though Laon makes a dying appeal that Cythna be allowed to flee to America, where "Freedom and Truth" are still worshiped (X.xxxix,XI.xxii). The request is denied. But in light of the subsequent history of feminism, which began as an organized movement in the United States and which owes its second incarnation to the same "chainless" people, the request is startlingly prophetic.

With the death of Laon and Cythna, the new order is extinct, and once more "the winter of the world," the arctic reign of Jupiter, is restored (IX.xxv). Yet hope is not irrecoverable. Though the lovers perish, they will "meet again/Within the minds of men, whose lips shall bless/[Their] memory, and whose hopes its light retain/When [their] dissevered bones are trodden in the plain" (II.xlviii). It may be winter, but "the seeds are sleeping in the soil" and with them, as in the poet's later ode, the promise, indeed the necessity, of renewal (IX.xxiv-xxvii). "We derive tranquility and courage and grandeur of soul," as Shelley explains in *A Philosophical View of Reform*, "from contemplating an object which is, because we will it, and may be, because we hope and desire it, and must be if succeeding generations of the enlightened sincerely and earnestly seek it" (VII.43). Laon and Cythna live on, joined eternally in the temple of the human spirit, whose portrayal opens and closes the poem. Here they are equal members of the "mighty" senate of the departed great, whose company is highlighted, in Shelley's sanguine preview of the future, by "female forms, whose gestures beamed with mind" (I.liv).

Though Shelley, perhaps more than any other man of his time, was predisposed by temperament, experience, and intellectual makeup to take the side of women in his writing and, in his actual practice, to tender them unqualified respect as persons rather than sex objects, his defense of women did not take shape in an ideological vacuum. His feminism was influenced by a variety of published sources, including Helvétius, d'Holbach, and Condorcet among the French Encyclopedists and Godwin and James Lawrence in his own country.[69] But the writings of Wollstonecraft, partly because of the personal connection, were the most significant. The main outlines of the poet's feminist ideology trace directly to her work, and it was above all her example that caused him to take up the active defense of women. In her own person Wollstonecraft seemed the embodiment of what he sought in the emancipated woman. If her daughter represented the promise of what such a woman might be, she herself was the reality.

Observers have often remarked that it was the mother, not the daughter, who should have been Shelley's companion and wife. His first wife was convinced that the younger Mary had succeeded in alienating her husband's affections by reviving the memory of her mother.[70] Shelley was familiar with Wollstonecraft's appearance through John Opie's celebrated portrait which hung over the fireplace in the upstairs living room of the Godwin home at Skinner Street. Harriet, on first encountering the Godwin household, remarked on the striking resemblance between Mary Godwin and her mother, little foreseeing the irony her remarks were to carry for posterity. First describing Fanny Imlay, the feminist's older daughter by the American Gilbert Imlay, Harriet observes: "There is one of the daughters of that dear Mary Wollstonecraft living with him [Godwin]. She is 19 years of age, very plain, but very sensible." In a patently Shelleyan comment, she adds, "the beauty of her mind fully overbalances the plainness of her countenance." Meanwhile there is "another daughter of hers who is now in Scotland. She is very much like her mother, whose picture hangs up in the study. She must have been a most lovely woman. Her countenance speaks her a woman who would dare to think and act for herself."[71]

In the months immediately following their elopement Shelley and Mary often returned to Wollstonecraft's grave in St. Pancras Churchyard where they had first declared their passion.[72] During the same period Shelley had Mary go through with him most of her mother's published work. The title of his first poem to Mary emphasizes her feminist heritage. In the Dedication to *The Revolt of Islam* Shelley acknowledges his hopes for Mary in terms of the legacy she inherits from her mother: "still her fame/Shines on thee, through the tempests dark and wild/Which shake these latter days" (Ded.xii).

Just what the memory of the pioneering feminist meant to the poet is best expressed in his 1817 review of Godwin's *Mandeville*, where he describes her as Godwin's "late illustrious and admirable wife" and finds it "singular that the other nations of Europe should have anticipated . . . the judgment of posterity" by pronouncing her name "with reverence"; her writings "have been translated and universally read in France and Germany long after the bigotry of faction has stifled them in our country" (VI.220). The phrase "the bigotry of faction," restating the Dedication's "the tempests dark and wild/Which shake these latter days," refers to the anti-Jacobin reaction of the century's opening decades which made Wollstonecraft's name, when remembered at all, a dirty word to her countrymen.[73] In his clear-sighted humanity, Shelley correctly prophesies that her name will one day be honored in the fashion it deserves.

The exact date of Shelley's first acquaintance with Wollstonecraft's work is uncertain. Nor is it certain which of her works he read first. What is certain is that from the first her arguments left a strong impression on his thinking, even though he was more utilitarian and antireligious, and that in time he came to know all her work intimately. Her beliefs, hopes, ideals, even rhetoric, sound again and again in his own work.

Like the poet, the feminist is deeply disturbed by the hypocritical sexist values permeating her society and poisoning the intercourse between the sexes. Conceding in *A Vindication*, perhaps to a greater degree than Shelley, that woman may be designed by nature to fulfill different duties in life, namely domestic and maternal, from those of man, Wollstonecraft insists that these are nevertheless "human duties" and thus the same principle should regulate them.[74] Under the system of the day, however, since woman receives an "education of the body" only, her mind is left "to rust," sacrificed to "libertine notions of beauty." The problem, Wollstonecraft recognizes, involves the miseducation of both sexes. Young men, sequestered in single-sex boarding schools during their formative years, learn to view women exclusively as sex objects, "very early rush[ing] into the libertinism which destroys the constitution before it is formed." The remedy, she believes, is the establishing of state-supported coeducational day schools where the sexes can mingle naturally and receive the same mental training. Only in this way will the relations between the sexes ever "deserve the name of fellowship."

To put the intercourse of the sexes on a more civilized and harmonious footing was thus a principal aim of Wollstonecraft's, as it was of Shelley's. But as long as the sexes were unnaturally divided and woman's intellectual growth deliberately stunted, this ideal was out of reach and the progress of both sexes at a standstill. Wollstonecraft acknowledges it a futile hope that any man will correct the situation. If anything is to be done, women must do it themselves. Like Shelley in *The Revolt of Islam*, she urges "a revolution in female manners," so as "to restore to [women] their lost dignity—make them, as a part of the human species, labour by reforming themselves to reform the world." The task will be difficult, for most women are engaged rather in burnishing than snapping their chains; long ages of servitude have conditioned them to "despise the freedom which they have not sufficient virtue to attain." Yet such a reformation will bring about a new dawn of harmony between the sexes, instead of the present "insidious state of warfare" that "undermin[es] morality, and divid[es] mankind"; and even love will acquire "more serious dignity," "purified"— as with Shelley's Laon and Cythna—"in its own fires."

Both writers were working toward the creation of a society that would allow for the full flowering of human potentiality within the coordinates of sympathetic relationship. Such a society would for the first time, in Shelley's terminology, make possible a genuinely antitypal connection between the sexes, all sympathies harmoniously blended, the archetypal need for which was embedded in the human psyche. If, however, woman's nature were consciously delimited to the merely sensual, such a flowering would be impossible, and both sexes were doomed to disappointment. But for Shelley mind had no sex, and the best answer to the sexist norms of the period was Wollstonecraft herself, a living refutation of woman's allegedly inferior intellectual capabilities. What she had been able to achieve alone and unaided, in the teeth of tradition, many women could do if granted equal opportunity with men. What Shelley saw in his mother-in-law's career was, in short, the successful socialization of "intellectual beauty," and it was to the release of this beauty in all women that his own efforts were dedicated.

Shelley's worship of "intellectual beauty" is usually thought of in terms of its metaphysical overtones as solemnized in the *Hymn to Intellectual Beauty*, composed at Lake Geneva in 1816. Because the poem implies fundamental notions about the nature of ontological reality, the concept of "intellectual beauty" is ordinarily viewed in the context of Shelley's philosophy of mind, labeled "intellectual," which has affinities with both Berkeleian idealism and Plato's philosophy of Ideas, though it is basically a version of Humeian skepticism. The expression's literal signification, "beauty of mind or intellect," is thus easily overlooked. But time and again Shelley speaks of "intellectual beauty" in the sense of mental endowment, powers of mind and the mind's products.[75] His hope is that all humankind will one day be raised from its present grossness in the "scale of intellectual being" to the possession of this true intellectual beauty.[76]

Since the stuff of reality, though not the cause, is mental, the gateway to its apprehension lies through the expansion of human mental powers. The more these are developed, the more a person takes on the coloration of the spirit that gives them their beauty. Shelley endues this process with moral as well as metaphysical significance. Expansion of "human kind's" mental powers necessarily leads toward humanitarian enlightenment and the evolution of a perfectibilitarian social order or, in the packed language of the poem, humankind's liberation from the "dark slavery" which hitherto has bound it. Feminism supplies an important key to this liberation, for the emancipation of women, one half of humankind, is the most vital single step toward propagating intellectual BEAUTY—toward fostering it, perpetuating it, making its visits less fleeting and disappointing.

Not only does the concept of intellectual beauty have feminist implications, but the very expression itself is probably feminist in origin. Shelley's adoption of this expression has been traced to his reading in a number of recondite sources, none of them overwhelmingly convincing.[77] But he would have also encountered it in a much more familiar place, his mother-in-law's *Vindication*, and in a context particularly meaningful to him. In examining "the poisoned source of female vices and follies," Wollstonecraft finds the trouble to lie in "the sensual homage paid to beauty," that is, "to beauty of features; for it has been shrewdly observed by a German writer, that a pretty woman, as an object of desire, is generally allowed to be so by men of all descriptions; whilst a fine woman, who inspires more sublime emotions by displaying intellectual beauty, may be overlooked or observed with indifference, by those men who find their happiness in the gratification of their appetites."[78]

Beginning with the book's Dedication and continuing throughout the body of the text, Wollstonecraft inveighs against the exclusively sexual elevation of women and insists that a woman's real beauty consists in "mental" or "intellectual" distinction. Mere physical beauty is acceptable in girls, but "the springtide of life over, we look for soberer sense in the face . . . We then wish to converse, not to fondle, to give scope to our imaginations as well as to the sensations of our hearts." Most men unfortunately look only for "more *tangible* beauty." In a very Shelleyan passage she defends "that superior gracefulness which is truly the expression of the mind. The mental grace, not noticed by vulgar eyes, often flashes across a rough countenance, and irradiating every feature, shows simplicity and independence of mind. It is then we read characters of immortality in the eye, and see the soul in every gesture."[79] This is that same "Spirit of Beauty" apostrophized by Shelley in the *Hymn*, a spirit whom both writers perceive to be "intellectual." The feminist, no less than the poet, possessed the soul-enwoven eyes that were the coefficient of this beauty. "Her eyes," marvels an enraptured Southey at their first meeting, "are the most meaning I ever saw."[80]

The "German writer" alluded to in the *Vindication* is almost certainly Shelley's old favorite, C. M. Wieland. In *The History of Agathon*, the poet's especial favorite, the beauteous Danae observes that "no passions were excited by intellectual beauty."[81] The remainder of the novel, however, gives the lie to this assertion. Wieland, like Wollstonecraft and like Shelley, is bent on demonstrating the possibility of an "intellectual love" supplying meaning and dignity to mere physical attraction (II.4). His hero Agathon, unlike most men, does not make the "dazzling whiteness and inviting contours of a beautiful bosom" the foundation of his love, but rather the intellectual and moral qualities lying behind such superficial "corporeal" charms. When looking at his mistress, he sees, just as does the Shelleyan lover, "all the excellencies of her mind" brightly shining through the "charming earthly veil" (II.29).[82]

But while Wieland, Shelley, and Wollstonecraft all agreed on the importance of intellectual beauty to full sympathetic partnership, Wieland did not mean quite the same thing by this attribute as did the other two. For Wieland intellectual beauty consists chiefly in moral qualities—innocence, purity, virtue, qualities of "soul"—while Shelley and Wollstonecraft place their faith in woman's powers of mind. This is not to say that both writers do not recognize moral beauty in women likewise. Shelley remarks in the *Discourse* on the "moral" as well as the "intellectual loveliness" with which "the acquisition of knowledge and the cultivation of sentiment animates as with another life of overpowering grace the lineaments and gestures of every form which it inhabits" (220), and Wollstonecraft in *A Vindication* acknowledges the "beauty of moral loveliness."[83] But their primary interest is in heightening woman's mental beauty. If sympathetic relations between the sexes are to be fully realized, both sexes must possess equal access to Shelley's Spirit of Beauty, a quality traditionally denied to women except in the rare instances of "the intellectual women of England & Germany," with their soul-enwoven eyes.[84]

In the actual careers of both Wollstonecraft and Shelley, the road to intellectual beauty takes a sharp turn back on itself, the "intellectual" faculty more and more subsumed under the faculty of the imagination. Both writers inaugurated their careers under the spell of Enlightenment rationalism, idealizing reason and defining intellect in terms of this traditionally male faculty. As their thinking matured, they grew increasingly restless with the limitations of analytic reasoning, substituting in its stead, as was typical of the age, the cohesive powers of the sympathetic imagination. This intuitive, synthesizing faculty seemed to represent a surer pathway to the reality of things, and it had been the traditional prerogative not only of the seer and the artist but of women. If true intellectual beauty were ever to light up the collective face of humankind, making it one with the "Light whose smile kindles the Universe," the "beauty in which all things work and move" (*Ado*.liv), it would require not only the liberation of the patriarchally fettered female intellect from its traditional bondage to the male, but its elevation as a model, a paradigm, for the male. Neither writer ever consciously saw the problem in precisely these terms. Shelley insists that there is no generic intellectual distinction between the sexes (220), and Wollstonecraft essentially agrees, believing that at least until the sexes have been given the same educational opportunities, it cannot be proved that women are intellectually inferior. But a feminist transvaluation is implicit in the developed thinking of each.

For both writers the archetypal embodiment of the male intellect would have been found immediately before them in the mind of William Godwin, at first admired but at last recognized as lacking in the highest kind of intellectual power. When Godwin praises Shelley's Chancery paper and his review of *Mandeville*, simultaneously depreciating the recently completed *Laon and Cythna*, the poet heatedly demurs. "I [have] long believed," he writes, "that my power consists in sympathy & that part of imagination which relates to sentiment & contemplation.—I am formed,—if for any thing not in common with the herd of mankind—to apprehend minute & remote distinctions of feeling whether relative to external nature, or the living beings which surround us, & to communicate the conceptions which result from considering either the moral or the material universe as a whole. Of course I believe these faculties, which perhaps comprehend all that is sublime in man, to exist very imperfectly in my own mind. But when you advert to my Chancery paper,—a cold, forced, unimpassioned, & insignificant piece of cramped & cautious argument; & to the little scrap about Mandeville, which expressed my feelings indeed, but cost scarcely two minutes thought to express, as specimens of my powers, more favorable than that which grew as it were from 'the agony & bloody sweat' of intellectual travail—surely I must feel that in some manner, either I am mistaken in believing that I have any talent at all, or you in the selection of the specimens of it" (*L.I.*577-578). By this date "intellectual" has incorporated the warm, feminine powers of sympathy, imagination, and sensibility, while excluding the cold, cramping, masculine restrictions of Godwinian analytical reasoning and argumentation. Imagination for Shelley is now "the Sun of Life," reason "the cold & uncertain & borrowed light of . . . the Moon." Reason's gaze is owl-like, imagination's that of the eagle.[85]

In the same way Wollstonecraft, when replying to Godwin's criticism of her uncompleted *The Wrongs of Woman*, objects: "I am compelled to think that there is something in my writings more valuable, than in the productions of some people on whom you bestow warm eulogiums—I mean more mind—denominate it as you will—more of the observations of my own senses, more of the combining of my own imagination—the effusions of my own feelings and passions than the cold workings of the brain on the materials procured by the senses and imagination of other writers."[86] Godwin himself, shortly after his wife's death, momentarily acknowledges that there was something in her cast of mind raising it to a plane in certain respects superior to his own. In the tribute to his wife's genius with which he closes the *Memoirs of the Author of the "Vindication of the Rights of Woman"* (1798), he reflects: "I did not possess, in the degree of some other men, an intuitive perception of intellectual beauty. I have perhaps a strong and lively sense of the pleasures of the imagination; but I have seldom been right in assigning to them their proportionate value, but by dint of persevering examination, and the change and correction of my first opinions. What I wanted in this respect, Mary possessed, in a degree superior to any other person I ever knew. The strength of her mind lay in intuition." In the strict sense of the word, he goes on, Mary "reasoned little," but "spontaneously, by a sort of tact, and the force of a cultivated imagination," she surprised by the "soundness" of her conclusions. This "light," he relates, was "lent to me for a very short period, and is now extinguished for ever."[87]

In the second edition of the *Memoirs*, published later in the same year, Godwin makes clear that the differences he is describing are essentially sexual in derivation. "A circumstance by which the two sexes are particularly distinguished from each other," he explains, is that "the one is accustomed more to the exercise of its reasoning powers, and the other of its feelings. Women have a frame of body more delicate and susceptible of impression than men, and, in proportion as they receive a less intellectual education, are more unreservedly under the empire of feeling." It is possible that he and Mary "each carried farther than to its common extent the characteristic of the sexes to which we belonged." At the same time Mary's particular ability, which he lacks, the intuitive perception of intellectual beauty, he now defines more exactly as the possession of "an intuitive sense of the pleasures of the imagination," whereas "intellectual" has become reserved for analytical reasoning.[88]

This is precisely the sort of traditional sexist distinction that Wollstonecraft rebels against so strongly in the *Vindication*. There, imagination is the culprit, "lying," the faculty of immature minds, while reason and understanding are extolled.[89] Unfortunately the rational faculty is denied to women because of their meager education. Hence women are doomed to the role of inferiors—intuitive, imaginative, but childlike, at the mercy of their emotions and instincts. By the end of her career, however, she seems to have reversed the ordering. In the uncompleted *The Wrongs of Woman* the stress is on the imagination, which is constantly praised, while reason has largely disappeared. Whether she would have accepted Godwin's distinction that the possession of such a mind was sexual in origin, there is no doubt that she valued its possession over the merely analytic intellect and was prepared to champion its value. If the sexes were complementary in this respect, as claimed by Godwin, the inferiority was no longer on the side of women.

For Shelley the highest type of mind united acute reasoning ability with superior intuitive powers. The supreme example was Plato, who exhibited "the rare union of close and subtle logic" with the "most remarkable intuitions." But the latter faculty weighed most heavily with the mature Shelley, allowing him to rank Plato far higher on the scale of intellectual being than his principal rival in antiquity, Aristotle.[90] The key to intuition was the faculty of the imagination, just as Wollstonecraft and Godwin had assumed, however different their evaluations. Through the Promethean power of the creative imagination human beings are enabled to ascend "to bring light and fire from those eternal regions where the owl-winged faculty of calculation dare not ever soar" (VII.135). Shelley's own poetry is a deliberate appeal to the "imagination" of his readers rather than "a reasoned system on the theory of human life," for "until the mind can love, and admire, and trust, and hope, and endure"—qualities personified in his regenerate Prometheus—"reasoned principles of moral conduct are seeds cast upon the highway of life which the unconscious passenger tramples into dust, although they would bear the harvest of his happiness."[91]

Shelley nowhere gives the intuitive perception of intellectual beauty a specifically sexual emphasis. While he believes in the "diversity . . . of the powers" that distinguish the sexes, these distinctions apparently do not include intellectual difference (VII.129). At the same time it is a feminine presence whose loveliness irradiates the *Hymn* as well as the many other poems where intellectual beauty is apostrophied: its personification is glowingly female. The whole movement of Shelley's thought is away from the traditionally masculine apprehension of reality toward a feminine or at least androgynous one. What was once woman's weakness becomes her strength, and the way is paved for the latter-day exaltation of woman's traditional intuitive and imaginative faculties by contemporary feminists, seeking a way out of the dead end at which male syllogistic and technological thinking has arrived: a dehumanized, computerized society. Woman's intellectual beauty becomes a saving grace for all mankind.

But the message is still more complicated, for Shelley's psychology of intellectual beauty involves a paradox. Describing the visitations of this power as being akin to the oceanic oneness with nature that is typical of children and is recaptured by adults only in moments of profound reverie preceding, accompanying, or following an unusually intense apprehension of life, Shelley argues that as human beings grow older and the "intellectual" powers mature, the ability to apprehend the spirit of intellectual beauty correspondingly declines. If this is the case, then education in the formal sense, the development of rational and analytical powers, is not what is needed at all, and ironically woman in her traditional state of childlike ignorance is nearer the Spirit of Beauty than is the educated adult man. Shelley himself first became intellectually conscious of the Spirit of Beauty at boarding school and apparently in reaction to the tyranny of conventional learning.[92] If man is to regain touch with that spirit, then it must, paradoxically, be through the deliberate fostering of his unintellectual self: the man must become as the woman and both as the child.

Such thinking is more than feminist in its reverberations. It portends this century's countercultural revulsion of the young and of educational reformers to the canonization of technological achievement. How far Shelley meant to pursue the implications of his thinking, or how far he himself was conscious of them, is problematic. Yet a dangerous anti-intellectualism and obscurantism are endemic in both the Romantic revolt against reason and its contemporary reincarnation which is antithetic to the Shelley born of the Enlightenment and is alien to the spirit of his best work. The light of the mind can too easily find itself extinguished in the cloudy waters of the irrational, which is not a result that Shelley, nor for that matter Wollstonecraft, would have welcomed. Both were liberal humanists at heart, and it is this bias, not romantic unreason, which is their enduring legacy to women.

9

The Eye of Sane Philosophy

THOUGH SHELLEY was almost uniquely far-sighted for his period, not all his views on women are compatible with subsequent developments in feminism, either today's or those emerging in the nineteenth century. The winning of the vote was to become the primary goal of the first women's movement. Mary Wollstonecraft had spoken in its favor as early as the *Vindication*. Yet Shelley was opposed to votes for women under existing social conditions.[1] While Jeremy Bentham and others had advocated the immediate institution of female suffrage, the proposal was "immature," he held in *A Philosophical View of Reform* (1819), adding the important qualification that if his objection were merely "the result of despondency," he would be "the last to withhold his vote from any system which might tend to an equal and full development of the capacities of all living beings" (VII.54).

Shelley's position on women was consistent with his position on the enfranchisement of the masses. He was equally opposed to universal male suffrage under existing social conditions. Despite the radicalism of his visionary prophecies, he was a gradualist when it came to practical politics.[2] Above all, he feared anarchy or mob rule, with the consequent reinstitution of even severer forms of repression, as had happened in France. Only when the masses, and women, were fully educated to their duties and responsibilities would he be ready to concede them the privilege of the ballot.[3] These were the "difficult and unbending realities of actual life" (VII.43).

Shelley's views on woman's suffrage, though realistically cautious, were at least basically feminist. His views on birth control, however, would appear antifeminist by the standards of the modern women's movement. Reproductive autonomy is one of the fundamental planks of twentieth-century feminism. Yet Shelley was strongly opposed to birth control. In his view, sex is reproductive by definition—"that gratification upon which the perpetuity of our species depends" (221)—and any attempt to bypass this function results in a "gross violation in the established nature of man." For this reason among others, homosexuality is wrong. That the poet made no efforts to limit conception in his own sexual practice is abundantly clear, as he was the father of at least six children in his brief lifetime, and in his eyes the joys of parenthood obviously represented one of the chief pleasures to be derived from the sexual act, as it did for his wives. For the participants to be concerned exclusively with "their mutual pleasure," as was possible with the use of mechanical contraceptive devices, defeating the normal reproductive consequences of the act, was illegitimate. Shelley underscores the "false delicacy" shrouding the subject which prevents his "explaining" himself more fully.

Shelley jotted down these observations in the same notebook containing portions of *A Philosophical View of Reform*, which attacks Malthusian population doctrine.[4] The jottings were apparently elicited by Godwin's just written reply to Malthus, *Of Population* (1820), for they cite Godwin's "comprehensive & penetrating intellect." Shelley, together with Godwin, opposed Malthusian doctrine on perfectibilitarian grounds. Malthus, who was after all a "priest," no more condoned artificial means of family limitation than did Shelley or Godwin; his only remedy was moral restraint. But his doctrines were already finding themselves associated in the popular mind with artificial birth-control practice, and later in the century his name would become synonymous, in a major historical irony, with the birth control movement. When Shelley satirizes Malthusianism in the contemporaneously written *Swellfoot the Tyrant*—"spay those Sows/ That load the earth with Pigs; cut close and deep./Moral restraint I see has no effect" (I.i.72-78)—he is evidently extending Malthus' doctrine to include neo-Malthusian techniques of birth control, specifically sterilization, and by implication contraception and abortion.[5] His detestation of abortion, deplored along with infanticide in the contraception jottings as one of the "expedients" too often resorted to by parents unable to support new life in the bleakly necessitarian world of the Rev. Malthus—"Abortions are dead in the womb,/And their mothers look pale"—is unmistakable from his outrage at the charge he had once done such a thing himself.[6] Of the Hoppners' scandalous assertions that while in Naples in 1818 he gave Claire Clairmont, supposedly pregnant with his child, "the most violent medicines to procure abortion," he vehemently protests: how can anyone believe him guilty of such "unutterable crimes" (L.II.319).

By today's standards Shelley's views may strike the reader as benighted, especially for a champion of women. In his defense, however, in his own day even the most advanced thinkers, with rare exceptions such as Jeremy Bentham and Francis Place, shared the same traditional belief in the authority of nature, though rationalist and utilitarian in every other respect.[7] The divorcing of sex from reproduction, while normal practice in the ancient world, has only become respectable again during the twentieth century. During the nineteenth, nature was defined by Judeo-Christian pronatalist norms which made procreation the sole legitimate end of the sexual instinct. Contraception was viewed as the unnatural practice of libertines and prostitutes and was forbidden by law. Sale of contraceptive information was actionable as "obscenity." Not surprisingly, the burgeoning feminist movement steered clear of associating its demands with birth control agitation. The primary end of sex was procreation. Wollstonecraft took this position, "the parental design of nature," in the *Vindication*, and it remained the standard feminist position until the closing years of the century, when birth control won a small but growing body of adherents among feminists.[8] Until then contraception was seen as merely another attempt by the "bestial male" at the sexual exploitation of women. What was wanted were fewer sexual opportunities, not more; continence, not lust. Men were expected to practice the same restraint demanded of women.[9] Shelley's position, though now outdated, is thus consistent with the historical development of feminism.

What to do with unwanted offspring, once conception had actually occurred, presented a serious problem under a system where birth control was not an option. Unlike ancient times, no one condoned infanticide. Yet the practice was not uncommon, especially in Protestant countries, and so was a concern of Shelley's. He bemoans the problem from his earliest poetry, as in "The Crisis" (11. 11-12), and a letter from Keswick during the period complains that "Children are frequently found in the River which the unfortunate women employed at the manufactory destroy," making the place "more like a suburb of London than a village of Cumberland" (*L.*I.223).[10] He adverts to the problem in the "Love is sold" Note to *Queen Mab*, ironically contrasting society's ferocious attitude toward the prostitute, guilty of nothing more serious than "having followed the dictates of a natural appetite," with its seemingly "lighter" treatment of the infanticide, she who "destroys her child to escape reproach" (I.142).

Infinitely preferable to child murder or exposure in Shelley's view, though scarcely an ideal solution, was the Continental institution of the foundling hospital. Of the Pisa Foundling Hospital, "where a hole in the wall admits at all hours the new born Babes, whom their Mothers commit to Asylum," Shelley observes to Medwin that "it was a disgrace to our boasted civilization that no similar one should exist in London or our large Cities which he said would prevent a crime here unknown and there too common. Infanticide, originating in a sense of shame and the inadequacy of means to support the fatherless offspring of prostitution."[11] Despite Shelley, a foundling hospital actually did exist in England, the famed London Foundling Hospital, established in 1739 through the heroic efforts of Thomas Coram, who had been appalled at the frequent sight of "newly-born children left deserted, to die, on the dunghills" in and around the city. At one time the hospital had branches at Acksworth, Shrewsbury, Westerham, Aylesbury, and Barnet, but it had long since abandoned the Continental policy of "indiscriminate" or unrestricted admission, favored by Shelley, as being too costly and impractical and also as encouraging to prostitution.[12] In any case even the foundling hospital along Continental lines was a last ditch resort for Shelley. When protesting the scandalous accusations of the Hoppners, who charged that after Claire's abortion had proved unsuccessful, he immediately tore the child from its mother and "sent it to the foundling hospital," Shelley contends that child abandonment is no less a "crime" than is abortion.[13] The responsibility for rearing a child belongs to the parents unmarried just as much as married.

While the march of time has not been kind to Shelley's thinking on women and birth control, his view of women in relation to the patriarchal family is far from obsolete in light of the latest feminist opinion. His insistence that the marriage contract "degrades" the female, turning her into chattel property, coupled with his espousal of free love and communal property sharing, puts him in the vanguard of feminist theory (L.I.81). In this respect his ideas have not dated at all and could still serve as inspiration today.

They once did serve as inspiration to feminists in the early stages of the nineteenth-century woman's movement, when feminists were not yet afraid of challenging the traditional family structure and envisioning radical social alternatives. As pointed out by modern historians of the movement, the minds of a number of the early feminists were open to the possibility that the "entire domestic system would have to be re-structured as a pre-condition for sexual equality."[14] Fanny Wright, like Shelley, attacked marriage, the church, private property, and the sanctity of patriarchal paternity rights. An intimate associate of Robert Dale Owen, she was well versed in Shelley's sexual doctrines through the writings of the Owenites, to which she herself contributed. At one time she even tried to enlist Mary Shelley's interest in the utopian colony at Nashoba, an experiment partly inspired by the memory of Shelley, Godwin, and Wollstonecraft.[15] As the movement developed, however, it grew increasingly conservative, frightened in America by Wright's example and later by Victoria Woodhull's, and in England by Wollstonecraft's, so that sexual programs such as Shelley's came to be viewed with alarm. Today his thinking is once again very much alive and to the point. In one respect, indeed, his eschewal of sexual jealousy—"the mean & envious motive"—Shelley's thinking reached a stage far in advance of all but the most optimistic feminist hopes, and at a period when birth control was not yet an option. Anyone who can treat the question of a child's biological paternity as a matter of little significance, as Shelley does from the Gothic novels onward, has reached a plateau of liberation shared only by the most emancipated sexual revolutionaries.[16]

There is nothing utopian, however, about one aspect of Shelley's feminism, which is certain to strike sparks in the modern woman's movement. Prostitution is today widely viewed as the ultimate in sexual politics, patriarchal oppression in its nakedest form. Its stubborn persistence is consequently a burning issue in contemporary feminism and a target for fiery rhetoric. "Prostitutes are our political prisoners—in jail for cunt," explodes Kate Millett. Prostitution is "paradigmatic, . . . the very core of the female's social condition. It not only declares her subjection right in the open, with the cash nexus between the sexes announced in currency, rather than through the subtlety of a marriage contract . . . but the very act of prostitution is itself a declaration of our value, our reification."[17] The movement wants first of all the decriminalization of prostitution, particularly since the laws are so discriminatory in their application. But ultimately the movement seeks not the regulation of prostitution, but its eradication. The movement has no interest in legalizing what it feels is the most obtrusive form of sexual exploitation.

One of the most characteristic elements of Shelley's work is his hatred of prostitution. Whereas the liberation of woman's intellectual beauty was the most important blessing to be anticipated from her longed-for emancipation, the total disfigurement of her higher nature was the certain outcome of her present sexual imprisonment, the prototype of which was prostitution. In the *Discourse* Shelley describes coition without sentiment, or intercourse that is merely "diseased habit," as a "brutal prostitution of the most sacred impulses of our being" (222). Prostitution as an institution is fully as degrading and "unnatural" as the crudest forms of homosexuality. It is a direct violation of all those propositions, based on the "indestructible laws of human nature," which Shelley regards as preconditions for proper sexual indulgence: that the person selected be beautiful in both mind and body, thereby uniting all sympathies in one; that the act be temperate and linked to the higher emotions; and that it be performed according to nature.

Shelley does not accept the facile and complacent assumption that the theoretically more enlightened sexual morality of modern times is significantly superior to that of the ancient Greeks so long as the equally unnatural practice of female prostitution underlies modern sexual relations. "A person must be blinded by superstition," he expostulates, to suppose that Greek pederasty, even as practiced in its "grossest sense," is "more horrible than the usual intercourse endured by almost every youth of England with a diseased and insensible prostitute." It cannot be more unnatural, because "nothing defeats and violates nature, or the purposes for which the sexual instincts are supposed to have existed, than prostitution. Nor is it possible that the society into which the one plunges its victims should be more pernicious than the other." Nothing, he protests, is "more melancholy and ludicrous than to observe that the inhabitants of one epoch or of one nation harden themselves to all amelioration of their own practices and institutions and soothe their consciences by heaping invectives upon those of others while in the eye of sane philosophy their own are no less deserving of censure" (223).

As usual, the framework of Shelley's argument is utilitarian. The "eye of sane philosophy" which corrects the faulty vision of all those blinded by superstition is none other than the "enlightened philosophy" that "must condemn the laws by which the sexual instinct is usually regulated" (221). It is the philosophy of that higher hedonism, with its delicately adjusted calculus of higher and lower pleasures, which Shelley takes as the starting point of all his ethical theory and which he opposes to the prevailing moral code of his time, one in his view setting up absolutes that do violence to the permanent instincts of human nature. The evils of prostitution are thus weighed by the same principles that inform all his other moral judgments.

That the evils were indeed great was a belief held not just by Shelley alone. Contemporary witness is virtually unanimous on the point. Prostitution was one of the great evils of the age, *the* "social evil." In the *Vindication* Wollstonecraft protests against "the shameless behaviour of the prostitutes, who infest the streets" of London.[18] The "harlot's curse" pollutes the night air of Blake's London, as it does Wordsworth's and Byron's.[19] The city "swarms" with prostitutes, agree contemporary journals; "Sin wears a front of brass among us."[20] The situation was the same in the cities and towns outside the metropolis. In short, a "great army of prostitutes," in Trevelyan's phrase, infested the cities of early nineteenth-century England, making them "hideous at nightfall."[21] Nor did the situation improve as the century advanced.

Estimates as to the exact number of prostitutes inhabiting London itself varied, but they were invariably spectacular. A letter to the *Examiner* in 1812 put the figure at 50,000.[22] Other estimates were 30,000, 40,000, or even 100,000.[23] A source that would have impressed Shelley, James Lawrence's *The Empire of the Nairs*, put the number at 70,000 for the opening years of the century, "so that every eighth female that we meet in the streets is a prostitute" (I.4-5). Shelley himself claims in the "Love is sold" Note to *Queen Mab* that "one-tenth of the population of London" is formed of prostitutes (I.142). He later warns his friend Maria Gisborne that on her visit to London she must expect to meet such sights as a "wretched woman reeling by," shouting curses with the watchman, "partner of her trade" (*Letter*, 269-270). Leigh Hunt recalls of Shelley after his death that "the unhappy mass of prostitution which exists in England . . . was always one of the subjects that in a moment's notice would overshadow the liveliest of his moods."[24]

Although the true extent of prostitution was enormously exaggerated by contemporary moralists, there is no doubt that prostitution was a serious, far-reaching, and steadily worsening evil during Shelley's time. The more society came to place a premium on the chastity of the respectable female and the sanctity of the home, the more prostitution became a necessity. As explained by Brian Harrison, the prostitute "necessarily featured in a society of frequent female confinements, of middle-class gratification-postponement, and of widespread celibacy."[25] This society took seriously the Malthusian ideal of moral restraint, an ideal that could only be realized in practice, as Francis Place ironically noted, at the expense of "vice and prostitution."[26] The remedy for Place was contraception. But for Shelley it was the abolition of what he considered society's absurd overestimation of female chastity and the monopolistic exclusiveness of the patriarchal marriage contract.

Through his study of Lawrence, Shelley was early taught to regard prostitution as primarily the fault of marriage. "So long as Hymen continues a monopolist," Lawrence declares in *The Nairs*, "Love will continue a smuggler," and "Wherever marriage is a profession, love will be a trade" (I.xvi,II.4-5). Were there no marriage, there would be no prostitutes. As Shelley protests to Lawrence in the summer of 1812 after first reading *The Nairs*, marriage is itself nothing more than a sort of "*legal*" prostitution, the woman bartering her body for economic gain. Neither institution could exist without the other. Previously, Shelley admits, he was blind to this connection, but now he sees that the existence of prostitution is "the greatest argument" of all against marriage—a view shortly to be repeated in the "Love is sold" Note to *Queen Mab*, where he affirms that "Prostitution is the legitimate offspring of marriage and its accompanying errors."[27] According to this view, if no artificial patriarchal restraints stood in the way of natural sexual fulfillment, prostitution would vanish. It can flourish only where it supplies a covert need.

The trouble stems from the fact that the traditional Christian marital ethic demands just such restraint. Historically a rigidly monogamous sexual ethic has been one of the cornerstones of Christian teaching. But in actual practice strict ideals of chastity have been found workable only when combined with a tacit condonation of extramarital outlet. In this way prostitution, while admittedly an evil, becomes a necessary evil, and in some instances is openly defended as such.[28] Shelley himself seems to have such an understanding in mind in his fragmentary and enigmatic remark toward the end of the *Discourse*: "If it be inquired how an individual ought to act in the [blank in original; probably "circumstances"]—the reply is—make the best of a bad matter" (223). In terms of traditional morality, prostitution is simply the inevitable price exacted for sexual purity.

In principle, the burden of sexual purity falls equally on both sexes. But in practice society cares only about woman's purity, described as "the great law of nature" by the *Quarterly Review* in 1819, woman's very "first virtue," or in Shelley's phrase, "the female criterion of virtue."[29] Ironically, the effects of such an unyielding ideal of chastity rebound cruelly on the heads of those it is designed to protect. "To this," explains Lawrence in *The Nairs*, "may be ascribed the number of involuntary courtesans who infest the metropolis" (I.xxv). Shelley concurs in *Peter Bell the Third*, portraying London as an infernal city where one is sure to encounter "mincing women, mewing . . ./Of their own virtue, and pursuing/Their gentler sisters to that ruin,/Without which what were chastity?" (III.i,viii). What, he asks in a caustic note, "would this husk and excuse for a virtue be without its kernel prostitution, or the kernel prostitution without this husk of a virtue? I wonder the women of the town do not form an association like the Society for the Suppression of Vice, for the support of what may be called the 'King, Church and Constitution' of their order. But this subject is almost too horrible for a joke."

Owing to the ferocity with which breaches of the sexual code were punished, prostitution was indeed often involuntary. In the words of the Victorian social historian W. E. H. Lecky, because of the "religious feeling" on the subject, "a single fault of this kind," at least in the upper and middle classes, is sufficient to "affix an indelible brand which no time, no virtues, no penitence can wholly efface. Infanticide is greatly multiplied, and a vast portion of those whose reputations have been blasted by one momentary sin, are hurled into the abyss of habitual prostitution."[30] So severe was public opinion against the woman who had "erred," as Lawrence stresses in *The Nairs*, that "no family would receive her" even as their menial servant, nor would any "manufactory . . . employ her."[31] Economic necessity left the unhappy outcast with no choice, and prostitution was the result.

The libertine practices of the day had under the euphemistic disguise of "gallantry" become for many men almost a national sport.[32] According to Shelley in the *Discourse*, such practice was censurable not only because of its debasing effects on the individual, yielding only an inferior sort of pleasure, but because of its wider effects on the social organism, producing "on the whole, greater pain than pleasure." Owing to an unnatural veneration of female purity, libertinism and seduction were inevitably swelling the tide of prostitution.[33] Such practices were condemned by the fundamental test of social utility. In Shelley's eyes the nation was hobbled by an inhuman sexual ethic. As long as this ethic retained its ecclesiastical authority, there was apparently no appeal, even though the most obvious evils were the result. That the solution was at once so near at hand and yet so impossible of attainment only compounded the misery.

Some reformers wished to ameliorate the situation by amending the nation's legal code, making seduction punishable by law.[34] Shelley opposes such a solution, believing that seduction and adultery cannot be legislated out of existence. He is quite severe on earlier attempts to do so. The solution will come about only through the free operation of the natural laws of utility, "until mankind shall have enough" of the unhappiness produced by the present system (222). A complete reversal of society's sexual ethic is needed, bringing it under the rule of the pleasure-pain principle.

Although seldom the subject of more than incidental comment, the theme of seduction, abandonment, and prostitution holds a significant place in Shelley's prose and verse. The poem "Ballad," or "Young Parson Richards," is entirely devoted to the subject. It belongs to a series of incendiary sociopolitical broadsides, including *The Mask of Anarchy*, fired off by Shelley in the years 1818-1819 in a deliberately rough-and-ready style in the hope of capturing a mass audience.[35] Rude and unpolished though the "Ballad" is, it discloses an important side of Shelley's thought, however offensive to conventional opinion. The poem relates the pathetic, albeit scandalous, history of a hapless country girl, who is ruthlessly seduced then heartlessly abandoned by a sanctimonious Church of England parson. Pregnant and unable to obtain employment, she is driven to the brink of prostitution. As a last resort, she returns to her seducer's door, babe in arms, only to find herself disowned, whereupon, partly from hunger but more from sheer despair, she collapses and dies. Shelley's polemical intent is the exposure of what he considers the gross moral hypocrisy of the nineteenth-century church. Directly responsible for conditions conducive to seduction and prostitution, it nevertheless remains coldly neglectful of the consequences. Underlining his message, Shelley has the parson remain grimly silent throughout the poem.[36]

This poem does not represent a momentary aberration; its sentiment goes very deep. The denouement of *Zastrozzi*, Shelley's first novel and the earliest of his published work, hinges on exactly the same situation, though without the anticlerical overtones. The seemingly motiveless malignity of the villain toward the hero, which gives the work its faint thread of plot, turns out to have good reason, for Zastrozzi's mother had been seduced by the hero's father on the promise of marriage and then abandoned. Subsequently, when she "begged a pittance to keep her[self] from starving, her proud betrayer spurned her from his door, and tauntingly bade her exercise her profession" (V.101-102). The virtuous Eloise meets the same galling fate in Shelley's next novel, *St. Irvyne*. In his first published verse, the "Victor and Cazire" volume, written with his sister Elizabeth, the story is the same.[37] The "Ballad" is thus plainly no anomaly. Its theme is present in Shelley from the outset, encouraged by the sentimental and Gothic traditions in which he was working, but recognized as a real-life plague spot in the nation's sexual conduct. The principal difference is that in the more mature piece he places the blame where it belongs, on society, rather than on the lustful machinations of the individual male.

This change occurred in the years immediately succeeding his expulsion from Oxford, no doubt fostered by his extensive readings in Godwin, Lawrence, and Wollstonecraft. It can be glimpsed in the social radicalism of the Esdaile Notebook's gruesome "Zeinab and Kathema" and later in *The Revolt of Islam*, an elaborately expanded version of the earlier poem.[38] The "Love is sold" Note to *Queen Mab* is Shelley's most scathing prose pronouncement on the subject, setting it firmly in its social context. "Women," he charges, "for no other crime than having followed the dictates of a natural appetite, are driven with fury from the comforts and sympathies of society." When the hapless outcast turns to prostitution, which is the only choice left to her, society "declares war" against her: "*She* is in fault; *she* is the criminal; *she* is the froward and untamable child; and society, forsooth, the pure and virtuous matron, who casts her as an abortion from her undefiled bosom. Society avenges herself on the criminals of her own creation; she is employed in anathematizing the vice today, which yesterday she was the most zealous to teach." This is what comes of obeying the "bigoted morality of [our] forefathers," for prostitution is the inevitable outcome of marriage and "its accompanying errors," namely legal monopoly, chastity, libertinism, seduction, and social disgrace (I.142).

But while Shelley sympathized with the plight of the prostitute and the unjust conditions that compelled her to her trade, he had nothing but loathing for the act itself and the degradation forced on its participants. The act is an overwhelming denial of his own ideal of sexual connection.[39] Sexual relations degenerate into an unnatural mercenary transaction in which the woman is reduced to the level of an object, to be bought and exploited in brutal terms for the man's selfish sensual gratification, reifying the woman in modern terminology, robbing her of a sense of self-worth and human dignity, and turning her into something hard, vicious, and unfeeling (I.142;V.234). "Even love is sold" is the biting rhetoric of *Queen Mab*, whereby the "solace of all woe" is transformed to "deadliest agony, old age/Shivers in selfish beauty's loathing arms,/And youth's corrupted impulses prepare/A life of horror from the blighting bane/Of commerce."[40] All this because of a "fanatical idea of chastity" which excludes men from "the society of modest and accomplished women . . . destroying thereby all those exquisite and delicate sensibilities whose existence cold-hearted worldlings have denied; annihilating all genuine passion, and debasing that to a selfish feeling which is the excess of generosity and devotedness" (I.142).

Shelley shared with his contemporaries a highly colored and overdramatic picture of the prostitute's lot and the fate to which she was condemned. Later in the century William Acton and others maintained that prostitution was merely a "transitory state" through which hordes of women passed before being reabsorbed back into respectable society, usually through marriage, often above their original station. Others through their savings set themselves up in business as milliners, shophelpers, or lodging house operators. The "fallen" woman's irremediable ruin was thus largely a myth.[41]

The threat posed by prostitution to health, however, was a serious one. "It is impossible to gain a sympathetic insight" into the period's thinking about prostitution, or sexual relations in general, notes Kellow Chesney, "without giving full weight to the significance of venereal disease. It was undoubtedly widespread, though just how common nobody knew."[42] Prostitutes were the chief agents of infection. All of them periodically contracted gonorrhea, and resort to their ministrations was so established a part of the era's sexual practice that it was a rare male who escaped gonorrheal infection at some period in his life.[43] Syphilis, however, not gonorrhea, was the real fear, though the two diseases were not clearly distinguished until well into the century. Fear of contagion was so widespread, in the words of Ronald Pearsall, "as to give currency to its own name—syphilophobia."[44]

This aspect of prostitution elicits Shelley's most horrified attention: "prostitution's venomed bane," in the language of *Queen Mab*, or the "pestilence that springs from unenjoying sensualism," filling all human life with "hydra-headed woes" (IX.87;V.194-196). No one, he charges elsewhere, can emerge untainted from the "poisonous embraces of a prostitute." She herself is "irrecoverably doomed to long and lingering disease," while her customers find their bodies and minds crumbling into "a hideous wreck of humanity; idiocy and disease become perpetuated in their miserable offspring, and distant generations suffer."[45] More destructive than the physical consequences of prostitution, however, are the psychological, which Shelley also conveys in the language of poisonous infection: vice "converteth . . ./Its food to deadliest venom."[46] All sex not connected with sentiment is poisonous in Shelley, a "nightshade" or "hemlock" (VI.181). More broadly still, all social evils whatsoever are a kind of venereal infection, a corruption of the healthy body politic—the sound of "King" has "poison in it, 'tis the sperm/Of what makes life foul, cankerous, and abhorred."[47] Only in a future regenerate society will humankind be free of infection: "Like passion's fruit, the nightshade's tempting bane/Poisons no more the pleasure it bestows" (QM.VIII.129-130).

That the mature Shelley would himself have been "quite incapable of gross amours with prostitutes," as maintained by Trelawny, is scarcely open to doubt.[48] Yet given the poet's preoccupation with the evils of prostitution and his patent horror at the dangers of venereal infection, it is not surprising someone might charge that he had more than an academic interest in the subject, that the later attitudes were the immediate result of the sort of youthful baptism into sex which he said very few young men of his day could escape. In fact Thornton

Hunt, the son of Shelley's friend Leigh, reported in the mid-Victorian period that the poet while in college had contracted a venereal infection: "accident has made me aware of facts which give me to understand that, in passing through the usual curriculum of a college life in all its paths, Shelley did not go scatheless, —but that, in the tampering with venal pleasures, his health was seriously, and not transiently, injured. The effect was far greater on his mind than on his body . . . Conscientious, far beyond even the ordinary maximum amongst ordinary men, he felt bound to denounce the mischief from which he saw others suffer more severely than himself, since in them there was no such reaction."[49]

As Hunt discloses neither the nature of his "facts" nor their authority it is possible the story rests on nothing more solid than intelligent deduction. Still, as Hunt was a reputable member of the Victorian literary community and personally sympathetic to Shelley, the story cannot be rejected out of hand. Hunt lends support to his assertion by pointing to the confessedly autobiographical section of *Epipsychidion* in which Shelley sketches an idealized history of his youthful erotic experience, including temptation by "One" who "sate by a well, under blue nightshade bowers," and "whose voice was venomed melody":

> The breath of her false mouth was like faint flowers,
> Her touch was as electric poison,—flame
> Out of her looks into my vitals came,
> And from her living cheeks and bosom flew
> A killing air, which pierced like honey-dew
> Into the core of my green heart, and lay
> Upon its leaves; until, as hair grown gray
> O'er a young brow, they hid its unblown prime
> With ruins of unseasonable time. (256-266)

These lines, according to Hunt, are a "plain and only too intelligible reference to the college experiences to which I have alluded." Shelley "indicates even the material consequences to himself in his injured aspect and hair touched with gray."[50]

As Kenneth Neill Cameron points out, this explanation has much to recommend it, even to the comment on graying hair, since "it was a commonly accepted belief that venereal disease turned hair gray prematurely, and Shelley's hair . . . was prematurely graying."[51] The passage also makes extensive use of the poet's poison and disease imagery. Particularly striking is the "nightshade bower," elsewhere associated with prostitution. Without external corroboration, however, the lines stop far short of being conclusive. It is equally possible that the imagery conveys a strictly emotional experience, the withering psychological consequences of a passionate but blighted love such as that described in the youthful "Passion: (to the [Nightshade])," probably referring to Shelley's loss of Harriet Grove.[52] Another point against the Hunt interpretation is that the gray hair of *Epipsychidion* is treated not as a literal consequence of what happened to Shelley but as a metaphor of decay.

More convincing support for Hunt's view is found in *Una Favola,* Shelley's unfinished Italian love allegory and plainly idealized auto-biography. *Una Favola* recounts the history of a youth, the poet him-self, who at the age of fifteen is awakened to the vision of love. He follows the vision into the wood of Life and there is "nourished by the fruit of a certain tree" growing in its midst, "a food sweet and bitter at once, which being cold as ice to the lips, appeared fire in the veins" (VI.283). That this is an allusion to sex with "a diseased and insensible prostitute" in the words of the *Discourse*—Shelley may first have written "cold" for "insensible"—seems more possible than the passage from *Epipsychidion,* which is more likely a reference to the soul-withering effects of Harriet Grove's betrayal.[53]

It has seemingly always been assumed that by "college" Hunt was referring to Shelley's brief stay at Oxford and that it was here Shelley infected himself. If there is any truth to the story at all, however, the probability is that the poet's "poisoning" must have happened earlier, during the Eton period, since his life at Oxford is fully documented, while there are gaps in the knowledge of his activities before his ar-rival at the university. There is no evidence of his being seriously ill or laid up for any length of time at Oxford. Certainly there is nothing to indicate he was in any way physically incapacitated or suffering bodily discomfort. Just how discomforting venereal infection could be, Byron's letters of the same year underscore. Nor is there evidence of anything psychologically traumatic dating from this period which could conceivably be connected to a disagreeable experience with a prostitute.

It makes more sense to think of the episode, if indeed it took place, as occurring at Eton, which was also a "college," the OED noting that the word *colleger* was applied originally to the "70 boys on the foun-dation of Eton College," and which also supplied the necessary op-portunities. For example, Lawrence, who was Montem Poet for the year 1790, just two decades ahead of Shelley, states in *The Empire of the Nairs* that the college was notorious for both the number and the repulsiveness of the whores frequenting its neighborhood, and these odious creatures were responsible for the sexual baptism of most of the young collegers.[54] This account is supported by Wollstonecraft in *The Wrongs of Woman*. Henry Darnford, recalling the less innocent activities of his school days at Eton for the benefit of the appalled Maria Venables, shudders: "I will not disgust you with a recital of the vices of my youth, which can scarcely be comprehended by female delicacy. I was taught to love by a creature I am ashamed to mention."[55] Eton historians Cheetham and Parfit say of the period simply that the boys "wenched," citing the *Gentleman's Magazine* for 1798 on the sexual immorality of the school.[56] The evidence of both the opportunities and the general practice at Eton, coupled with Hunt's claim that the poet's tampering with venal pleasures occurred in his "early youth," suggest that Shelley's hypothetical "poisoning" took place in a period well antedating the Oxford days.[57] Certainly it was at Eton that the evils of prostitution and the sexual double standard first appeared in his work.

What Shelley would have thought of subsequent attempts to control venereal disease through the state regulation of prostitution can only be surmised. By a curious irony the Contagious Diseases Acts of the 1860s, in which such legislation was attempted, became a major target of the first woman's movement under the leadership of Josephine Butler. The Acts were intended to safeguard the health of the military by making prostitutes in garrison towns subject to enforced medical inspection. What the feminists objected to was, first of all, the official state recognition of prostitution implicit in the Acts and, second, the blatant sexual discrimination inherent in the licensing and inspection of the prostitutes. The Acts thus violated, in the words of William O'Neill, "Christian moral standards, feminine integrity, and the most fundamental principles of English justice."[58] Unquestionably Shelley would have sympathized with the libertarian, if not the religious, opposition to the Acts. The real issue, as he was aware, is not the spread of venereal disease but the persistence of the double standard. So long as men and women are judged by a different sexual morality, prostitution will thrive. Victorian feminists wished to impose a single standard of continence on both the sexes, men observing the same restraint exacted of women. But modern-day feminists want sexual freedom for both the sexes. True sexual equality demands no less. And with woman's "purity" no longer an issue, the attitudes fostering prostitution will gradually fade. This was Shelley's position also, and it gives his sexual philosophy continuing force.

10

The Detestable Distinctions of Sex

In *Laon and Cythna*, the suppressed version of *The Revolt of Islam*, Shelley's hero and heroine are not only lovers but brother and sister. In view of the universality of the incest taboo, Shelley might be expected to depict such a relationship as unnatural, one of those varieties of sexual connection implicitly forbidden in the *Discourse* as not *"according to nature"* (222). This is not the case. The passionate attachment of brother and sister is portrayed in glowing colors, and the forced erasure of their consanguineous relationship—demanded when the publisher, Charles Ollier, realized exactly what had been foisted on him—mortified Shelley, leading him to protest that the poem was "spoiled." According to Peacock, Shelley was "for some time inflexible" about making any changes at all in the poem and although he had "no hope of another publisher," he "for a long time refused to alter a line." Only with his friends acting as a sort of "literary committee," proposing alterations, was the text eventually modified. But Shelley never originated any of the changes and insisted to the end that his poem was ruined.[1]

To a notorious degree Shelley shared the period fascination with incest, which colored the literature not only of his own country but of America and the Continent as well. Far from condemning this sort of love as unnatural, the Romantics seemed bent on elevating it into an ideal, at least as between brother and sister. Part of the attraction of incestuous love was its illicitness. Prohibited by Old Testament injunctions still enforced in England by the ecclesiastical courts, incestuous attachment appealed to the Romantic sensibility precisely because of its sinfulness, and its portrayal became a prominent element of the Romantic satanism characteristic of the age. The appeal of incest also stemmed from the Romantic eagerness to explore new sensations, to push the boundaries of sexual experience to their furthest limits. Part of the interest was literary in origin, deriving from the Gothic love of the horrific, to which incest contributed its mite. And part was a natural extension of Romantic Prometheanism, the revolt against anachronistic social custom and usage. The last motive Shelley gives as his principal one in the original Preface to *Laon and Cythna*: "In the personal conduct of my Hero and Heroine, there is one circumstance which was intended to startle the reader from the trance of ordinary life. It was my object to break through the crust of those outworn opinions on which established institutions depend. I have appealed therefore to the most universal of all feelings, and have endeavoured to strengthen the moral sense, by forbidding its energies in seeking to avoid actions which are only crimes of convention. It is because there is so great a multitude of artificial vices that there are so few real virtues. Those feelings alone which are benevolent or malevolent, are essentially good or bad."

It was possible to adopt this essentially utilitarian stance, in language directly predicting the *Discourse*, because the extent of the incest taboo was not yet recognized. Free thinkers during the eighteenth century, immune to ecclesiastical preachments on the subject, could argue the case for cultural relativity with some plausibility, since incest had seemingly had the sanction of certain non-European societies.[2] Shelley introduces the dual incest motif into *Rosalind and Helen* on somewhat the same grounds, directing the emotional thrust of the poem against the murderous prejudice, social as well as religious, which can lead to martyrdom for incestuous lovers (156-166). Even in *The Cenci*, where the subject is scarcely viewed in the most favorable light, the thinking is fundamentally utilitarian. The Count's crime is not incest per se but incest done to wound, degrade, defile—an act committed out of hatred, not love. As Shelley was noting at the same time of Calderón's *Los Cabellos de Absalón*: "Incest is like many other *incorrect* things a very poetical circumstance. It may be the excess of love or of hate. It may be that defiance of every thing for the sake of another which clothes itself in the glory of the highest heroism, or it may be the cynical rage which confounding the good & bad in existing opinions breaks through them for the purpose of rioting in selfishness & antipathy" (L.II.154).

Shelley's emphasis makes clear the utilitarian foundations of his thinking: incest is a violation of the laws of society and thus "incorrect," not a violation of the laws of human nature and hence unnatural. As always, the mode in which the act is performed determines its morality, and incest may be good or evil depending on whether it eventuates in an overbalance of pleasure or pain for the participants. *The Cenci* is a play about "moral error" (L.II.190), but the error springs from the motives of its principals, Beatrice as well as her father, and not from the mere act of incest as such. In the draft

Preface to the drama Shelley attributes Beatrice's horror at her father's incestuous assault to "superstitions & customary persuasions," that is, to "religion, education, a sense of modesty."[3] To Shelley himself the Count's behavior is "disgusting," an act of extreme libertine obscenity. But this is no justification for the sort of superstitious loathing—"the necessity of circumstance and opinion" described in the published version of the Preface—which creates in Beatrice a murderous passion, causing her to rise against her normally gentle and pacific nature to commit the unnatural crime of patricide. The ultimate source of the tragedy is Christian sexual morality.

Aside from *The Cenci*, however, incest is nearly always a positive good in Shelley, whether introduced literally, symbolically, or as merely a figure of speech, and the act is portrayed as clearly within the bounds of nature.[4] The incest of nature is an integral part of "Love's Philosophy," and in the regenerate world of the future incest is projected even at the cosmic level in the love of the spheres. What this means in human terms is that in a society governed by lawless love, in which the proprietary nuclear family has disappeared, the incest interdiction will lose its significance.

Whether Shelley was so liberated in his own sexual practice has been the subject of speculation from his own lifetime on. In the Preface to *Laon and Cythna* he is careful to dissociate himself from the "sentiments connected with and characteristic of" the blood relationship of the poem's lovers; these have "no personal reference to the writer." And in a letter to Byron in 1816 he gladly disbelieves the rumors about Byron's guilty liaison with his half-sister, Augusta Leigh, which he calls "the only important calumny that ever was advanced against you."[5] Yet rumors abounded about his own supposed participation with Byron in a "League of Incest," as their allegedly promiscuous relations with Mary Godwin and Claire Clairmont at Lake Geneva in 1816 were maliciously labeled, since intercourse even with half-sisters, as Mary and Claire were erroneously believed to be, constituted incest in the period. These allegations, when combined with the witness of his own poetry, made him for many of his contemporaries literally that "incestuous wretch." Although Shelley burlesqued the image in *Peter Bell the Third* (478-479), it was no joke to either him or Byron. "These calumnies were monstrous," as Shelley explains to Teresa Guiccioli, "and really too infamous to leave us, their victims, even the refuge of contempt . . . They said that we had formed a pact to outrage all that is regarded as most sacred in human society. Allow me, Madam, to spare you the details. I will only tell you that atheism, incest, and many other things—sometimes ridiculous and sometimes terrible—were imputed to us" (*L.*II.328). Both poets believed, mistakenly, that Southey was responsible for carrying the rumors back to England. "The Son of a Bitch," fulminates the incensed Byron, "on his return from Switzerland two years ago—said that Shelley and I 'had formed a League of Incest and practiced our precepts with &c,'—he lied like a rascal—for they *were not Sisters*—*one* being Godwin's daughter by Mary Wollstonecraft— and the other the daughter of the present Mrs. G. by a *former* husband . . . He lied in another sense—for there was no promiscuous inter- course—my commerce being limited to the carnal knowledge of the Miss C—I had nothing to do with the offspring of Mary Wollstonecraft—which Mary was a former Love of Southey's—which might have taught him to respect the fame of her daughter."[6] Their untruth notwithstanding, these slanders continued to distort the popular image of the two poets long after their lifetimes.

Later in the century the image of the incestuous Shelley was widened to include the relationship with his sister Elizabeth. This came about through the machinations of Hogg, who in his *Life of Shelley* garbled the texts of the poet's letters to himself so as to disguise his own love for Elizabeth. Owing to Hogg's artful alteration of personal pronouns, the reader was left with the unavoidable con- clusion that the poet must have been dying of love for his own sister. Freudian critics in the twentieth century seized on this possibility, coupled with the serious Oedipal overtones of Shelley's relationship with his mother and the conflict with his father, to help unlock the riddle of Shelleyan psychosexuality.[7] But in view of Hogg's tamperings and Shelley's real modes of thinking and practice, there is little reason to believe that he ever knowingly harbored incestuous designs on any members of his family, whatever may be speculated about his unconscious desires. It is true that the painter Benjamin Haydon, on the basis of his acquaintance with Shelley in 1817, wrote that the poet "would lie with his sister" and "sophisticate himself into a conviction of its innocence."[8] But this is a reference to the perfected world of the future, not the present sad reality.

Of most interest today is not Shelley's putative desire for incestuous connection, conscious or repressed, nor even his perfectibilitarian be- lief in its ultimate innocence, but rather the deeply felt symbolic significance that he read into the act of incest, with implications extending to the deepest roots of sexual relationship as he understood it. When Shelley protested that the alterations in his vision of the liberation of women had "spoiled" *Laon and Cythna*, he was think- ing of more than simply its erotic emasculation. He was lamenting the destruction of its symbolic core, the metaphor of total sexual equality which serves as the dramatic heart of the original poem and which provides it with a formal artistic symmetry otherwise lacking. *Laon and Cythna* is founded on the psychology of sympathetic or sentimental connection, the desire for which Shelley believes lies embedded in the human psyche from birth. Ordinarily in Shelley's love poetry the psychodynamics of sentimental connection are portrayed as the quest of the individual psyche for union with its personal sympathetic antitype. But in *Laon and Cythna* sentimental connection is projected as a universal linking of antitypes, man and his sister woman joined in complete and sympathetic bonding. The poem is "a story of human passion in its most universal character," as Shelley explains in its Preface. Thus consanguineous love functions as an all-encompassing paradigm of sympathetic communion between the sexes, like mated to like in perfect harmony, sexual division overcome in a total fusion of sentimental affinities, "intellectual, imaginative, sensitive"—"all sympathies harmoniously blended."

The sympathetic nature of this sort of communion demands that Laon and Cythna be brother and sister. Not only does the relationship underscore the drama's basic feminist theme, but it demonstrates in the strongest possible terms the psychosexuality that is to bring about the longed-for community of the sexes. What can be firmer, deeper, or more founded on an identity of interest and being than a love whose wellsprings trace to infancy and whose growth is accomplished with the principals side by side? In what other sort of attachment can the principals see each other most fully mirrored or echoed, the boundaries of the self most completely broken down, and the rapprochement of the sexes most nearly a living reality? "Disguise it not," asserts the impassioned language of the poem, "we have one human heart—/All mortal thoughts confess a common home" (VII.xix). Therefore, "Those/Who grow together cannot choose but love,/If faith or custom do not interpose,/Or common slavery mar what else might move/All gentlest thoughts." This is "Nature's law divine" (VI.xxxix). Laon and Cythna are literally "kindred" spirits, brother and sister to one another's souls; and so by implication are the sexes generically, were it not for the alienating intervention of sexist socialization and patriarchal tyranny. Shelley draws out the feminist implications of this metaphor until it becomes the poem's overarching symbol. This is the real explanation of incest in the poem and of Shelley's dogged resistance to its excision.[9]

As an image of sympathetic identification, incest was not original with Shelley. Drawing on the Platonic tradition of the twin or double

The Detestable Distinctions

soul, a number of writers during the period had already exploited the motif in a sympathetic love context, including C. M. Wieland in the novel of which Shelley was so fond, *The History of Agathon*.[10] Shelley's originality comes in placing the lovers in a feminist relationship. This adds a wholly new dimension to the motif and, when viewed in the light of the complex psychodynamics underlying the relationship, gives the motif a subtlety and psychological depth previously absent. The psychoerotic level of the poem is carefully developed in terms of the socialization of the lovers, and the equality of their relationship is stressed from its beginnings.

For all practical purposes Cythna from childhood has been Laon's embodied antitype. Reared solely by her brother, she has come to resemble him so fully, to share the same thoughts, interests, and ideals, that he is under no further compulsion to search the world for his sympathetic counterpart, to "weave a bondage of . . . sympathy,/As might create some response" (II.xvi). He describes her literally in terms of his antitype, in language recalling *On Love*: "As mine own shadow was this child to me,/A second self, far dearer and more fair" (II.xxiv). In place of "far dearer," Shelley has Laon say "far purer" in the original draft, making the association with the psychology of *On Love* even plainer: the ideal inner prototype, of which the antitype is the embodied replica, is as "a mirror whose surface reflects only the forms of purity and brightness" (VI.202).[11]

Deserted by the "false" and "heartless" friends with whom he had tried to establish sympathetic relations in his youth, Laon falls back entirely on his association with Cythna. Hand in hand they explore the country of their birth, Cythna eagerly participating in her brother's intellectual pursuits. At night the two sleep twined in one another's arms. The couple share but a single purpose, so intimately are their consciousnesses interconnected through intellectual sympathy. Cythna's thoughts are all her brother's, while in him, "communion with this purest being/Kindled intenser zeal, and made me wise/In knowledge, which, in hers mine own mind seeing,/Left in the human world few mysteries."[12] Of particular importance is Cythna's solitary upbringing, outside the traditional confines of patriarchal custom. This nurturing has left her "female mind/Untainted by the poison-clouds which rest/On the dark world" (II. xxxv). Because brother and sister share in a hatred of all forms of tyranny, political, social, and religious, and because woman's immemorial subjection constitutes one of the chief manifestations of this tyranny, they are convinced feminists. But this oppression was "coldly felt" by Laon until his sister, already sympathetically identified with her own kind, raised his consciousness and heightened his sympathies. While both agree that woman's "slavery must be broken," Cythna appropriates this task specifically to herself (II.xxxv-xxxvii). The leading of a feminist revolution becomes her consuming goal, one triumphantly, if only momentarily realized, when, as the militant Laone, she pre-empts the male role and leads the battle for the patriarchal city (V.xix).

With the "sweet brother of [her] soul" back again at her side, Cythna resumes her natural feminine self, and the two are free to consummate that love which has never wavered through ages of sexist tyranny (II.xlvii). Everything in their past, their common experience and their shared biological heritage, has prepared for this act. Their final physical merging is simply the last step in a process of commingling and fusion that has gone on all their lives. "Few," observes Laon, "were the living hearts which could unite/Like ours, or celebrate a bridal-night/With such close sympathies" (VI.xxxix). This is literally the climax of Shelley's vision—mankind and womankind joined on every level of being as brother and sister, seeming in each other's "breath and blood to live and move" (IX.xx). But since the world is not yet ready for such a consummation, their union cannot last; it founders on the shoals of overwhelming patriarchal reaction. Yet though brother and sister must die, the memory of their example lives on in the temple of the human spirit. Humankind has been shown a type of community that cannot be expunged and may one day become a reality if future generations are prepared to will it.

The feminist implications of Shelley's love psychology are not limited to *Laon and Cythna* but underlie many of his other poems as well. Man can find the sympathetic antitype of himself, his complete mirror image, only if woman receives the same development, shares the same rights and opportunities, as her brother the male. Incest becomes the natural symbol of this identity. Thus the incestuous relationship of the lovers in *Rosalind and Helen* is not gratuitous but fully in keeping with Shelley's basic purposes. It is his way of symbolically underscoring the lovers' likeness and therefore their sympathetic identification, possible only if the woman is liberated from sexist values. In this fashion alone can each sex truly be "the soul's soul" of the other—that is, its twin soul or antitype—in a mating that threatens the very foundations of patriarchal sexual relationship. Love in Shelley's work is always verging on incest, figuratively if not literally. "Would we two had been twins of the same mother!" is Shelley's frenzied plea in *Epipsychidion* (45) of his antitypal and therefore metaphorically incestuous love for Emilia Viviani. The desire for sympathetic identity is total. Even if in real life lovers bound to each other at the biological level are rare, in symbolical terms sympathetic lovers are always blood relations, kindred spirits, sisters and brothers of each other's souls.

This rhetoric becomes meaningful only if the sexes truly share the same experience and life opportunities. Without full sexual equality the sympathetic identification that is the cornerstone of Shelleyan love is unattainable; but with sexual equality, the sympathetic union of the sexes is as natural as the rhythms underlying the cosmos, urging all things in one spirit to meet and mingle. Such a union is figured at the end of *Rosalind and Helen* in the wedding of the protagonists' children. "Fed/From the same flowers of thought" since childhood, the two had grown together "until each mind/Like springs which mingle in one flood became." As a result, in the children's union their unhappy parents, themselves martyrs to tyrannical patriarchal custom, were permitted to glimpse the "shadow of the peace denied to them" (1288-1291). The idea is repeated in *Fiordispina* where the betrothed are portrayed as

> two cousins, almost like to twins,
> Except that from the catalogue of sins
> Nature had rased their love—which could not be
> But by dissevering their nativity.
> And so they grew together like two flowers
> Upon one stem, which the same beams and showers
> Lull or awaken in their purple prime,
> Which the same hand will gather—the same clime
> Shake with decay.[13]

In the close childhood relationship of the lovers Shelley is possibly reviving the memory of his own youthful engagement to his first cousin Harriet Grove, with whom he was nearly as intimate in childhood as he was with his own sisters and with whom he shared a startling facial resemblance, making the two appear almost twins.[14] Not that there was anything exceptional in the attachment: love among the English squirearchy featured extensive intermarrying of blood relations, and the Shelley family had twice previously been inbred in this fashion. A semi-incestuous love psychology was thus Shelley's natural familial inheritance.[15] But more important, a close early relationship between lovers was built into the very structure of Shelley's love psychology, a relationship that could be figured symbolically as incest.

The philosophy behind this symbolism is set forth in Adam Smith's

Sexuality and Feminism in Shelley

The Theory of Moral Sentiments, the most influential statement of the period on the doctrines underlying Shelley's love psychology. "After himself," declares Smith, "the members of his own family . . . are naturally the objects of [a man's] warmest affections . . . He is more habituated to sympathize with them: he knows better how every thing is likely to affect them." Consequently his sympathy is "more precise and determinate than it can be with the greater part of other people." His feelings, in short, are more like what "he feels for himself." Sympathetic affection is earliest elicited in the friendships among brothers and sisters. "By the wisdom of nature, the same situation, by obliging them to accommodate to one another, renders that sympathy more habitual, thereby more lively, more distinct, and more determinate."[16] This primal sympathetic bonding becomes in Shelley the model or paradigm for his doctrine of ideal sexual relationship, and its realization is possible only if the sexes share the same experience from earliest consciousness.

The feature of Shelley's love psychology that gives it central feminist significance, however, is its demand that sympathetic likeness or affinity operate at every level of identification, not excluding the intellectual. In practice, this can only mean woman's full social emancipation and her complete educational equality with man. Even before Shelley developed his doctrine of sympathetic love, his youthful ideal of "congeniality" between the sexes compelled such a conclusion. In the earliest work Shelley insists that the "congeniality of sentiment and union of idea" which makes lovers "coincide . . . in everything" is the basis of sentimental love, whose archetype he is later to postulate as connate in the human psyche. His lovers are ceaselessly on the watch for "congenial minds," "congenial souls," with whom they can merge in total sympathetic communion, mirror images who can *"understand"* or *"sympathize in"* their every thought, feeling, and sensation, who can even *"anticipate"* them in this regard. This love is "unshakable" and "everlasting" because, as explained in the later work, it rests on the fundamental laws of the higher hedonism.

From the beginning these views made Shelley contemptuous of the sort of sexist "love" typical of his age, founded on "heated admiration" of woman's "person and accomplishments, independently of mind." Such love "was like the blaze of the meteor at midnight, which glares amid the darkness for awhile, and then expires." It was unworthy of man's best self. But "congenial minds," searching for fullness of "sympathetic connexion" and lasting relationship in love, will ever "seek their kindred soul."[17] Translated into

The Detestable Distinctions

terms of the poet's mature love psychology, this thinking leads directly to the antitypal connections of a Laon and Cythna, a Prometheus and Asia, even a Shelley and Mary, all sympathies harmoniously blended in a relationship of perfect equality, man and woman joined at every level of being. The happy result is that woman's "intellectual beauty," so long veiled through dark ages of patriarchal neglect, now shines forth as her greatest glory, and the progress of humankind toward its perfectibilitarian destiny is assured.

Thomas Hardy, in a novel filled with echoes of Shelley, includes an extremely significant conversation about his hero and heroine, Jude Fawley and Sue Bridehead: " 'I have been struck with these two facts: the extraordinary sympathy, or similarity, between the pair. He is her cousin, which perhaps accounts for some of it. They seem to be one person split in two! . . . it is not an ignoble, merely animal, feeling between the two . . . [but] an extraordinary affinity or sympathy . . .' 'Platonic!' 'Well no. Shelleyan would be nearer to it. They remind me of—what are their names—Laon and Cythna.'" Described as "counterparts," almost each other's double, Sue and Jude share a "complete mutual understanding, in which every glance and movement was as speech for conveying intelligence between them," a kinship making them "almost the two parts of a single whole."[18] *Jude the Obscure* both brings to a climax a literary tradition spanning the century and links it explicitly with Shelley. The novels of the Brontë sisters, for example, conform to the same pattern of lovers paired on the basis of sympathetic likeness or correspondence, as do those of George Eliot, George Meredith, and particularly Charles Brockden Brown, whose works at the beginning of the century did so much to influence Shelley.[19] The examples are in fact legion.

For all these writers love is sympathetic; love goes wrong only when couples are joined as opposites or when they share nothing but physical desire. Unlike Shelley, however, rarely do these novelists make explicit the feminist meaning built into the tradition, though most imply it in one way or another. The effect of their work was nevertheless considerable in promoting an attractive psychosexual alternative to the conventional standard of sexual complementarity or "compensatory unlikeness." In Tennyson's classic formulation of the conventional ideal which dominated the century and did so much to keep women in an inferior position, each of the sexes fulfilled a "defect" in the other. Love's "dearest bond" was "not like to like, but like in difference."[20] The traditional male valued the female for her "exquisite unlikeness"; she "completed" him.[21] "We are foolish, and without excuse foolish, in speaking of the 'superiority' of one sex to the other, as if they could be compared in similar things," explains Ruskin in "Of Queens' Gardens," the century's most uncompromising rationale of sexual complementarity: "Each has what the other has not: each completes the other, and is completed by the other: they are in nothing alike, and the happiness and perfection of both depends on each asking and receiving from the other what the other only can give."[22] Woman's "defect" unfortunately was that her mind, unlike the "larger mind" of man, was "childlike."[23] Her "proper sphere" was therefore the home, together with the rest of the children. As modern feminism has pointed out, the Victorian ideal of sexual complementarity was in reality a convenient excuse for perpetuating the patriarchal status quo, each sex locked in its separate sphere. And in sexual politics, separate has never meant equal. An ideal of sympathetic likeness consequently ran counter to the period's sexual norm and helped prepare the way, if only psychologically, for the growing rapprochement of the sexes in the twentieth century, instead of their time-honored division, although the tradition of sexual complementarity is far from dead.

The full feminist implication of the sympathetic love tradition was spelled out, not by the novelists, but by the polemicists Mary Wollstonecraft, Fanny Wright, Margaret Fuller, and John Stuart Mill, whose message forms a striking parallel with Shelley's. "The man who can be contented to live with a pretty, useful companion, without a mind," affirms Wollstonecraft, "has never felt the calm satisfaction that refreshes the parched heart . . . of being beloved by one who could understand him . . . 'The charm of life,' says a grave philosophical reasoner [Adam Smith], is 'sympathy; nothing pleases us more than to observe in other men a fellow-feeling with all the emotions of our own breast.' " But affection between husband and wife cannot be genuine "when so little confidence is established at home, as must be the case when their pursuits are so different."[24] "Let [men] not imagine that they know aught of the delights which intercourse with the other sex can give," concurs Wright, "until they have felt sympathy of mind with mind, and heart with heart; until they bring into that intercourse every affection, every talent, every confidence, every refinement, every respect."[25] Fuller, emphasizing the sympathetic kinship of the sexes, scorns the old divisive sexual complementarity: "the time has come . . . when Man and Woman may regard one another as *brother and sister*, the pillars of one porch, the priests of one worship."[26] Mill clinches the argument in *The Subjection of Women*: "Intimate society between people radically dissimilar to one another, is an idle dream. Unlikeness may attract, but it is likeness, which retains; and in proportion to the likeness is the suitability of the individuals to give each other a happy life." While women are subject to their present sexist rearing, "a man and a woman will but rarely find in one another real agreement of tastes and wishes as to daily life." But when they are "not too much unlike to begin with, the constant partaking in the same things, assisted by their sympathy," will work "a gradual assimilation of the tastes and characters to one another," leading to the real enrichment of both (as often happens between two friends of the same sex). In short, "the moral regeneration of mankind will only really commence, when the most fundamental of the social relations is placed under the rule of equal justice, and when human beings learn to cultivate their strongest sympathy with an equal in rights and in cultivation."[27]

These statements underscore the central position that Shelley's psychology of sexual relationship occupies within the developing ethos of nineteenth-century feminism. But in his subtle exploration of the complex psychodynamics of sexual relationship, Shelley goes beyond anything else ever attempted during the century from a feminist point of view. Not often does a genuine contribution to the understanding of human psychosexuality come garbed in the highest poetry.

Yet Shelley's love psychology has frequently been viewed in a less than sympathetic light, not as high-minded idealism but as an elaborate excuse for authorial self-love, for narcissistic reduplication or ego-aggrandizement, for a sort of sexual solipsism or autosexuality that denies the reality of others. According to such criticisms, "only by finding his female duplicate, a sort of spiritual *Doppelgängerin*," could Shelley "satisfy his desire to love another without violating his love of himself." He believed "in the divine Spirit of Love as a man standing before a magnifying shaving-glass believes in his own enlarged reflection."[28] It is true that the logic of Shelley's psychology implies narcissism and that there was a pronounced element of narcissism in the poet's own psychological makeup, which colored all his relationships with women. But because of the epistemology of the day, Shelley's psychology had no other choice but to be narcissistic or centered on the self. Since this epistemology was inherently solipsistic, the only avenue to transcending the boundaries of the self was through sympathetic self-projection into others, and the closer the other resembled the self, the greater the possibility of genuine sympathetic identification or love. In other words, the sympathetic love tradition was a priori narcissistic, and in this Shelley shared an element with all his fellow Romantics. No one, however, defined the tradition's psychodynamics more closely than Shelley nor attached it more firmly to its philosophical base. And no one throughout the century portrayed its liberating importance for women more dynamically. In all of this Shelley's psychology of sexual relationship is objectively valuable and not to be dismissed as the self-deceiving rationalizations of a man in love with his own reflection.

Moreover Shelley's psychology remains important today. Congeniality between the sexes, sympathetic cross-gender identification, stands to many as humankind's one positive hope for terminating the immemorial sex war and allowing men and women to join hands on a basis of friendship and equality. The traditional patriarchal standard of sexual complementarity and polarization needs to be discarded in favor of a new ideal of mono- or unisexuality. No more can man afford to regard woman as the mysterious "Other." While reproductive dimorphism is a biological fact, at every other level of being the sexes seem potentially kindred, woman sharing the same life-possibilities as her brother man.[29] As an autonomous being, she ought therefore to be allowed the same right to self-determination historically permitted the male. This is the gospel of Simone de Beauvoir, which set the modern woman's movement on its way.[30] But it is equally the preaching of Shelley, Wollstonecraft, and Mill. The message has lost none of its force.

What is needed, as stressed by the new feminists, is the total annihilation of the traditional gender stereotypes and sex roles which have kept the sexes locked inside the prisons of their separate spheres and complementary identities, alien and unknown to each other except at the most superficial levels of being. Unlike the first woman's movement, the goal of the second is therefore "not just the elimination of male *privilege* but of sex *distinction* itself."[31] The new feminists are "tired of the gender of things," in Anne Sexton's phrase ("Consorting with Angels"). The ideal is now the "androgynization" of the sexes or the release of opposite-sex elements of the self, so that in their increasing synthesis or integration, men and women will truly reflect or reduplicate one another, revealing their common humanity or kinship, genuinely type and antitype in Shelleyan terminology. Elements of this ideal have already entered into contemporary culture at every level, from monosexual hair styles and dress to a loosening up of sex roles and a toleration of cross-gender personality traits and behavior. Unfortunately, however, "there are few places in our culture where women are actively *supported* for manifesting psycho-sexually androgynous or 'male'-like behavior," points out the feminist psychotherapist Phyllis Chesler.[32] The obverse is true to an even greater degree for men. The opening up of gender possibility is thus the goal of feminist androgyny. The Stanford psychologist Sandra Bem has argued the need for a whole new standard of psychological health which deliberately fosters androgynous behavior rather than behavior based on sexual complementarity. Not only does "traditional sex typing necessarily restrict behavior," but evidence is accumulating that it is actually psychologically unhealthy, making social adjustment more difficult.[33]

The androgynous ideal is not entirely new in a feminist context. Earlier in the century it was central to Virginia Woolf's vision of a feminist rapprochement between the sexes.[34] She in turn traced the idea back to the Romantics, specifically to Coleridge and his ideal of "the androgynous mind," in opposition to what she labeled the "single-sexed" mind, and like Shelley, she recognized the ideal as necessitating "sympathy" between the sexes.[35] The interest in androgyny was in fact pervasive throughout the nineteenth century, if only occasionally feminist in orientation as with the Fourierists and Saint-Simonians.[36] And the impulse toward androgyny has been present in Western society since earliest times, often associated with the incest of brother and sister.[37] But it has taken the modern era to recognize its full feminist import.

Except for his translation of the *Symposium* (189D–190B), Shelley nowhere uses the term *androgyny*. Nevertheless the idea is implicit throughout his work, particularly in his portrayal of the sexes, with their harmonious blending of the traditionally masculine and the traditionally feminine. Moreover in his own person he most nearly incorporated this ideal.[38] In appearance, habits, attitudes, and modes of thought, he was a living type of what humanity might become—prophesied as such more than a century ago by the pioneering American feminist Fuller, perhaps the first writer to realize the feminist message of Shelley's androgyny: "Shelley . . . like all men of genius, shared the feminine development, and unlike many knew it. His life was one of the first pulse-beats in the present reform-growth . . . and, by his system and his song, [he] tended to reinstate a plant-like gentleness in the development of energy. In harmony with this, his ideas of marriage were lofty, and, of course, no less so of Woman, her nature, and destiny."[39]

No longer, in short, does Shelley stand convicted, as has traditionally been the case, for his womanishness, his maternalism, his emotionality, his airy fancifulness, his pacifism, his elevation of sentiment over sex, his dislike of obscenity and dirty jokes, in sum his general lack of conventional manly virility. Nor is he to be credited for these things only in an impractical sense, as the attributes of an other-worldly visitant who is too pure and spiritual for the crude realities of this world, in a masculinized version of the Victorian angel in the house. With the slow turning of the zeitgeist, Shelley emerges as an ideal type of humanity, beaconing the way toward the future. His irresistible attraction to Greek sculpture, with its celebration of epicene beauty and hermaphroditism, need no longer represent the suspect yearnings of a repressed homosexual but can stand as the recognition of a beauty valuable in its own right and one reflected in his own being—the androgynous merging of masculine and feminine in a higher unity transcending patriarchal definitions of gender. Whether this merging reflected a literal androgynization in the poet's case, the result of some sort of hormonal imbalance or physiological malfunction in utero, can only be guessed. The findings of modern researchers in this field, particularly those of John Money, make speculation tempting.[40] They might explain, among other things, the hitherto mysterious lines from *Julian and Maddalo* (463-466) that seemingly hint at some sort of anatomic anomaly.[41] But whatever may have been Shelley's physiological or hormonal difficulties, there is no reason to doubt that, in the psychological sense, he achieved a condition of androgynization so complete that sexual differentiation or distinction could only be experienced as seriously frustrating, an unwelcome limitation of human possibility: "these detestable distinctions will surely be abolished in a future state of being."[42]

Unisexuality is not the only solution to the sex war latent in the sympathetic love tradition. At the opposite pole, a perhaps more logical resolution, is homosexuality, the total separation of the sexes on the basis of same-sex identification, a sexual nationalism presupposing gender reduplication or likeness rather than the elimination of gender differences implicit in the sexual integration of androgyny. This solution has been advanced by the Lesbian wing of the contemporary woman's movement as the necessary meaning of full sexual correspondence. As Jill Johnston expresses this view, same-sex identification stands as the one infallible means of transcending traditional sexual division or otherness: "Women who love their own sex love the sameness in the other." The psychology of this love is avowedly narcissistic, leading to "the enhancement of self through narcissistic identification," or the "miracle of the mirror." The ultimate feminist solution is accordingly for women to "cease to think of themselves as the 'other' in relation to the 'other,' " and to unite with their "own kind or species."[43] The obverse, though not dwelt upon, is for men to keep to themselves sexually as members of their own species.

The Detestable Distinctions

To a degree same-sex identification has always been inherent in the psychosexuality of Western society, owing to the patriarchally dictated segregation and polarization of the sexes. Like can only sympathize with like, and the sexes have been very unlike. Greek love acknowledged the implications of this dissimilarity openly. But homosexual identification is also implicit in the twin traditions, common throughout history, of male comradeship and female sisterhood, the sexual element of which has occasionally been acknowledged in even the most puritanical of times by a Byron or Rachilde, a George Sand or Oscar Wilde.[44] The Lesbian feminists are simply accepting the given conditions of patriarchal sexuality and pressing them to their logical conclusion.

Such a solution, however, seems merely to translate the patriarchal doctrine of separate spheres into even more absolute terms. The ideal of one world, one race, prevails in most other areas of modern life. Why divide humanity at so fundamental a level? And if such an absolute separation should ever be established, what will prevent the old Jupiter order of patriarchy from reimposing itself in even more oppressive form? In the battle of the sexes, the male still holds the trump cards of superior size and strength. With all the sympathetic bridges between the sexes down, there is no guarantee that man will choose a peaceful coexistence with his opposite, instead of brutally exploiting his advantage, particularly if the latest sex research is correct in implying that he is neurologically more aggressive than the female. As the tradition of sympathy has continually stressed, dissimilarity of interests, qualities, and aims leads to sympathy's contrary, antipathy: unlike equals dislike. With the two sexes confronting each other across the psychological barricades of alien worlds, woman may find herself abruptly returned to a role of enforced servitude more savage and unfeeling than anything she has hitherto known. Or even more drastic, she may find herself face to face with the final solution, total extinction as a sex.[45]

Far more rewarding is the future held out by androgyny, with the increasing resemblance of the sexes, type sympathetically mirrored by type across the whole spectrum of human possibility, independent of sex stereotyping, until, as with Shelley's Cythna and Laon or Asia and Prometheus, the two consolidate as one. Only then will the sexes find themselves genuinely friends as well as lovers and know at last the satisfaction of the unalloyed pleasure that, according to Shelley, comes from satisfying the laws of the true utility which make love and friendship synonymous.

These ideas receive their most exalted statement in the context of

Shelley's metapoetics. Interpenetrating and ultimately undergirding the material world is a unifying power or spirit of love which, he holds, sweeps through the resistant world of sense shaping all objects to its own likeness as each sustains its impress (*Ado*.xliii). The source of this spirit is imaged as a burning fountain of stainless light for whose fire the whole creation "thirsts" (*Ado*.xxxviii,liv). This is the same spirit that Shelley apostrophizes as intellectual beauty. Upon the visitations of this spirit depend all human "Love, Hope, and Self-esteem." Connecting the spirit with his erotic psychology, Shelley portrays it as the "messenger of sympathies,/That wax and wane in lovers' eyes" (*Hymn*.iv). But if these sympathies are ever to be made enduring and psychological identification between the sexes is to be rendered permanent, men and women equally must take on the likeness of the spirit, becoming its "mirrors" (*Ado*.liv).

This position stands as the culmination of Shelley's erotic philosophy. While he acknowledges a primal "thirst" for purely physical sympathy which animates all of nature (*Ado*.xix), he states that as humankind leaves behind its animal origins and draws together under the forms of society, it thirsts for more complex satisfaction. The psychodynamics of this thirst are described as a pairing of erotic ego ideals, the lovers "thirsting" for these to duplicate the entire range of human personality, intellectual and imaginative as well as sensitive. The ideals themselves are imaged as "mirrors" whose surfaces reflect "only the forms of purity and brightness" (*On Love*). They reflect the spirit of intellectual beauty, in other words, whose pure bright light irradiates and sustains the entire cosmos, according to the poet's deepest hope, a beauty "in which all things work and move" (*Ado*.liv). Insofar as men and women merge their separate identities in mirroring this light, they leave behind them the barriers of sexual distinction and participate in a transcendent unity, whose nature is love.

Abbreviations and Short Titles

Notes

Index

Abbreviations
and Short Titles

Ado.	*Adonais*
Alr.	*Alastor*
Bostetter, *Romantic Ventriloquists*	Edward E. Bostetter. *The Romantic Ventriloquists*. Seattle: 1964.
Cameron, *Golden Years*	Kenneth Neill Cameron. *Shelley: The Golden Years*. Cambridge, Mass.: 1974.
Cameron, *Young Shelley*	Kenneth Neill Cameron. *The Young Shelley: Genesis of a Radical*. New York: 1950.
Chernaik, *Lyrics*	Judith Chernaik. *The Lyrics of Shelley*. Cleveland & London: 1972.
Claire's *Journals*	*The Journals of Claire Clairmont*, ed. Marion Kingston Stocking. Cambridge, Mass.: 1968.
Clark	*Shelley's Prose, or the Trumpet of a Prophecy*, ed. David Lee Clark. Albuquerque: 1954.
Dowden, *Life of Shelley*	Edward Dowden. *The Life of Percy Bysshe Shelley*. London: 1886.
Epi.	*Epipsychidion*
Esdaile	Percy Bysshe Shelley. *The Esdaile Notebook: A Volume of Early Poems*, ed. Kenneth Neill Cameron. New York: 1964.
Gisborne & Williams	*Maria Gisborne & Edward E. Williams: Shelley's Friends, Their Journals and Letters*, ed. Frederick L. Jones. Norman, Okla.: 1951.
Godwin, *Political Justice*	William Godwin, *Enquiry Concerning Political Justice and Its Influence on Morals and Happiness*, 3rd ed., ed. F. E. L. Priestley. 3 vols. Toronto: 1946.

Hogg, *Life of Shelley*	Thomas Jefferson Hogg. *The Life of Percy Bysshe Shelley*, ed. Humbert Wolfe, vols. I-II. London: 1933.
Holmes, *Pursuit*	Richard Holmes. *Shelley: The Pursuit.* London: 1974.
Hymn	*Hymn to Intellectual Beauty*
J&M	*Julian and Maddalo*
Julian *Works*	*The Complete Works of Percy Bysshe Shelley*, ed. Roger Ingpen and Walter E. Peck. 10 vols. London, New York: 1926-1930.
Kendall, *Descriptive Catalogue*	Lyle W. Kendall, Jr. *A Descriptive Catalogue of the W. L. Lewis Collection, Part One.* Texas: 1970.
Koszul, *Shelley's Prose Bod.*	*Shelley's Prose in the Bodleian Manuscripts*, ed. A. H. Koszul. London: 1910.
L	*The Letters of Percy Bysshe Shelley*, ed. Frederick L. Jones. Oxford: 1964.
L&C	*Laon and Cythna*
L&J (M)	*Byron's Letters and Journals*, ed. Leslie A. Marchand. Cambridge, Mass.: 1973-1977. Vols. I-VIII.
L&J (P)	*The Works of Lord Byron: Letters and Journals*, ed. Rowland E. Prothero. 6 vols. New York: 1898-1901.
Letter	*Letter to Maria Gisborne*
Locock, *Shelley MSS Bod.*	C. D. Locock. *An Examination of the Shelley Manuscripts in the Bodleian Library.* Oxford: 1903.
Marchand, *Byron*	Leslie A. Marchand. *Byron: A Biography.* 3 vols. New York: 1957.
Mary's *Journal*	*Mary Shelley's Journal*, ed. Frederick L. Jones. Norman, Okla.: 1947.
Mary Shelley, *Letters*	*The Letters of Mary W. Shelley*, ed. Frederick L. Jones. 2 vols. Norman, Okla.: 1946.
Medwin, *Revised Life*	Thomas Medwin. *The Life of Percy Bysshe Shelley*, ed. H. Buxton Forman. Oxford: 1913.
New Shelley Letters	*New Shelley Letters*, ed. W. S. Scott. New Haven: 1949.
Note Books	*Note Books of Percy Bysshe Shelley*, ed. H. Buxton Forman. 3 vols. St. Louis: 1911.

Notopoulos	James A. Notopoulos. *The Platonism of of Shelley: A Study of Platonism and the Poetic Mind.* Durham, N.C.:1949.
Peacock, *Memoirs of Shelley*	Thomas Love Peacock. *Memoirs of Shelley,* in *The Life of Percy Bysshe Shelley,* ed. Humbert Wolfe, vol. II. London: 1933.
Peck, *Shelley*	Walter Edwin Peck. *Shelley: His Life and Work.* Boston & New York: 1927.
Poetical Works	*The Complete Poetical Works of Percy Bysshe Shelley,* ed. Thomas Hutchinson. London: 1956.
Poetry, ed. Coleridge	*The Works of Lord Byron: Poetry,* ed. Ernest Hartley Coleridge. 7 vols. London: 1904.
Pr.Ath.	*Prince Athanase*
Pr.Unb.	*Prometheus Unbound*
QM	*Queen Mab*
R&H	*Rosalind and Helen*
Rev.Is.	*The Revolt of Islam*
Rogers, *Shelley at Work*	Neville Rogers. *Shelley at Work: A Critical Inquiry.* Oxford: 1956.
Rossetti Papers	*Rossetti Papers: 1862 to 1870, a Compilation,* ed. William Michael Rossetti. New York: 1903.
S&C	*Shelley and his Circle, 1773-1822,* ed. Kenneth Neill Cameron, vols. I-IV; ed. Donald H. Reiman, vols. V-VI. Cambridge: 1961, 1970, 1973.
SP	*The Sensitive Plant*
TofL	*The Triumph of Life,* in *Shelley's Poetry and Prose,* ed. Donald H. Reiman and and Sharon B. Powers. New York, 1977.
Trelawny, *Letters*	*Letters of Edward John Trelawny,* ed. H. Buxton Forman. Oxford: 1910.
Trelawny, *Records*	Edward John Trelawny. *Records of Shelley, Byron, and the Author.* London: 1878.
Verse & Prose	*Verse and Prose from the Manuscripts of Percy Bysshe Shelley,* ed. Sir John C. E. Shelley-Rolls, Bart., and Roger Ingpen. London: 1934.
Vindication	Mary Wollstonecraft. *A Vindication of the Rights of Woman, with Strictures*

	on Political and Moral Subjects, ed. Charles W. Hagelman, Jr. New York: 1967 [1792].
Wasserman, *Critical Reading*	Earl R. Wasserman. *Shelley: A Critical Reading.* Baltimore & London: 1971.
Wasserman, *Shelley's Prometheus*	Earl R. Wasserman. *Shelley's Prometheus Unbound: A Critical Reading.* Baltimore: 1965.
Webb, *Violet in Crucible*	Timothy Webb. *The Violet in the Crucible: Shelley and Translation.* Oxford: 1976.
White, *Shelley*	Newman Ivey White. *Shelley.* New York: 1940.
White, *Unextinguished Hearth*	Newman Ivey White. *The Unextinguished Hearth: Shelley and His Contemporary Critics.* Durham, N.C.: 1938.
Witch	*The Witch of Atlas*

Notes

1. A Discourse on Love

1. *Essays, Letters from Abroad, Translations, and Fragments*, ed. Mrs. Shelley (London, 1840). The break occurs at the paragraph beginning, "From this distinction arose that difference of manners." The original MS in the Bodleian Library (Shelley adds. e. 6, pp. 44-59; e. 11, pp. 17-41) shows that Shelley wrote "A Discourse *of* the Manners" in his own title, not *on* as subsequently published.

2. In 1931 Roger Ingpen still labeled the essay "A Fragment" and held it "probable that Shelley may have intended to develop the subject further" (*Plato's Banquet, Translated from the Greek, A Discourse on The Manners of the Antient Greeks Relative to the Subject of Love, Also A Preface to the Banquet, Revised and Enlarged by Roger Ingpen, From MSS in the Possession of Sir John C. E. Shelley-Rolls, Bart.* [Plaistow, London, 1931], pp. 3, vii). However, Notopoulos (p. 390n34) convincingly asserts that "The last paragraph of the essay . . . shows clearly that Shelley had finished with the subject of the essay and that he was deliberately making for the reader the transition to the reading of the translation of the *Banquet*."

3. Because the 1931 edition of the *Discourse* was privately printed and limited to a hundred copies, its impact on Shelley criticism was muffled. With the appearance of Notopoulos (1949), which includes the complete text plus cancellations, and Clark (1954), which includes the unexpurgated version without cancellations, the effect of the *Discourse* has at last been felt. See esp. Bostetter, *Romantic Ventriloquists*; Gerald Enscoe, *Eros and the Romantics* (The Hague, 1967).

4. July 10, 1818 (*L*, II, 20). The sometimes chaotic spelling in Shelley's letters is silently regularized in all quotations.

5. July 25, 1818 (*L*, II, 26).

6. July 25, 1818 (*L*, II, 22). In a note to this passage Jones refers only to the bowdlerized version of the *Discourse*, an unfortunate slip.

7. Aug. 16, 1818 (*S&C*, VI, 656-657, quoted by permission of The Carl H. Pforzheimer Library). That the subject of the *Discourse* was on Shelley's mind during this time also appears later in the letter when he writes of "the manners & feelings of those divine people—who in their very errors are the mirrors as it were in which all that is delicate & graceful contemplates itself."

The "Discourse" of his title plainly derives from his translation of Plato's dialogue, where the word is repeated some thirty-four times, in each case denoting one of the speeches on love declaimed by the guests at the banquet. Having just finished the translation of a collection of "discourses" on the meaning of love, Shelley apparently came to think of his own essay as another such discourse. The letters posted while he was working on the essay show the title taking shape. For the essay's subsequent textual history, see Notopoulos, pp. 383-385, 520-521.

8. *The Works of Thomas Love Peacock* (New York, 1967), IV, 95. Cf. VII, 202-203: "You have done well in translating the *Symposium*," Peacock wrote in reply to Shelley's letter of July 25, "and I hope you will succeed in attracting attention to Plato, for he certainly wants patronage in these days, when philosophy sleeps and classical literature seems destined to participate in its repose." See also Hogg to Shelley, June 15, 1821 (*L*, II, 359n1).

9. See Notopoulos, pp. 388-390, 541-555; Mary Shelley, Pref. to *Essays, Letters from Abroad*; Mary Shelley, *Letters*, II, 139-140.

10. *Preface to the Banquet of Plato* (1818), in Julian *Works*, VII, 161. Unless otherwise noted, parenthetical references in the text to Shelley's prose are to this edition, with the exception of the *Discourse*, where Clark is followed.

11. *A Discourse of the Manners of the Antient Greeks* (Clark, p. 223). For "to cast off the cloak of self-flattering prejudices," Shelley first wrote, "to prevent the preconceived notions of" (Notopoulos, p. 539).

12. Specifically the "period which intervened between the birth of Pericles and the death of Aristotle," c.400-322 B.C. (Clark, p. 217). In the MS of the *Discourse* both the "birth of Pericles" and "Aristotle" are canceled but no substitutes supplied (Notopoulos, p. 521).

13. Shelley to Leigh Hunt, Nov. 3, 1819 (*L*, II, 145). On Aug. 17, 1818, when Shelley was writing his introduction to the *Symp.*, Mary Shelley explains to Maria Gisborne that while "in many particulars" the dialogue "shocks our present manners," "no one can be a reader of works of antiquity unless they can transport themselves from these to other times and judge not by our but by their morality" (*Letters*, I, 56). On ancient literature in early nineteenth-century England, see the article by Hogg on Longus in *The Liberal* 1 (1822): 357; Helen E. Haworth, " 'The Virtuous Romantics': Indecency, Indelicacy, Pornography and Romantic Poetry," *Papers on Language and Literature* 10 (Summer 1974): 287-306.

14. 7 vols., 5th ed. (Paris, 1817); Mary's *Journal*, p. 219. Mary also read the work, and Claire Clairmont was reading it as early as Jan. 18, 1818, before the departure from England (*S&C*, VI, 451), and was still reading it on Jan. 22-28 (Claire's *Journals*, p. 80). Byron knew the work also, mentioning it in a note to *Hints from Horace* (1811) and in a note to Canto II of *Childe Harold's Pilgrimage*.

15. Abbé Barthélemy, *Travels of Anacharsis the Younger in Greece* (London, 1796), I, xii-xiii.

16. Mar. 16, 19, 20, 21, 1818 (Mary's *Journal*, p. 93; *S&C*, VI, 528). The only other candidate is the *Lectures on the History of Literature, Ancient and*

Modern by Schlegel's brother Friedrich von Schlegel (Edinburgh, 1818), but it is unlikely that Shelley could have obtained the work before leaving England.

17. August Wilhelm Schlegel, *Lectures on Dramatic Art and Literature*, trans. John Black (London, 1894 [1815]), pp. 48-49. William Hazlitt, who reviewed the *Lectures* in *The Edinburgh Review* 26 (Feb. 1816): 57-99, may have called Shelley's attention to their significance.

18. Shortly after arriving in Italy Shelley lent his "Schlegel" to the Gisbornes (*L*, II, 17). "How do you like Schlegel?" wrote Mary to Maria not long afterward: "how much finer a view does he take of the tragic poets than that Frenchman Barthelemy, who, if he could without an anachronism in his work, would, I doubt not, have preferred Racine to Sophocles" (F. L. Jones, "Mary Shelley to Maria Gisborne," *Studies in Philology* 52 [Jan. 1955]: 45). Claire's *Journals* record that she was reading the "second Volume of Schlegel's criticism" in Rome, Mar. 18, 1819 (p. 109).

19. Hogg, *Life of Shelley*, II, 533; Mary's *Journal*, pp. 33, 27.

20. C. M. Wieland, *The History of Agathon* (London, 1773), III, 58; II, 107-108. The novel contains one overtly homosexual episode, treated unsympathetically (I, 30).

21. Thomas Mitchell, in *The Quarterly Review* 21 (Apr. 1819): 271-320; *L*, II, 145.

22. *Lectures*, I, 46-57. Two eighteenth-century tomes on classical antiquity with which Shelley was familiar, Charles Rollin's *Histoire ancienne* (1726) and John Gillies' *The History of Ancient Greece* (1786), make no overt references to Greek pederasty but only veiled, infrequent allusions to "shameful vices" and "impurity."

23. See e.g. Noel Perrin, *Dr. Bowdler's Legacy* (New York, 1969); Norman St. John-Stevas, *Obscenity and the Law* (London, 1956); Donald Thomas, *A Long Time Burning* (London, 1969); Peter Fryer, *Private Case—Public Scandal* (London, 1966); Fryer, *Mrs. Grundy: Studies in English Prudery* (London, 1963).

24. Cf. Notopoulos, pp. 384-385.

25. See e.g. Friedrich von Schlegel, *Lectures*, I, 55-57; Cornelius de Pauw, *Philosophical Dissertations on the Greeks*, 2 vols. (London, 1793); Henry David Hill, *Essays on the Institutions, Government, and Manners of the States of Ancient Greece* (London, 1823 [1819]), pp. 266-267; [Thomas Mitchell], review of Friedrich von Schlegel's *Lectures*, *The Quarterly Review* 21 (Apr. 1819): 272, 318; [Mitchell], "State of Female Society in Greece," *The Quarterly Review* 22 (July 1819): 163-203.

26. Barthélemy, *Travels of Anacharsis*, I, 74-75; II, 15-16, 485; Schlegel, *Lectures*, pp. 193-194; Madame de Staël-Holstein, *The Influence of Literature upon Society* (Boston, 1813), I, 103, 206-207. Another likely source is Gillies, *History of Ancient Greece* (1786). Although Shelley is not known to have read Gillies before the fall of 1820, he ordered the *History* from his bookseller as early as 1812, which would make Gillies the first modern authority to influence his views about the ancient Greeks. Not only Gillies' picture of the

Athenian matron's degraded status but also his very language are reminiscent of Shelley's. That women's status was in fact degraded has been challenged by recent scholars. For the controversy, see Donald C. Richter, "The Position of Women in Classical Athens," *The Classical Journal* 67 (Oct.-Nov. 1971): 1-8; Marylin B. Arthur, "Early Greece: The Origins of the Western Attitude Toward Women," *Arethusa* 6, no. 1 (Spring 1973): 19n13; Sarah B. Pomeroy, *Goddesses, Whores, Wives, and Slaves: Women in Classical Antiquity* (New York, 1975), pp. 58-60.

27. *Kalos* and *eueidēs* are transliterated from the original Greek in Shelley's text. Shelley first wrote, "The epithet beautiful now scarcely applied but the female sex, was then appropriate to the male" (Notopoulos, p. 531).

28. David M. Robinson and Edward J. Fluck, *A Study of the Greek Love-Names*, The Johns Hopkins University Studies in Archaeology, no. 23 (Baltimore, 1937), pp. v, 9; see also Jean Marcadé, *Eros Kalos: Essay on Erotic Elements in Greek Art* (Geneva, 1962), p. 8; P. E. Arias, *A History of 1000 Years of Greek Vase Painting*, trans. and rev. B. Shefton (New York, [1963]), p. 15; K. J. Dover, *Greek Homosexuality* (Cambridge, 1978), pp. 9, 86, 121-122.

29. Robert Flacelière, *Love in Ancient Greece*, trans. James Cleugh (New York, 1962 [1960]), p. 224; K. J. Dover, *Greek Popular Morality in the Time of Plato and Aristotle* (Berkeley and Los Angeles, 1974), p. 70.

30. See e.g. Hill, *Essays*, p. 267; [Mitchell], "State of Female Society in Greece," p. 194.

31. *Philosophical Dissertations*, I, 2-3, 74, 78, 82. Byron cites the *Dissertations* in his notes to *Childe Harold's Pilgrimage*, Canto II.

32. See Pomeroy, *Goddesses, Whores, Wives, and Slaves*, p. 74; Robert Flacelière, *Daily Life in Greece at the Time of Pericles*, trans. Peter Green (New York, 1965), p. 71; W. K. Lacey, *The Family in Classical Greece* (Ithaca, 1968), pp. 106-107.

33. See [Mitchell], "State of Female Society in Greece."

34. See de Pauw, *Philosophical Dissertations*, I, 77; Johann Joachim Winckelmann, *The History of Ancient Art*, trans. G. Henry Lodge (Boston, 1880 [1764]), II, 393; Charles Burton Gulick, *The Life of the Ancient Greeks* (New York, 1902), p. 171.

35. *Pr.Unb.*II.i.116-117; II.v.52-53.

36. Mary Shelley, Pref. to *Poetical Works* (1839); Charles and Mary Cowden Clarke, *Recollections of Writers* (London, 1878), p. 152.

37. *Esdaile*, pp. 50, 85, 43, 88; "To Mary Wollstonecraft Godwin" and "To Mary—" (cf.*Rev.Is.*Ded.98-99); "To Constantia [Singing]"; "To Sophia"; "Lines to Emilia Viviani" (*Note Books*, I, 189); *Epi.* 37-38, 88-90; *L*, II, 445.

38. "How eloquent are eyes!" exclaims Shelley in one of his earliest verses: "Not the rapt Poet's frenzied lay . . . Can speak so well as they" (*Esdaile*, p. 110).

39. *Pr.Ath.*60-63, 128-131.

40. Koszul, *Shelley's Prose Bod.*, p. 10.

41. *L*, I, 539. Later Shelley wrote Byron of Allegra's "extraordinary

degree of animation & intelligence" (*S&C*, V, 242; cf. *J&M*.147-150). When Byron finally saw the child, he remarked on "her very blue eyes" and her "re-markabl[e] intelligen[ce]" (*S&C*, VI, 750; cf. *L&J*[M], VI, 62, 150).

42. *Rev.Is.*VIII.xxix, II.xxi. Of his own little Ianthe, Shelley writes: "when o'er thy fitful slumber bending/Thy mother folds thee to her wakeful heart,/Whilst love and pity in her glances blending,/All that thy passive eyes can feel, impart" (*Esdaile*, p. 163).

43. "Stanzas.—April, 1814"; early draft of *Ginevra* (*Verse & Prose*, p. 60); "Passion" (*Esdaile*, p. 41). The Madman in *J&M*, whose mind is at once enlightened and beclouded, has eyes which are "lustrous and glazed" (285).

44. *S&C*, VI, 583 (quoted by permission of The Carl H. Pforzheimer Library); see also *L*, II, 9.

45. *L*, II, 58; *S&C*, VI, 764; see also *L*, II, 67.

46. *L*, II, 92-93. Byron said of upper-class Italian women at this period: they "remain children in mind long after maturity had stamped their persons" (*Lady Blessington's Conversations of Lord Byron*, ed. Ernest J. Lovell, Jr. [Princeton, 1969], p. 180; cf. *L&J* [M], VII, 98). Madame de Stael's novel *Corinne; or, Italy* (1807), which Shelley read at the end of his first year in Italy, reports of upper-class Italian women: "many are so ignorant that they cannot even write, and confess it without scruple. They engage a *Paglietto* to answer letters for them." She also mentions their "Oriental indolence": they "appear like so many beauties of a harem" (trans. Isabel Hill [New York, 1859], pp. 103-104).

47. *L*, II, 363. Following "sentimental" Shelley originally wrote "stupid." The reference is to Byron's mistress, the Countess Teresa Guiccioli.

48. *L*, II, 334-335. Claire Clairmont, Allegra's mother, protested to Byron: everyone "joins in condemning [convents] without adverting to the state of ignorance and profligacy of the Italian women, all pupils of convents" (*L&J*[P], V, 498).

49. *The Cenci* (V.ii.66; IV.i.135; I.ii.84; II.i.48; II.i.370; V.iv.133-134).

50. Medwin, *Revised Life*, p. 281. "It is grievous," Mary Shelley protests to Leigh Hunt, "to see this beautiful girl wearing out the best years of her life in an odious convent where both mind and body are sick from want of the appropriate exercise of each." Yet she "writes so beautifully" and possesses ideas which "lift her so far above the rest of the Italians" (*Letters*, I, 124).

51. *L*, II, 256, 360, 276.

52. See also *A Philosophical View of Reform* (VII, 50).

53. *Lectures*, p. 24; *History of Agathon*, I, 164-165. The theory appears to have originated with Abbé Du Bos, who sought to find in climatic variation an explanation for national and racial differences, and who attributed the mental superiority of the Athenians to climate (Abbé [Jean Baptiste] Du Bos, *Critical Reflections on Poetry, Painting and Music*, trans. Thomas Nugent [London, 1748], II, 190-191).

54. II, 286-287, 307; cf. Gillies, *History of Ancient Greece*, p. 160. Barthélemy and de Pauw both rejected this theory, however.

55. Dec. 24-29, 31, Jan. 2-3, Mar. 14 (to himself) (Mary's *Journal*, pp.

114, 115, 117); cf. Claire's *Journals*, p. 110.

56. Claire was reading Barthélemy in London as early as January 1818 (*Journals*, pp. 80-81). It seems unlikely that Shelley also read the book before leaving England, since he spent so much time over it later in Italy. If, however, his reading of the *Voyage* was dependent on his reading of Schlegel, he must have first read Schlegel well before he left England, assuming Claire's copy to be the same one he read. Claire was also reading Oliver Goldsmith's *History of Greece* (*Journals*, Jan. 24), but this contains nothing of significance about the manners of the ancient Greeks or the status of women except for brief references to the marriage and adultery laws.

57. See e.g. Gillies, *History of Ancient Greece*, ch. 14.

58. *History of Ancient Art*, II, 286-287; see also Gillies, *History of Ancient Greece*, ch. 14.

59. "A people of the most perfect physical organization," Shelley wrote to John Gisborne of the ancient Greeks (*L*, II, 156).

60. See Stephen A. Larrabee, *English Bards and Grecian Marbles* (New York, 1943), ch. 8; John Buxton, "Shelley's Neo-Classical Taste," *Apollo* 96 (Oct. 1972): 276-281.

61. *L*, II, 80, 112. Shelley's distaste may have originated in Winckelmann's *History*, which depreciates Michelangelo (II, 305, 452).

62. *On the Devil and Devils* (VII, 101); *L*, II, 81.

63. See Shelley's note on the Ganymede ("A statue of surpassing loveliness"), stressing the boy's delicacy, lightness, gentleness, prettiness, and innocence. "Idaean Ganymede" is Jupiter's cup-bearer in Shelley's *Pr.Unb.* (III.i. 25-26).

64. Mary Shelley, *Letters*, I, 63. Two years later, while house-hunting in Florence, Shelley reported that he had spent a morning at the Uffizi Palace looking at "a favourite Apollo" (*L*, II, 313).

65. K. J. Dover, "Classical Attitudes to Sexual Behavior," *Arethusa* 6, no. 1 (Spring 1973): 66, notes that in Greek art women were sometimes depicted with male waists and hips, "as if a woman's body was nothing but a young man's body plus breasts and minus external genitals." Marie Delcourt, *Hermaphrodite*, trans. Jennifer Nicholson (London, 1961 [1956]), pp. 56-57, notes that "critics have even gone so far as to claim that sculptors studied only male anatomy, that the portrayers of the *Corai* put feminine heads on draped masculine bodies . . . Modern authorities have more than once made mistakes, restoring an ephebe as a girl, or giving a beard to a feminine figure in a vase painting."

66. Larrabee, *English Bards and Grecian Marbles*, p. 196, identifies this hermaphrodite statue as the one at Florence, but Shelley could as well have seen others at Paris and Rome. Though these statues have a variety of attitudes and postures, the most common is reclining or recumbent, modeled on a bronze prototype supposedly executed by Polycles in the second century B.C. (Delcourt, *Hermaphrodite*, pp. 58-64).

67. In another *Epi.* fragment Shelley remarks on "Agathon's sweet lips"

(104-108). The reference is to the *Symposium* and the dramatist, and pathic, Agathon, whom Shelley always mentions glowingly. In one of Shelley's favorite novels, Wieland's *History of Agathon*, the hero is described as "of such exquisite beauty, that the Rubens and Girardons of that age, as they despaired of finding a more perfect form, or of collecting such an one from the scattered beauties of nature, took him for a model, when they wanted to represent an Apollo or a Bacchus" (I, 8).

2. Love's Typology

1. *The Allegory of Love* (London, 1953 [1936]), p. 4. Other influential proponents of this view are Denis de Rougemont, *Love in the Western World*, trans. Montgomery Belgion (Garden City, N.Y., 1957); M. C. D'Arcy, *The Mind and Heart of Love* (New York, 1956); J. Huizinga, *The Waning of the Middle Ages* (Garden City, N.Y., 1947); Robert S. Briffault, *The Troubadors* (Bloomington, 1965 [1945]).

2. *A Problem in Greek Ethics* (London, 1901), pp. 52-55.

3. Review of Henry T. Finck, *Romantic Love and Personal Beauty*, *The Nation* 45 (Sept. 22, 1887): 237-238.

4. *Do What You Will* (Garden City, N.Y., 1929), p. 145.

5. *In Praise of Love* (New York, 1958), p. 6; cf. Peter Dronke, *Medieval Latin and the Rise of European Love-Lyric* (Oxford, 1965), I, 2, 164; J. B. Broadbent, *Poetic Love* (London, 1964), p. 18; Flacelière, *Love in Ancient Greece*, p. 212.

6. *Lectures on Dramatic Art and Literature*, pp. 193, 24; cf. Gillies, *History of Ancient Greece*, p. 158.

7. Love's archetypal nature was occasionally defended in the preceding century, as in Oliver Goldsmith, "Whether love be a natural or fictitious passion," *The Citizen of the World* (Letter CXVI).

8. Modern-day scholars, disputing the earlier view, cite the *Iliad*, Greek mythology, Herodotus, Xenophon, and Euripides to show that an undercurrent of genuine heterosexual love existed from earliest times, though largely suppressed in the classic period. This submerged current broke through in the Alexandrian era and later dominated the sentimental Greek romances. Shelley became familiar with these romances, but not apparently before the summer of 1820.

9. Mary Shelley, *Letters*, I, 5-6. Once, visiting the Westbrooks, Shelley reported that Eliza began talking "about *l'amour*; I philosophised" (Shelley to Hogg, Apr. 28, 1811? [*L*, I, 71]). He wrote to his friend Edward Graham, Sept. 14, 1810, enclosing a lyric, "You will know I am not much of a hand at *love* songs you see I mingle metaphysics with even this, but perhaps in this age of Philosophy that may be excuse[d]" (*L*, I, 16).

10. The *Discourse* is associated with the more famous *On Love* in Shelley's notebooks (*S&C*, VI, 638-639).

11. Conversely, Byron employs "romantic" and "sentimental" almost

interchangeably, the latter having been a major vogue word of the preceding century, introduced into the language in 1741 by Laurence Sterne.

12. Shelley's *Speculations on Morals* similarly associates "chivalry" with "sentimental love" (VII, 76).

13. *L&J*(M), VIII, 147-148; *L&J*(M), VII, 202; *L&J*(P), VI, 429-430; *Lord Byron's Correspondence*, ed. John Murray (London, 1922), II, 176; see also *L&J*(M), VI, 112; VII, 174. In April 1822 the Countess gave Byron permission to continue the poem on condition that it be "more guarded and decorous and sentimental in the continuation than in the commencement" (*L&J*[P], VI, 95).

14. *The History of the Decline and Fall of the Roman Empire*, 12 vols. in 1 (London, 1811 [1776-1788]), p. 91.

15. See Roy R. Male, "The Power of Sympathy: A Study of Shelley's Moral Ideas" (Ph.D. diss., University of Texas, 1950), abridged as "Shelley and the Doctrine of Sympathy," *Studies in English* 29 (1950): 183-203.

16. Henry Home, Lord Kames, *Essays on the Principles of Moral and Natural Religion* (1751), in Walter Jackson Bate, "The Sympathetic Imagination in Eighteenth-Century English Criticism," *ELH* 12 (June 1945): 156.

17. *The Theory of Moral Sentiments* (London, 1822 [1759]), I, 1-4, 153-156.

18. See Glenn R. Morrow, "The Significance of the Doctrine of Sympathy in Hume and Adam Smith," *The Philosophical Review* 32 (Jan. 1923): 60-78.

19. *A Treatise of Human Nature*, ed. L. A. Selby-Bigge (Oxford, 1965 [1739]), pp. 363-365, 575-576.

20. *L*, I, 303, 51. Hogg, *Life of Shelley*, II, 266, declares that Harriet "read aloud to Shelley" Smith's *Theory of Moral Sentiments*. Mary Wollstonecraft, *A Vindication of the Rights of Woman*, with which Shelley shortly became familiar, was strongly influenced by the work. Later, when reading Robert Forsyth, *The Principles of Moral Science* (Edinburgh, 1805), Shelley found Smith's theory summarized (I, 97).

21. "With a spirit ill fitted to sustain such proof, trembling and feeble through its tenderness, I have every where sought sympathy and found only repulse and disappointment." So Shelley begins the essay *On Love* (VI.201).

22. "Before [an infant] can feel sympathy, he must have been led by a series of observations to perceive that his nurse, for example, is a being possessed of consciousness, and susceptible like himself of the impressions of pleasure and pain" (*Political Justice* [London, 1793], II, 348-349).

23. *A Defence of Poetry* (VII, 109); see also VII, 121: "Neither the eye nor the mind can see itself unless reflected upon that which it resembles."

24. "Power of Sympathy," p. 161n38. In *A Treatise* Hume wrote, "the agreeable sentiment . . . excited by sympathy is love" (bk. III, pt. II).

25. Cf. *QM*: the "stranger-soul" from birth "looks abroad/For happiness and sympathy" (IV.122-123).

26. See e.g. *QM* (VI.104-107, 128-129); *Rev.Is.* (I.xxxv); *The Mask of*

Anarchy (xlviii); *Witch* (vii); *Ado.* (xxxviii, liv); Julian *Works* (I, 239, 240; III, 56; VI, 77; VII, 9-10, 13, 87). Shelley may have first been struck by the motif in an erotic context in Lucretius, who describes love in terms of an unquenchable thirst (IV.1097-1105). Another possible source is Rousseau, *Confessions* (see *Shelley's Poetry and Prose*, ed. Donald H. Reiman and Sharon B. Powers [New York, 1977], p. 454). The motif first appears in one of Shelley's earliest poems, "I will kneel at thine altar" (1809).

27. "Up until the end of the nineteenth century the chief colloquial expression for the orgasm was 'to spend.' It had not yet been displaced by the modern 'to come' " (Steven Marcus, *The Other Victorians* [New York, 1964], p. 22).

28. Cf. Godwin on man's inborn necessity for total sympathetic communion: "He pines for an ear into which he [may] pour the story of his thoughts, for an eye that shall flash upon him in dumb, but eloquent discourse, for a heart that shall beat in unison to his own" (*Fleetwood*, in White, *Shelley*, I, 700-701; see also Godwin, *St. Leon* [London, 1832 (1799)], pp. 62-63).

29. *Essay on Christianity* (VI, 249). Cf. *A Refutation of Deism* (VI, 52): "the beings in whose welfare we are compelled to sympathize by the similarity of their conformation to our own" (in a note Shelley cites Godwin, *Political Justice*, I, 449).

30. Cecil Lang argues that the Romantic concept of sympathetic identity or likeness in love originated with Goethe's *Elective Affinities* and entered into English literature by way of Shelley ("Romantic Chemistry," *The Courier* 10, no. 4 [Syracuse, 1973]: 35-46). But there is no evidence that Shelley was familiar with the novel, and the similarities between the two writers are at best strained. Shelley's manifest inspiration was the native sympathetic love tradition, in which he was thoroughly grounded.

31. *Treatise of Human Nature* (bk. 3, pt. 3; bk. 2, pt. 2); *Essays Moral, Political and Literary* (London, 1904 [1741-1742]), p. 555. Shelley ordered the *Essays* from Hookham, Dec. 17, 1812 (*L*, I, 342).

32. Shelley's translation (Notopoulos, pp. 432-433), little of which is strictly Platonic.

33. "To Jane: The Invitation" (26); Pref. to *Alr.*

34. In a note Shelley adds: "These words are inefficient and metaphorical—Most words so—No help" (*Shelley's Poetry and Prose*, ed. Reiman and Powers, p. 474n2).

35. The word *antitype* can also mean "an opposite type" and is often confused with its homophone *antetype*. See Fowler, *Modern English Usage*, under "type."

36. See esp. Ross Greig Woodman, *The Apocalyptic Vision in the Poetry of Shelley* (Toronto, 1964); James C. Evans, "Masks of the Poet: A Study of Self-Confrontation," *KSJ* 24 (1975): 70-81.

37. See e.g. *A Defence*: "A child at play by itself will express its delight by its voice and motions; and every inflection of tone and every gesture will

bear exact relation to a corresponding antitype in the pleasurable impressions which awakened it" (VII, 110). See also *L*, II, 353, 438; *Peter Bell III* (Prol., 16); *A Philosophical View of Reform* (VII, 29): Shelley first wrote "proto type" (*S&C*, VI, 1017).

38. Shelley uses this language as early as 1812 in describing his "sympathetic" relationship with Elizabeth Hitchener (*L*, I, 240).

39. The quest is discernible as early as Shelley's Gothic romance *St. Irvyne*. Olympia says of her "burning attachment" for Wolfstein that "although the object of her attachment had never before been present to her mind, the desires for that object, although unseen, had taken root long, long ago" (V, 144). She is experiencing sentimental love, whose "object or its archetype forever exists in the mind which selects among those who resemble it that which most resembles it."

40. This experience is dated at "the dawn of the fifteenth spring" in Shelley's Italian love allegory *Una Favola* (VI, 283). Fifteen may seem late, but as explained by John Money and Anke Ehrhardt, "The age of puberty has been becoming progressively lower for at least the last century and a half, judging by the evidence of records preserved in Europe and the United States" (*Man & Woman, Boy & Girl: The Differentiation of Dimorphism of Gender Identity from Conception to Maturity* [Baltimore, 1972], p. 197).

41. See Shelley to Leigh Hunt, June 19, 1822 (*L*, II, 438). This was a coterie expression, used originally by the Shelley circle to mock the obscurities of Kantian "psychologics" (see *L*, II, 321; *Peter Bell III*, 11. 518-532, 534n; Peacock, *Melincourt* [London, 1896 (1817)], p. 233n1). Peacock satirizes Shelley's use of the term in a typological context in *Nightmare Abbey* (ch. 3).

42. See Locock, *Shelley MSS. Bod.*, p. 13, for draft lines and fragments of *Epi.* dealing with the shadow. The concept has usually been traced to the *Republic*, but it was present in Shelley's thought in embryo long before his serious study of Plato. See Shelley to Elizabeth Hitchener, Nov. 23, 1811, where he calls her his "second self, the stronger shadow of that soul whose dictates I have been accustomed to obey" (*L*, I, 189).

43. *Unfinished Drama* (52); *Epi.* (42).

44. Adam Smith had written that the individual's every faculty "is the measure by which he judges of the like faculty in another. I judge of your sight by my sight, of your ear by my ear, of your reason by my reason, of your resentment by my resentment, of your love by my love. I neither have, nor can have, any other way of judging them" (*Theory of Moral Sentiments*, p. 18).

45. Cf. Shelley to Peacock, July 12, 1816, describing an evening in the Alps: "the imagination surely could not forbear to breathe into the most inanimate forms, some likeness of its own visions" (*L*, I, 481).

46. Cf. *Unfinished Drama* (1-4, 51-60).

47. *S&C*, III, 481 (quoted by permission of The Carl H. Pforzheimer Library); "Hymn of Pan" (31-32). In the *Discourse*, when describing the "universal thirst" for sympathetic communion, Shelley observes in a canceled

passage that the thirst, when "individualised . . . seldom . . . if ever fails of producing . . . disappointment" (Notopoulos, p. 530).

48. The only direct reference in Shelley's poetry to the nympholeptic theme is a canceled passage connected with stanza 11 of *Witch*: herdsmen and mountain maidens wild with an inward want "as men with [blank] nympholepsy stricken" (*Verse & Prose*, p. 32).

49. The stanzas are 115-124. Cf. Byron, *The Lament of Tasso* (vi). Shelley commented that these lines "have a profound and thrilling pathos which . . . make[s] my head wild with tears" (*L*, I, 556-557).

50. *S&C*, II, 612-613; *Love Against Hate* (New York, 1942), pp. 280-281; see also Northrop Frye, *A Study of English Romanticism* (New York, 1968), pp. 123-124.

51. *Group Psychology and the Analysis of the Ego* (New York, 1951), p. 74.

52. *Of Love and Lust: On the Psychoanalysis of Romantic and Sexual Emotions* (New York, 1957), pp. 14-16, 65, 42-43, 87-88.

53. *The Psychology of Sexual Emotion* (New York, 1957); see also Grant, "Sexual Love," in *The Encyclopedia of Sexual Behavior*, ed. Albert Ellis and Albert Abarbanel (New York, 1964), pp. 646-656.

54. "Sexual Love," pp. 646-652; *Psychology of Sexual Emotion*, pp. 41, 69-74.

55. "Sexual Love," p. 655. Money and Ehrhardt recognize the "falling-in-love" experience as a discrete psychosexual state dependent on the body's biological clock, coinciding with the onset of "hormonal puberty, though the correlation between the two is not perfect" (*Man & Woman, Boy & Girl*, p. 22). More experimental study is needed in order to determine the exact characteristics of the state's releaser-stimuli. Its origin may lie in nature's desire not only to guarantee the mating of the species but also to keep "the couple together long enough for sexual affection to be joined by parental affection" and thus ensure nurturant protection of the young. The duration of the state varies, but two years represents the maximum (pp. 191-192). The authors say nothing, however, about same-sex love, nor do they make clear whether the state is a purely biological mechanism, independent of social context, both of which problems are significant to Shelley.

3. Love's Visible Link

1. A. Clutton-Brock, *Shelley: The Man and the Poet* (New York, 1909), p. 112; *Poems of Shelley*, ed. Stopford A. Brooke (London, 1897), pp. xlvi-xlvii.

2. Ian Jack, *English Literature, 1815-1832* (Oxford, 1963), p. 199.

3. Harry Levin, *The Broken Column* (Cambridge, 1931), p. 53. John Peale Bishop, "Percy Shelley," questions whether he had "any balls" or what he used to "piss" with. A character in Aldous Huxley, *Point Counter Point*, describes Shelley as a "kind of fairy slug" who was "always pretending . . .

that going to bed with women wasn't really going to bed with them but just two angels holding hands . . . The women loved it, of course—for a little. It made them feel so spiritual—that is, until it made them feel like committing suicide."

4. Benjamin Bailey to John Taylor, Aug. 29, 1818 (*The Keats Circle*, ed. Hyder Edward Rollins [Cambridge, 1948], I, 35). Bailey was upset that Keats was succumbing to Shelley's putative philosophy that "*Sensual Love* is the principle of *things.*"

5. Though the notion of the incorporeal Shelley is still widespread, its revision, beginning in 1959 with Edward Bostetter, "Shelley and the Mutinous Flesh," *Texas Studies in Literature and Language,* I, 203-213, has been gathering momentum. See Seraphia Deville Leyda, "*The Serpent Is Shut Out from Paradise*" (Salzburg, 1972), pp. 7-12.

6. Walter M. Gallichan, *The Poison of Prudery* (Boston, 1929), p. 30. Ford Brown, *Fathers of the Victorians* (Cambridge, 1961), cites the growing horror of nudity in the nineteenth century, the "eunuch century" as D. H. Lawrence would baptize it. See also Eric Trudgill, *Madonnas and Magdalens* (New York, 1976), pp. 3-5.

7. The quotation from Claire Clairmont is from her 1814 journal and is by permission of The Carl H. Pforzheimer Library. Trelawny's not always reliable *Records* describes Shelley enlivening a staid supper-party at the Villa Magni by appearing clad only in his native dignity—"unprecedented licence even in a poet" (pp. 111-115).

8. *Peter Bell III* (313-332; see also 751-752). A stanza dropped from the poem when Mary Shelley published it in 1840 shows that Shelley was familiar with contemporary gossip that Wordsworth had not always been so prudish. Shelley speaks of Wordsworth's having committed a "concealed Don Juanism . . . in his seventeenth year"—an apparent reference to a putative affair with a local Hawkshead girl named Mary who figured in Wordsworth's schoolboy poems (F. W. Bateson, "Exhumations V. Shelley on Wordsworth: Two Unpublished Stanzas from 'Peter Bell the Third,' " *Essays in Criticism* 17 [Apr. 1967]: 125-129). A canceled stanza, alluding to contemporary gossip about Wordsworth's supposed incest with his sister Dorothy, comments that he probably "never even kissed her"—further evidence of his prudery apparently.

9. In his early "Mary to the Sea-Wind" Shelley speaks of a "sense-enchanting" bloom left by the kisses of young love (*Esdaile*, p. 94; cf. *Rev.Is.*XII.xvii). The pleasures of the senses are often an enchantment in Shelley, a necessitarian spell (*Pr.Unb.*II.ii.41-45; *Rev.Is.*IX.xxxii).

10. *Pr.Unb.* (III.iv.198, 134-135, 156-163).

11. A rejected passage printed in *Verse & Prose*, p. 66, makes clear that the "loving game" refers to the woman's traditional sexual coyness in response to the man's advances.

12. VI, 180; cf. *L*, II, 9.

13. "Henry and Louisa" (1809), 11. 30-31 (*Esdaile*, p. 132).

14. *Rev.Is.* (IV.xiii-xiv); *Pr.Unb.* (III.iv.156-158). In the early Gothic novels Shelley adheres to the traditional norms of female modesty, delicacy, and sexual decorum for his heroines, while the villainesses "shamelessly" acknowledge their passion, thus "disgusting" their lovers; but these novels are probably deliberate burlesques of the conventions demanded by the genre. From then on, women receive nothing but praise for casting off the traditional sexual restraints.

15. Canceled passage from *A Defence*, discussing the bucolic or erotic poets of Egypt and Sicily (Koszul, *Shelley's Prose Bod.*, p. 88). Shelley continues, "It is not what the erotic writers have, but what they have not, in which their imperfection consists."

16. "After feast and music," Shelley writes in his review of Peacock's *Rhododaphne*, "the natural result of the situation of the lovers is related by the poet to have place," that is, sexual intercourse (VI, 275).

17. "Love is sold" note to *QM* (I, 142); "The Devil's Walk," 1. 80; *On the Devil and Devils* (VII, 92); *Peter Bell III* (230-231, 573-578); *Refutation of Deism* (VI, 38).

18. Malthus' injunction first appeared in the second edition of the *Essay on Population* (1803). Byron notes in *Don Juan* that the *Essay* had become "the eleventh commandment,/Which says, 'Thou shalt not marry,' unless *well*" (XV.xxxviii).

19. *Essay on the Principle of Population*, 4th ed. (London, 1807), II, 241-242, 245, 247, 252-253, 257, 260-271, 292-293, 317-336, 339.

20. Cf. "Song to the Men of England" (1819): "Have ye leisure, comfort, calm,/Shelter, food, love's gentle balm?" Shelley's contempt for the Malthusian "remedy" dates to well before 1819 according to Peacock's satirical treatment of the subject in *Melincourt* (1817), p. 93. Shelley laments the "misery . . . of unsatisfied celibacy" as early as *QM* ("Natural diet" note).

21. Shelley also links "priests" and "eunuchs" together as "unmanly" (VII, 16; cf. *L*, II, 299). Yet Malthus was no eunuch and set as high a value on sexual gratification, where legitimate, as did Shelley (*Essay on Population*, II, 236-237).

22. Note to *Rhododaphne*; see also Patricia Merivale, *Pan The Goat-God* (Cambridge, 1969), pp. 63-65; Notopoulos, pp. 68-70. Shelley's "Pan cult" included Peacock, Hogg, and Hunt.

23. An exception is Shelley's sympathetic quotation of a passage in Peacock's *Rhododaphne* portraying "a Bacchanalian dance" (VI, 275-276). In an early draft of his translation of Plato's *Ion* Shelley uses the term "orgasm" to describe bacchanalian possession (Koszul, *Shelley's Prose Bod.*, p. 121).

24. Showing that Christian asceticism can sometimes be literally emasculating, Shelley has the Maniac in *J&M* exclaim that, had he known his love would become poisoned, "like some maniac monk," he would have "torn out/The nerves of manhood by their bleeding root" (424-428).

25. Shelley found the personification of this ideal in the Greek Venus Anadyomene, the "Deity of superficial or sexual desire," whose sculptural

representation he describes as "all soft and mild enjoyment," her face expressing "a breathless yet passive and innocent voluptuousness . . . it is at once
desire and enjoyment and the pleasure arising from both." The Virgin Mary,
he adds, "might have this beauty" too, "but alas!" (VI, 321).

26. *Revised Life*, p. 25; marginalia to Medwin, *Conversations of Lord
Byron*, in Ernest J. Lovell, Jr., *Captain Medwin* (Austin, 1962), p. 22.

27. This was the opinion of the books' reviewers (White, *Unextinguished
Hearth*, pp. 34-35).

28. Shelley to Edward Graham, Nov. 30, 1810 (*L*, I, 23). Cameron claims
that these lines depict fellatio, Shelley's meaning made clear by his letter to
Graham (*Golden Years*, p. 223). But neither the poem nor the letter supports
such a reading; the idea would have been repugnant to Shelley and unthinkable to his audience. What is being described is kissing.

29. *Life of Shelley*, I, 262-263. But H. Buxton Forman notes: "the traces
of burlesquing are not at all obvious"; the verses are "no more extravagant
than others written by Shelley as a youth" (*The Shelley Library* [London,
1886], p. 11).

30. The "quenchless fire" of "youthful passion," Shelley was writing at
the same time in the *Esdaile* verses ("Passion," 1. 31).

31. *Poetical Works*, p. 870; "Passion," *Esdaile*, p. 52; QM (IX.77).

32. *Esdaile*, p. 85.

33. "To Harriet," 11. 42-43; "The Retrospect," 1. 157 (*Esdaile*, pp. 86,
160).

34. Louise Schutz Boas, *Harriet Shelley* (London, 1962), p. 7; Winifred
Scott, *Jefferson Hogg* (London, 1951), p. 51.

35. Clellan S. Ford and Frank A. Beach, *Patterns of Sexual Behavior*
(New York, 1951), p. 266.

36. *Life of Shelley*, II, 5; I, 440, 459.

37. *Memoirs of Shelley*, p. 336.

38. *L*, I, 395, 403 (with emendations from Kendall, *Descriptive Catalogue*, p. 108); Mary's *Journal*, Aug. 4, 1814. Stanzas 3-4 of "To Mary Wollstonecraft" apparently record this scene. Harriet Westbrook wrote Catherine
Nugent, Nov. 14, [1814], that Mary had told Shelley she was "dying in love
for him, accompanied with the most violent gestures and vehement expostu-
lations" (*L*, I, 421n2).

39. *L*, I, 401-402. If the Maniac's ravings in *J&M* refer to Shelley's difficulties with Harriet, as is probable, this is further evidence of the couple's
sexual estrangement. See e.g. 11. 420-422: "That you had . . . ne'er endured/
The deep pollution of my loathed embrace." See also 11. 460-467.

40. "Stanzas, Written at Bracknell, March, 1814," 1. 5.

41. The blank was left by the legal transcriber of the letter during the
Chancery suit over the custody of Shelley's children and, as Cameron, *Golden
Years*, p. 19, notes, "presumably read 'bodies'; as he seemed to have no diffi-
culty with Shelley's hand elsewhere, the omission must have been deliberate."

42. An aborted version is repeated in Canto XI.i-vi, preceding Laon and
Cythna's forced separation.

43. Carlos Baker, "The Traditional Background of Shelley's Ivy Symbol," *MLQ* 4 (June 1943): 205-208, notes the erotic overtones in Shelley's use of ivy here and elsewhere. Besides the "traditional connection between ivy and Bacchus," he gives as Shelley's principal source Spenser, *The Faerie Queene*. In one of Shelley's earliest love poems, "Henry and Louisa" (1809), "the Ivied Thorn" is described as overshadowing the lovers' "most blissful bower" (pt. 1, xv).

44. In Act I, II. 347-348, Shelley calls both perverted love and hate a "poisoned wine."

45. The Earth has been literally revivified by the Titan's kiss, her nerves electrified to the innermost depths of being (III.iii.84-87).

46. "Love, as might be expected, is made to perform a variety of extraordinary functions," sardonically notes one of the poem's first reviews (*Quarterly Review* 26 [Oct. 1821]; also in White, *Unextinguished Hearth*, p. 244).

47. That Shelley is describing young love in its fecund prime is reinforced by *SP* (I.66-69), where the vernally blooming flowers, "interpenetrated/With the light and odour" shed by their neighbors, are likened to "young lovers whom youth and love make dear/Wrapped and filled by their mutual atmosphere."

48. "To—'One word is too often profaned'" (ii); *Epi.* (12). Both poems date from 1821.

49. In *Rev.Is.*IX.1.2-5, Shelley writes, "and sleep no more around dared to hover/Than, when all doubt and fear has passed away,/It shades the couch of some unresting lover/Whose heart is now at rest." This passage conveys the same restless rest that comes from spending the night with one's lover.

50. Hunt replied, "I . . . shall put it, *incontinently*, into the Indicator" (*S&C*, VI, 1091). This was a joke of long standing in the Shelley circle. Cf. Mary Shelley to Hogg, Apr. 26, 1815 (*New Shelley Letters*, p. 89).

51. For the unbowdlerized text, see Julian *Works*, III, 295.

52. Helen Rossetti Angeli, *Shelley and His Friends in Italy* (New York, 1911), pp. 96-102.

53. First published in 1934 in *Verse & Prose*, p. 5. See also the draft of one of Shelley's letters in Italian to Emilia: "Your form, visible, to my mind's eye, surrounds me with the gentle shadow of its divine beauty. Many times you thus [?] me. Your dark eyes ever most beautiful, are above me. I seem to feel your hand on mine and your lips—but then I close my eyes until you cease to love it—then it will be quenched like a flame which lacks fuel" (*L*, II, 449).

54. Mary is compared to "The cold chaste Moon," whose "wandering shrine of soft yet icy flame" "warms not but illumines," and who "smiled or frowned" on him as he lay within "a chaste cold bed," asleep in spirit and limb (281-300).

55. *L*, II, 254, 256. Yet Shelley concludes with the comment, "So much for sentiment," which suggests that he thinks of Emilia in terms of his archetype of sentimental love, a passion that does not exclude the desire for physical connection.

56. In a rejected Preface to the poem Shelley writes: "The love of woman

which these verses express was but the form of that universal Love which Plato taught," presumably transsensual (Wasserman, *Critical Reading*, p. 443).

57. As early as 1812 Shelley speaks of "minds unisonous in reason and feeling" joining to form a "Paradise" defying the world (*L*, I, 245).

58. "To Edward Williams"; "To Jane: The Invitation"; "To Jane: The Recollection."

59. "The Magnetic Lady to Her Patient."

60. "Lines Written in the Bay of Lerici" (9-23). The passions that Jane aroused, according to the poem's cancellations, were "desire" and "fear." See Chernaik, *Lyrics*, pp. 273-276.

61. "Lines: 'We Meet Not as We Parted' " (text from Julian *Works*, IV, 207). Exactly when the episode in the poem took place—if indeed it existed outside Shelley's imagination—is not known, though some commentators have associated it with the events related in "Lines Written in the Bay of Lerici," which can be dated May or June 1822. The claim has been made that Shelley's devotion to Jane was rewarded by more than just a kiss. Walter Peck writes, "if we are to trust an unpublished letter written by Shelley to Byron, it led to the actual fulfillment of passion, one evening, after an Italian *festa* which they together had attended" (*Shelley*, II, 199). But since the letter has never been forthcoming, White concludes that it was either a forgery or Peck's invention (*Shelley*, II, 626-628).

62. William H. Masters and Virginia E. Johnson, *Human Sexual Response* (Boston, 1966), p. 214.

63. William H. Masters and Virginia E. Johnson, *Human Sexual Inadequacy* (Boston, 1970), p. 71; see also pp. 46-49.

64. *Purity of Diction in English Verse* (London, 1952), pp. 144-152; cf. John Atkins, *Sex in Literature* (London, 1970), pp. 36-37, 119-120.

65. My analysis is based primarily on the *Shelley Concordance*, comp. F. S. Ellis (London, 1892), which records the verse, but I have also drawn on the prose.

66. "The diaphanous Veils, in which those sweet ladies oft array/Their delicate limbs, who would conceal from us/Only their scorn of all concealment" (*Witch*.lxv). The attractions of the transparently veiled woman go back to Shelley's earliest work. See e.g. *St. Irvyne* (V, 152).

67. "Mingling" is Shelley's most common expression for coitus. Only once does he use the vulgarism "sleeping with" (*The Cenci*.I.iii.63).

68. The *Shelley Concordance* records 135 entries under the term "faint." It is Shelley's principal expression for intense physiological response.

69. See draft passages of *Epi.*, where Shelley experiments with "pulse," "blood," "veins" (Locock, *Shelley MSS Bod.*, pp. 6-13).

70. The only directly physiological postcoital change remarked by Shelley is the seeming disappearance of the sex flush from Cythna's breasts, her now "pale bosom" (*Rev.Is.*VI.xxxviii.4), though this may simply be the effect of moonlight.

71. *Human Sexual Response*, p. 344.

72. In *Childe Harold* (IV.cxix), Byron speaks of "The dull satiety" which destroys sentimental love.

73. *St. Irvyne* (V, 167-168, 136); *Zastrozzi* (V, 77). In both novels Shelley advances the uncharacteristic notion that women, unlike men, far from growing tired of sex through repetition, are inflamed: "Possession, which, when unassisted by real, intellectual love, clogs man, increases the ardent, uncontrollable passions of woman even to madness" (*St. Irvyne*, V, 138). This can hardly have been drawn from experience at such an early date. Matthew G. Lewis' *The Monk* reveals its derivation: "Possession, which cloys man, only increases the affection of women" (New York, 1952 [1796], pp. 236-237).

74. The *Shelley Concordance* contains a page and a half of entries, many of them erotic in nature, under the term "joy."

4. Civilized Sex

1. Shelley explains the physics behind this notion in *A Refutation of Deism* (VI, 50).

2. *SP* (I.1-12). Because of its phallic properties, the mimosa or sensitive plant had been a euphemism for the penis since 1779 and James Perry's bawdy poetic satire *Mimosa: or, The Sensitive Plant*. See Peter Fryer, *Mrs. Grundy*, p. 263; Robert M. Maniquis, "The Puzzling *Mimosa*: Sensitivity and Plant Symbols in Romanticism," *Studies in Romanticism* 8 (Spring 1969): 136. However, it is improbable that Shelley intended any such reading of his poem.

3. "West Wind" (iv.3); "Zucca" (55-56); *Witch* (ix); *QM* (IV.145-146); *Pr.Unb.* (IV).

4. See e.g. the daring ingenuity of the metaphors underlying 11. 155-170 of *TofL* and its drafts, with their erotically laden vocabulary of *mingling, dying, spending, foaming*, etc.

5. *L*, II, 218-219; see also Shelley to Hogg, Nov. 28, 1817 (*S&C*, V, 330-331).

6. Shelley found a precedent in Erasmus Darwin, *The Loves of the Plants*. See Desmond King-Hele, *Erasmus Darwin* (New York, 1963), ch. 8; King-Hele, "The Influence of Erasmus Darwin on Shelley," *KSMB*, no. 13 (1962): 30-36; King-Hele, "Erasmus Darwin's Influence on Shelley's Early Poems," *KSMB*, no. 16 (1965): 26-28.

7. VI, 131, 137; see also VII, 116. *Witch* (569-573) involves essentially the same figure. In a stanza in *Ado.* later rejected, Shelley has one of the mourners seize "with sudden grasp/The unseen strings of the aeolian air,/ Dallying with them until he might unclasp/The zone of the coy Music, and lay bare/Its inmost bosom" (*Verse & Prose*, p. 39). Since the mourner is Thomas Moore, the figure, though astonishing, is at least appropriate.

8. *Three Fragments on Beauty* (VII, 154); "Henry and Louisa" (126-127); "A Summer Evening Churchyard" (4-5); fragment from *Note Books*, I, 161.

9. The passage was later canceled (Notopoulos, p. 522).

10. *The Autobiography of Leigh Hunt*, ed. Roger Ingpen (New York,

1930), II, 35-36. Trelawny remarked that with Shelley, "love as a passion was never dissociated with sentiment" (*Rossetti Papers*, p. 502).

11. *The History of Clarissa Harlowe*, letter 19. Exactly when Shelley read *Clarissa* is not known, but both Mary and Claire had been reading an Italian translation as recently as April 1818, shortly after their arrival in Italy (Mary's *Journal*, pp. 96-97; Claire's *Journals*, p. 92).

12. Francis Place, *Illustrations and Proofs of the Principle of Population*, ed. Norman E. Himes (Boston, 1930), App. B.

13. *Revised Life*, p. 13. Sir Timothy Shelley was himself rumored to have produced at least one natural son, for whom, true to his code, he provided in later life. Shelley's grandfather, Sir Bysshe Shelley, acknowledged four illegitimate children in his will.

14. *L*, I, 142, 305.

15. "To Harriet" (11-14). Though the poem is dated May 1813 in the Esdaile notebook, Cameron argues that it was probably written in the summer of 1811 (*Esdaile*, p. 302; see also "To Harriet," pp. 85-87).

16. V.90. In IV.162, selfish sensualism "quench[es] the flame/Of natural love," i.e. sentimental love, natural to civilized beings.

17. VI, 248, 231. Shelley was still pointing to the problem in his last work, *TofL*, which depicts "the ribald crowd" swept up in the "wild dance"—"swift, fierce and obscene"—swirling round the triumphal car of life (137-140). This is love at its lowest common denominator, the reverse of civilized connection. An enigmatic fragment probably connected with *Charles the First* also refers to the problem (*Note Books*, II, 20).

18. Of the Venetians, Shelley relates that, until living among them, he had "no conception of the excess to which . . . passionless lust, & all the inexpressible brutalities which degraded human nature could be carried." As for Byron, Shelley believes him to be "heartily & deeply discontented" with his behavior which is basically unnatural to him (*L*,II, 43, 58; see also *L*, II, 317). In 1821 Byron recollected his disgust at Cambridge on being introduced to "the common place libertinism of the place and time," an attitude that persisted all his life, however much in periods of disillusion he might ridicule the seeming self-deception of higher or sentimental connection (*L&J*[P], V, 445).

19. *S&C*, VI, 764 (quoted by permission of The Carl H. Pforzheimer Library); *L*, II, 349.

20. *L&J*(M), VI, 66; cf. VI, 193. Byron writes to Richard Hoppner, July 2, 1819, that he is sick of "libertinism," and to Hobhouse, Apr. 6, 1819, that he is "tired of promiscuous concubinage" (*L&J*[M], VI, 175; *L&J*[M], VI, 108).

21. *L*, II, 330, 363; see also II, 322, 336.

22. Though not the only reason Shelley turned against Byron, this was one of them.

23. *Symp*. 181B-C (Shelley's translation, in Notopoulos, p. 422). Shelley also interpolates "libertinism" into 192A to convey profligate sexual behavior.

24. Cf. Robert Forsyth, *The Principles of Moral Science* (1802), which Shelley may have been reading at this time: "The pleasures which arise from

the indulgence of the appetites diminish, like all other pleasures, by repeated enjoyment" (I, 210).

25. *Zastrozzi* (V, 84); *St. Irvyne* (V, 178); *QM* (V.247-248); "To Harriet" (*Esdaile*, pp. 168-169).

26. *A Vindication of Natural Diet* (VI, 17). Cf. Shelley on Byron and his "concubines." The idea was perhaps suggested by Hume, "Of Polygamy and Divorce": "Solomon . . . with his seven hundred wives and three hundred concubines [wrote] pathetically concerning the vanity of the world" (*Essays Moral, Political and Literary*, p. 189). Other possible sources are James Lawrence, *The Empire of the Nairs* (London, 1811), I, ix-x; Mary Wollstonecraft, *Letters Written During a Short Residence in Sweden, Norway and Denmark* (London, 1796), p. 20; Peacock, *Nightmare Abbey*, ch. 1. Claire Clairmont wrote in her *Journals*, Apr. 1, 1822: "A clergyman in his Sermon defended the character of Solomon saying he was a libertine upon a principle of Enquiry."

27. Cf. Forsyth, *Principles of Moral Science*, I, 217-218.

28. Harry Harlow in Arno Karlen, *Sexuality and Homosexuality* (New York, 1971), p. 400.

29. See e.g. William H. Masters and Virginia E. Johnson, *The Pleasure Bond* (Boston, 1974). While recognizing intrinsic differences between individuals in the strength of the sex drive, they stress the importance of psychological and cultural factors. See also Lester Kirkendall, "Sex Drive," in *The Encyclopedia of Sexual Behavior*, pp. 942-943.

30. A. H. Maslow, *Motivation and Personality* (New York, 1954), pp. 242-243.

31. In the "Love is sold" note to *QM* Shelley distinguishes between the "natural temperance" of civilized connection and its opposite, the "unintellectual sensuality" of the libertine (I, 142). Cf. Masters and Johnson, *Pleasure Bond*, pp. 94-95, stating that sex for its own sake quickly reaches the law of diminishing returns and results in boredom and satiety, to be rekindled only with a new partner, while sex involving emotional commitment, intimacy, and caring never loses its pleasure and tenderness. The emphasis is on the necessity for total interpersonal connection, not simply sensual gratification, if lasting fidelity is to be achieved.

32. *Symp.* 187E, 182 (Shelley's translation, Notopoulos, pp. 428, 422).

33. Both Mary and Claire were reading *Tristram Shandy* in the opening weeks of 1818 before leaving for Italy (Mary's *Journal*, p. 91; Claire's *Journals*, p. 86).

34. Cf. Webb, *Violet in the Crucible*, p. 137: Shelley would "never indulge in sniggering" about sex. "Sex was too serious and man's dignity too precarious to be the subject of a joke."

35. Medwin, *Life of Shelley* (1847), I, 24; II, 355-356; Hogg, *Life of Shelley* (1858), II, 114; cf. *L*, I, 287; Arthur H. Beavan, *James and Horace Smith* (London, 1899), p. 171; Mary Shelley, *Letters*, I, 121; see also Claire's *Journals*, p. 194; Medwin, *Revised Life*, pp. 331-332.

36. *Fathers of the Victorians*, p. 18.

37. In a note to *Hellas* Shelley holds that even the intemperate and un-

chaste Greek gods are "personally more innocent" than the deities of other pagan mythologies.

38. Shelley read *Lysistrata* June 21, 1818 (Mary's *Journal*, p. 218). He also read through most, if not all, of the remaining comedies in this same period immediately before the composition of the *Discourse*. In Schlegel's *Lectures*, read a short while earlier, Shelley found a determined defense of Aristophanes against modern strictures, which may have stimulated his own reading of the dramatist (pp. 41, 154-156).

39. "I will beget a son" note to *QM* (I, 156). Shelley labels the Incarnation "monstrous and disgusting," his chief epithets for obscenity. Obscenity implies a corruption or perversion of the sexual nature, a feeding on filth or putrefaction which is ultimately nauseating to man's civilized self. Concubinage and libertinism are obscene because they are literally "sickening vice."

40. Webb, *Violet in the Crucible*, examined the MS texts of the translations against the published versions. Some of the omissions in the latter are the responsibility of Mary Shelley rather than the poet.

41. *L*, II, 361. Shelley first wrote "many" in place of "some" scenes (Kendall, *Descriptive Catalogue*, p. 125). Dante, whom Shelley also admired and was eventually to translate, was nevertheless slightly marred in his view by certain "distasteful passages" in the *Inferno* with their "gross & strong outlines" (*L*, II, 112).

42. Reported by Maria Gisborne, June 25, 1820 (*Gisborne & Williams*).

43. *Faust* 3960-3961. "Goethe's obscenely brilliant couplet," Francis George Steiner calls the lines ("Shelley and Goethe's Faust," *Rivista di Letteratura Moderne* n.s., 2 [April-June 1951]: 273); cf. Curtis C. D. Vail, "Shelley's Translations from Goethe's *Faust*," *Symposium* 3 (Nov. 1949): 199.

44. Sc. ii.234-270 (Shelley's translation). Goethe actually wrote "suitor" (*Werber*), not "pimp." But Shelley apparently "suspect[ed] Mephistopheles of the worst," notes Webb (*Violet in the Crucible*, pp. 174-175).

45. Ll. 169-171, trans. William Arrowsmith, in *Complete Greek Tragedies*, ed. David Grene and Richmond Lattimore (Chicago, 1958), II, 241. Webb's examination of the MS text showed that Shelley in fact translated ll. 179-181, which describe gross libertine sexuality, but in softened language (*Violet in the Crucible*, p. 135). Webb speculates that Shelley took the trouble to translate *The Cyclops*, though so opposed to obscenity, owing to his interest, shared with Leigh Hunt and Mary Shelley, in Polyphemus as a Frankenstein monster type, committing evil because of being denied social sympathy (pp. 80-87; cf. *S&C*, VI, 1086-1087).

46. Whether Shelley ever read Burns's suppressed bawdry is questionable, but he probably knew of its existence through Byron, who in 1813 had been lent "a quantity of Burns's unpublished, and never-to-be published, Letters," which, as Byron notes in his Journal, Dec. 13, 1814, were "full of oaths and obscene songs." See also (*L&J*[M], III, 202, 239); *Bowles Letter* of 1821. Many of the songs had led an underground existence since the beginning of the century in the pornographic collections *The Merry Muses of Caledonia* and *The Giblet Pye*, and their authorship was common knowledge. See Helen

E. Haworth, " 'The Virtuous Romantics': Indecency, Indelicacy, Pornography and Romantic Poetry," pp. 298-301; G[ershon] Legman, *The Horn Book* (New Hyde Park, N.Y., 1964), pp. 117-180.

47. *Revised Life*, p. 435.

48. Cf. Shelley to Maria Gisborne, July 1820, and to Medwin, July 20, 1820 (*L*, II, 218, 220). *Note Books*, II, 172-174, includes particularly gross fragments apparently connected with *Peter Bell III*, followed by a prose memorandum of Shelley's, probably related to the verses, which reads, "To say that I am in earnest—Many people would think it a better joke than any in the poem."

49. I. i. 233-235. In a draft passage from *Fiordispina*, the nurse wants to know why her description of Fiordispina's wedding night makes the young bride blush: "the violets pale and blue/Play the same game, but never change their hue" (*Verse & Prose*, p. 66). Cf. the blushing lovers in *Witch* (lxxvi).

50. *L*, II, 323. This episode later inspired one of Shelley's choicest epistolary witticisms. Of the arrival at Lerici of his sailboat, the *Don Juan*, Shelley writes Trelawny: "nothing can exceed the admiration *she* has excited, for we must suppose the name to have [been] given during the equivocation of sex which her godfather suffered in the Harem" (*L*, II, 421). The Don had been disguised as a ravishing odalisque.

51. *L*, II, 239-240; cf. II, 261, 276.

52. "We sate linked in the inwoven charm/Of converse and caresses sweet and deep,/Speechless caresses, talk that might disarm/Time" (*Rev.Is.* VII.i; cf. VI.xxxi). This motif appears in Shelley's earliest verse: "love and converse sweet" ("Wandering Jew," canto II). "Delightful converse," with its alternative "delightful talk," were Shelley's phrases for his initial happiness with Mary following their elopement in 1814. While a harmony of sympathies is fundamental to Shelley's erotic psychology, the condition is also part of his attempt in the *Discourse* to explain the *Symp*. for a modern audience. According to Plato, "Love is the desire of generation in the beautiful, both with relation to the body and soul" (*Symp*. 206B, Shelley's translation, Notopoulos, p. 445; see also 181C).

5. Lawless Love

1. The MS contains a number of false starts before Shelley managed to work out this notion to his satisfaction (Notopoulos, p. 533). The idea grew out of his continuing effort in the *Discourse* to elucidate for a modern audience the sexual distinctions set forth in the *Symp*., in particular the Platonic discrimination between Pandemian and Uranian love. The act of love "in itself," just like any other action, such as "drinking, singing, talking," is "neither good nor evil"; the "mode" in which it is done makes it so (*Symp*. 180E-181).

2. VII.131-133; Notopoulos, p. 485.

3. *Pr.Unb.*IV.127-128; "The Birth of Pleasure."

4. Notopoulos, p. 533. The law stated that a man might "with impunity kill an adulterer caught in the act with any of the women in his *kyrieia*"—

mother, sister, daughter, as well as wife (Lacey, *Family in Ancient Greece*, p. 114). The Athenian attitude was primarily civic, not moral, the result of a patriarchal obsession with the legitimacy of paternity. See also Robert J. Bonner and Gertrude Smith, *Administration of Justice from Homer to Aristotle* (Chicago, 1938), II, 203-204.

5. Shelley's translation, Notopoulos, p. 422.

6. Notopoulos, pp. 533-534.

7. Shelley takes an occasional poetic swipe at the traditional attitude toward adultery from which he himself had to suffer. *R&H* shows the serious social consequences of one charged with this "crime": Helen experiences complete ostracism and, like the author, is nearly deprived of her children. In a less serious vein *Swellfoot the Tyrant*, a burlesque of the current trial of Queen Caroline for infidelity—"The heaviest sin on this side of the Alps!" (I.i.371)—reduces the subject to absurdity.

8. Notopoulos, p. 533.

9. See Rogers, *Shelley at Work*, p. 8, for the notebook citation.

10. *L*, I, 323. In the early days of Christianity seduction was the forerunner of more than social ruin. In the "Love is sold" note to *QM* Shelley cites Gibbon on the savage penalties instituted against this act by the first Christian emperor, Constantine (I, 141n). He returns to the subject in *A Refutation to Deism* (VI, 38).

11. In a canceled and fragmentary passage later in the essay, Shelley writes, "As to the distinctions which endless legislators set up between debauchery of different kinds, if . . ." (Notopoulos, p. 537).

12. Notopoulos, p. 533.

13. *L*, II, 238. Gossip had it that Byron and Shelley had thrown dice for the honor of fathering Claire Clairmont's Allegra.

14. *L*, II, 94; I, 517; *Letter to Maria Gisborne* (5).

15. *The Literary Gazette and Journal of Belles Lettres*, May 19, 1821, pp. 300-308. Even before anything was known about the poet personally, the freedom of his unorthodox sexual views had been found censurable. *The Anti-Jacobin Review and Magazine*, Jan. 1812, reviewing *St. Irvyne*, complained that the author's "notions of *innocence* and *virtue* are such as, were they to pass current in the world, would soon leave society without one innocent or virtuous being," because the two heroines on principle neglect to legalize their numerous sexual liaisons.

16. Shelley lampooned these attacks in *Peter Bell III* where a reviewer protests of Peter's verse: "Is incest not enough?/And there be adultery too?" (VI.v). A doggerel fragment is composed in the same vein: "he was of the Atheistic scism/Many an [action of] Don Juanism/Had he committed" (*Note Books*, II, 108).

17. Leigh Hunt, "The Quarterly Review and The Revolt of Islam," *The Examiner*, Sept. 26, Oct. 3, 10, 1819; also in White, *Unextinguished Hearth*, pp. 143-150. In 1817 Southey wrote Wordsworth that "Hunt with all his family is on a visit to—Shelley, and in a fair way of becoming as infamous in his domestic conduct" (*New Letters of Robert Southey*, ed. Kenneth Curry [New

York, 1956], II, 156). Benjamin Haydon, who knew both Hunt and Shelley during this period, lumped the two together, with Byron, in his conventional abhorrence of advanced sexual doctrine.

18. Supplement to 1822; also in White, *Unextinguished Hearth*, p. 338.

19. *Divorce in England* (London, 1957), p. 11.

20. See *QM* (I.126-128; V.189-196; IX.38-40, 46-56, 76-88, 144-146, 200-202); *Rev.Is.* (Ded.vii; V.li.4; VI.xxxix-xl; VII.xxxv; VIII.xii); *R&H* (846-854); *Pr.Unb.* (III.iii.45-48; iv.185-188); *Epi.* (148-173 & Adv.); *Ginevra* (34-47). The antimatrimonialism of the Gothic novels is complicated by the fact that the most daring speculations often issue from the mouths of the villains and are undercut by authorial comment. But the fact that the hero of the second novel is an antimatrimonialist discloses Shelley's true position. He is dramatizing the complexities of "lawless love," seeking to distinguish, as throughout his career, the differences between licentious or libertine love and sentimental or sympathetic love, both of which are antipathetic to marriage and thus superficially justifiable by the same arguments. The literary sources of the novels' antimatrimonialism have proved puzzling. It is not certain that Shelley read Godwin's *Political Justice* or Abbé Barruel's *Memoirs Illustrating the History of Jacobinism* until after the novels were written. A more likely source is Rousseau's *Julie, ou La Nouvelle Héloise*, one of Shelley's favorite novels and one containing many parallels with *St. Irvyne*.

21. Also valuable is the draft of a paper defending his matrimonial views and practice which Shelley introduced at the Chancery hearing before Lord Eldon in 1817 over the custody of his children by Harriet Westbrook (Dowden, *Life of Shelley*, II, 86-88). At one point he apparently planned to introduce Milton as a precedent (cf. Pref. to *Pr.Unb.*: "the sacred Milton was . . . a bold inquirer into morals"). Cameron believes that the paper should be included among Shelley's works (*Golden Years*, p. 51n179).

22. Cameron, *Young Shelley*, pp. 266-270.

23. *Political Justice*, II, 508-509.

24. Sources for this belief include Hume's "Of Polygamy and Divorce," Lucretius (V.962-965), Diodorus Siculus, Herodotus, and Lord Monboddo, *Of the Origin and Progress of Language* (I, 221-229), which Shelley ordered in 1812. The evolutionary hypothesis of marriage was standard at the time, though much debated subsequently.

25. "I knew a very interesting Italian lady last winter [Emilia Viviani], but she is now married; which . . . is you know, the same as being dead." Shelley to Hogg (*L*, II, 360). The poet says he is quoting Peacock, presumably *Nightmare Abbey* (ch. 9), where Marionetta complains of marriage, "we might as well be dead."

26. "Fragments Connected with *Epipsychidion*" (17); *Epi.* (160). This connection may not have been conscious, for "true love" also recalls Emilia's own essay on "Il vero Amore," and the passage is indebted to Dante's definition of divine love in *Purgatorio*, Canto XV.

27. "Fragments Connected with *Epipsychidion*" (27-35). In the notebook containing *On Marriage*, Shelley jotted a note before it, "The similitude of

doctrine between Jesus Christ and the Cynics on the subject of marriage and love," and one after it, "Jesus Christ' idea of marriage" (Koszul, *Shelley's Prose Bod.*, p. 56). These notes are apparently related to the canceled opening of a paragraph in the contemporaneous *Essay on Christianity*, "The wise man neither married nor is given in marriage." In Shelley's reading, Christ is not recommending celibacy, the usual interpretation, but is attacking the institutional absolutism of marriage. The connection with the Cynics is through Diogenes, as described in Diogenes Laertius, *Life of Diogenes*, 72: "He advocated community of wives, recognizing no other marriage than a union of the man who persuades with the woman who consents" (Notopoulos, "The Dating of Shelley's Prose," *PMLA* 58 [June 1943]: 482-483; *Lives of Eminent Philosophers*).

28. "Fragments Connected with *Epipsychidion*" (16). Trelawny later told W. M. Rossetti that "M[ary] was excessively jealous of S[helley], both sexually and as regards the influence of other women over his mind" (*Rossetti Papers*, p. 500).

29. *L*, I, 173; cf. I, 194-195. This attitude persisted to the end of Shelley's life. Trelawny quotes him as observing in 1822, "Jealousy is gross selfishness; it looks upon everyone who approaches as an enemy: it's the idolatry of self, and, like canine madness, incurable" (*Records*, p. 73).

30. Larry and Joan Constantine note that, although there is no single model of jealousy, property, possession, ownership, and rights are the underlying bases (*Group Marriage* [New York, 1973], p. 172). See also the Constantines' "Sexual Aspects of Multilateral Relationships," in *Beyond Monogamy*, ed. James R. Smith and Lynn G. Smith (Baltimore, 1974), pp. 268-290; Ewald Bohm, "Jealousy," *The Encyclopedia of Sexual Behavior*, pp. 568-570; Anna K. and Robert T. Francoeur, *Hot & Cool Sex* (New York, 1974), ch. 6. On the possibly mammalian origins of jealousy Shelley would have had the support of Kinsey (*Sexual Behavior in the Human Male* [Philadelphia, 1948], p. 411).

31. The Shelley circle was debating these questions as late as 1819 in Rome, when Claire Clairmont records Shelley, Mary, Amelia Curran, and herself as holding a "discussion concerning Jealousy" (*Journals*, p. 111). On modern experiments in group marriage, the Constantines comment: "In the long run . . . people in multiple relationships who develop effective exploratory styles of dealing with jealousy outgrow certain forms of jealousy. In this sense we regard jealousy based on status, control, possession, ownership, and exclusivity as less mature." Some participants "genuinely take pleasure in the pleasure of someone they love"; some "focus on the secondary, more personal gains which can accrue from having a happier spouse"; and some— much as in Shelleyan love—experience "a form of ego extension" in which they regard "the experiences of an intimate as being in some sense [their] own" (*Group Marriage*, pp. 186-187). The Smiths argue that "The conquest of sexual jealousy, if achieved, could be the greatest advance in human relations since the advent of common law or the initiation of democratic processes" (*Beyond Monogamy*, p. 38).

32. *L*, I, 37, 135, 144, 194-195, 242, 323.

33. *L*, I, 167-208; *S&C*, III, 47 (quoted by permission of The Carl H. Pforzheimer Library).

34. *L*, I, 174-184; *S&C*, III, 47 (quoted by permission of The Carl H. Pforzheimer Library).

35. *L*, I, 171-202.

36. *L*, I, 174-184. Shelley had probably first tried to get Harriet to return Hogg's love, but when he realized how deeply this went against her principles, he discouraged the idea. Cf. *The Diary of Dr. John William Polidori, 1816*, ed. William Michael Rossetti (London, 1911), pp. 127-132.

37. *S&C*, III, 67; *L*, I, 203 (cf. I, 131).

38. *L*, I, 144-145, 234-235, 244, 252, 274, 288, 294, 296.

39. *L*, I, 331, 336. Joseph Gibbons Merle, who knew both Shelley and Elizabeth Hitchener slightly, remembered that when the latter returned to her father's house at Hurst, she found her reputation in ruins and was unable to obtain a single pupil for her school. People spoke of her "elopement" to Wales with Shelley; "if [the two] were to be credited, their union was purely platonic. This might be true, but worldly people did not believe it" ("A Newspaper Editor's Reminiscences," *Fraser's Magazine* 33 [June 1841]: 709-710).

40. Shelley to James Lawrence, Aug. 17, 1813 (*L*, I, 323).

41. Southey to Shelley, Sept. 1820? (*L*, II, 232-233).

42. Shelley to Hogg, Oct. 4, 1814, notes his "inconsistent & indisciplinable" behavior during the breakup of his marriage with Harriet and the ensuing elopement with Mary (*L*, I, 401).

43. The novel is a roman à clef whose protagonists are intended to represent Wollstonecraft and Godwin. It seeks to demonstrate the unworkableness of Godwin's antimatrimonial doctrine in practice, the principal stumbling block being the blasting of the woman's reputation. The novel also rejects the Shelley-Godwin belief that "natural constancy" can serve as a substitute for binding marriage: "unbridled licentiousness would soon be in general practice" (*Adeline Mowbray; or, The Mother and Daughter* [1804], in *The Works of Mrs. Amelia Opie* [Philadelphia, 1843], I, 214).

44. *L*, I, 242, 397-399.

45. Shelley to Southey, Aug. 17, 1820 (*L*, II, 231).

46. When Hogg first met Shelley after the elopement, he jokingly asked after "his *two* wives" (Claire's *Journals*, p. 59). David Booth, the husband of Mary's friend Isabel Baxter, believed that Shelley was sharing the favors of both Mary and Claire, speaking of its being now "Mary's turn to live" with the poet, "now Clare's." He suspected that the little Alba (Byron's Allegra) was the child of Shelley and Claire (*S&C*, V, 390-391; quoted by permission of The Carl H. Pforzheimer Library).

47. *L*, I, 391, 398. In his 1816 diary Polidori wrote that Shelley "paid Godwin's debts, and seduced his daughter; then wondered that he would not see him" (John Buxton, *Byron and Shelley* [London, 1968], p. 7). Cf. *The Diary of Benjamin Robert Haydon*, ed. Willard Bissell Pope [Cambridge, 1960], II, 89).

48. *Memoirs of Mary Wollstonecraft*, ed. John Middleton Murry (London, 1928), p. 101n9; see also *Political Justice*, III, 86-87.

49. In the philosopher's defense, the security of his book business, which supported his family, depended upon safeguarding his reputation (Ford K. Brown, *The Life of William Godwin* [London, 1926], p. 297).

50. By 1817 Shelley's revulsion against Harriet had become so complete that he apparently acquitted Hogg of all blame in the earlier affair (*Rev.Is.* V.v).

51. See *S&C*, III, 423-434, for a textual history of the letters and a summary of scholarly response to them.

52. *S&C*, II, 437; III, 456 (cited by permission of The Carl H. Pforzheimer Library).

53. See e.g. *S&C*, III, 451, 471-472 (cited by permission of The Carl H. Pforzheimer Library).

54. *S&C*, III, 471 (quoted by permission of The Carl H. Pforzheimer Library).

55. Cameron believes the relationship "did not go beyond flirtation" (*Golden Years*, pp. 24-25).

56. A letter from Mary Shelley to Hogg in 1823, after Shelley's death, refers to her "often . . . erroneous conduct with regard" to Hogg, but this misconduct seems to refer to her later hostility and rudeness to him when their natural lack of sympathy surfaced rather than to anything sexual (*New Shelley Letters*, p. 139).

6. The Male Eros

1. *L*, II, 58. This letter has been taken to mean that Shelley imputed these practices to Byron himself (see Lord Lovelace, *Astarte* [London, 1921], p. 214n1). But this would have been unthinkable to Shelley, who ridiculed the homosexual rumors circulating about his friend as "innocent from their very extravagance, if they were not still more so from their silliness" (*L*, I, 506).

2. *L*, II, 63. For photographs of this statue, see Jean Marcadé, *Roma Amor* (Geneva, 1961), pp. 112-113.

3. The Count was thrice arrested on this charge but each time managed to buy his way off for the sum of 100,000 crowns. In his drama Shelley changes the crime to murder and in his translation of the MS source omits some sexual details, referring "the curious" to the Italian text.

4. Blackstone, *Commentaries*, bk. 4, ch. 15; cf. Coke, *Institutes*, ch. 10.

5. Notopoulos, p. 535.

6. Notopoulos, p. 535.

7. See e.g. H. I. Marrou, *A History of Education in Antiquity*, trans. George Lamb (New York, 1956), pp. 26-35; Dover, *Greek Popular Morality*, p. 214; Dover, *Greek Homosexuality*, passim.

8. Pref. to *Hellas* and *Essay on the Revival of Literature* (VI, 213).

9. *Decline and Fall*, ch. 64.

10. First published in 1824 as *Apophoreta*.

11. Of the "vulgar imputation" Shelley first wrote that it could have been "nothing resembling" (Notopoulos, p. 535).

12. *Satyricon* 114, trans. Michael Heseltine, Loeb Classical Library (1939), pp. 239-240.

13. See also *Satyricon* 132; cf. J. P. Sullivan, *The Satyricon of Petronius* (London, 1968), p. 234.

14. Lucretius is not a good example, since he bases love, including pederastic, on lust, the desire for physical connection and release (*De Rerum Natura* IV.1035-1279). Nevertheless the passage on love was Shelley's favorite section of the poem (*L*, I, 545). He must simply have chosen to ignore its pederastic implications. Virgil is an appropriately sentimental example, but not Horace. Shelley read Horace's *Odes* on Aug. 8, 1818, while writing the *Discourse*.

15. Notopoulos, pp. 535, 536. For the allusions, see Dover, *Greek Homosexuality*; Jeffrey Henderson, *The Maculate Muse* (New Haven, 1975), ch. 7.

16. Encouraging a "pure" interpretation of Greek pederasty are Plutarch, *Lives*, Xenophon, *Memorabilia*, and Diogenes Laertius, *Lives of Eminent Philosophers*, all of which Shelley knew well. Plutarch's *Amatorius*, from the *Moralia*, paints a different picture, but Shelley is not known to have read it, though Peacock cites it twice in his notes to *Rhododaphne*, written in 1817. Also casting doubt on the purity of Greek practice is the *Amores*, traditionally ascribed to Lucian, whom Shelley read in the fall of 1816 and again in the summer of 1818 while at work on the *Discourse*, but presumably not the dialogue on love nor the *Dialogues of the Courtesans* and the *Saturnalia*. Shelley was also reading Athenaeus, *Deipnosophists*, at this time (Rogers, *Shelley at Work*, p. 169). Bk. 13, containing a lengthy account of ancient pederastic practice, includes among boy-lovers such celebrated names as Agamemnon, Pindar, Sophocles, Epaminondas, and Alexander the Great. But since Athenaeus nowhere suggests that the passion to which these figures were subject was purely emotional, Shelley must not have read this far. The most damning evidence is Aeschines, *Against Timarchus*, but the speech was apparently unknown to Shelley.

17. A year later *The Quarterly Review* 21 (Apr. 1819): 296, took much the same approach in a review of Schlegel, *Lectures*, where Thomas Mitchell speaks of Aristophanes and Plato as "the two great painters of the higher and lower classes of society in Athens," and of their "manners."

18. *Phaedrus* 251-252, trans. Harold North Fowler, Loeb Classical Library (Cambridge, 1960), I, 487-489.

19. Notopoulos, p. 535.

20. *Human Sexual Response*, p. 55. Psychologists classify the ability to fantasy to orgasm a form of autoeroticism or "psychic masturbation." It seems to be of rare occurrence, more so among men than among women, though there are "no valid statistics" (William Masters, personal communication). Kinsey, on the basis of his sample study groups, reported an 0.81%

occurrence for the male and approximately 2% for the female. In the male, "spontaneous ejaculation is almost wholly confined to younger boys just entering adolescence," although there were "stray cases of males of college age ejaculating under the excitement of class recitation or examination, in airplanes during combat, and under other rare circumstances," and two "older males" in the sample were capable of this response (*Sexual Behavior in the Human Male*, pp. 190-191; *Sexual Behavior in the Human Female* [Philadelphia, 1953], p. 163). According to Masters, the etiology of spontaneous orgasm is unknown: "We have no concept of the neurological process that triggers orgasm or ejaculation"; but the psychogenic process is "in all probability" identical with that causing nocturnal emission. There seem to be no physiological differences between "orgasm occasioned by the sexual object and that released by fantasy," but those capable of achieving spontaneous orgasm exhibit "an advanced degree of sensitivity to the psychosocial input" triggering the response, as Shelley maintains (Masters, personal communication).

21. Pref. to *Poetical Works* (1839).

22. *Revised Life*, pp. 27-28.

23. *Revised Life*, pp. 89-90.

24. Wasserman, *Critical Reading*, p. 142n34, from the Morgan Library MS; see also "Fragments Connected with *Epipsychidion*" (134-169). *Verse & Prose*, pp. 17-19, includes rejected stanzas probably intended for Canto I of *L&C*, which also seem connected with this experience.

25. Both Godwin and Drummond use the term "intellectual system" (*Political Justice*, bk. 4, ch. 9; Sir William Drummond, *Academical Questions* [London, 1805], p. 135).

26. *On Life* (VI, 196); *On Metaphysics* (VII, 59).

27. *On Metaphysics* (VII, 62-64).

28. "Pornography in the Home: A Topic in Medical Education," in *Contemporary Sexual Behavior*, ed. Joseph Zubin and John Money (Baltimore, 1973), p. 412. In spite of woman's greater ability to fantasy to orgasm, erotic fantasies and particularly erotic dreams play a less prominent role in female psychosexuality (pp. 420-421). See also Money and Ehrhardt, *Man & Woman, Boy & Girl*, pp. 149-187; Kinsey, *Human Female*, p. 521. Although these phenomena may be related to the level of androgen in the bloodstream, the associated imagery is "not inaugurated by the hormones of puberty, whether in boys or girls, but simply activated to be more vivid, frequent, insistent, and associated with genitopelvic arousal and orgasm. The origin of images that demonstrate their erotic arousal power at puberty lies earlier in the biography" (Money and Ehrhardt, pp. 253, 149).

29. *Man & Woman, Boy & Girl*, p. 354.

30. The "spontaneous appearance at puberty of sex dreaming—wet dreaming—independent of sexual experience may be programmed into the brain pathways by prenatal male sex hormones" (Money and Patricia Tucker, *Sexual Signatures* [Boston, 1975], p. 163).

31. Kinsey, *Human Male*, p. 521.

32. In the novels erotic dreaming is, unrealistically, a propensity of

women. Even in the later work it is often Shelley's women who dream erotically. This may be partly owing to the influence of the Gothic tradition where the erotic dream is the experience as much of the female as of the male.

33. Since Shelley apparently placed the onset of puberty at fifteen (*Una Favola*), and since nocturnal emissions "almost invariably begin a year or more after the other adolescent developments (pubic hair, voice change, growth in height, etc.) are under way" (Kinsey, *Human Male*, p. 523), Shelley's earliest work must have been produced at the time he was first experiencing the graphic joys of the wet dream. Presumably the veiled maid of *Alr.* comes to the poem's youthful protagonist at the same age. The nocturnal emission was to become an increasing cause of concern to nineteenth-century physicians, who termed it a kind of "disease" ("spermatorrhea") and laid at its door such ills as consumption, epilepsy, and madness. There was even the curious notion that the nocturnal emission was "a form of contagious clap," physicians dousing their patients "with salivatory doses of mercury" (John S. Haller, Jr., and Robin M. Haller, *The Physician and Sexuality in Victorian America* [Urbana, 1974], pp. 211-212). As for masturbation, the other chief expression of adolescent sexuality, often accompanied by active fantasying, period horror was unbounded. Frequent masturbation could lead, among other things, to "involuntary emission." See e.g. E. M. Sigsworth and T. J. Wyke, "A Study of Victorian Prostitution and Venereal Disease," in *Suffer and Be Still: Women in the Victorian Age*, ed. Martha Vicinus (Bloomington, 1972), pp. 85-86; G. J. Barker-Benfield, *The Horrors of the Half-Known Life* (New York, 1976), pp. 164-181. Shelley's experience of onanism can only be guessed, although the practice was presumably one of the abuses implicitly condemned in the *Discourse* as going against nature because defeating the purpose of the sex act, namely procreation (222-223).

34. *Alr.* 42. "Most individuals wake up when there is an orgasm" (Kinsey, *Human Male*, p. 521).

35. Pref. to *Alr.* Cf. "Fragment: *Igniculus Desiderii.*"

36. Money and Ehrhardt, *Man & Woman, Boy & Girl*, p. 187.

37. "On Leaving London for Wales," 1812 (*Esdaile*, p. 55).

38. The last line contains a parallel with or even a reminiscence of Peacock, *Rhododaphne*, Canto VI: "The lamps grow dim/And tremble, and expire. No more./Darkness is there, and Mystery." This is just before Anthemion and the nymph have intercourse, after he has been treated to a preview of her charms in a scene resembling the veiled maid episode of *Alastor*.

39. Cf. the little death in *R&H* when "limbs are interwoven" (1125-1129). The lines from "The Boat on the Serchio" echo Virgil's "Fourth Georgic" (IV.359-374), which Shelley translated, probably in 1818 (Joseph Raben, "Shelley's 'The Boat on the Serchio': The Evidence of the Manuscript," *PQ* 46 [Jan. 1967]:66). But the metaphor of coition is not in the original.

40. "Fragment" (*Poetical Works*, p. 660).

41. For "Indian Serenade" as an Oriental love song, see G. M. Matthews, "Shelley's Lyrics," in *The Morality of Art*, ed. D. W. Jefferson (New York, 1969), pp. 203-204; Chernaik, *Lyrics*, p. 160.

42. Chernaik, *Lyrics*, pp. 153-154. The "wild & joyous" is from the draft text.

43. A variant reading sets out the complainant's symptoms in logical sequence: "I faint I fail I die away" (*Verse & Prose*, p. 55). Sources suggested for this formula include Erasmus Darwin, *The Loves of the Plants*.I.451;II.331-332;IV.263 (King-Hele, *Erasmus Darwin*, p. 149); Charles Wesley, "Jesu, Love of My Soul" (Murray Roston, *Prophet and Poet* [Evanston, 1965], p. 105). See also Geoffrey Bullough, *Mirror of Minds* (Toronto, 1962), pp. 155-156; Chernaik, *Lyrics*, pp. 152-153; Richard Levin, "Shelley's 'Indian Serenade': A Re-Evaluation," *College English* 24 (Jan. 1963): 306-307.

44. Money and Ehrhardt, *Man & Woman, Boy & Girl*, p. 253.

45. Notopoulos, p. 535.

46. Notopoulos, p. 539. Lawrence Zillman, *The Complete Known Drafts of Shelley's Prometheus Unbound* (Ann Arbor, 1967), pp. 14-15n57, transcribes "social intercourse" for "sexual intercourse" and connects the passage not with the *Discourse* but with the Preface to *Prometheus Unbound* (see also Wasserman, *Critical Reading*, p. 290n71). The context seems to favor the Notopoulos reading, however. In any case Shelley could hardly have enjoyed the sexual explicitness into which the examination of Greek love was taking him. Christopher Ricks, *Keats and Embarrassment*, (Oxford, 1974), p. 60, takes Shelley's unease as evidence that, unlike Keats, he was "chary" and "defensive" about sex. But this charge is unfair, since Shelley was more intellectually inquiring about sex than any of his contemporaries.

47. *Paideia: The Ideals of Greek Culture*, trans. Gilbert Highet (New York, 1945), III, 187; cf. Jerry Stannard, "Socratic Eros and Platonic Dialectic," *Phronesis* 4 (1959): 122-123; Hans Kelsen, "Platonic Love," *The American Imago* 3 (Apr. 1942): 55-56, 58, 82. H. I. Marrou maintains that pederastic relationship "was the normal mode, the standard type of all education" in ancient Greece. Greek *paideia* "found its realization in *paiderasteia*" (*History of Education in Antiquity*, pp. 31-32; see also Victor Ehrenberg, *The Greek State* [New York, 1960], pp. 99-100).

48. In his translation of the *Symp.* Shelley toned down the sexual implications of the original, doubtless with publication in mind, for complete textual fidelity would have defeated his purpose. When the translation was finally published by Mary Shelley in 1840, the text was heavily bowdlerized, "friendship" being substituted throughout for "love" and Alcibiades' attempted seduction of Socrates dropped altogether.

49. "Be every thing to me love," writes Mary Godwin to Shelley shortly after their elopement, "& indeed I will be a good girl and never vex you any more I will learn Greek and—but when shall we meet when I may tell you all this & you will so sweetly reward me" (*Letters*, I, 5).

50. "Shelley's 'Disinterested Love' and Aristotle," *PQ* 32 (Apr. 1953): 214-217.

51. See Godwin, *Political Justice*, bk. 4, ch. 10.

52. "Of Self-Love," *An Enquiry Concerning the Principles of Morals*, in

Hume's Moral and Political Philosophy, ed. Henry D. Aiken (New York, 1948), pp. 270-275.

53. Julian *Works*, V, 175, 188. The source was probably less philosophic than literary, for Lewis' *The Monk*, to which Shelley's novels are indebted, stresses the concept of disinterestedness.

54. This view was reinforced by Hogg's attempted seduction of Harriet Westbrook: "Your crime has been *selfishness*" (*L*, 171, 178; *S&C*, III, 47-48). In happy contrast was Shelley's rapidly developing friendship with Elizabeth Hitchener, perhaps unfortunately for her, a model of "disinterestedness" (*L*, I, 173, 191-192).

55. *Political Justice*, bk. 4, ch. 10.

56. The date of "Speculations on Morals" remains obscure, though MS evidence indicates the composition extended over 1815-1821 (*S&C*, IV, 733-738). In *A Philosophical View of Reform*, written in 1819, Shelley speaks of the "generous emotions of disinterested affection which the records of human nature and our experience teach us that the human heart is susceptible of" (Clark, pp. 240-241).

57. VI, 76-77, reconstructed by Mary Shelley from the fragmentary MS draft (*S&C*, IV, 733-738). She supplied the "dis" of "disinterestedness" and prefixed "propensities" with "natural."

58. *Life of Shelley*, I, 437.

59. II.xvii; V.v; V.xlv; VI.xi; VI.xv. Cf. Mary Shelley's notes on the text: "There exists in this poem a memorial of a friend of [Shelley's] youth." See also *Witch* (lxxvii); *Assassins* (VI, 167).

60. *New Shelley Letters*, pp. 138, 144. "All Shelley's friends preyed upon him shamefully except Hogg," Trelawny remarked to Claire Clairmont, but "his love was pure—and the one bit of romance in his life" (*Letters of Trelawny*, p. 232).

61. See e.g. Arthur Wormhoudt, *The Demon Lover* (New York, 1949), p. 110. Eustace Chesser claims that Shelley's "very horror" when the subject of homosexuality was raised "betrays his inclinations: he protested too much" (*Shelley & Zastrozzi: Self-Revelation of a Neurotic* [London, 1965], pp. 34-35). But this attitude was universal in the period. Despite his obvious repugnance, Shelley was in fact more tolerant of homosexuality than was usual in his day. By contemporary standards, he protested too little, not too much.

62. White and Ingpen place the experience at Syon House (*Shelley*, I, 27-28; Julian *Works*, VII, 358); Hogg (*Life of Shelley*, I, 30) and Dowden (*Life of Shelley*, I, 20) conclude it could be either but Syon House is more likely. Shelley himself was unable to remember the "precise epoch." If eleven, he was still at Syon House, while twelve marked his first year at Eton. The identity of the boy remains unknown (Dowden, I, 20; White, *Shelley*, I, 28). Mary Shelley's MS notes for her uncompleted biography of her husband, later used by Hogg in his *Life of Shelley*, remark on his "several sincere friendships" at Eton and add, "Among his papers there is the commencement of an essay on friendship & in it he has thus commemorated this youthful attachment," followed

by the canceled sentence, "I do not remember the name of this friend." Elizabeth Nitchie, "Shelley at Eton: Mary Shelley vs. Jefferson Hogg," *KSMB*, no. 11 (1960): 48-54, finds no MS source for the dedication to a friend—taken by Hogg to mean himself—with which the essay is prefaced in Hogg's *Life of Shelley*: "I once had a friend, whom an inextricable multitude of circumstances has forced me to treat with apparent neglect. To him I dedicate this essay. If he finds my own words condemn me, will he not forgive?" This was most likely written by Hogg himself, she believes (cf. Julian *Works*, VII, 358). Forman, however, prints the fragment in the *Note Books* (II, 15) from the same notebook containing "Follow to the deep wood sweetest" where it immediately precedes a jotting for the "down, down" lyric of *Pr. Unb.*, followed by the "Mighty Eagle" lines to Godwin. Forman says the fragment is "duly headed:—'Friendship.' "

63. When Hogg printed the essay in his *Life of Shelley*, he prudently interpolated "like children, as we still were!" (I, 31). While Shelley found schoolboy kissing harmless, he was not so permissive when such practice extended to adult males. When traveling down the Rhine in the summer of 1814, he and Mary reacted with horror to the actions of their fellow German passengers, who "swaggered and talked, and got tipsy, and what was hideous to English eyes, kissed one another" (*History of a Six Weeks Tour*). The original *Journal* entry records an even stronger reaction, as do Claire's *Journals*.

64. A recurring dream recorded by Shelley in *On Metaphysics* (VII, 66) may be connected with this episode (cf. Holmes, *Pursuit*, p. 295).

65. Alfred Zimmern, *The Greek Commonwealth*, 5th ed. rev. (London, 1931), pp. 343-344, compares the pederastic relationships of fifth-century Athens to the "manly and fortifying . . . modern friendships which, knit at our boarding-schools and Universities, continue through the vicissitudes of divergent careers, and sometimes make history." He speaks of them in terms of "romantic devotion," stressing their purity and chastity, but admits a "physical element" may occasionally have been "abused"—the "black horse" of Plato's *Phaedrus*.

66. *The Autobiography of Leigh Hunt*, ed. J. E. Morpurgo (London, 1949), pp. 83-84. Benjamin Disraeli, *Coningsby* (1844), contains a similar rhapsody on schoolboy friendship at Eton, equated with "sympathy."

67. *L&J*(M), II, 155.

68. Byron later wrote, "I was never in friendship but once, in my nineteenth year," but "it gave me as much trouble as love" (*L&J*[M], III, 67). It is now believed the "Thyrza" poems are addressed to Edleston.

69. *L&J*(P), V, 168-169, 455, 463; VI, 30, 80, 366.

70. "From his boyhood," according to Lady Caroline Lamb, Byron admitted having been "in the practice of unnatural crime" and "mentioned 3 schoolfellows" at Harrow "whom he had thus perverted." Subsequently in the Levant he engaged in this practice "unrestrictedly" ("Lady Byron's Minutes of Conversation with Ly C. L. March 27th 1816," in Doris Langley Moore, *The Late Lord Byron* [Philadelphia, 1961], pp. 243-244). The early letters, now available unexpurgated, are strewn with allusions to homosexual activities

and feelings, both his own and others'. He successfully repressed this side of his nature on his return to England, but it was revived in the last weeks of his life by an attachment to the Greek youth Loukas, recalling the tender feelings of his boyhood at Harrow.

71. "And embraces enough to have ruined the character of a county in England," Byron adds (*L&J*[M], II, 6).

72. H. Montgomery Hyde, *The Love That Dared Not Speak Its Name* (Boston, 1970), p. 150; cf. p. 170.

73. *Eton Microcosm*, ed. Anthony Cheetham and Derek Parfit (London, 1964), pp. 16, 93.

74. *John Addington Symonds* (London, 1964), pp. 32-33.

75. *The Love That Dared Not*, p. 110.

76. Cf. Hyde, *The Love That Dared Not*, p. 116; Bernard Grebanier, *The Uninhibited Byron* (New York, 1970), pp. 31-32; *Don Leon*, 11. 377-389 and notes (p. 333).

77. Ethel Colburn Mayne, *The Life and Letters of Anne Isabella Lady Noel Byron* (New York, 1929), p. 331. In later life Lady Byron had a "fanatical abhorrence of public schools," labeling them "nurseries of corruption and crime" (p. 331).

78. See e.g. J. R. Ackerley, *My Father and Myself* (New York, 1969); Robin Maugham, *Escape from the Shadows* (New York, 1973); Michael Davidson, *Some Boys* (London, [1971]); Brian Aldiss, *The Hand-Reared Boy* (London, 1970); John Reed, *Old School Ties: The Public School in British Literature* (Syracuse, 1964); Jonathan Gathorne-Hardy, *The Old School Tie: The Phenomenon of the English Public School* (New York, 1978).

79. Edward Carpenter, *The Psychology of the Poet Shelley* (London, 1925), p. 37, remarks "the filthy talk, the gross and insolent habits . . . the beguilement of the time by sex-indulgences," which Shelley must have encountered at Eton.

80. The usual practice was mutual masturbation. Arthur Freeman, "Schoolboy Homosexuality," *Mattachine Review*, May 1960, pp. 11-20, reports that in his public school, "buggery and other récherché practices" were unknown to him. "The normal practice was mutual masturbation, accompanied when the elder partner was more unselfish or imaginative by love-play not unlike that of adult heterosexuality."

81. *Lord Dismiss Us* (London, 1967). Michael Davidson remarks of his school: "there was a great deal of emotional homosexuality—bigger boys 'in love' (yet why put it in inverted commas? It was *love!*) with the unapproachable younger" (*Some Boys*, pp. 175-176). See also Freeman, "Schoolboy Homosexuality," pp. 15-16.

82. Hogg dates the fragment 1822, "not long" before the poet's death (*Life of Shelley*, I, 22-24). However, internal evidence suggests that it must have been composed earlier, not long after the *Discourse*. Notopoulos, "The Dating of Shelley's Prose," p. 492, assigns "On Friendship" to late 1818 or early 1819. This seems to be confirmed by the introductory fragment in *Note Books*, which apparently dates from 1819.

83. Cf. Godwin on his growing attachment to Wollstonecraft, "It was friendship melting into love" (*Memoirs of Mary Wollstonecraft [Godwin]*, ed. W. Clark Durant [London, 1927 (1798)], p. 233).

84. In place of "sentimental" Shelley first wrote "passionate," the substitution underscoring his desire to bring the experience within the boundaries of a single psychological archetype (Notopoulos, p. 538).

85. Cf. Shelley, "Note on the Hundred and Eleventh Sonnet of Shakespeare" (VII, 152), where Shakespeare addresses "a dear friend."

86. *Political Justice*, I, 441, 447. Shelley considered these matters as early as the winter of 1810-1811. See his letter to Hogg (*L*, I, 47). The "alloy" of pain, evil, selfishness, and carnal lust recurs as a motif throughout Shelley's work, beginning with his earliest poetry.

87. Actually, the passive partner in Greek pederasty was not expected to derive bodily pleasure from the act. He submitted only to please his lover. If he did exhibit pleasure, he was considered "perverted," a "prostitute" (Dover, *Greek Homosexuality*, pp. 52-53, 87, 91).

88. Stanley Rosen observes that this passage in the original Greek implies a desire not simply for the company of the loved one but for sexual intercourse with him (*Plato's Symposium* [New Haven, 1968], p. 274).

89. *Symp.* 211C-212. In his own translation of this passage Shelley does not employ "unalloyed" but clearly means it: "What, then, shall we imagine to be the aspect of the supreme beauty itself, simple, pure, uncontaminated with the intermixture of human flesh and colours, and all other idle and unreal shapes attendant on mortality" (Notopoulos, p. 450). The phrases "wholly divested of the smallest alloy of sensual intermixture" and "exempt from the smallest alloy of sensuality" from "On Friendship" and "wholly divested of any unworthy alloy" from the *Discourse* (in the original MS "sensual" is canceled in favor of "unworthy" [Notopoulos, p. 538]) are reworkings of the passage from Plato. The vocabulary of Diotima's speech becomes pervasive in Shelley's later work. The material world is invariably an "alloy" which "stains" the pure white light or fire of eternity.

90. Rosen notes that the dialectical progression of the *Symp.* is to transform *eros* into *philia* (*Plato's Symposium*, pp. 84, 180-189).

91. Shelley to Leigh Hunt, Jan. 25, 1822: "I consider you as a piece of sterling gold in the midst of the baser metals that surround you" (*L*, II, 382). That is, Hunt's friendship brings Shelley pleasure unalloyed.

92. *Epi.* (160-183). Using similar language, Shelley works this out on the metaphysical level in *Ado*.

93. Notopoulos, pp. 210-211. Nothing is actually known about Plato's sex life. Ancient tradition, depending solely on gossip-mongering and inferences from the dialogues, is historically worthless. The epigrams are Plato's by attribution only.

94. [Thomas Mitchell], "View of Grecian Philosophy.—The Clouds, &c," *The Quarterly Review* 21 (Apr. 1819): 271-320. Hogg also noticed the article, describing its views to Peacock as "sufficiently perverse" and imagining Shelley's reaction (*New Shelley Letters*, pp. 123-124).

95. *The British Essayists* 40 (London, 1819): 216-217, 223, 174, 224, 225-

226; see also Thomas Gould, *Platonic Love* (London, 1963), p. 193; W. K. C. Guthrie, *Socrates* (Cambridge, 1971), pp. 70-77. But the evidence remains inconclusive.

96. Apparently Shelley did not know *Charmides* 155D, where Socrates kindles to the "flame" of pederastic desire. To defend Socrates, Shelley could have drawn on Xenophon, *Memorabilia*, which stresses the purity and disinterestedness of his relations with his pupils, and which Shelley read on June 13-14 and 16-17, 1818, not long before he composed the *Discourse*. But Athenaeus, whose work Shelley also knew, suggests a different view (*Deipnosophistae* XIII).

7. *Love's Dominion*

1. Shelley first wrote, "their claim[s] are more harmoniously united" (Notopoulos, p. 531), associating the passage directly with his sentimental archetype, "all sympathies . . . harmoniously blended."

2. See Jérôme Carcopino, *Daily Life in Ancient Rome*, ed. Henry T. Rowell, trans. E. O. Lorimer (New Haven, 1940); Mary Johnston, *Roman Life* (Chicago, 1957); Moses Hadas and The Editors of Time-Life Books, *Imperial Rome* (1965); Pomeroy, *Goddesses, Whores, Wives, and Slaves*, pp. 149-189; Judith P. Hallett, "The Role of Women in Roman Elegy: Counter-Cultural Feminism," *Arethusa* 6 (Spring 1973): 103-124; J. V. P. D. Balsdon, *Roman Women* (London, 1962). Shelley's source for woman's status in Rome was most likely Gibbon, *Decline and Fall of the Roman Empire*, ch. 44.

3. See e.g. E. Royston Pike, *Love in Ancient Rome* (London, 1965), ch. 20; J. P. Sullivan, *The Satyricon of Petronius*, pp. 232-235; Marcadé, *Roma Amor*; George Luck, "The Woman's Role in Latin Love Poetry," in *Perspectives of Roman Poetry*, ed. G. Karl Galinsky (Austin, 1974), pp. 15-31.

4. *Sexual Life in Ancient Rome*, trans. Gilbert and Helen Highet (New York, 1953), pp. 179-180; *History of European Morals*, II, 303. Cf. *TLS*, June 18, 1964: the Romans were "a sophisticated people with coarse tastes and immensely dirty minds."

5. *Essay on Christianity* (VI, 228); "Fragment: A Roman's Chamber" (1819).

6. In a note on "A Statue of Minerva" Shelley defends the Greek orgy, but his perturbation is obvious. There is no ambivalence, however, in his attitude toward the Roman imitation: "In Rome it had a more familiar, wicked and dry appearance—it was not suited to the severe and exact apprehensions of the Romans, and their strict morals once violated by it sustained a deep injury little analogous to its effects upon the Greeks, who turned all things—superstition, prejudice, murder, madness—to Beauty" (VI, 323).

7. In an 1818 review of Peacock, *Rhododaphne*, Shelley writes: "it is a Greek and Pagan poem," but the "story itself represents a modern aspect, being made up of combinations of human passion which seem to have been developed since the Pagan system has been outworn" (VI, 273-274). Trelawny has Shelley make the same point (*Records*, p. 73).

8. See e.g. Joseph Berington, *A Literary History of the Middle Ages*

(London, 1814), p. 227. Claire read this in 1818 (*Journals*, p. 85), and Shelley may have looked into it because Claire was living with the Shelleys at the time. Berington was a popularizer of medieval culture, whose *Lives of Abelard and Heloise* (1787) Mary read in 1815. Unlike Shelley, he did not confuse *trouveur* with *troubadour*, though like the poet, he noticed that the word means "inventor."

9. In the *Discourse* Shelley observes, "Perhaps nothing has been discovered in the fragments of the Greek lyric poets equivalent to the sublime and chivalric sensibility of Petrarch" (218). Cf. "Lines Written Among the Euganean Hills" (200-203); *L*, II, 20.

10. Dante's *Vita Nuova* is also "an inexhaustible fountain of purity of sentiment," or sentimental love (VII, 128).

11. Richard Barber, *The Knight & Chivalry* (New York, 1970), p. 80. Maurice Valency notes that it is "still in vain that we look for any immediate source or influence out of which the courtly lyric could have come . . . The various hypotheses which have been adduced . . . are not mutually exclusive. Most are in some degree acceptable; none is certain" (*In Praise of Love*, p. 36). Urban Tigner Holmes, Jr., *A History of Old French Literature from the Origins to 1300* (New York, 1936), p. 172, lists ten different theories. The Hispano-Arabic theory of origins presently has the most adherents.

12. Chs. 7-8, 18 (*Tacitus on Britain and Germany*, trans. H. Mattingly [Harmondsworth, 1951]).

13. *Decline and Fall of the Roman Empire*, ch. 9.

14. Richard Hurd, *Letters on Chivalry and Romance*, ed. Hoyt Trowbridge, The Augustan Reprint Society, no. 101-102 (Los Angeles, 1963 [1762]), p. 19; Thomas Percy, *Reliques of Ancient English Poetry* (London, 1910 [1765]), II, 169; Thomas Warton, *The History of English Poetry, from the Eleventh to the Seventeenth Century* (London, 1870 [1774-1781]), p. 75.

15. [Paul-Henri Mallet], *Northern Antiquities: or, A Description of the Manners, Customs, Religion and Laws of the Ancient Danes, and Other Northern Nations*, trans. [Thomas Percy] (London, 1770), I, 315-318, 320-321, published originally as *Introduction à l'histoire de Dannemarc, où l'on traite de la religion des lois des moeurs & des usages des anciens Danois* (1755).

16. Pref. to *Northern Antiquities*, I, ii-iii.

17. Shelley ordered "Dr. Percy's Northern Antiquities" Aug. 8, 1817 (*L*, I, 552). Mary Shelley read vol. 1 during Sept. 2-19 (*Journal*), p. 84). Pelloutier, *Histoire des Celtes*, which was one of Mallet's sources, is cited by Gibbon, as is Hume, *History of England*, Abbé Du Bos, *Histoire de la monarchie française*, and Tacitus, *Germania*. Since Shelley read Hume, Tacitus, and possibly Du Bos after reading Gibbon, he may similarly have read Pelloutier and Mallet. Gibbon himself generally distinguishes between Celtic and Germanic. Whatever Shelley's source, he took it as authoritative, since he repeats the confusion in his poetry ("Lines Written Among the Euganean Hills," 11. 152, 223). However, see *Shelley's Poetry and Prose*, ed. Reiman and Powers, p. 495n6.

18. *French Chivalry* (Baltimore, 1940), pp. 96-98.

19. *Allegory of Love*, pp. 8-9.

20. *Lectures on Dramatic Art and Literature*, trans. John Black, pp. 24-25, 155-156. Shelley would also have seen Schlegel's views summarized in Hazlitt's review of the *Lectures*, *Edinburgh Review* 26 (Feb. 1816). Schlegel's brother Friedrich adopted the same view in his *Lectures* (I, 305), translated into English in 1818, but whether Shelley read these is uncertain.

21. See Mary Daly, *The Church and the Second Sex* (New York, 1968), pp. 4-56; Rosemary R. Ruether, "Misogynism and Virginal Feminism in the Fathers of the Church," in *Religion and Sexism*, ed. Rosemary R. Ruether (New York, 1974), pp. 157-158; Derrick Sherwin Bailey, *Sexual Relation in Christian Thought* (New York, 1959), p. 61.

22. Eleanor C. McLaughlin, "Equality of Souls, Inequality of Sexes: Woman in Medieval Theology," in *Religion and Sexism*, pp. 215-233; Joan M. Ferrante, *Woman as Image in Medieval Literature* (New York, 1975), p. 26.

23. Eileen Power, "The Position of Women," in *The Legacy of the Middle Ages*, ed. C. G. Crump and E. F. Jacob (Oxford, 1951), p. 402.

24. The church's preaching of a single sexual standard has also been cited as an advance over the sexual standards of the ancient world, even if it had little practical effect (McLaughlin, "Equality of Souls," p. 227).

25. Ferrante, *Woman as Image*, pp. 21-22; Valency, *In Praise of Love*, p. 20.

26. Lewis, *Allegory of Love*, p. 8; Moshe Lazar, *Armour Courtois* (Paris, 1964), p. 254; W. T. H. Jackson, *Literature of the Middle Ages* (New York, 1961); McLaughlin, "Equality of Souls," pp. 246-252.

27. Cf. *Refutation of Deism* (VI, 38n1); *Essay on Christianity* (VI, 251-252). After the days of his youthful radicalism, Shelley centered his opposition to Christianity on Paul, not Jesus (see *Autobiography of Leigh Hunt*, II, 36).

28. *Decline and Fall*, ch. 18.

29. *The History of England* (Oxford, 1826 [1759-62]), II, 125, which Shelley was reading in 1818, before and during the writing of the *Discourse*. Hume, "Of the Rise and Progress of the Arts and Sciences," which Shelley probably read, also deals briefly with the subject. Shelley read more on the subject in 1820 in William Robertson, *The History of the Reign of the Emperor Charles the Fifth* (1769). In 1819 both Mary and Claire read what Claire called "a history of chivalry" (Claire's *Journals*, Apr. 17-18; Mary's *Journal*, Apr. 15, May 1, 3). This was the *Bibliothèque universelle des dames: Romans*, vol. 11, Class 5 (Paris, 1787), summarizing chivalric romances centering on Charlemagne's court. If Shelley read the work, its effect would have been negligible, since it deals mainly with warfare, not love.

30. *Medievalism and the Ideologies of the Enlightenment* (Baltimore, 1968), p. 286. Sainte-Palaye admits "there was much licentiousness on many occasions," including adultery and concubinage (*Memoirs of Ancient Chivalry* [London, 1784], pp. 335-336).

31. *Memoirs*, pp. 75-76; cf. pp. 228-239. The troubadours "may be justly styled painters from life," insists Sainte-Palaye's English translator, Mrs. Dobson (*The Literary History of the Troubadours* [London, 1807 (1779)], p. xi).

32. In *A Philosophical View of Reform* Shelley observes, "The French were what their literature is (excluding Montaigne & Rousseau,) weak, superficial, vain, with little imagination, & with passions as well as judgements cleaving to the external forms of things" (*S&C*, VI, 979; quoted by permission of The Carl H. Pforzheimer Library). He could hardly have held such a view if he had been familiar with French erotic literature.

33. June 21, 1821 (Mary's *Journal*). This entry does not preclude an earlier reading.

34. *History of English Poetry*, pp. 75-76. Later Warton gives the troubadours credit for being the first to establish the vernacular as a vehicle for serious literature and for popularizing a taste for poetry in feudal courts (pp. 105-106).

35. *Edinburgh Review* 24 (June 1815). Shelley read Sismondi, *Histoire des républiques italiennes*, Jan. 20, 1819 (Mary's *Journal*), but no record exists of his having read *De la littérature*.

36. James Lawrence, with whom Shelley corresponded in 1813, was also knowledgeable about the medieval love-lyric (see e.g. his *The Etonian Out of Bounds* [London, 1828], II, 14).

37. *Prose of the Romantic Period*, ed. Carl R. Woodring (Boston, 1961), p. 575. Peacock refers to the "exaggerated love" of the troubadour lyric, a characterization that would not altogether have pleased Shelley.

38. Mary's *Journal*, p. 19; Claire's *Journals*, pp. 81-82.

39. *Coleridge's Miscellaneous Criticism*, ed. Thomas Middleton Raysor (London, 1936), pp. 20-21. In an earlier lecture he explains that the Goths "were elevated by that respectful and chivalrous feeling towards women perfected by the influence of Christianity" (pp. 8-9).

40. [George Ellis], *The Quarterly Review* 7 (Mar. 1812): 194.

41. *Poetical Works*, ed. E. H. Coleridge, II, 6-7. In his support Byron cited Sainte-Palaye—somewhat unorthodoxly, since most readers derived exactly the opposite conclusion from his work—and "Rolland," a reference to *Recherches sur les prérogatives des dames chez les Gaulois, sur les cours d'amours* (Paris, 1787) by [Barthélemy Gabriel] M. le Président Rolland [D'Erceville] de l'Académie d'Amiens. Its extensive notes make Rolland's treatise a mine of scholarship on these questions, but despite Byron, he supports the traditional view of chivalry, the troubadours, and the courts of love, taking their ideals seriously.

42. *In Praise of Love*, pp. 4-5.

43. "Clio and Venus: An Historical View of Medieval Love," in *The Meaning of Courtly Love*, pp. 19-20; see also Marc Bloch, *Feudal Society*, trans. L. A. Manyon (Chicago, 1964 [1961]), II, 309.

44. Power, "The Position of Women," p. 406; Valency, *In Praise of Love*, p. 5; cf. Herbert Moller, "The Meaning of Courtly Love," *Journal of American Folklore* 73 (Jan.-Mar. 1960); Frederick Goldin, "The Array of Per-

spectives in the Early Courtly Love Lyric," in *In Pursuit of Perfection: Courtly Love in Medieval Literature*, ed. Joan M. Ferrante and George D. Economou (Port Washington, N.Y., 1975), p. 58.

45. The trend today is to view the problem as spurious. It is dangerous to lump the many varieties of medieval Eros under the one heading "courtly love," a term invented long afterward by Gaston Paris in the mid-nineteenth century. The literary conventions of individual genres should also be kept separate from the social conventions of the courts where they arose. Some scholars are for abandoning the term altogether. Yet the ultimate effect of courtly literature was revolutionary, even if several centuries had to pass for its attitudes to be internalized and thus translated into practice.

8. In Defense of Women

1. Victorian critics calling attention to Shelley's feminism include G[eorge] H[enry] L[ewes], "Percy Bysshe Shelley," *Westminster Review* 35 (Jan.-Apr. 1841): 67-82; [Mathilde Blind], Review of *The Poetical Works of Percy Bysshe Shelley*, ed. W. M. Rossetti, *Westminster Review* 37, n.s. (July, Oct. 1870): 75-97; Charles Sotheran, *Percy Bysshe Shelley as Philosopher and Reformer* (New York, 1876); John Todhunter, *A Study of Shelley* (London, 1880); Todhunter, *Shelley and the Marriage Question* (London, 1889); Henry Salt, *Shelley's Principles* (London, 1892); Salt, *Percy Bysshe Shelley: Poet and Pioneer* (London, 1896).

2. Defoe, who in *An Essay upon Projects* (1697) has been called the first important writer to champion woman's cause, still considered her essentially man's subordinate, and he did little imaginatively to champion her cause. The novels of James Lawrence, Charles Brockden Brown, Mary Hays, and Mary Wollstonecraft were earlier attempts at literary consciousness-raising, but these today have only historic interest.

3. The Owenite journal *The New Moral World* in the 1830s drew on Shelley to expose the slavery of women, and later the militant suffragette leaders drew sustenance from Shelley's work.

4. *Principles of Social Reconstruction* (London, 1916), pp. 225-226; see also Gerald McNiece, *Shelley and the Revolutionary Idea* (Cambridge, 1969), pp. 180, 183, 198-200; Seraphia Leyda, "*The Serpent Is Shut Out from Paradise*"; Holmes, *Pursuit*; Cameron, *Golden Years*; John V. Murphy, *The Dark Angel: Gothic Elements in Shelley's Works* (Lewisburg, Pa., 1975).

5. Because his father inculcated a relationship of "passive obedience," exacting love as a "*duty*," Shelley "never loved" him, according to his letters to Godwin in 1812 (*L*, I, 227, 250). These sentiments, written after Shelley's break with the family, probably overstate the truth. According to his sisters, he was "exceedingly fond of his father" when young (Hogg, *Life of Shelley*, II, 459); but the relationship can hardly have been close.

6. Medwin, *Revised Life*, p. 104. Julian *Works* (VIII, lv) calls Shelley's mother a good letter-writer but "no reader of books."

7. G. Rattray Taylor, *Sex in History* (New York, 1954), pp. 98, 198-

201, notes Shelley's "mother-fixation." Cameron, *Young Shelley*, pp. 3-5, finds Mrs. Shelley's influence considerable but the effects ambiguous.

8. *Young Shelley*, p. 5.

9. Virtually everyone who knew Shelley spoke of his traditionally feminine characteristics: his "flushed, feminine, artless face" "blush[ed] like a girl[s]" (Trelawny); his "port had the meekness of a maiden" (Hogg); his "most feminine and gentle voice" (Benjamin Haydon); his "feeble frame and girlish voice" (John Taafe); his countenance, "when joyful, was singularly bright and animated, like that of a gay young girl" (Thornton Hunt); he was "as incapable of cruelty as the softest woman" (Mary Shelley). Supposedly in Italy Shelley was once taken for a woman in man's clothing (William Michael Rossetti, *Memoir of Percy Bysshe Shelley* [London, 1886], p. 122). Amelia Curran's portrait of the poet, taken in his last years, also shows a very womanish figure.

10. Eleanor E. Maccoby and Carol Nagy Jacklin, *The Psychology of Sex Differences* (Stanford, 1974), p. 365. This failure to differentiate normally may in some cases be due to "an as yet undiscovered fetal or hormonal component which acts to induce a predisposition to ambiguity or incongruity of postnatal gender identity differentiation," but in others "it is relatively easy to implicate familial interaction" (Money and Ehrhardt, *Man & Woman, Boy & Girl*, p. 21).

11. *Life of Shelley*, I, 15; Dowden, *Life of Shelley*, I, 16; cf. Sir John Rennie, *Autobiography* (London, 1875), pp. 1-2.

12. Kendall, *Descriptive Catalogue*, p. 95.

13. Claire to Jane Hogg Williams, c.1832-1833, in Mrs. Julian Marshall, *The Life and Letters of Mary Wollstonecraft Shelley* (London, 1889), II, 248.

14. *The Early Victorian Woman* (London, 1953), p. 20.

15. *L*, I, 202, 413; cf. I, 414.

16. *Child of Light* (Hadleigh, Essex, 1951), p. 3. Mary's indifference to domestic accomplishments continued throughout her marriage with Shelley. Trelawny recalls that Mary "had none of the habits of a housewife, and dinner etc. had very much to take care of themselves" (*Rossetti Papers*, p. 398).

17. Medwin remembers that Shelley often used to read what Mary had written during the day "in whose progress he took great delight and interest, now and then altering in pencil a word" (*Revised Life*, p. 374).

18. *L*, II, 324. In a note to *The Cenci* Mary observes that Shelley "was always most earnest and energetic in his exhortations that I should cultivate any talent I possessed, to the utmost."

19. Medwin describes Claire in 1821 as possessing eyes "that flashed with the fire of intelligence" and as having "considerable talents," speaking "French and Italian, particularly the latter, with all its nuances and niceties" (*The Angler in Wales* [London, 1834], II, 987). She also became proficient in German. But Claire's mind, while quick, lacked Mary's intellectual depth and perseverance.

20. Mary, despite her early aggressiveness, was basically reserved, retiring, and conservative, longing for domestic security and social pleasures.

Although after Shelley's death she occupied a position of potential leadership in the dawning woman's movement, she found the pressures of being her mother's daughter increasingly burdensome and in the end dissociated herself from the cause of militant feminism. She was temperamentally unsuited to feminist autonomy, needing the strength of a man to lean on (Mary's *Journal*, pp. 204-209; Mary Shelley, *Letters*, I, 366).

21. Claire to Byron, Jan. 12, 1818, in *"To Lord Byron,"* ed. George Paston and Peter Quennell (London, 1939), p. 233.

22. Claire's *Journals*, pp. 40, 406, 408. Mary's *Journal* (Oct. 7, 1814) records that Claire and Shelley stayed up late, talking of "oppression and reform . . . Jane states her conception of the subterranean community of women"—an apparent reference to woman's traditional patriarchal subjection.

23. *L&J*(P), III, 434, letter 5.

24. Shelley wrote that Jane Williams was "extremely pretty & gentle" but was "not *very* clever" and lacked "literary refinement" (*L*, II, 256-257, 376, 435); see also Mary Shelley, *Letters*, I, 130).

25. *L*, II, 120, 180, 186.

26. *L*, II, 105, 92; see also I, 384.

27. Shelley wrote to Godwin in 1812 that Elizabeth, though of very humble birth, had early in life developed "a very deep & refined habit of thinking" which enabled her to overleap "the bounds of prejudice." Although when he first met her, she had not read *Political Justice*, her life appeared in great part "modelled upon its precepts" (*L*, I, 311-312).

28. *L*, I, 196, 218, 240, 245.

29. *Revised Life*, pp. 117-118; *Life of Shelley*, II, 365. Harriet's first impression was in essential agreement (*L*, I, 320n).

30. Medwin, *Revised Life*, pp. 117-118.

31. *Vindication*, pp. 154, 61, 210, 157, 190, 45. Godwin later noted that "the spirited and decisive way in which the author [Wollstonecraft] explodes the system of gallantry, and the species of homage with which the sex is usually treated, shocked the majority" of the reading public, who "were in arms against the author of so heretical a doctrine" (*Memoirs*, pp. 54-55).

32. Typically the arch-libertine Lovelace of Richardson's novel uses the rhetoric of gallantry toward Clarissa—"my goddess," "my empress"—even as he plots her ruin.

33. See e.g. Byron to Douglas Kinnaird, Oct. 26, 1818 [1819], *L&J*(M), VI, 232.

34. *L&J*(M), I, 52.

35. See *Don Juan* (I.cxvi). Byron was especially sarcastic about Shelley's idol, Petrarch (*L&J*[M], III, 240).

36. *L&J*(M), I, 165; II, 21; III, 228; see also Katharine M. Rogers, *The Troublesome Helpmate: A History of Misogyny in Literature* (Seattle, 1966), pp. 204-206; Bruce Wallis, *Byron: The Critical Voice* (Salzburg, 1973), I, 83-84; II, 448-451. Byron devoted a verse satire to mocking "blue-bottles" (*The Blues* [1821]).

37. *L&J*(M), V, 126; Mayne, *Lady Byron*, p. 165; *L&J*(M), I, 161. After

Byron's break with his wife, he savaged her as the pedantically "learned" Donna Inez and then as the "blue" Miss Millpond in *Don Juan* (I.x-liii; XV.xli).

38. *L&J*(M), II, 132. Anna Seward is the object of this sneer. Byron is free with "bitches" in his letters when referring to women he does not like.

39. *L&J*(M), II, 170, 95; cf. III, 204-205. This is the antithesis of Shelley's ideal of "interesting converse."

40. *Conversations of Lord Byron*, ed. Ernest J. Lovell, Jr. (Princeton, 1966), p. 73.

41. *Don Juan* (I.xxi).

42. *L&J*(M), VIII, 15.

43. Byron to John Murray, Jan. 2, 1817 (*L&J*[M]).

44. See e.g. *L&J*(M), III, 246; II, 208; III, 109.

45. *Don Juan* (II.cxix-cci; XIV.xxiii-xxv).

46. Malcolm Elwin, *Lord Byron's Wife* (London, 1962), p. 283.

47. John Stuart Mill, *The Subjection of Women* (Cambridge, 1970 [1869]), pp. 76, 42-43.

48. *Life of Shelley*, I, 303.

49. Bod. MS Shelley e. 4; see also Locock, *Shelley MSS Bod.*, p. 73.

50. *Sexual Politics* (Garden City, 1970), p. 73; cf. Germaine Greer, *The Female Eunuch* (New York, 1971), p. 23.

51. *The Dialectic of Sex: The Case for Feminist Revolution* (New York, 1970), pp. 23, 166.

52. *L*, I, 83; see also Cameron, *Golden Years*, pp. 27, 180, 353.

53. *L*, I, 30; cf. Hogg to Elizabeth Shelley, May 25, and to Mrs. Shelley, Aug. 22, 1811 (*New Shelley Letters*, pp. 42-44, 47-50).

54. *L*, I, 180-181. Hogg was still playing the gallant years later with Mary and then Jane Williams (*New Shelley Letters*, p. 147).

55. *Life of Shelley*, I, xxiii.

56. This practice receives the support of modern psychology. "In some extremely important ways, people are what you expect them to be, or at least they behave as you would expect them to behave," notes the feminist psychologist Naomi Weisstein, which reveals the "influence of social expectation," and thus "one must understand social expectations about women if one is going to characterize the behavior of women" (" 'Kinder, Kuche, Kirche' as Scientific Law: Psychology Constructs the Female," in *Sisterhood Is Powerful*, ed. Robin Morgan [New York, 1970], pp. 215-220).

57. *Life of Shelley*, II, 324.

58. Kendall, *Descriptive Catalogue*, pp. 94-95.

59. *Dialectic of Sex*, p. 256.

60. White, *Unextinguished Hearth*, pp. 237-238.

61. Todhunter, *A Study of Shelley*, p. 55.

62. *Westminster Review* 38, n.s. (July, Oct. 1870): 88-89.

63. Shelley to Hogg, Apr. 28, 1811?, speaks of the despotism of "the Asiatic tyrant who renders his territory wretched to fill his seraglio" (*L*, I, 71). He was still dealing with the harem motif in *Hellas* (1821).

64. Pref. to *Rev. Is.* notes that one consequence of the despotic social system portrayed in the poem is "an utter extinction of domestic affections."

65. "*The Cause*" (London, 1928), pp. 16-17.

66. "Institutionalized Oppression vs. the Female," in *Sisterhood Is Powerful*, pp. 438-440.

67. *Sexual Politics*, p. 63.

68. In a copy of *Rev. Is.* presented by Shelley to Leigh Hunt's sister-in-law, Elizabeth Kent, passages on the equality of women are scored by Shelley in the margins (Peck, *Shelley*, II, 22n.72).

69. These three French Encyclopedists are cited in the notes to *QM*, though their feminism is not mentioned. See also H. C. Barnard, *Education and the French Revolution* (Cambridge, 1969), pp. 93-95; Jacob Bouton, *Mary Wollstonecraft and the Beginnings of Female Emancipation in France and England* (Philadelphia, 1975 [1922]), pp. 150-153; H. N. Brailsford, *Shelley, Godwin and Their Circle* (New York, n.d.), pp. 196-199. D'Holbach, *Système social* (1774), contains an assault on gallantry as masking woman's fundamental subjection to man. Although Shelley is not known to have read the *Système*, its views may have reached him through Mary Wollstonecraft, *A Vindication*, which possibly reflects a familiarity with the work. Godwin, *Political Justice*, is explicitly feminist only in its denunciation of marriage with its patriarchal reduction of woman to chattel status, but Shelley's growing knowledge of Godwin's practice—his egalitarian relationship with Wollstonecraft and his enlightened upbringing of his daughters—doubtless exerted an effect. Lawrence, *Empire of the Nairs*, an avowedly feminist work, doubtless supplied ammunition for Shelley's feminism in *Rev. Is.*, particularly for the harem symbolism, which is a principal motif in the *Nairs*.

70. Mary "heated his imagination by talking of her mother, and going to her grave with him every day" (Harriet to Catherine Nugent, Nov. 20, 1814, in Alfred Webb, "Harriet Shelley and Catherine Nugent, II," *The Nation* 48 [June 13, 1889]: 485). Hogg, Peacock, and Trelawny give a similar impression.

71. Harriet to Catherine Nugent, c. Oct. 1812, in Webb, "Harriet and Catherine Nugent, I," pp. 466-467.

72. Returning to the scene in 1824 after Shelley's death, Mary writes: "Such, my loved Shelley, now ten years ago, at this season, did we first meet, and there were the very scenes—that churchyard, with its sacred tomb, was the spot where first love shone in your dear eyes" (Mary's *Journal*, p. 194).

73. Much of the abuse was inspired, not by the work that had made Wollstonecraft famous, the *Vindication*, but the later *Posthumous Works* and Godwin's *Memoirs*, which reveal her heterodox sexual beliefs and practice. As noted by Ralph Wardle, "in short order she became a symbol of the hated Jacobinism," and her memory was mercilessly vilified by the Tory press. By the time of Shelley, however, her name was largely forgotten (*Mary Wollstonecraft* [Lawrence, Kan., 1951], pp. 317, 331).

74. While Shelley favored emancipating women from domestic slavery and liberating their intellects to the same degree as men's, he recognized a

"diversity . . . of powers" distinguishing the two sexes (*Defence of Poetry* [VII, 129]) and believed woman's maternal role was biologically programmed. In defending Claire Clairmont's desire not to yield total control of her infant daughter Allegra to its father Byron, Shelley expatiates on the inborn power of woman's maternal instinct: "the strongest affections & even the most unappeasable instincts of our nature" (*S&C*, VI, 564-565; quoted by permission of The Carl H. Pforzheimer Library). Claire would be condemned as "an unnatural mother even by those who might see little to condemn in her becoming a mother without the formalities of marriage" if she should give up all claims to her daughter.

75. By "intellectual beauty" Shelley means "specifically the beauty of the mind and its creations" (Cameron, *Golden Years*, p. 238).

76. Prometheus is "the type of the highest perfection of moral and intellectual nature" (Pref. to *Pr. Unb.*). Shelley himself possessed this beauty to an exceptional degree: his "countenance painfully intellectual" (Joseph Severn); this "intellectual-looking creature" (Benjamin Haydon); "his countenance, whether grave or animated, strikingly intellectual" (Medwin); "Bysshe looked, as he always looked . . . intellectual" (Hogg); "His face was singularly engaging, with strongly marked intellectuality" (Sophia Stacey). Teresa Guiccioli remembered that Shelley's features, though not regularly beautiful like Byron's, gave the "impression" of beauty: "It was the fire, the enthusiasm, of his Intelligence that transformed his features" (*La Vie de Lord Byron en Italie*, in Doris Langley Moore, *Lord Byron: Accounts Rendered* [New York, 1974], p. 335).

77. Suggested sources include Spenser, Platonic "Hymns" (Shelley substituting "Intellectual" for Spenser's "Heavenly Beautie"); Plotinus, *Enneads* (though there is no evidence that Shelley read this); Monboddo, *Of the Origin and Progress of Language* (Monboddo [I, 95-97] uses the expression in connection with Diotima's speech in the *Symp.* describing the ladder of love); and Robert Forsyth, *Principles of Moral Science* (I, 513-515).

78. *Vindication*, p. 86.

79. *Vindication*, pp. 116-117, 149; cf. pp. 181, 255-257.

80. *Life and Letters of Robert Southey*, ed. C. C. Southey (London, 1850), I, 305.

81. *History of Agathon*, II, 4; see also II, 78; IV, 48-49.

82. Wieland associates these ideas with Plato only in the popular, nontechnical sense conveyed by the "Platonic maxim, that external beauty is the reflection of the intellectual beauty of the soul" (IV, 48-49; see also II, 196). The implication is more feminist than Platonic, especially considering the medium of such beauty, female rather than male. Wieland, *History of Peregrinus Proteus*, likewise read by Shelley, again employs the vocabulary of "intellectual beauty," here tied to the concept of sympathetic love (I, 177; II, 351-352).

83. *Vindication*, p. 223; see also p. 256.

84. Shelley would also have encountered the expression "intellectual beauty" in an essentially feminist context in the works of Amelia Opie and his

friend Peacock. In Opie, *Adeline Mowbray*, read by the poet as early as the summer of 1811, the expression is used as an equivalent of mental capability (p. 129) and almost certainly derives from the *Vindication*, of whose doctrines the novel forms a critique, or possibly even from the author herself, with whom Opie was at one time closely acquainted. "Intellectual beauty" is also associated with Wollstonecraft's doctrines in Peacock, *Melincourt* (London, 1896[1817]), pp. 117-119, the phrase obviously deriving from the *Vindication*. The novel's exponent of intellectual beauty in women, Mr. Forester, is modeled on Shelley.

85. Shelley to Charles Ollier [Mar. 1821] (*L*, II, 273). Shelley's values have changed radically since 1812 and his *Letter to Lord Ellenborough*, where Newtonian reason possesses "the eagle-eye of truth" that "darts through the undazzling sunbeam of the immutable and just, gathering thence wherewith to vivify and illuminate a universe" (V, 284). See also his "Devil's Walk" (137); "I will beget a Son" note to *QM* (I, 156); *Association of Philanthropists* (V, 264).

86. [Sept. 4, 1796], in *Godwin & Mary: Letters of William Godwin and Mary Wollstonecraft*, ed. Ralph M. Wardle (Lawrence, Kan., 1966), p. 28; see also *S&C*, I, 55.

87. *Memoirs of Mary Wollstonecraft*, ed. Durant, pp. 124-126. In "My First Acquaintance with Poets" Hazlitt quotes Coleridge's remark that the mental superiority of Wollstonecraft over Godwin was an "instance of the ascendancy which people of imagination exercised over those of mere intellect."

88. *Memoirs*, ed. Murry, pp. 130-131. Neither Shelley's letters nor the list of his reading in Mary's *Journal* contains any mention of the *Memoirs*, but it was read by Mary, June 3, 1820 (*Journal*, p. 134), and by Claire, Sept. 3, 1814 (*Journals*, p. 35), while journeying down the Rhine with Mary and Shelley. As just two days previously Shelley had been reading aloud from his mother-in-law's *Letters from Norway*, the trio must have been making a concerted effort to learn the details of the feminist's life. See James Rieger, *The Mutiny Within* (New York, 1967), p. 47; McNiece, *Shelley and the Revolutionary Idea*, p. 183; Burton R. Pollin, "Godwin's *Memoirs* as a Source of Shelley's Phrase 'Intellectual Beauty,'" *KSJ* 13 (1974): 17-18.

89. *Vindication*, pp. 170, 175-176.

90. Pref. to *Symp.* (VII, 162).

91. Pref. to *Pr.Unb.*

92. Ded. to *Rev.Is.*iii-iv. Cf. F. D. Maurice: "All little children are Platonists and it is their education that makes men Aristotleians" (*The Life of Frederick Denison Maurice* [London, 1884 (1836)], I, 206-207).

9. The Eye of Sane Philosophy

1. Technically women as a class were not disenfranchised until the Great Reform Bill of 1832, but by the end of the eighteenth century few, if any, voted.

2. "The gradual paths of an aspiring change" (*QM*.IX.148); cf. Shelley

to Leigh Hunt, Nov. [16], 1819 (*S&C*, VI, 1080).

3. Cf. *A Proposal for Putting Reform to the Vote* (VI, 68).

4. MS notebook, quoted by permission of the Pierpont Morgan Library. See also *S&C*, VI, 956, 961.

5. Harold Boner, *Hungry Generations: The Nineteenth-Century Case Against Malthusianism* (New York, 1955), pp. 99-100; cf. Cameron, *Golden Years*, pp. 357-358.

6. "Lines Written During the Castlereagh Administration," 11. 3-4.

7. See Norman E. Himes, *Medical History of Contraception* (Baltimore, 1936); Peter Fryer, *The Birth Controllers* (New York, 1966); John Noonan, *Contraception* (Cambridge, 1966); St. John-Stevas, *Life, Death and the Law* (Bloomington, 1961). Himes considers Francis Place, Richard Carlile, Robert Dale Owen, and Dr. Charles Knowlton the most important English writers on contraceptive technique in the period 1823-1850. Shelley knew Place, who was a friend of Godwin. Place disliked Shelley, but Owen admired him, even soliciting subscriptions for the publication of *QM* on the same page of the *Free Enquirer* (Oct. 23, 1830) containing the prospectus of his forthcoming book on *Moral Physiology* which described contraceptive techniques. Owen had originally been a Godwinian but was converted to neo-Malthusianism by reading Carlile—once defended by Shelley, but not for his contraceptive views.

8. *Vindication*, Ded. and pp. 208-210. Wollstonecraft also condemns abortion (p. 209). The only important nineteenth-century writer to connect feminism with birth control was John Stuart Mill, and even he did not advocate its practice openly, except once in his youth—an act that was to haunt him at his death, preventing his burial in Westminster Abbey.

9. William L. O'Neill, *The Woman Movement* (London, 1969), p. 41.

10. Brown notes that "there were many infanticides, the newspapers continually printing notices of serving-maids in particular destroying their infants" (*Fathers of the Victorians*, p. 21). Wollstonecraft points to the evil in *Vindication* (p. 209). William Langer estimates that as late as 1878 about 6% of all violent deaths in England were infanticides ("Checks on Population Growth: 1750-1850," *Scientific American* 226 [Feb. 1972]: 96).

11. *Revised Life*, pp. 238-239.

12. R. H. Nichols and F. A. Wray, *The History of the Foundling Hospital* (London, 1935). Infanticide and child abandonment continued as major problems throughout the nineteenth century. See Bracebridge Hemyng in Henry Mayhew, *London Labour and The London Poor* (New York, 1968 [1861-1862]), vol. IV; William Acton, *Prostitution*, 2nd ed., ed. Peter Fryer (New York, 1969 [1870]), p. 25. Statistical records demonstrate that illegitimate births were dramatically on the rise all over Europe during the century, primarily among the lower classes, dislocated by the rise of industrialization and growing urbanization. See Edward Shorter, "Illegitimacy, Sexual Revolution, and Social Change in Modern Europe," *The Journal of Interdisciplinary History* 2 (Autumn 1971): 273-277.

13. *L*, II, 319. Shelley's "Neapolitan infant," Elena Adelaide Shelley, whose origin remains a mystery, may represent his attempt to save an unwanted child from the Foundling Hospital in Naples. He registered the child as his own, but it died in infancy. Cf. Cameron, *Golden Years*, pp. 66-73.

14. O'Neill, *The Woman Movement*, p. 29.

15. Wright and Mary Shelley later became good friends, though Mary never completely succumbed to her friend's social radicalism (Mary Shelley, *Letters*, I, 366; Robert Dale Owen, "Frances Wright, General Lafayette, and Mary Wollstonecraft Shelley," *The Atlantic Monthly* 32 [Oct. 1873]: 448-459).

16. In *St. Irvyne* Fitzeustace loves Eloise even though she is pregnant by the libertine seducer Nempere, and when the child is born, he "cherishe[s] it with the affection of a father" (V, 194-195). In *Rev.Is.* Laon has a similar reaction to Cythna's child by the libertine Tyrant Othman (V.xxxiv; XII.vi; XII.xxiv).

17. "Prostitution: A Quartet for Female Voices," in *Woman in Sexist Society*, ed. Vivian Gornick and Barbara K. Moran (New York, 1971), p. 65.

18. *Vindication*, p. 186. The elimination of prostitution is one of the work's major concerns.

19. "London" (13-14); *The Prelude* (VII.385-387); *Don Juan* (XI.xxx.4-5).

20. *The Anti-Jacobin Review*, Jan. 1816; *Christian Guardian*, Feb. 1809, p. 65.

21. G. M. Trevelyan, *English Social History* (London, 1943), pp. 490-491.

22. Jan. 5, 1812. The correspondent based his figures on Patrick Colquhoun, *Treatise on the Police of the Metropolis* (1796), the principal source for such estimates during these years (Cameron, *Young Shelley*, p. 126). Colquhoun also lists 2000 "Houses of ill Fame, Brothels, Lodging Houses for Prostitutes" (4th ed. [London, 1797], p. x).

23. Peter Fryer, Intro. to Acton, *Prostitution*; E. M. Sigsworth and T. J. Wyke, "A Study of Victorian Prostitution and Venereal Disease," in *Suffer and Be Still*, pp. 77-79. Claire Clairmont wrote in her *Journals*, Apr. 7, 1820, "Paris is called an immoral city because it contains but 8,000 prostitutes— London a very moral one because it possesses one hundred thousand of these poor wretches" (p. 139). She subsequently tried to cross out the entry.

24. Leigh Hunt, *Lord Byron and Some of His Contemporaries* (Philadelphia, 1828), p. 187.

25. "Underneath the Victorians," *Victorian Studies* 10 (1966-1967): 257-258.

26. Himes, *Medical History of Contraception*, p. 213.

27. *L*, I, 323; Julian *Works* (I, 142). Shelley says that even before reading the *Nairs*, he "retained no doubts of the evils of marriage,—Mrs. Wollstonecraft reasons too well for that," but that he had not previously grasped the notion of marriage as "legal" prostitution. Yet Wollstonecraft makes the point at least twice in the *Vindication* (pp. 104, 222). The notion was a cliche in ad-

vanced circles by the eighteenth century and was to become a rallying cry for feminists in the nineteenth. It was also adopted by socialist polemics and featured in Engels, *Origin of the Family*. Today it is a standard weapon in the radical feminist arsenal, except the wife is now seen as morally more corrupt than the prostitute, who simply eliminates the "games" and "bullshit" and sells the commodity openly (Ellen Strong, "The Hooker," in *Sisterhood Is Powerful*, pp. 290-291).

28. Bracebridge Hemyng wrote later in the century that "the legislature, by refusing to interfere, have tacitly declared the existence of prostitutes to be a necessary evil, the suppression of which would produce alarming and disastrous effects upon the country at large" (*London Labour and The London Poor*, IV, 212; cf. Lecky, *History of European Morals*, II, 283).

29. July 1819, p. 198; *L*, I, 242.

30. *History of European Morals*, II, 283-285.

31. II, 15. In Wollstonecraft, *The Wrongs of Woman*, the prostitute Jemima complains that "even to be employed at hard labour is out of the reach of many whose reputation misfortune or folly has tainted" (*Posthumous Works* [London, 1798], I, 112, cf. II, 16).

32. "It cannot be denied by anyone acquainted with rural life, that seduction of girls is a sport and a habit with vast numbers of men married . . . and single, placed above the ranks of labour" (Acton, *Prostitution*, p. 199).

33. While seduction as a principal cause of prostitution was a commonplace throughout the century, the assertion was disputed by some, including Acton, who blamed the problem on poverty (*Prostitution*, pp. 127-129).

34. See e.g. Michael Ryan, *Prostitution in London* (London, 1839), p. vi. Others, such as Wollstonecraft, favored making the seducer legally responsible for maintenance of the victim and her children (*Vindication*, pp. 118-119). Acton, *Prostitution*, pp. 203-207, thought this would substantially reduce the incidence of seduction.

35. While the value of the other broadsides is admitted, the "Ballad," with the exception of Julian *Works*, is rejected as uncanonical on the specious ground of being unworthy of Shelley. A first draft appears in one of Shelley's Italian notebooks (Bod. MS Shelley adds. e. 6) on the verso of pages containing drafts of the *Discourse* and the Pref. to the *Symp.* (Rogers, *Shelley at Work*, pp. 7-8). It may have been inspired by his discussion of prostitution in the *Discourse*. See William J. McTaggart, *England in 1819: Church, State and Poverty* (London, 1970); Edmund Blunden, *Votive Tablets* (London, 1939), p. 236; Rogers, *Shelley at Work*, p. 318; Holmes, *The Pursuit*, pp. 562-564.

36. In the original draft the parson calls his victim an "idle trull" and other unpleasantnesses, finally ordering her on her way before he sets the dog on her (McTaggart, *England in 1819*, p. 34). The revision is far more effective. The first draft also includes stanzas ironically connecting the parson with the Rev. Thomas Malthus and his doctrine of moral restraint: it is permissible for the rich to increase and multiply but is forbidden for the poor on penalty of starvation (p. 34).

37. Song III, "Cold, cold, is the blast" (July 1810). This was one of several poems attributed to Elizabeth Shelley for Hogg's benefit (*Life*, I, 126). But Shelley's authorship is now generally accepted on the basis of internal evidence (Cameron, *Esdaile*, pp. 258-259). *The Esdaile Notebook* (pp. 129-130) contains an earlier version dated 1808, a date that quite probably makes it the earliest poem in the notebook, which contains several other poems playing variations on the same theme, as does the "Victor and Cazire" volume. See also "The Wandering Jew," Canto II. According to Leigh Hunt, *Lord Byron and Some of His Contemporaries*, p. 162, Shelley personally came to the defense of a victim of seduction during this same period.

38. Cythna's career and fate repeats Kathema's. Both poems are social allegories attacking the inequities of the sexual code as it affects women. Prostitution, whether legal or illegal, is shown to be the fundamental condition of all women. See esp. "Zeinab and Kathema," ll. 165-166; *Rev.Is.*, Canto IV. Among the women released from patriarchal bondage by Cythna's temporary overthrow of the Tyrant are prostitutes (xxii). Later, when the earth is returned to the misrule of the Tyrant, women are again forced into prostitution (X.xix).

39. It was usually a sterile practice, "defeat[ing] or violat[ing] nature, or the purposes for which the sexual instincts are supposed to have existed" (*Discourse* [223]). The object was to avoid conception, prostitutes and their clients being the chief users of the crude contraceptive devices of the period, and if conception did result, abortion or infanticide was often the fatal consequence. For this reason prostitution is ridiculed in the Malthusian satire *Swellfoot the Tyrant*, where along with "moral restraint," "Starvation, typhus-fever, war, [and] prison" it curbs population (I.i.72-78). In *TofL* the landscape framing the dance of libertine sex is appropriately a desert. The dance itself derives from the witches' Sabbath in Goethe's *Faust* which is described in terms of commercialized sex. Winter or desert landscapes are characteristic of all non-procreative sex in Shelley's poetry, and in his visions of the regenerate world love is always literally generative.

40. V, 189-194. Shelley continues to use this imagery through his last poem, *TofL* (1. 175), where of the old trying to make love he writes, "And frost in these performs what fire in those [maidens and youths]."

41. Acton, *Prostitution*, pp. 71-75. See also George Bernard Shaw, *Mrs. Warren's Profession*.

42. *The Anti-Society* (Boston, 1970), pp. 354-355.

43. Not one man in ten between the ages of twenty and thirty, according to Ryan, *Prostitution in London*, escaped infection, at least in large cities (p. 405).

44. *The Worm in the Bud* (New York, 1969), p. 226. Mercury was the most common form of therapy for syphilis, and silver nitrate for gonorrhea, but until the twentieth century there was no real cure for the infections. Condoms, such as they were, more often served to prevent infection than conception.

45. VI, 178; I, 142; cf. I, 159.

46. QM.III.50-52, cf. IV.250-252; *Essay on Christianity* (VI, 249-250).

47. "Ode to Liberty" (222-223); possibly such a social canker is also suggested by the symbolism of *SP*, pt. 3. Only once does the phrase "venereal infection" appear in Shelley, in connection with writers of the Restoration period who "infected" literature with their obscenity (*Discourse* [223]). A jotting in the notebook containing the *Discourse* reads "Loathsome diseases the cause of modern obscenity exceeding the worst of antiquity in hideousness and horrors" (Bod. MS Shelley adds. e. 2, p. 73 rev., in Holmes, *The Pursuit*, p. 434).

48. *Rossetti Papers*, p. 502.

49. "Shelley—by One Who Knew Him," *Atlantic Monthly*, Feb. 1863, in *Shelley and Keats: As They Struck Their Contemporaries*, ed. Edmund Blunden (London, 1925), pp. 30-31.

50. "Shelley—by One Who Knew Him," p. 50.

51. *Young Shelley*, p. 126; see also Cameron, *Golden Years*, pp. 56-57; White, *Shelley*, I, 107; Peck, *Shelley*, I, 107.

52. *Esdaile*, pp. 41-42.

53. *Discourse* (Notopoulos, p. 536); cf. *On Love*'s "lips of motionless ice" (VI,201). For the psychological explanation, see not only "Passion" but also "The Retrospect. Cwm Elan 1812," ll. 39-42 (*Esdaile*, p. 156), which *Epi.* (259-263) seems to echo directly.

54. VII, 46-47. See also Lawrence, *The Etonian Out of Bounds*, I, i.

55. *Posthumous Works*, I, 56-57. Wollstonecraft who had herself stayed in 1786 at the home of an Eton teacher and housemaster, the Rev. John Prior, found the atmosphere of the school detestable. Godwin writes that this confirmed his wife's preference for day schools, which did not interfere, in her words, with "domestic affections, the foundation of virtue" (*Memoirs*, ed. Murry, p. 39; cf. *Vindication*, pp. 237-239, 246).

56. *Eton Microcosm*, pp. 16-17.

57. See also *Una Favola*'s age fifteen.

58. *Woman Movement*, pp. 37-39; see also Marian Ramelson, *The Petticoat Rebellion* (London, 1967), chs. 10-11; Strachey, *"The Cause,"* pp. 194-217; Josephine Kamm, *Rapiers and Battleaxes* (London, 1966), pp. 116-126.

10. The Detestable Distinctions of Sex

1. Peacock, *Memoirs of Shelley*, II, 365; see also Shelley to Ollier, Dec. 11, 13 and to Thomas Moore, Dec. 16, 1817 (*L*, I, 578-582; *S&C*, V, 347-350); Keats to George and Thomas Keats, Dec. 21, 1817 (*The Letters of John Keats*, ed. Maurice Buxton Forman, 2nd ed. rev. [Oxford, 1935], p. 72); *Poetical Works*, pp. 886-888. Frederick L. Jones, "The Revision of *Laon and Cythna*," *JEGP* 33 (July 1933): 368-371 (also in *L*, I, 581n5), challenges Peacock's account of Shelley's resistance to the poem's alterations, arguing that as soon as Shelley's friends had convinced him that the original text would destroy his

chances with the public, he "assented at once, even cheerfully." Ben W. Griffith, Jr., "The Removal of Incest from *Laon and Cythna*," *MLN* 70 (Mar. 1955): 181-182, concludes from a marginal comment at Canto V, xxix, of the Bod. MS of *L&C* that during the poem's composition Shelley himself considered changing Cythna into Laon's cousin and thus would have had no objection when subsequently asked by Ollier to alter the lovers' relationship. However, another notation on a page directly preceding the draft Dedication to the poem, which suggests that Shelley was much concerned with justifying incestuous relationship in the text and which could have been as late as 1817 after the main text was completed, reads: "Solomons Song Cap. 4—v. 9 particularly 4. v. 12 or Cap. 5 v. 2" (Bod. MS Shelley adds. ed. 14; in Claude C. Brew, *Shelley and Mary in 1817: The "Dedication" of The Revolt of Islam* [London, 1971], p. 25). As Wasserman, *Critical Reading*, observes, these variants of the "my sister, my spouse" or "my sister, my love" theme indicate that Shelley was trying to "validat[e] his use of the sister-spouse relationship" in his poem "by noting its spiritual significance in the Song of Songs." Leigh Hunt's articles on the poem in the *Examiner*, Sept. 26, Oct. 3, 10, 1819, further imply that Shelley's friends forced the changes. Finally, erasure of the lovers' blood relationship undermines the poem's most important symbolic effects, indicating conclusively that Shelley had no choice but to protest.

2. See e.g. Alfred Owen Aldridge, "The Meaning of Incest from Hutcheson to Gibbon," *Ethics* 61 (1950-1951): 309-310; Peter L. Thorslev, "Incest as Romantic Symbol," *Comparative Literature Studies* 2 (1965): 41-58; James D. Wilson, "Incest and American Fiction," *Studies in the Literary Imagination* 7, no. 1 (Spring 1974): 31-50.

3. *Note Books*, II, 96-97.

4. The one exception is *Pr.Unb.*I.346-349, where the incest of Oedipus with his mother is called "unnatural love" and the conflict between his sons "more unnatural hate" (349). In a marginal note opposite this line in the original draft Shelley wrote: "The contrast would have been completer if the sentiment had been transposed: but wherefore sacrifize the philosophical truth, that love however monstrous in its expression is still less worthy of horror than hatred" (Locock, *Shelley MSS Bod.*, p. 34).

5. *L*, I, 506. Despite Shelley, the calumny was probably justified. And to a greater degree even than Shelley, Byron evinces a preoccupation with incest in his own work.

6. *L&J*(M), VI, 76; see also VI, 82, 126; VII, 102.

7. See e.g. Thomas Verner Moore, "Percy Bysshe Shelley: An Introduction to the Study of Character," *Psychological Monographs* 31 (1922): 24-29, 61; Wormhoudt, *The Demon Lover*, pp. 88-111; John V. Hagopian, "A Psychological Approach to Shelley's Poetry," *The American Imago* 12 (Spring 1965): 28.

8. *Diary of Benjamin Robert Haydon*, II, 372-373.

9. Literal incest is not normally the result when brother and sister grow up side by side. On the contrary, they generally evince a marked aversion to

sexual relations or marriage. The reason, according to modern research, is that "the intimacy of close proximity, including sexual play in infancy," leaves an imprint that precludes "subsequent establishment in adolescence of a new, falling-in-love imprint" (Money and Ehrhardt, *Man & Woman, Boy & Girl*, p. 190). Shelley, however, is primarily concerned with incest as a metaphor and not with the literal coupling of siblings.

10. II, 120, 197-198; IV, 183-184.

11. Bod. MS e. 19, p. 67 (Wasserman, *Critical Reading*, p. 24).

12. II.xvii-xxxii; see also IV.xxx.

13. Ll. 11-19; cf. Peacock's *Rhododaphne*, Canto VI. Both poets stress the importance of shared childhood experience for the development of true sympathetic identification in adulthood.

14. Medwin, *Revised Life*, p. 48.

15. Recalling his first acquaintance with the Shelley family, Hogg observes: "they were evidently consanguineous; it was all, my uncle, and my aunt; my cousin this, my cousin that, and my cousin the other; my nephew and my niece . . . Bysshe fell in love at an early age,—violently, desperately in love, with a fair cousin" (*Life of Shelley*, II, 117).

16. *The Theory of Moral Sentiments*, pp. 321-322.

17. *Zastrozzi* and *St. Irvyne* (V, 59, 190-191, 194-195, 136); "Epithalamium" (42). Although "congeniality," once Shelley's principal term for describing sympathetic connection (see e.g. *L*, I, 135, 150, 193), is entirely replaced by the more sophisticated terminology of the mature psychology, the Shelley circle occasionally employed the term in a bantering fashion as late as 1820. Mary Shelley, chiding Maria Gisborne for not writing, quizzes her: "do you think, as Hogg does, that there is an instinctive intercourse between congenial souls that needs not the slow and troublesome formality of letter-writing?" (*L*, II, 214). Peacock frequently uses "congeniality" in the Shelleyan sense in his novels of the period.

18. Thomas Hardy, *Jude the Obscure* (New York, 1961 [1896]), pp. 228-230, 144-145, 288. In addition to borrowing Shelley's ideal of sympathetic love, Hardy shares his antimatrimonial and free love doctrines. He also quotes directly from *Epi.* (p. 243) and alludes to *SP* (p. 340).

19. See e.g. *Jane Talbot*, where Jane is described as desiring in a husband "one who could divide with [her her] sympathies; who saw every thing just as [she] saw it; who could emulate [her] enthusiasm, and echo back every exclamation which chance should dictate to [her]"; she believes in "kindred among souls, of friendship and harmony of feelings" (Charles Brockden Brown, *Jane Talbot* [Philadelphia, 1887 (1801)], pp. 66, 69). Cf. Brown, *Ormond* (New York, 1937 [1799]), p. 155, where Constantia sighs "for a companion fitted to partake in all her sympathies."

20. *The Princess* (VII.283-289, 261-262). In reviewing the poem, the *Sun* explained that sexual complementarity was providential in origin (Jan. 8, 1848); in Edgar Finley Shannon, Jr., *Tennyson and the Reviewers* (Cambridge, 1952), p. 99.

21. The words are those of Sir Willoughby Patterne, George Meredith's portrait of the archetypal Victorian male in *The Egoist* (New York, 1963 [1879]), p. 46.

22. John Ruskin, "Of Queen's Gardens," *Sesame and Lilies*, in *The Complete Works of John Ruskin* (New York, n.d.), XII, 59.

23. *The Princess* (VII.268). Period science held that woman's brain was smaller in cubic content than man's. See e.g. Elizabeth Fee, "Science and the Woman Problem: Historical Perspectives," in *Sex Differences: Social and Biological Perspectives*, ed. Michael S. Teitelbaum (Garden City, N.Y., 1976), pp. 182-195; Haller and Haller, *The Physician and Sexuality in Victorian America*, pp. 49-57.

24. *Vindication*, pp. 145, 247, 285.

25. *Course of Popular Lectures* (1829), in Miriam Schneir, ed., *Feminism: The Essential Historical Writings* (New York, 1972), p. 23.

26. *Woman in the Nineteenth Century* (New York, 1971 [1844]), p. 172.

27. *Subjection of Women*, pp. 91-93, 95. Harriet Taylor, who was to become Mill's wife, made much the same point in her article in the *Westminster Review* (1851) advocating sexual equality (LV, 307). See also d'Holbach, *Système social* (pt. 3, III, ch. 11, pp. 369-371), which may have influenced Wollstonecraft's *Vindication*.

28. Hoxie Neale Fairchild, *Religious Trends in English Poetry* (New York, 1949), II, 344, 366; see also Bostetter, *Romantic Ventriloquists*, pp. 210-213; F. A. Lea, *Shelley and the Romantic Revolution* (London, 1945), pp. 6, 173-174, 186; Herbert Read, *In Defence of Shelley & Other Essays* (London, 1936), pp. 27, 36, 53-54, 60; W. H. McCulloch, "The Last Night at Tan-yr-allt, February 26, 1813," *KSMB*, no. 8 (1957): 22-29; Chesser, *Shelley & Zastrozzi*, pp. 23, 29-30.

29. As the sexes are presently socialized, sex-linked traits are real, and a few traits, such as aggressiveness, may owe their origin to biology through the hormones rather than to socialization. But modern research indicates that these are much less extensive or deep-seated than traditionally supposed, and that the likeness of the sexes, not their disparity, is fundamental. Even where sex differences are demonstrated to exist, it is more expedient socially to minimize than to stress them. Sexual monism rather than dualism seems to hold out the best hope for the future harmony of the sexes (Maccoby and Jacklin, *The Psychology of Sex Differences*).

30. *The Second Sex*, trans and ed. H. M. Parshley (New York, 1953), pp. xix-xx, xxix, 142.

31. Firestone, *Dialectic of Sex*, pp. 11-12.

32. *Women & Madness* (Garden City, N.Y., 1972), p. 173n.

33. Sandra Lipsitz Bem, "Androgyny vs. the Tight Little Lives of Fluffy Women and Chesty Men," *Psychology Today* 9 (Sept. 1975): 57-62; see also Ashton Barfield, "Biological Influences on Sex Differences in Behavior," in *Sex Differences*, p. 110.

34. See e.g. Herbert Marder, *Feminism and Art* (Chicago, 1969); Nancy

Topping Bazin, *Virginia Woolf and the Androgynous Vision* (New Brunswick, 1973); Carolyn G. Heilbrun, *Toward a Recognition of Androgyny* (New York, 1973); Elaine Showalter, *A Literature of Their Own* (Princeton, 1977).

35. *A Room of One's Own* (New York, 1929), pp. 170-171. *Orlando* is the most explicit novelistic illustration of the ideal of "sympathetic" cross-gender identification, associated directly with Shelley through Orlando's androgynous mating with the symbolically named Marmaduke Shelmerdine (pp. 257-262).

36. A. F. L. Busst, "The Images of the Androgyne in the Nineteenth Century," in *Romantic Mythologies*, ed. Ian Fletcher (New York, 1967), pp. 1-95; Mircea Eliade, *Mephistopheles and the Androgyne*, trans. J. M. Cohen (New York, 1965), pp. 98-103; Raymond Furness, "The Androgynous Ideal: Its Significance in German Literature," *MLR* 60 (Jan. 1965): 58-64. Fourier's feminism—he is credited with coining the term—is based on cross-gender identification. In the phalanxes of his ideal state, lovers would be matched according to their "sympathies," or similarities of character and interests, so that they need not fall back on "purely sensual intrigues" or "trivial, simple sex." Sympathetic relationship would be "based on both physical and spiritual affinities" (*The New Amorous World*, in *The Utopian Vision of Charles Fourier: Selected Texts*, trans. and ed. Jonathan Beecher and Richard Bienvenu [Boston, 1971], pp. 378-390).

37. Heilbrun, *Toward a Recognition of Androgyny*, pt. 1; Delcourt, *Hermaphrodite*, passim. Delcourt notes the connection of androgyny with brother and sister incest in Greek and Roman mythology as well as in primitive folklore and alchemy (pp. 81-82). See also Busst, "Images of the Androgyne," p. 53; Furness, "The Androgynous Ideal," p. 61.

38. See Edward Carpenter and George Barnefield, *The Psychology of the Poet Shelley* (London, 1925); G. Wilson Knight, *Lord Byron's Marriage* (New York, 1957), pp. 256-257; Knight, *The Starlit Dome* (London, 1959), pp. 238-242; Knight, *The Mutual Flame* (London, 1955), pp. 212-213; John Cowper Powys, *Visions and Revisions* (New York, 1915), pp. 176-177; Cameron, *Golden Years*, p. 298; Holmes, *Pursuit*, p. 517.

39. *Woman in the Nineteenth Century*, pp. 113-114.

40. See e.g. John Money, "Psychosexual Differentiation," in *Sex Research*; Money, *Sex Errors of the Body* (Baltimore, 1968); Money and Ehrhardt, *Man & Woman, Boy & Girl*; *Transsexualism and Sex Reassignment*, ed. Richard Green and John Money (Baltimore, 1969); John L. Hampson, "Determinants of Psychosexual Orientation," in *Sex and Behavior*, ed. Frank A. Beach (New York, 1965); Robert J. Stoller, *Sex and Gender* (New York, 1968); Alice S. Rossi, "Maternalism, Sexuality, and the New Feminism," in *Contemporary Sexual Behavior*, ed. Joseph Zubin and John Money (Baltimore, 1973).

41. This reading assumes that the Madman is Shelley. Carl Grabo, *The Magic Plant* (Chapel Hill, 1936), p. 271, notes "the sex pathology suggested in

these lines." Jean Overton Fuller, *Shelley* (London, 1968), p. 271, finds evidence of hermaphroditism in *Epi.* and in a doodle Shelley traced in a notebook, but if the figure is indeed an hermaphrodite, its male genital is located in an unusual place.

42. Shelley's final opinion of Elizabeth Hitchener as an "ugly, hermaphroditical beast of a woman" suggests that the androgynous ideal was not physically reversible, at least not to the same degree. It might be consistent with the envisioned merging of sexual difference for a man to resemble a woman, but not the reverse.

43. *Lesbian Nation: The Feminist Solution* (New York, 1973), pp. 167, 267-269, 172. Charlotte Wolff, *Love Between Women* (London, 1971), explains that Lesbian love is "essentially different from any other kind of love" because "the sameness" of the lovers' "psycho-physical reactions entails the possibility of an understanding on every level so complete as to be incomparable to any other form of love. There is no need to grope for the right response; it is given per se" (pp. 87-88).

44. Not only was a sublimated male homoeroticism endemic throughout the nineteenth century, owing to the rigid segregation of the sexes, but so was its female complement. Unpublished letters, diaries, and accounts books reveal the pervasiveness of a Lesbian sensibility among middle class women, conveyed in terms of a romantic friendship corresponding to male romantic friendship and often expressed in the same vocabulary of sympathetic love. As with men, these friendships occasionally passed the boundaries of the sentimental to become overtly sexual. See Carroll Smith-Rosenberg, "The Female World of Love and Ritual: Relations Between Women in Nineteenth-Century America," *Signs* 1 (Autumn 1975): 1-29.

45. Valerie Solanis, in the notorious *SCUM Manifesto*, has drawn this lesson, but stood it on its head. It is man who will be erased, not woman.

Index

Abortion: and *Swellfoot the Tyrant*, 198; Shelley and Claire Clairmont, 198, 200

Acton, William, 207

Adonais: and the "thirst" of love, 53, 228; and Shelley's metapoetics of love, 228

Adultery: and pleasure-pain philosophy, 93; Athenian attitude to, 93-94; and Shelley, 94; and English marriage law, 97; and gallantry, 173; nineteenth-century attitude to, 205; and utility, 205

Alastor, 65, 68; and wet dream, 1, 129; love defined in Preface to, 27; sexual intercourse in, 58; erotic vocabulary of, 58

Allegra, 15, 17, 90

Androgyny: and Shelley, 3, 166, 172, 225-226; and modern feminism, 3, 195, 224-225, 227; in Greek sculpture, 20-23; and sympathetic identification, 224-225; and Virginia Woolf, 225; and nineteenth-century feminism, 225; and incest, 225

Antimatrimonialism: and Shelley, 2, 95-105 *passim*; literary sources of, 98nn20-21; and Wollstonecraft, 98, 201; and Fanny Wright, 200-201; and prostitution, 203, 207

Antitype: defined, 36; components of, 37-38; and Theodor Reik, 43; in *Epipsychidion*, 66, 67; and Shelley's incest symbolism, 216, 217, 218

Archetype. *See* Sentimental love

Ariosto, 155, 166

Aristophanes, 9, 148, 149

Aristotle, 194

"Ballad: Young Parson Richards," 205-206

Barthélémy, Abbé Jean Jacques, 9, 12; *Voyage du jeune Anacharsis*, 12

Beach, Frank A., 55

Beauty: female, 12-14, 16-18; male, 12-14, 20-23; and sexual intercourse, 90. *See also* Intellectual beauty; "Soul-enwoven" eyes

Beauvoir, Simone de, 224

Bem, Sandra, 225

Bentham, Jeremy, 197, 198

Birth control: Shelley on, 197-201 *passim*; and homosexuality, 198; Malthus on, 198; Godwin on, 198; and *Swellfoot the Tyrant*, 198; Wollstonecraft on, 199. *See also* Abortion; Contraception

Blake, William, 202

Blind, Mathilde, 181

Bluestockings, 170, 171, 174

"Boat on the Serchio, The," 131

Boccaccio, Giovanni, 48, 87, 94; *Decameron*, 48

Boinville, Mrs. Jean Baptiste Chastel de, 170-171

Brontë sisters, 221

Brown, Charles Brockden, 221

Burns, Robert, 47, 87

Butler, Josephine, 211

Byron, George Gordon, Lord, 2; and Allegra, 17; on sentiment, 27-28, 41; and Teresa Guiccioli, 28, 80, 173; on nympholepsy, 41; *Childe Harold's Pilgrimage*, 41, 161; and libertinism, 79-80, 96, 173; *Don Juan*, 88, 174, 176; homosexuality of, 117, 141, 175, 227; on troubadour love lyric, 161, 162; on chivalry, 161, 175; and Claire Clairmont, 169, 214-215; and gallantry, 173; on women, 173-176; and Annabella Milbanke, 174; and Augusta Leigh, 174; on prostitution, 202; and venereal disease, 210; and incest, 214, 215

Calderón de la Barca, Pedro, 155, 213; *Los Cabellos de Absalón*, 213

Cameron, Kenneth Neill, 165, 209

Cenci, The, 17-18, 79, 118, 213

Chastity: Shelley on, 49, 89-90, 93; Christian attitude to, 49, 100; and sexual temperance, 89; and libertinism, 89, 205, 207; and free love, 90, 100; Plato on, 124; and prostitution, 204, 205, 207, 211

Chaucer, Geoffrey, 160, 161

Chesler, Phyllis, 224

Chivalry: and courtly love, 154; and Germanic attitude to women, 156-159 *passim*; Shelley's knowledge of, 159; eighteenth-century scholarship on, 159-161; Coleridge on, 161; Byron on, 161, 175; of Shelley to women, 162, 179-180; and eighteenth-century gallantry, 172; John Stuart Mill on, 176-177

Circle of the self: defined, 32, 33, 39; and sympathetic love, 35

Clairmont, Clara Mary Jane (Claire): and Shelley, 14, 167, 169-170, 198, 214-215; and Byron, 169, 214-215; feminism of, 169-170; and abortion, 198, 200; and "League of Incest," 214-215

Climate: Shelley on, 13, 18; and ancient Greeks, 13, 18-19; and eighteenth-century scholarship, 19

Coleridge, John Taylor, 10

Coleridge, Samuel Taylor, 86; 1818 lectures, 161; and androgyny, 225

Coliseum, The, 14, 32

Condorcet, Marquis de, 187

Congeniality: and sympathetic love, 135, 220; and feminism, 220

Consciousness-raising, 3, 165, 184, 218

Contraception: Godwin on, 165, 198; Mary Wollstonecraft on, 173, 199; Shelley on, 175, 198, 199; and *Swell-*

foot the Tyrant, 198; Malthus on, 198; and libertinism, 199; and prostitution, 199

Coram, Thomas, 200

Cornwall, Barry (Bryan Waller Procter): *Dramatic Scenes*, 88-89

"Crisis, The," 199

Cumberland, Richard, 148-149

Dante, 155, 163; *Vita Nuova*, 66; *Convito*, 66

Davie, Donald, 71

De Beauvoir, Simone. *See* Beauvoir, Simone de

Defence of Poetry, A: and social sympathy, 29; and sympathetic imagination, 32; and law of association, 39-40; erotic imagery in, 76; and pleasure-pain, 92, 144-145, 147

Devil's Walk, The, 87

Diogenes Laertius: *Lives of Eminent Philosophers*, 147

Discourse of the Manners of the Antient Greeks Relative to the Subject of Love, A: history of, 2, 5-7; sexual philosophy in, 2-3, 5-6; and modern sex research, 5-6; and social history, 11

Disinterested love: and eighteenth-century philosophy, 134, 136; and ancient Greeks, 134, 137, 146, 150, 151; in Shelley, 134-139; and eighteenth-century novel, 135; Shelley vs. Hogg on, 135, 156; and Godwin, 136, 145; and sentimental friendship, 137-139, 140, 145-147; and free love, 147

Dreams: "On Dreams," 126; Shelley on, 126, 127; erotic dreaming, 128-130. *See also* Reverie; Wet dream

Eliot, George, 221

Enlightened philosophy: defined in *A Discourse*, 77, 89, 95; and Shelley's sexual code, 95; and Christian sexual morality, 95; and equality of women, 151; and prostitution, 202

Epipsychidion, 18, 68, 76, 147; and Shelley's typology of love, 37, 38, 66, 67; and free love, 146; and venereal disease, 209, 210; and incest sym-

bolism, 218
"Epithalamium," 52
Erotic vocabulary: in Shelley's Gothic
novels, 52, 58, 71; in *Alastor*, 58; in
The Revolt of Islam, 59-60; in *Rosalind and Helen*, 60; in *Prometheus
Unbound*, 61; and Masters and Johnson, 71; summarized, 71-73; in Shelley's work, 75-77; subversion of, 79;
rhetoric of orgasm, 130-132
Euripides: *Hippolytus*, 94; *The Cyclops*, 86-87
"Even love is sold" Note to *Queen
Mab*: and antimatrimonialism, 98-
101, 104; and infanticide, 199; and
prostitution, 203, 204, 206-207
Eyes. *See* "Soul-enwoven" eyes

Favola, Una, 210
Feminism: and Shelley, 2-3, 5, 48-49,
97, 99-100, 164-165, 177-181 *passim*;
and modern woman's movement, 3,
165, 180, 184, 195, 197, 198, 200;
and Shelley's feminine ideal, 3, 167-
168, 171; and sympathy, 3, 220-224;
and androgyny, 3, 227; and nineteenth-century woman's movement,
165, 185, 186, 197, 199, 200-201; and
Shelley's relations with women, 167-
172; in *Queen Mab*, 180; in *Prometheus Unbound*, 180-181; and revolution, 180-186 *passim*; in *The Revolt
of Islam*, 181-186, 217-218; sources
of, 187-189; and incest symbolism,
216-221 *passim*. *See also* Sexual
equality; Women
"Fiordispina," 48, 131, 219
Firestone, Shulamith, 177-178, 180
Ford, Clellan S., 55
Foundling hospital: Shelley on, 199-
200; and Hoppner scandal, 200
Free love: Shelley on, 3, 100-103; and
chastity, 90; vs. sexual promiscuity,
101-103; and imagination, 103; in
Epipsychidion, 103, 104, 116; and
enlightened philosophy, 103, 107;
and sexual jealousy, 104, 106; Shelley's practice of, 105-116; and *A Defence*, 147
Freud, Sigmund, 42-43

Friendship: and love, 92; sympathetic,
111-112; worldly, 112; vs. love, 136;
of Shelley and Hogg, 137-139; between the sexes, 224, 227. *See also*
Sentimental friendship
Fuller, Margaret, 3, 22, 225

Gallantry: and seduction, 105, 205; and
Germanic attitude to women, 156,
159; and *Childe Harold's Pilgrimage*,
161; defined, 172-173, 176; Wollstonecraft on, 172-173, 177; and
Peter Bell III, 173; and libertinism,
173, 205; and Regency sexual code,
173-175; Shelley on, 173-180 *passim*;
Shelley vs. Hogg on, 178-180; Shelley's practice of, 179-180; and prostitution, 205. *See also* Libertinism
Gibbon, Edward, 28, 120, 156, 159, 177
Gisborne, Maria, 6, 170
Godwin, William, 6, 7, 167; and sympathy, 31; *Political Justice*, 31, 98,
111, 112; Shelley on, 40, 188, 192;
and Malthus, 49, 198; and antimatrimonialism, 98, 111; on disinterestedness, 136, 145; on contraception and
abortion, 165; as source of feminism,
187; and intellectual beauty, 193-
194; *Memoirs of the Author of the
"Vindication of the Rights of
Woman,"* 193-194; *Of Population*,
198
Goethe, Johann Wolfgang von: *Faust*,
86
"Good-Night," 63-64
Grant, Vernon, 43-44
Greek sculpture: Shelley's attraction to,
20-23, 155, 226; and English schoolboy friendship, 139-140, 145-146
Grove, Harriet, 52; Shelley's love for,
40, 54, 101, 219; and disinterested
love, 135-136; and "Passion: (to the
[Nightshade])," 210; and *Epipsychidion*, 210; and "Fiordispina," 219
Guiccioli, Countess Teresa, 28, 80, 173

Hardy, Thomas: *Jude the Obscure*,
221; and *Laon and Cythna*, 221
Haydon, Benjamin, 215
Hazlitt, William, 160

Hellas, 20-21

Helvétius, Claude A., 187

Hermaphroditism: and Greek sculpture, 22-23, 226; and Shelley, 22-23, 226n41; of Elizabeth Hitchener, 172, 226n42; and modern sex research, 226

Hitchener, Elizabeth: and Shelley, 108-109, 171-172; as hermaphroditical, 172, 226n42

Hogg, Thomas Jefferson: and Elizabeth Shelley, 40, 106, 137-138, 166-167, 178-179; and Harriet Shelley, 53-54, 105-108, 113, 137, 179; friendship with Shelley, 137-139; and gallantry, 178-180

Holbach, Baron Paul H. D. d', 187, 223n27

Home, Henry (Lord Kames), 29

Homosexuality: Shelley on, 2, 6-11 *passim,* 117-118; nineteenth-century attitude to, 6-11 *passim,* 117-118; and Byron, 117-118; and *The Cenci,* 118; and nineteenth-century English public schools, 141-143; and birth control, 198; and prostitution, 201. *See also* Lesbianism; Pederasty

Hunt, Leigh, 64, 77, 87, 96, 160-161

Hunt, Thornton, 208-211 *passim*

Hurd, Richard, 156

Huxley, Aldous, 25

Hymn to Intellectual Beauty, 126; and intellectual philosophy, 189; and feminism, 190-191, 195; and sympathetic love, 228

Imagination: and sympathy, 30, 31-32, 137, 192-195 *passim;* and sex, 75-77; and disinterestedness, 136, 137; and intellectual beauty, 192-194; vs. reason, 192-196

Imlay, Fanny, 187

Incest; and sympathetic love, 185, 216, 217, 218; Romantics on, 212-213, 216-217; Shelley on, 212-215; in *Laon and Cythna,* 212-218 *passim;* in *The Cenci,* 213-214; in *Rosalind and Helen,* 213, 218, 219; in "Love's Philosophy," 214; in *Prometheus Unbound,* 214; in *Peter Bell III,* 214; and

Byron, 214, 215; and Shelley, 214, 215; symbolism of, 216-218; in *Epipsychidion,* 218; and androgyny, 225

"Indian Serenade," 65, 132

Infanticide: Shelley on, 198-200; and prostitution, 199

Intellectual beauty: and ancient Greek women, 12; English and German vs. Italian women, 16-18; and Mary Shelley, 168; and Elizabeth Shelley, 178-179; and Wollstonecraft, 189, 190-191; in Shelley, 189-196; and imagination, 192-195; and sympathetic love, 221; and Shelley's metapoetics of love, 228

Intellectual philosophy, 127-128, 189

Jacklin, Carol N., 1, 166n10, 224n24

Jaeger, Werner, 133

James, William, 25

Jealousy, sexual: in ancient Athens, 94; Shelley on, 94, 100, 106, 113, 201; and free love, 104-112 *passim;* modern sex research on, 105

Johnson, Virginia E., 1, 46, 70-71, 73, 125, 137

Johnston, Jill, 226

Julian and Maddalo, 226

Kames, Lord. *See* Home, Henry

Keats, John, 46n4, 133n46; *The Eve of St. Agnes,* 67

Kennedy, Florynce, 184

Kinsey, Alfred, 1, 44, 105n30, 125n20, 128n28, 129nn31, 33

Laon and Cythna; and sympathetic love, 185, 217-218; Shelley on, 192-193; and incest, 212, 213, 214; revision of, 212, 215-216; and feminism, 216, 217. See also *Revolt of Islam, The*

League of Incest, 214-215

Lecky, W. E. H., 152, 205

Leigh, Augusta, 174, 214

Lesbianism: and narcissism, 226; and feminism, 226, 227

Lewis, C. S., 24, 157

Lewis, Matthew Gregory; *The Monk,* 51

Libertinism: Shelley on, 3, 77-80 *passim*; charges of, 78, 95, 96; in Shelley's work, 78-79, 207n39; and Byron, 79-80, 96; and *Symposium*, 80; vs. civilized love, 80-83, 90; and pleasure-pain philosophy, 98, 205; and gallantry, 173, 205; and prostitution, 205, 207

"Lines: 'We Meet Not as We Parted,'" 69-70

"Lines Connected with *Epipsychidion*," 23, 102-103, 144

"Lines Written in the Bay of Lerici," 69

Love, Shelley's psychology of, 2, 3, 24, 27, 228; and feminism, 3, 223, 224; compared with modern psychological theories, 42-44; and incest, 219, 220; as narcissistic, 223-224. *See also* Romantic love; Sentimental friendship; Sentimental love; Sexual love; Sympathetic love

"Love's Philosophy," 64, 75, 77, 214

Lucian, 87

Maccoby, Eleanor E., 1, 166n10, 224n24

Mallet, Paul-Henri: *Northern Antiquities*, 156, 157

Marriage. *See* Antimatrimonialism

Mask of Anarchy, The, 205

Maslow, A. H., 82

Mason, Mrs. (Lady Mountcashell), 170

Masters, William H., 1, 46, 70-71, 73, 125, 137

Masturbation, 125n20, 129n32

Medwin, Thomas, 19, 51, 87, 126

Meredith, George, 221

Metapoetics of love, 228

Michelangelo, 21

Milbanke, Annabella (Lady Byron), 174, 176

Mill, John Stuart, 3, 165, 199n8, 222-223, 224; *The Subjection of Women*, 176-177, 222

Millett, Kate, 177, 184, 201

Mitchell, Thomas, 148

Money, John, 1, 38n40, 44n55, 166n10, 216n9, 226

Narcissism: and Shelley, 15, 223-224; and Lesbian feminism, 226

Necessity of Atheism, The, 8

Nocturnal emission. *See* Wet dream

Nympholepsy: and Shelley, 40-41; and Byron, 41; and Peacock, 41

Obscenity: Shelley on, 83-87, 120, 121; and Byron, 84, 88-89; and Shelley's translations, 86-87; and contraception, 199; and incest, 214

"Ode to the West Wind," 132, 186

Ollier, Charles, 19, 212

On Beauty, 33

O'Neill, William, 211

"On Friendship": and English schoolboy friendship, 139; and Greek pederasty, 139, 143-144; and Byron's "Childish Recollections," 140; and *A Discourse*, 143, 144; on friendship vs. love, 143-144; and *A Defence*, 144-145

On Life, 39, 126, 127, 130

On Love: defines love, 27; and "thirst" of love, 33, 34; and sympathetic likeness, 33, 35-39 *passim*; on love's typology, 34-41 *passim*; and *Epipsychidion*, 66, 67; and *Laon and Cythna*, 217; and metapoetics of love, 228

On Marriage, 28-29, 100

On the Devil and Devils, 51

Opie, Amelia: *Adeline Mowbray*, 111

Orgasm, 51, 53; Shelley on, 72-73, 130-131; vocabulary of, 130-132. *See also* Spontaneous orgasm; Wet dream

Owenites, 165, 200; Robert Dale Owen, 200

Pan, 50-51, 75

"Passion: (to the [Nightshade])," 210

Patriarchal nuclear family: Shelley on, 3, 99, 200-201; and incest, 214

Pausanias, 19, 20; *The Description of Greece*, 19

Pauw, Cornelius de, 13, 14; *Philosophical Dissertations on the Greeks*, 13

Peacock, Thomas Love, 6, 41, 55, 160-161, 212; *Crotchet Castle*, 7; *Rhododaphne*, 19; *The Four Ages of Poetry*, 161

Pederasty: nineteenth-century attitude to, 6-9, 10-11; in ancient Greece, 6-9,

11, 23, 25, 117, 118-123 *passim*, 149, 150; and women in Greece, 12, 14, 179, 227; and pleasure-pain philosophy, 119, 145, 146; in ancient Rome, 120-121, 144; and spontaneous orgasm, 124-125, 139, 146. *See also* Homosexuality

Percy, Thomas, 156, 157

Peter Bell the Third, 47-48, 87, 204, 214; and Wordsworth, 47-48

Petrarch, 155, 174n35

Petronius Arbiter: *Satyricon*, 121

Philosophical View of Reform, A, 50, 186, 197, 198

Place, Francis, 50, 78, 199, 203

Plato: and *A Discourse*, 2, 5, 6; and Shelley's translation of *Symposium*, 2, 6, 7, 35, 123, 225; and nineteenth-century attitude to male love, 6-7; *Symposium*, 22, 122, 123, 146, 149; on Greek pederasty, 25, 122-125, 133-134, 146, 150; and *On Love*, 35; on sexual temperance, 83; on adultery, 93; *Phaedrus*, 122, 123, 124-125; Shelley on sexual practice of, 147-148; epigrams, 148; and intellectual philosophy, 189; vs. Aristotle, 194; and incest, 216-217; and androgyny, 225

Pleasure-pain: and utility, 91, 92, 94, 202; as basis of Shelley's sexual code, 91-93, 202, 205; and higher hedonism, 92, 144-145, 147; and enlightened philosophy, 95; and Greek pederasty, 119, 145, 146

Pliny, 19, 20; *Natural History*, 19

Prince Athanase, 15

Prometheus Unbound, 48, 76, 88, 185; sex in, 61-63; antimatrimonialism in, 98; feminism in, 180-181

Promiscuity, 46; and promiscuous concubinage, 29, 79, 82, 102; Shelley on, 78-79; vs. free love, 101-102

Prostitution: and contraception, 199; and woman's movement, 201, 211; Shelley on, 201-204 *passim*, 210; in nineteenth-century, 202-205, 207; and "Ballad: Young Parson Richards," 205-206; Shelley's experience with, 208-211

Prototype: defined, 36; and Preface to

Alastor, 37, 38; and *On Love*, 41; and Theodor Reik, 43; and *Laon and Cythna*, 217

Prudery: Shelley on, 8-11, 46-49; Shelley's lack of, 47; and Wordsworth, 47-48; and Harriet Shelley, 54-55

Queen Mab, 46, 96; antimatrimonialism in, 98; feminism in, 180; and prostitution, 207

"Question, The," 76

Regency sexual code. *See* Gallantry

Reik, Theodor, 43

Reverie: and *Hymn to Intellectual Beauty*, 126; Shelley's psychology of, 126, 127; and *On Life*, 126, 130; and Wordsworth, 126-127; and sexual fantasy, 128-130; modern sex research on, 128-130; and spontaneous orgasm, 130-133; in *Epipsychidion*, 131; and intellectual beauty, 195. *See also* Wet dream

Revolt of Islam, The: sexual intercourse in, 59-60; and libertinism, 79; feminism in, 181-186, 217-218; and Wollstonecraft, 187-188; and prostitution, 206. See also *Laon and Cythna*

Richardson, Samuel, 77

Roman sexuality, 152-153

Romantic love, 43-44; Shelley on, 3; and medieval courtly society, 24, 25; in antiquity, 24-26; and Byron, 27n11, 173; and gallantry, 173, 177, 178; vs. romantic realism, 174. *See also* Sentimental love

Rosalind and Helen: sexual intercourse in, 60; and incest, 213, 218, 219

Rousseau, Jean Jacques, 27, 107, 155; in *The Triumph of Life*, 16, 147; *Julie*, 135; *Emile*, 169

Ruskin, John: "Of Queens' Gardens," 222

Russell, Bertrand, 165

Sainte-Palaye, La Curne de, 159, 160, 161n41; *Mémoires sur l'ancienne chevalrie*, 159; *Histoire littéraire des troubadours*, 159

St. Irvyne, 17, 52, 206

Schlegel, August Wilhelm von, 9-10,

11, 12, 19, 25-26, 157-158; *Lectures,*
9, 25-26, 157-158
Schlegel, Friedrich von: *Lectures,* 10,
148
Seduction: charges against Shelley, 46,
112, 113; Hogg's attempt on Harriet
Shelley, 53, 105-108; Shelley on, 93,
94, 95, 205; Greek attitude to, 94;
Christian attitude to, 95; and English
marriage law, 97; and prostitution,
205-207
Sensitive Plant, The, 16, 76, 170
Sentiment: Shelley on, 27; Byron on,
28; and sentimental love, 29; and
sex, 53, 77, 201
Sentimental friendship: Shelley and
Hogg, 137-139; and Greek pederasty, 139-140; and English schoolboy
friendship, 139-141; in "On Friendship," 139, 143-144; vs. sentimental
love, 143-147
Sentimental love, 3; and medieval
courtly society, 24, 25, 153-154; as
psychological archetype, 24, 26, 28,
29, 151, 153, 216, 220; and ancient
Greeks, 24-26, 27, 143; defined, 27;
and ancient Romans, 28, 152, 153;
and civilization, 28-29, 77; psychodynamics of, 34, 36; and Freud, 42;
delusive character of, 39-41, 68; vs.
libertinism, 80, 92; and antimatrimonialism, 98-99; and disinterestedness, 135, 136, 137; and congeniality,
135, 137, 220; and sentimental
friendship, 140, 141, 143. *See also*
Romantic love
Sexton, Anne: "Consorting with Angels," 224
Sexual complementarity; and doctrine
of separate spheres, 3, 181, 221, 222,
224, 227; and Tennyson's *The Princess,* 221, 222; and Ruskin's "Of
Queens' Gardens," 222
Sexual double standard: Shelley on, 3,
89-90; and prostitution, 204
Sexual equality: Shelley on, 3, 150,
151, 164, 177, 180, 184, 224; and utility, 150, 151. *See also* Feminism
Sexual fantasy. *See* Reverie
Sexual imagery. *See* Erotic vocabulary

Sexual impulse, 28, 29, 45, 53, 54, 60
Sexual intercourse: in *Alastor,* 58; in
The Revolt of Islam, 59-60; in *Rosalind and Helen,* 60; in *Prometheus
Unbound,* 61-63; in *The Triumph of
Life,* 63; in *Epipsychidion,* 65, 66-68;
composite portrait of, 71-73; conditions for, 77, 82-83, 90, 117; social
ethics of, 91
Sexual love: Shelley on, 1-2, 45-50 *passim,* 73-74; animals and savages vs.
civilized beings, 28, 81-82; as sensation, 53-54, 136; intensity and duration of, 81-83
Shakespeare, William, 144, 155
Shelley, Elizabeth (sister), 52; Hogg's
love for, 40, 101, 166-167; *Original
Poetry* by "Victor and Cazire," 166,
206; and Shelley's feminism, 166-
167; supposed incest with Shelley, 215
Shelley, Elizabeth (mother), 52; and
Shelley, 165
Shelley, Harriet Westbrook: Hogg's attempted seduction of, 53-54, 105-
108; prudery of, 54-55; marriage to
Shelley, 54-55, 56; separation from
Shelley, 109-112; and Shelley's feminism, 167, 171; and Wollstonecraft,
187
Shelley, Mary Godwin, 5, 6; as Shelley's antitype, 39, 57, 58, 68; Shelley's feelings for, 55-59 *passim,* 63-69
passim, 162-163; and Wollstonecraft,
167, 187-188; and Shelley's feminism, 167-169; intellectual beauty of,
168; *Valperga,* 168; *Frankenstein,*
169; and nineteenth-century woman's movement, 169n20; and League
of Incest, 214-215
Shelley, Percy Bysshe: discarnate myth
of, 1, 3, 5, 45-46, 50, 226; as androgynous, 3, 166, 225-226; sexual
humor, 16-17, 87-89; sexual imagination, 75-77; relation with parents,
165; relation with sisters, 165, 166,
167; femininity, 166, 225
Shelley, Sir Timothy, 78, 165
Sismondi, Simonde de, *De la littérature
du Midi de l'Europe,* 160
Smith, Adam: and sympathy, 3, 29-30,

219-220; *The Theory of Moral Senti-ments*, 29, 220

Socrates: and free love, 104, 146; and Greek pederasty, 133, 148-149, 150, 163

Sodomy, 118-124 *passim*, 142

"Soul-enwoven" eyes, 14-18 *passim*, 59, 191

Southey, Robert, 109, 110, 191, 214-215

Spark, Muriel, 168

"Speculations on Morals," 31-32, 136

Spenser, Edmund, 155, 161

Spontaneous orgasm: and Shelley, 123, 130-133; and Greek pederasty, 124-125, 139, 146; modern sex research on, 125n20. *See also* Orgasm; Wet dream

Stacey, Sophia, 63-65, 170

Staël, Madame de: *De la littérature*, 12

Sterilization, 198

Sterne, Laurence: *Tristram Shandy*, 83

Suffrage, woman's, 197

Swellfoot the Tyrant, 87, 88; and Malthus, 198, 207n39

Sympathetic love: and sympathetic likeness or identification, 3, 32, 33, 39, 218-228 *passim*; psychodynamics of, 32-40 *passim*; and imagination, 39-40; and incest, 218-220; and nineteenth-century novel, 221; and narcissism, 223-224; and Shelley's metapoetics of love, 228

Sympathy, doctrine of: and Adam Smith, 3, 29-30, 219-220; as basis of Shelley's sexual psychology, 3, 29-42 *passim*; and Hume, 3, 30, 35; and feminism, 3, 219-223; and Wollstonecraft, 3, 222; and Fanny Wright, 3, 222; and Margaret Fuller, 3, 222; and John Stuart Mill, 3, 222-223; laws of, 29-32, 219-220; and Godwin, 31

Tacitus, 156, 157, 159

Tasso, 155, 161

Taylor, Thomas, 7, 19

Temperance, sexual: and *Symposium*, 83; Shelley on, 83, 89, 117; and *Phaedrus*, 124

Tennyson, Alfred, Lord, 181, 221, 222; *The Princess*, 181

"Thirst" of love, 27, 28, 29, 40, 53, 59, 73; defined, 33-34; and women, 48-49; and Shelley's metapoetics, 228

"To: 'When passion's trance is over-past,'" 74

"To a Skylark," 73

"To Constantia [Singing]," 131-132

"To Edward Williams," 69

"To Emilia Viviani," 65

"To Jane: The Invitation," 69

"To Jane: The Recollection," 69

"To Sophia," 65

Triumph of Life, The, 16, 63, 147, 148

Troubadour love lyric: Shelley on, 154; and Sainte-Palaye, 159-160; Shelley's knowledge of, 160-161; Byron on, 161, 162

Turner, Cornelia, 56, 170-171

Type: and sexual impulse, 34; and typology of love, 36, 37; and sympathetic identification of sexes, 224, 227

Unisexuality, 3, 224, 226, 227. *See also* Androgyny

Utility: and Shelley's sexual code, 91, 92, 202, 205; and pleasure-pain philosophy, 91-92; true, 92; and seduction, 95, 205; and antimatrimonialism, 98, 102; and free love, 103, 105, 107, 146; and feminism, 150; and prostitution, 202, 205

Valency, Maurice, 25, 162

Venereal disease, 208-211

Viviani, Teresa Emilia, 15, 18; and Shelley, 34, 65-68, 147; and incest symbolism, 218

Warton, Thomas, 156, 160

Wet dream: and *Alastor*, 1, 129, 130; and *A Discourse*, 123; and spontaneous orgasm, 125; and Shelley, 128-130. *See also* Dreams; Reverie

Wieland, Christoph Martin, 9, 19, 26, 27; *Peregrine Proteus*, 10; *Aristippus*, 10; *History of Agathon*, 10, 25, 191

Wilde, Oscar, 141, 227

Williams, Jane, 15, 68-70, 147, 170

Winckelmann, Johann Joachim, 19-22;
The History of Ancient Art, 19, 20

Witch of Atlas, The, 23, 46, 48, 51

Wollstonecraft, Mary: and sympathy,
3, 22, 224; on birth control, 165, 199;
influence on Shelley, 172, 187-189; *A
Vindication of the Rights of Woman*,
172, 189-190, 191, 194; on gallantry,
172-173; and intellectual beauty,
189, 191-196; *The Wrongs of Woman*, 193, 194, 211; on woman's suffrage, 197; and nineteenth-century
feminism, 201; and prostitution, 202,
211

Women: Shelley on, 2, 3, 5, 48-49, 97,
99-100, 150-151, 162-163, 164-165; in
ancient Greece, 3, 11-14, 16-18, 23,
150-154 *passim*, 164, 175; in nineteenth-century Italy, 3, 16-18; in
modern Western society, 44; in nineteenth-century England, 151, 164-184
passim; in ancient Rome, 152, 153,
177; in Middle Ages, 153-163 *passim*;
Shelley's relations with, 164-174 *passim*; Shelley's ideal of, 167-168, 171.
See also Feminism

Woodhull, Victoria, 201

Woolf, Virginia, 225

Wordsworth, William, 126-127, 202

Wright, Frances (Fanny), 3, 200-201,
222

Zastrozzi, 52, 206

"Zeinab and Kathema," 206